BASIC WILDERNESS SURVIVAL SKILLS

Build Shelters * Safety and First Aid * Fire Building

Forage, Hunt, and Fish * And Much More

BRADFORD ANGIER
Edited by Lamar Underwood

THE LYONS PRESS

Guilford, Connecticut
An imprint of The Globe Pequot Press

The Lyons Press is an imprint of The Globe Pequot Press.

Printed in the United States

Designed by Compset, Inc.

10 9 8 7 6 5

ISBN 978-1-58574-226-4

Library of Congress Cataloging-in-Publication Data is available on file.

BASIC WILDERNESS SURVIVAL SKILLS

CONTENTS

FOREWORD

Beyond the places where the pavement ends . . . beyond the last graveled road . . . on beyond the final stretch of rugged, brush-choked ruts where even a four-wheel-drive ceases to stubbornly press ahead—here begins the back-country, the true wilderness. Here, we are on our own. No rescue squad vehicles can arrive, lights flashing, their professional crews ready to help us. It is true that some lakes and clearings might lie ahead, big enough for a floatplane or helicopter to pluck us from whatever misfortunes we have encountered. But the rescuers may not get the word in time. Probably won't, if you believe in the dictums of Murphy's Law.

What should we do? Stay home, head for the mall?

Nonsense. What Jack London labeled, "The Call of the Wild," and Bradford Angier references as, "The Call of the Trail," are spiritual marching orders for many of us. We are as committed to the wilderness experience as we are to breathing. We are going out there, with our eyes and ears wide open, to see what's over the next hill, what's around the next bend in the stream. Perhaps the day will come when the rocking chair beside the fire will be the only place we can live the bold, free wilderness life—as we allow our memories to sweep us back to precious times and places we can no longer attain. But as long as we can hack it out there, we're going to hit the trail.

"Hacking it" is exactly what this book is all about. And our guide is a man who has done everything he teaches. "Some teach, others do," goes a tired old bromide. No one ever tried to pin such a silly label on the late Bradford Angier. He is a great teacher—and we're all lucky for that—but beyond that distinction is the fact that Brad Angier learned every lesson he ever passed on by experiencing it himself. The man tied every knot, paddled with every stroke, built every shelter, started every fire that ended up in his tips on wilderness living and survival. What Brad Angier did not know about living in the woods probably wasn't very important.

When we're talking about wilderness ventures made for our personal satisfaction, the word "Survival" might seem more than a trifle heavy, as in some old nature expressions such as "red in tooth and fang." However, once one embraces the concept of being on your own in the wilderness, what starts as a voluntary venture can turn into a struggle for survival. Unlikely, yes, but a distinct possibility nevertheless.

Vilhjalmur Stefansson, the great explorer and adventure writer, in *My Life With the Eskimo* suggests that all should go smoothly out there, with the question of "survival" never an issue. "Having an adventure," he writes, "shows that someone is incompetent, that something has gone wrong."

Fair enough, but lamenting on the fact that the mess we're in never should have happened in the first place won't get us out of harm's way when the chips are down. Whether we've been plain foolish or just unlucky, getting back may depend entirely on our own skills for quite some time before help arrives.

For Brad Angier, the skills needed to "survive" what Stefansson called an "adventure" are no different than the wilderness living skills needed to follow the paths of the man Angier wished most to emulate, Henry David Thoreau. Like Thoreau, Brad Angier and his wife Vena—short for "Elvena"—dreamed of a wilderness life lived in peace and simplicity through self-sufficiency. A life stripped bare of non-essentials, far beyond the pavement's end, could only be attained by mastering the skills required to be on your own in the wilderness. "On your own!" Those are the key words, the code by which Brad and Vena set out to *live,* not merely *survive.* As the titles of so many of Brad's books (there are thirty-five of them by my last count) reveal, the lore and expertise he shares is directed toward using that knowledge to find contentment in the wilderness, whether for a visit or a permanent stay as a homesteader. This is wilderness living as a way of life. The skills are basics, but they are the same skills by which one might hope to survive one of Stefansson's "adventures"—the foul-ups or disasters that might truly leave one up that famous creek without a paddle.

Unless we stay home, such an adventure could happen to you or me. The many possible scenarios may seem far-fetched from your favorite reading chair, but they have happened before, certainly will happen again. An unscheduled plane goes down far out in the wilderness without sending a radio message; a canoe wraps around a rock on some remote wilderness river, the hapless canoe-trippers lucky to save themselves from drowning but now with injuries and all their gear gone; a boat is lost at sea; a backpacker loses his bearings in a jumble of mountain wilderness. In all these instances, the same skills that served Brad Angier in wilderness living become "survival" skills. They literally could mean life or death.

Mostly, Brad Angier's books have a less dramatic mission. He wished to share with others the wilderness living skills by which he and Vena enjoyed the idyllic life as wilderness homesteaders on the Peace River near the settlement of Hudson Hope north of Dawson's Creek in British Columbia. Although that area dominates the background of their books, they pursued the vigorous outdoor life in other locations as well.

Brad Angier is gone now, but Vena is still with us, active and vigorous back in Massachusetts where their adventures began. Born in 1910, Brad passed away on March 3, 1997, while living near Tucson, Arizona. Vena told me recently that though he was bedridden with a muscular problem and suffering from Alzheimer's, "Brad was a very lovable and uncomplaining patient. Even when he didn't know me, he would look up and say, 'You're a wonderful person.'"

Brad and Vena were both New Englanders before they started their life journey together in marriage and wilderness living. Born in Watertown, Maine, Brad became something of a teenage prodigy by writing and selling stories for *Boy's Life* magazine while he was in Beverly (Mass.) High School. At the age of thirteen, he sold a short story, called "A Romance and Barry," to the Beverly Evening Times, the daily newspaper where he would eventually have his first job as a reporter. In the years before he joined the paper, Brad went from Beverly High School on to Kimball Union Academy and then to Bates College.

Brad and Vena first met in the 1930s while Brad was New England editor of Box Office. Vena was a professional dancer then, well on her way to fulfilling what had long been her mother's wish that she become a *premiere danseuse*. "I first saw him backstage at the Met," Vena told me, "I didn't get to meet him, but I sure did notice him. Then in the late 1930s I was asked if I'd take a summer job at a lake outside of Boston where a choreographer was needed for a musical show at an open air theatre. I accepted and enjoyed the work. Brad was one of the so-called money men behind the venture. I believe they did quite well. We became acquainted, but then I went out on the road, then went overseas with a small unit of U.S. Camp Shows. It wasn't until after the war that we met again, and everything went along swiftly. We were married and eventually went North.

"I came from a large and rowdy family, while Brad was an only child of older people, brought up to be a very proper New Englander. He was to me a very gentle gentleman. One wouldn't see him as a rugged outdoorsman. But when we headed North he was a true outdoorsman and eased me through the process, laughing with me at some of the things I thought and did.

"One day I was outside and heard what I thought was people in trouble on the river. Brad got up from his writing to help. When he came outside, he stood for a while then told me the sounds I was hearing were of geese heading south.

"Brad also told me not to worry about wild animals, as they would be more afraid than I. So I went picking raspberries one day and with the pail about full, I raised up and at the same time a black bear raised up about twenty feet from me on the other side of the berry patch. I don't remember much. The pail went one way, and I went the other back to the cabin. I think the bear went in another direction. So much for being calm and doing all the things Brad suggested I do in a situation of that kind."

Two wonderful autobiographical accounts of Brad and Vena's life on the Peace River have been published, but are not easy to find. I have paperback versions of each. *At Home In the Woods* by Vena and Brad was published by Collier Books, a division of Macmillan, in 1971, after being originally published in hardcover by Sheridan House, New York, in 1951. *We Like It Wild* by Brad was published in paperback by Collier in 1973 after being originally published in hardcover by Stackpole in 1963. These two books basically cover the same ground—Brad and Vena's life on the Peace River—and they are superb reading material for all us "armchair" homesteaders. Perhaps someday some enterprising publisher will reissue one of the titles.

Brad and Vena had been living on the Peace River only a short time when their writing efforts went through monumental change. They had been devoting their literary output to fiction, with very poor results. They just could not sell what they wrote. Finally, they turned to the materials at hand—writing about the ropes and tools and skills of wilderness living. Nice letters and checks instead of printed rejection slips began to arrive through Hudson Hope's primitive post office. They were finally on their way to producing the thirty-five books I mentioned earlier. The Sheridan House acceptance was their first big breakthough.

"I've been back to Hudson Hope and the Peace River a couple of times since Brad died," Vena told me. "Once for his ashes to be scattered on the Peace and another time to visit friends. Not many left now. It was sad to go back and see how civilization had taken over. We had the best of that area and terrific memories. It was a wonderful life, and he was a wonderful companion. I wonder where we could find another wilderness area these days. There is nothing like an eighteen-by-twenty-foot cabin to find out how compatible two people are."

In preparing this Brad Angier book, it has been my assignment and pleasure as editor to combine three of Brad's works into this single volume. The three original books are *Skills In Taming the Wilds,* published by Stackpole in 1967; *The Master Backwoodsman,* published by Ballantine Books in 1979; and *Bradford Angier's Backcountry Basics,* published by Stackpole in 1983.

In selecting the material to be included in this book, I have, of course, been guided by a mission to deliver the meat-and-potatoes, if you will, of basic wilderness survival skills. At the same time, I have endeavored to include as much of Brad Angier's prose as possible on the aesthetics of the outdoor experience—his "Call of the Trail."

With the exception of a few of the titles and updated material on where-to-go and addresses, all the text in this book was written by Brad Angier. As you realize, Brad wrote his books long before the coming of the Internet and long before the publication of numerous maps and books that are available today on important backcountry destinations. In addition, the backpacking equipment and information revolution, with writers like Colin Fletcher and magazines like *Backpacker,* had not emerged when Brad was writing and hitting the trails to the backcountry.

But what you will find in the pages ahead is the very best of Bradford Angier on just about everything you need to know for wilderness living. You may never be called upon to use what you learn here to save your life. You may never have the opportunity to put the skills to work in making a permanent home in the wilderness as Brad and Vena did. But with Brad Angier as your trainer and mentor, the next time you hit the trail, for a long venture or a quick overnighter, you will feel that special deep satisfaction of knowing you can hack it out there. No matter what happens.

—Lamar Underwood
October 2001

INTRODUCTION

THE CALL OF THE TRAIL

Every outdoor trip is divided into three parts: the excitement of getting ready, the adventure itself, and finally the deep-down pleasure of reminiscence.

Although you may not plan to hit the trail again for a month or until next year, you will be missing one of the keenest joys of all if as soon as one such excursion is over you do not begin preparations for the next. You'll be passing up the pulse-quickening satisfaction of keeping your equipment ready, of purposefully thumbing catalogs and maps, and of sprawling terse reminders in a worn notebook carried for those moments when inspiration fires. Even in the midst of the steel bones and asphalt veins of the big city, all this can keep you mighty close to those other days and to those freer ones soon to come.

Then once again, almost before you know it, the wilderness night begins bulging from the west in a deep blue flood that drenches all but the last few warming embers of the sunset. Sweet ebony fumes lift from ready birch bark, and then the dry poplar with its clean medicinal odor catches hold. By you, in the forest's untroubled space, is everything you need; gun, fishing gear, camping outfit, grub, shelter, and friendly warmth.

* * *

Civilization these days seems to be closing in more and more stiflingly all about us. Yet on this continent there remains real wilderness where you can still make your own way, cut firewood and browse with no harm to anyone, and answer the instinctive call of the open places while eyes will never be keener or stride more lusty. This is good, for essentially we all need the tonic of our remaining backwoods.

The trail's call is instinctive, having nothing to do with our common sense. We realize we are perhaps fools for answering it, and yet we go. The comforts of worldly conveniences, to relegate the matter to its basic level, are not to be disregarded lightly: the burden-lightening ease of having our physical labor performed for us, the agreeableness of cultivated minds, of theaters and

television, of books, of keeping abreast of world developments. These we re-
nounce. In exchange, we undertake an existence in which there is considerable hard toil—work so admittedly long and exhausting that few men paid to
labor would consider it for a second.

We go back to the pioneer demands of eating simply, of enduring much, of
sleeping out in storms and wind. We deliberately put ourselves where such
discomforts as wet, cold and heat, hunger, thirst, danger, and monotony become a part of our lives. On numerous occasions in the self-reliance of a
wilderness existence even the stoutest of heart will admit to himself privately—very privately if he is really stouthearted, so that his companions will
not falter—that if destiny allows him to get through, he will never get in such
a position again.

Such occasions arise when lengthy continuances fray the spirit. We have
borne a pack until every muscle is strained taut; the woods are breathless, the
mosquitoes buzz about us unceasingly in spite of the repellent with which we
have doused ourselves. We beat all day windward in a lone canoe toward
what would normally be but a several hours' paddle: the gusts are relentless
and the wind-hurled water cold; there are looming rocks and no time to eat;

chill gray evening draws perilously near, and there are inches of water about our feet.

We have strived through clotting snow until every time we advance our snowshoes we have the sensation of an imp stabbing his little pitchfork into our thighs; it has darkened; the colored alcohol in the thermometer is an inch below zero, and with numbed fingers we must make an adequate camp which is only a forerunner of many more such camps to follow. For days it has driven down rain, so that we, pressing through the sodden brush, are soaked and comfortless and sweaty, and the undergrowth has lacerated our shriveling hide.

We have stealthily tracked a bull moose on the look for a lady love for two days, only dismayingly to realize he has looped back into the wind prior to coiling up for a rest, then crashed away in a black blur from an unsuspected patch of small spruce, keeping it between him and us so that we have no chance for a shot. Or we are just plain exhausted, not from a single day's tiredness but from the gradual wearing down of a long ride.

Then in our private hearts we echo these reactions: "We are idiots. This is not pleasure. There is no genuine call for us to do this. If we ever struggle out of here, we will stay home where common sense reigns!"

After a while we do get out and are thankful. But in the next few months we will have proved to ourselves the following truth—the most all-encompassing axiom the backwoods have to teach. It won't matter how difficult a time we have been subjected to, how little fun has been interwoven with it, for in a few months our overall reaction to that journey will be good. We will think back on the difficult times and triumph over the pictures of them with a certain joy of remembrance.

I recall one trip I took in the early fall, hunting and fishing along the wild Half Moon of New Brunswick's Southwest Miramichi River. It rained without ceasing for a week. We were wet to the hide all the time, ate standing up in the roaring campfire that evaporated some of the downpour, and slept soaked. So frosty was it in the mornings that the tarps over our sleeping bags were stiff with ice and snapped when we hauled out. But even in that torment we got our limits of fish and game. Despite that, I can appraise the ordeal as about the most ill-conceived I ever got into. Yet as a general impression, that Southwest Miramichi canoe trip comes back to me as a most enjoyable one.

Once we have been back home a bit the call of the trail starts to become audible. Initially it is extremely docile. But trifle by trifle a restlessness permeates us. At first we don't appreciate precisely what is the difficulty. We are concerned only that our everyday life has lost its savor, that we are performing tasks more or less automatically, that we are a modicum more touchy than our naturally intractable temperaments.

And slowly it comes over us precisely what is the trouble. Then we mutter to ourselves:

"Fellow, you've learned. You are no cheechako. You realize precisely how hard you will have to labor, and how many difficulties you are going to encounter, how famished, chilly, damp, weary, and generally worn out you are going to be. You've been in the bush often enough before, so it's especially vivid to you. You're getting into this thing with your eyes wide open. You know what you're going to be in for. You're mighty well set right here, and you'd be an idiot to go."

"Right you are," you agree with yourself. "You're plumb right about it all. I wonder where we can pick up another cayuse."

Destinations

Throughout this country there are vast stretches of unspoiled and practically uninhabited wilderness. Here you can take your pack. You can fish and photograph and live with nature for almost as long as you will, and have a glorious and totally different adventure you'll never forget.

All this can be done at hardly any expense. The most costly factor, as a matter of fact, is time. Once you have assembled a small outfit and reached a jumping-off place, you can journey and sightsee at no further outlay than for the food you'd eat anyway, for less than the cost of living at home.

Furthermore, you are completely footloose and independent, free to roam and sleep where you will. You need rely on no one, and there is none of the care and cost of boats, cycles, automobiles, and pack animals.

"Hiking a ridge, a meadow, or a river bottom, is as healthy a form of exercise as one can get," said former Supreme Court Justice William O. Douglas. "Hiking seems to put all the body cells back into rhythm. Ten to twenty miles on a trail puts one to bed with his cares unraveled. Hiking—and climbing, too—are man's most natural exercises. They introduce him again to the wonders of nature and teach him the beauty of the woods and fields in winter as well as in spring. They also teach him how to take care of himself and his neighbors in times of adversity.

"We need exercise as individuals. We need to keep physically fit and alert as people . . . 'History is the sound of heavy boots going upstairs and the rustle of satin slippers coming down.' Nations that are soft and sleek—people who get all their exercise and athletics vicariously—will not survive when the competition is severe and adversity is at hand. It is imperative that America stay fit. For today we face as great a danger, as fearsome a risk, as any people in history."

Although modern equipment and improved methods have been developed that ease hiking of its drudgery and hard physical work, and open it to all ages, there is nothing new about hiking and camping with only what can be easily packed on one's back. Our early frontiersmen traveled that way whenever they entered the wilderness. Daniel Boone spent two whole years more or less alone in the virgin wilderness of Kentucky, living off the country, with no outfit except that which he had been carrying when he left.

Those who have never done any backpacking in the right manner, with a good outfit, have the idea that it is the toughest kind of toil. One often hears the expression, "I don't propose to make a packhorse of myself." Many who have attempted such a vacation never repeat it because they have found it too much like hard work. Any resemblance to hard work, however, is due entirely to improper equipment and mistaken technique. Done right, there is nothing hard about vacationing with a packsack. You wander free and unfettered, with just enough exercise in the pure air to make life thoroughly enjoyable.

Those who have adopted the best methods of backpacking, formerly known to a few, are returning regularly to the trails and bringing others with them. Many are combining the satisfaction of hiking with camping and fishing in unspoiled wilderness, all at costs they could not even approximate in any other form of diversion.

Such trips are for anyone healthy and fairly vigorous. They can be enjoyed equally by parents, by teenagers of both sexes, elderly people in good health, and certainly by children. One of the most important sidelines of some of the packsack companies is child carriers. Some are designed so the youngster rides an adult's back, something like a papoose of yore, and can be carried either forward or—especially in bush country—backwards.

Today only two things are essential for backpacking vacations: drinking water, which you can purify if need be, and country where you can walk without trespassing.

Where to Go

Within the 154 national forests in thirty-nine states and Puerto Rico are 182,000,000 such acres and more than 105,000 miles of trails, all open to backpacking. National parks are crisscrossed with thousands of miles of maintained trails. Innumerable public campgrounds are enmeshed by well-marked webs of hiking paths which lead to every type of attraction. Considerable undeveloped countryside everywhere, within easy reach of even the largest cities, calls for exploration on foot.

Toting everything you need, you can rove in the woods of all our Atlantic states; in the forests of northern Michigan, Wisconsin, and Minnesota; in the Ozark Mountains; and in the piñon and cactus highlands around Taos, New Mexico, where Kit Carson made his camps earlier.

If you live near crowded New York, there are the Catskill Mountains only three hours away by car. North of Boston, beyond the inviting backways of Essex and Gloucester, are the White Mountains, with the Little Imp and other unforgettable trails. Just east of Philadelphia are the South Jersey pine barrens. From the capital of our country, the cloud-scoured Blue Ridge is only two hours distant.

Trails

Hiking the Long Trail

Vermont's Long Trail is a wilderness footpath for hikers. Extending from Canada to Massachusetts, it winds along or near the crest of the state's historic Green Mountains. Some ninety side trails, together with frequent crossings of country roads, provide such frequent access to supplies that it's possible to make this trip with ultralight equipment. All you have to do is crisscross the route beforehand in an automobile and cache food, preferably contained in large cans for easy storage and preparation, in convenient places such as under rock shelves. The fact that there are some sixty-three shelters, open or enclosed, along the way makes such a lightweight trip even more practical. These havens are never more than a day's hike apart.

The length of the Long Trail is a fraction over 255 miles, approximately a hundred miles longer than Vermont itself. The more than ninety side trails add another 170 miles, making a total of about 425 miles for the complete Long Trail system. Of this, the Green Mountain Club is responsible for maintaining a total of 265 miles, 175 miles of the Long Trail and 90 miles of side trails. The U.S. Forest Service is in charge of 80 miles of the Long Trail and of the largest part of the remaining side trails. The portion of the Long Trail between Vermont 100, near Sherburne Pass, and Massachusetts 2 at Blackinton, is associated with the younger Appalachian Trail.

There is one shelter for about every four miles of trail. If you'd like to earn the right to join the End-to-End Club of one of this country's major trails, here's a good place to start. Incidentally, the way to walk all these north-south footpaths is northward, if possible. Then you are considerably less troubled by sun in the eyes.

Detailed information on the Long Trail is available from the Green Mountain Club, which puts out an up-to-date guidebook to this footpath in the wilderness. This easily packed booklet gives the mapped, step-by-step story. [Some other publications also are available. Contact Green Mountain Club, 4711 Waterbury-Stowe Rd., Waterbury Center, VT 05677; (802) 244-7037. Their website is http://www.greenmountainclub.org]

Riding and Hiking Trails

With nationwide interest in wilderness hiking increasing at a remarkable rate, big new trail systems are still being developed. One of these is the projected 3000-mile California Riding and Hiking Trail, extending from San Ysidro near Mexico northward through the Tehachapi Mountains and the Sierra Nevada to near the Oregon line, and returning in a long loop through the breezy coast mountains. Something over a thousand miles of this new trail have already been completed and are being enthusiastically used.

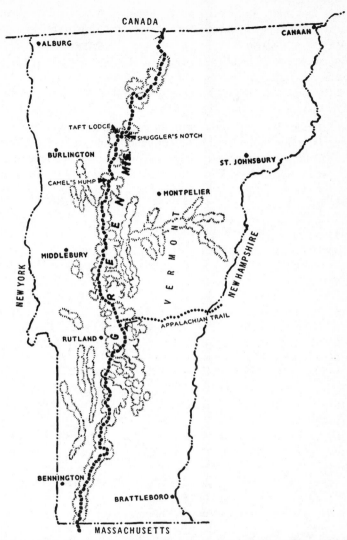

Vermont's Long Trail. This trail, over 255 miles long, roughly coincides with the Appalachian Trail between the Massachusetts border and a point slightly northeast of Rutland, where the latter trail branches off to the east.

Construction specifications call for a minimum trail width of thirty inches to be built through a twenty-foot right of way. A system of overnight camps has been started. Units are to be spaced some fifteen to twenty miles apart, with facilities consisting of stoves, tables, water, sanitation, and corrals.

Numerous secondary trails are already planned. All in all, the wilderness through which these three thousand miles loop is among the most magnificent in the West.

Although in several counties the trail is complete and in use, in some others the acquisition of rights of way has just been started. Where the trail goes through federal lands, construction and maintenance are being handled by the U.S. Forest Service and the National Park Service. In other areas the construction and maintenance are under the supervision of the Department of Parks and Recreation in Sacramento, California, from which current information is available.

The Big Ones

Then there is the 1,995-mile footpath known as the Appalachian Trail, with its chain of free lean-tos and fireplaces, which twists from Mount Katahdin in Maine to Springer Mountain in Georgia. On the other side of the continent,

The Appalachian Trail. Popular with hikers, this famous trail extends from Maine to Georgia.

the rugged 2,156-mile Pacific Crest Trail extends from Canada to Mexico in a country-long slash from near Mount Baker in Washington to Campo in San Diego County, California. Both are enlivened by hundreds of miles of secondary trails that invite side excursions.

The Appalachian Trail is a free, serene, slightly incredible footpath that crosses the sparkling lake and mountain country south of Maine, goes through the Green and White Mountains and the Berkshire Hills, and finally leads through the restful wild areas along the crests of the Catskill, Allegheny, Blue Ridge, and the Great Smoky Mountains to its southern terminus.

Among the feeder paths to this great wilderness thoroughfare is the Horseshoe Trail, which starts at the historic Valley Forge battlefield and joins the main Appalachian Trail at Manada Gap, Pennsylvania. The Horseshoe, unlike the parent route, is a riding lane as well as a footpath. There also are numerous motor roads that cross the summits of these mountains, thus tapping the Trail and providing easy access to it from any of the eastern states.

The wilderness way twines, for the most part, at elevations of 2,000–5,000 feet through high wooded mountains with many open crests. It passes through a well-watered country. There are campgrounds with fireplaces and a large number of lean-tos along it for those who do not choose to pack their own shelter. Innumerable camp spots exist everywhere for the more experienced.

Weather and travel conditions are best from about the middle of June to late September. The climate at these generally high altitudes is a relief during the summer months from the swelter of the lowlands—and from the noise and grime of nervous vacation traffic. Hiking and camping under nearly arctic conditions is possible for the more strenuous during the snowy months.

Here and there along the Appalachian Trail will be found an occasional lodge and small vacation resort. As a rule, however, it is still all wilderness. Those who plan to take fullest advantage of the outdoor opportunities the country affords must pack shelter and food on their backs, as it is a hiker's route and not a horse trail.

It is unnecessary to overburden oneself with weighty equipment and food. The mild sumer nights demand a minimum of bedding, except in the White Mountains area above timberline, where the weather is unpredictable. A very light down bag is ideal. Every three or four hiking days along the Trail there are branch paths, and sometimes roads, winding down to farming land and small villages where country stores afford a chance to replenish food supplies. Good fishing abounds in many of the streams that splash from the crests.

The Appalachian Trail is a volunteer recreational project. It is supervised and maintained by the Appalachian Trail Conference [799 Washington St., P.O. Box 807, Harpers Ferry, WV 25425-0807. Phone (304) 535-6331. Their website is http://www.atcom.org/]. This is a federation of organizations, mainly outing clubs, and individuals interested in the footpath. Its activities and objectives are entirely voluntary. Having no salaried employees, it furnishes complete information about the trail by means of its pamphlets, guidebooks, bulletins, and maps. A small charge is made for these. The funds so derived are used to republish the literature.

The Pacific Crest Trail extends from Canada to Mexico along the crests of the Cascade, Sierra Nevada, and Sierra Madre mountains. It incorporates seven major units, largely built and maintained by the National Park Service. These are almost entirely within government parks and forests. Only some 160 miles, in fact, lie outside these public lands.

The long path, skirting such famous mountains as Rainier, Adams, Hood, Shasta, and towering Whitney, is not a rustic lane for picnic parties. It is, in its rugged course from lodgepole pine to dusty cactus, a wilderness route for expert outdoorsmen. This does not imply that numerous scenic portions of the trail, particularly in California, are not entirely feasible for families with eight-year-old children and eighty-year-old grandparents. They are.

The Sierra Club [85 Second St., Second Floor, San Francisco, CA 94105-3441. Phone: (415) 977-5500. Website is http://www.sierraclub.org/] is the organization that has done the most work in bringing the Pacific Crest Trail to the attention of the public and in fostering all it stands for. Founded in 1892 with naturalist John Muir its first president, the Sierra Club with its present thousands of members each year organizes trips into the high hills and along the star-scouring routes where it maintains numerous campsites, huts, and cheerful lean-tos.

Much of the robust course is suitable for well-shod pack animals as well as for hikers. Most of it passes through very wild country with considerable distances between supply points. This is higher, steeper in spots, than the Appalachian Trail. Some of it zigzags to altitudes one and two miles above sea level. Because of snow in the high country, portions are not always penetrable until at least well into July.

Only a few railroads and highways cross the main trail. All along the mountains, however, there are numerous roads entering from the lowlands. These bring you to it after one or two days of travel from traffic-clogged highways. Some of these side trails are, as a matter of fact, equal in scenic and recreational features to the north-south wilderness path itself. At the ends of many of these approaches will be found outfitters with pack animals and supplies for trail travel.

You can arrange, if you want, for a packer with his train to take you along the trail as far as you wish, perhaps going in over one lateral road and coming out along another. The more popular plan, when you aren't going to do all the walking, though, is to have an outfitter pack your duffle into a more or less permanent camp in some favorably situated locality, and then pick you up to go out on some prearranged date. In the meantime, you can explore the region with a backpack. The country is so vast, and in most areas the scenery is so varied and

The Pacific Crest Trail. This rugged trail, extending from Canada to Mexico, is, for the most part, a wilderness route for expert outdoorsmen.

grand, that you can easily spend a month or more taking short trips from an established camp and never exhaust the possibilities for variety and enjoyment.

The Pacific Crest Trail is the roughest of the four. Too, the nights there are apt to be cooler than on the East's Appalachian Trail and the Long Trail. In the

West, therefore, depending, of course, on where you hike, some of your equipment may well approach that of the alpinist. Strong mountain shoes, preferably with cleated rubber soles that will cut through gravel and give you sure footing on rocks, are highly desirable. You'll probably appreciate a warm jacket, shirt, or sweater for the evenings. Bedding in general should be a little heavier than along the Atlantic heights of the continent. A down sleeping bag, a mummy type weighing not over five pounds, will be excellent.

Along neither route is a regular tent essential during moderate weather. A compact plastic poncho, weighing less than a pound, will pinch-hit perfectly for both raincoat and shelter.

A compass is always desirable, as it is everywhere in wild places. Although the main wilderness trails are well marked, it is easy to get mixed up on directions in the haze and clouds often encountered at high altitudes.

Available Maps

The trail organizations mentioned have available sometimes extremely detailed maps of their routes with, in some accompanying guide publications, almost step-by-step directions.

The best Pacific Crest Trail maps are those published by the U.S. Forest Service, Washington, D.C. If you will mention the particular sections of the trail in which you are interested, this division of the Department of Agriculture will suggest the names and the very low prices of the maps showing these.

[U.S.D.A. Forest Service, P.O. Box 96090, Washington, DC 20090-6090. Their home website is http://www.fs.fed.us/index.html. For maps the website is http://www.fs.fed.us/links/maps.shtml]

As none of these many widespread routes nor the regions adjacent to them can be reasonably negotiated nor thoroughly enjoyed without backpacking, a readily carried outfit containing equipment and food for each person is indispensable. Large tents and other heavy rigging are both unsuitable and handicapping, except for extended and rather expensive pack train trips. For backpacking, everything should be cut down in weight and bulk to absolute essentials. Food should be largely water-free.

Enchanted and Enchanting

And so, at the end of the paved road—shouldering your pack and striding into enchanted and enchanting country—you leave behind the unhealthy tension, bustle, noises, fumes, expense, and frustrations of civilization. There is no other kind of vacation that can compare to these backpacking trips, none that will take you so close to peace and utter freedom.

And when you return, what a tale you'll have to tell about this entirely different world in which you've been. Everyone who has made such a lightweight hike, and has sat at night by crackling campfires deep in the wilderness, wants to go back.

PART ONE
SOME BASICS: SKILLS, TOOLS, GEAR

CHAPTER ONE

USING THE WOODSMAN'S BASIC TOOLS

One doesn't need to be a lumberjack in order to acquire enough know-how in the use and care of axes, hatchets, saws, and knives to handle these tools effectively when undertaking such common tasks as felling, chopping, and sawing timber.

Even the greenest tenderfoot can fell his first trees in a given direction if he will follow the simple principles set forth here. Wind, incline, weight, and surrounding objects must, of course, be taken into consideration.

A small safety notch is first made to minimize any possibility of the butt's kicking back or the trunk's splitting. Below this on the opposite side, where the tree is to fall, a wide notch is cut. When this indentation is about three-fifths through, a few strokes at the first nick should send the tree crashing.

The two notches are so placed that they form a natural hinge. This hinge controls the direction of the fall and lessens the chance that the butt may thrust backward. However, one should have his eye on a safe place and should hurry there when the moment comes for the call of "Timber-r-r!"

It is even easier to drop a tree by using a saw. The principles remain the same. Make the same brief initial cut. Follow it with a deep slit opposite and below; then deepen the first incision.

An ax, or perhaps a wooden wedge cut on the spot, may have to be driven into one gash or the other to free the saw. Too, you often can topple a heavy tree that is pretty much on balance and come closer to pinpointing its fall by using a wedge in the higher cut.

AXES

The ax is an almost indispensable tool for woodsmen, many of whom rate it even above matches as the most valuable item to have along in the bush. It may be, however, a very dangerous instrument in the hands of a novice.

The ax is not really needed in the average warm weather camp. It is not necessary, either, on summer backpacking trips. It is, rather, the tool for heavy work, for getting in large wood for fires, for building big shelters, and for cutting out timber that may fall across horse trails and canoe streams.

How Heavy an Ax?

The ax with a 2½- or perhaps a 3-pound head is big enough for most outdoorsmen. Heavier axes bite deeper and therefore, in the hands of an expert,

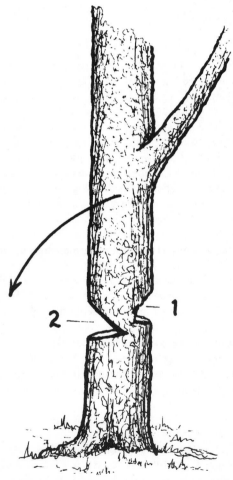

Controlling Direction of Timber Fall. Tree should fall in the direction of the arrow if a small notch is made at position 1, a larger notch at position 2, and a few additional strokes made at the first notch.

do faster work. That is why lumberjacks, frontiersmen, and others who grow up in ax country and who use these mobile wedges regularly, pick a heavy model. These, besides being tiring in the hands of a tyro, require a lot of skill and are, therefore, more potentially dangerous.

Double-bitted axes are very tricky in the hands of all but experienced and careful men. In addition, they cannot be used easily as hammers, for which purpose, although it is not to be recommended, the outdoorsman is sometimes apt to find himself employing it a dozen times a day.

The handiest ax for packing, although not for any great amount of work, is the Hudson Bay model, with a narrow butt and a face of normal width. Sometimes an occasional craftsman uses one of these painstakingly on a log cabin, but such an individual is usually a perfectionist who has more of the qualities of the cabinetmaker than of the carpenter. This model, because of its narrow poll through which the handle is attached, does not hold up too well in all cases.

But for ordinary outdoor requirements, where weight is a factor but you still want an ax, a Hudson Bay with a 1½-pound head and a 24-inch handle will do a lot of work. The Hudson Bay ax, incidentally, is a convenient one to tie behind your saddle.

Outdoorsmen who use an ax very much probably will be most satisfied with an ordinary single-bit ax with about a 2½-pound head. A handle or helve about 26 to 28 inches long is generally enough, although some may find they can swing the 36-inch handle more naturally. In any event, if you adopt one length of handle and use it exclusively, you will come to do better and safer work.

Sharpening an Ax

The edge on the ax you buy is probably sharp enough for the average two-weeks-a-year camper. The good axman will probably want to thin this edge for keener cutting. The best tool for this, and for rough sharpening as well, is a grindstone, kept wet during use.

In the woods a 12-inch or so flat file does a good job. To sharpen an ax, start about an inch back from its edge and carry that out straight. Taper very slightly to the edge itself. Do not overdo this, however, or the ax will bind. Finish the job with a sharpening stone.

It is false economy to look for ax bargains. This is especially true since well-balanced, expertly tempered, and conscientiously forged brands may be purchased for a very few dollars.

Hatchet

The light 1-pound ax with a 12-inch handle will do all the work necessary in many camps and on backpacking trails. The average outdoorsman can use it with more effectiveness and greater safety than a long-handled ax. As a matter of fact, some of the more skilled backwoods axmen often turn to such a hatchet, smoothing a pole or log so skillfully with one that you'd suppose it had been planed.

Such a hand ax works well in securing wood for a small campfire, when you bother to use an ax at all. It's a lot more useful than a knife for blazing a trail. Secure a substantial sheath for it, but don't ordinarily carry it on your belt. This is both inconvenient and uncomfortable. Stow it, instead, in a rucksack or saddle pocket.

Axmanship

A whole book could be written on the subject of axmanship. The best axmen almost all picked up the art as boys on the farm or in the woods, but with practice and care, anyone can learn well enough for all the usual outdoor chores. Incidentally, experienced golfers find the desirable free and easy swing to an exact point almost second nature.

The main thing is to be careful. You can ruin an outdoor trip in a hurry with just one stroke that lands a fraction of an inch from the place it should go. The best general precaution is to anticipate the worst and to be so placed that even if it does occur, no one will be hurt. Too, a sharp ax is safer than a dull one in that it is not so likely to bounce off the wood.

Be prepared, though, to have the ax glance off a knot, and have your feet and legs where they will not be hit. Instead of relying on a perfect swing, take the time to clear away any shrubs and branches that might catch the blade. Don't take the risk of steadying a billet with hand or foot.

Avoid, too, the common practice of leaning a stick against a log and half chopping and half breaking it in two. A lot of head injuries from flying wood have resulted from this all too prevalent habit. When you're felling a dead tree for firewood or for a cabin, watch out that another tree doesn't break off the top and send it crashing back toward you. In other words, there are a great many possible misadventures. The more of these you can foresee and protect yourself against, the less will be the possibility of an injury.

When you stop to think of it, axes are far less dangerous than such a very common substance as glass. Any shortcomings do not lie in the ax but rather in the individual. Use this wedge with a nice easy swing. Let the gravity fall of the ax do most of the work, and you'll be able to cut all morning without pressing. Keep your eye on the exact spot where you want the edge to strike, and practice until it always does strike there.

Replacing Handles

Ax handles, especially in the hands of beginners, occasionally break. If this should happen, cut off the remaining handle near to the head and try to drive it out the wider end of the slot. If this doesn't work, you'll have to burn it out.

This can be done without injury to the tempered metal. Just wet a small area of ground. Then shove the ax blade into this damp soil all the way to the

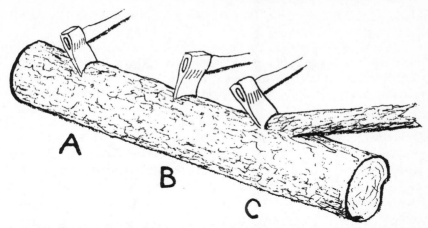

Axmanship Fundamentals. Always chop at an acute angle of the grain, as in *A*. An ax, hitting the grain at a right angle, as in *B*, will hardly bite at all. The way to chop limbs off a trunk is upward, the way they grow, as in *C*.

eye. Kindle a fire directly over the head. The heat and flames should so char the wood that it can be driven or broken out easily.

The driving on of a new handle should be accomplished by blows on the end of the upraised handle, not on the head itself. Finally, tighten the ax with a wooden wedge. Cut off any portions of the wedge and handle that protrude beyond the head. If you have salvaged a metal wedge from the old combination, use this to tighten the head further.

Incidentally, do not paint or varnish ax handles, as this causes your hands to blister.

Preserving the Temper of the Blade

Woodsmen may be seen on frosty mornings, warming axes in their hands. Another trick is to keep your ax in your shelter. An ax left out during a really frigid night may shiver to fragments at the first stroke. Incidentally, care must be taken not to bend a saw that has become brittle with frost.

Heat, whether from fire or from a too vigorously turned grindstone, endangers the temper of steel. A well-tempered blade is something to cherish. Some lumberjacks will not leave an ax in green wood on the theory that this may draw the precious temper.

Some Elementals

Chop at an acute angle to the grain. The ax, hitting at a right angle to the grain, will hardly bite at all.

The way to chop limbs off a trunk is upward, the way they grow.

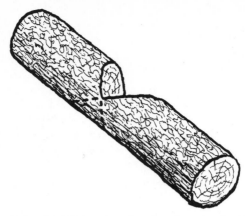

Chopping a Fallen Log in Two. Two V-shaped notches, started on opposite sides of the log, will do the job nicely.

Start each of the pair of side notches needed to chop a fallen log in two as wide apart as the log itself. Two such V's, joining at the stick's center, will sever it most economically.

As for squaring a log, methods vary with workmen. An easy way, however, is to walk along the top and score a side with an easy swing of the ax. That is, make naturally slanting cuts several inches apart to the same approximate depth. This latter may be indicated by a guide line. The chips are then hewn out by walking back the other way and cutting parallel along the real or imaginary guide line.

You can spend as much time as you want from then on in slicing off a shaving here and there until, with sufficient patience and skill, the surface becomes as smooth as if it were planed.

SAW

It is usually much easier and faster to saw all but small logs than it is to chop them. If you are using a wood-burning stove, such a tool will be invaluable for working available fuel into the right lengths to fit the firebox. Even when you're bivouacking in weather nippy enough to require the companionship of an overnight blaze, a saw will make the task of accumulating enough fodder for that campfire a comparatively easy one.

Swede Saw

The long slim blade of the Swede saw is a favorite of outdoorsmen in the cold climates. It is so thin that it speeds through wood with a minimum of effort. It is so light that it can be easily handled in any position. The long, narrow blade is so flexible that, except during extreme cold, it can be coiled to the circumference of a saucer, held together by a cord wound and tied among its teeth, and wrapped with a piece of canvas for carrying.

The two-piece, light, tubular handle is easily slid apart and packed. If you want, you can even dispense with this and bend a husky green sapling into place for a frame when necessary. Make a small hole through each end of the sapling, at right angles to the wood, with a knife or nail. Then split each end. The improvised handle can then be attached by inserting the blade in the slits and securing it, through each hole, by wire or whatever else is handy. Carrying two butterfly bolts for this purpose can save time.

The cranky side of a Swede saw is its disposition to twist and bind. Many select the heavier, comparatively rigid crosscut saw for this reason. The crosscut is of particular value in cabin construction for making the straight cuts necessary for window and door openings. Besides being surer and steadier than the temperamental Swede saw, it can be inserted in a wall in the space made by removing one log. The one-man crosscut, on which an additional handle can be slipped, will suffice.

Whatever saw you take into the bush, don't make the mistake some tenderfeet do and carry a blade with the small crosscut or rip teeth used by carpenters. See to it that your saw is designed for cutting rough timber.

Sawhorse

You will save time with one or two sawhorses if you are going to do much sawing. The simplest sawhorse is two poles driven into the ground to form an X. A chunk of wood jammed between the lower gap in this contrivance will steady it. The X often is wired together in the middle for further support. Two such sawhorses placed conveniently side by side can save a lot of maneuvering and stooping.

KNIVES

For all his mastery of earth and space, man is a weak creature, with inadequate teeth and scarcely any claws. He must rely on tools to perform the simplest functions, and since the earliest man picked up the first sharp-edged stone, the knife has been a primary tool in the wilderness. A man in the outdoors without one is a weakling, while the man with one is the master of a hundred situations. With the right kind of knife he can warm himself, feed himself, shelter himself, clothe himself, and defend himself.

Procuring a knife is a very personal undertaking. Your own preference will guide you, but a few rules apply to all knives. Buy the best you can afford, in a pattern designed for the use you have in mind. Beware of war surplus and import bargains. It's best to stick with a known brand from a dependable dealer.

A hollow-ground blade is not satisfactory on an outdoor knife because its thin edge, shaped in cross section like that of a straight-edge razor, is likely to chip. On the other hand, the blunt, chisel-like bevel found on the exceptionally hard-tempered knives that are advertised to cut through bone and metal will not take a keen enough edge to make them suitable for general wilderness use.

For a general-purpose knife, avoid those with stainless steel blades, as ordinarily they, too, won't take a keen edge. When they are dull, it takes forever and a day to bring them to an even half-decent sharpness on a whetstone. Stainless steel knives made by hand are harder than mass-manufactured products, for a tougher metal can be used than can be handled by die stamping. But usually, if you are going to put out the money for a handmade knife, you may as well have the very finest high carbon steel.

Care of Knife and Sheath

Your knife should always be thoroughly cleaned and dried after use. Never sheathe a wet blade. As a matter of fact, if you intend to store a knife for a prolonged period, coat it with oil, vaseline, or some other protection, and leave it out of the sheath.

Sporting knives need the same attention as carving knives. It is never advisable to immerse either in water. Wiping and drying the blade is generally sufficient.

All carbon steel blades, which are the best now available, will become stained from meat. Furthermore, a knife left for a very long time in a sheath will become stained from the acids present in all leather. Such discoloration does not harm the blade. It can be removed easily by polishing with a crocus cloth.

Any rust that appears on the blade should be removed before pitting sets in, by rubbing with fine grit emery cloth or steel wool. Then, for a fine finish, polish with a crocus cloth, available at most good hardware stores.

As is the case with an ax, a sharp knife is safer to use than a dull one.

Shoe polish or saddle soap should be used on leather handles to keep the leather from drying out. Metal polish will refurbish hilt and butt. Shoe polish or saddle soap should be used on the sheath, as well. Never use oil for this purpose, for this will soften the leather, making it flexible and causing difficulty in sheathing the blade.

How to Sharpen a Knife

W. D. Randall, who, in his Orange Blossom Trail shop in Orlando, Florida, makes by hand the finest sporting knives in the world, recommends the use of two hones, one with a medium or coarse grit for starting the sharpening process and the other with a fine grit for finishing. A single, two-sided pocket carborundum will do, too.

To sharpen a knife, just follow these step-by-step directions:

1. Lubricate the hone with a few drops of saliva.
2. Place the knife diagonally on the hone, at a forty-five-degree angle.

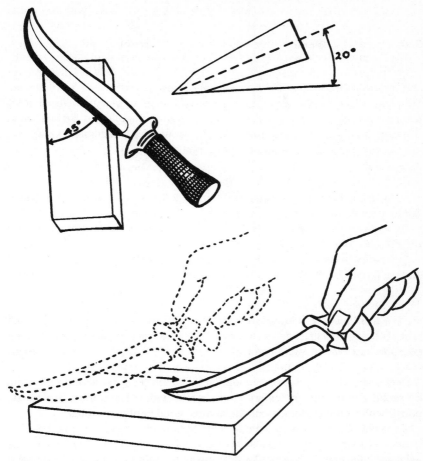

Sharpening a Knife. *Top Left:* Place the knife diagonally on the hone, at a 45° angle. *Top Right:* Raise the side of the blade to an angle of about 20° from the hone's surface. *Bottom:* Keeping the edge of the blade to the surface of the hone, holding both the diagonal position and the 20° angle, sweep the edge across the hone from hilt to point.

3. Raise the side of the blade away from the surface of the hone to an angle of about twenty degrees.
4. Keeping the edge of the blade to the surface of the hone, holding both the diagonal position and the twenty-degree angle, sweep the edge across the hone from hilt to point.
5. Turn the blade over and repeat the process.
6. Continue sharpening on alternate sides of the blade, one stroke at a time. Be sure to use even, sweeping strokes, and to maintain the same angle on

both sides of the blade throughout each stroke. Lessen the pressure as the edge is restored.

7. If a wire edge develops, hone it off by giving the blade a few light sweeps across the fine-grit hone at a high angle of about sixty degrees.

A New Concept in Sharpening

"If you want a professional edge, and have the time and patience to achieve it," adds Bo Randall, "here's a method of sharpening you may prefer.

"Follow the previous directions, but lay the blade flat and hone it until it is brought to a true razor edge, and light reflection on the cutting edge is no longer discernible. Since such a razor-like edge will not hold up under use, it should be strengthened by a few final sweeps across the hone on each side, with the blade held at a high angle (about 60°). This will leave a minute, edge-holding bevel that can hardly be seen by the naked eye.

"This method will, of course, leave hone marks across the blade bevel. In order to restore a fine finish, it is then necessary to polish the blade by rubbing it with emery cloth, starting with a medium grit, finishing with 600 grit, and following this with crocus cloth to attain the final polish."

The Crooked Knife

The famous crooked knife is one with a thin, curved blade about six inches long. It is the Indian's and occasionally the backwoodsman's substitute for a plane, drawknife, or spokeshave.

The crooked knife is used for making snowshoe frames, paddles, and thin planks for toboggans. It can be invaluable in the home manufacture of cabin furniture. The worker holds it in his hand, and, drawing it toward him, can easily shave wood to almost any curved or flat surface.

Crooked knives could once be had from many of the Hudson's Bay trading posts in Canada. Now often unheard of in a lot of these, they usually can be secured from Hudson's Bay Company headquarters in Winnipeg, Manitoba. They are made in both right-hand and left-hand models, generally without a handle. You put on your own handle.

KNOTS AND LASHINGS

Taking to the woods may seem to have nothing to do with the old saying that "for want of a nail a shoe was lost; for want of a shoe a horse was lost," etc. Many a camper, however, has painfully discovered that for want of a good knot or lashing a temper was lost, and along with it a tarpaulin, canoe, or valued pet.

Knots and lashings correctly and easily tied are a mark of the experienced outdoorsman. They can prevent a lot of trouble. Learning to tie a few basic knots and lashings is a fine way to pass an off-season evening in front of the fireplace. You may be surprised at how interesting such simple outdoor skills can become.

Knots vary a little in design, depending on their functions. The principles remain the same, however. What is desired in most instances is a knot that will not let go, but which, at the same time, can be untied in a hurry.

The easiest way to learn how to tie the various knots is by using real rope in real situations. This is not always practical, of course, and work at odd moments with a small length of cord carried in a pocket will accomplish wonders. So it will not be too unrealistically limp, this cord preferably should be at least an eighth of an inch thick.

A primary step in becoming familiar with knots is learning the names of the different parts of the rope and knots. A rope, for example, has only two parts. The end is the short, free section with which most knots are tied. The standing part is the remainder of the rope.

Knots are made by combining loops, bights, overhands, and underhands. A loop is formed by making the ends of the rope go in opposite directions. A bight, the beginning joint of many knots, is made by turning a portion of rope back upon itself. An overhand, or, for that matter, an underhand, knot is formed by passing the end through a loop.

BEST ROPE MATERIALS

Good manila hemp is the old reliable in most wilderness situations. Sisal is less expensive, but it also is weaker and less durable. Cotton is smoother, but when it gets wet and frozen, it's tempting to take an ax to the knots. Nylon is hard and strong, but it is expensive, slippery, and hard to keep tight, inasmuch as it will stretch as much as a fifth of its total length.

There are two primary kinds of rope. Laid rope is composed of hemp, sisal, cotton, or jute fibers. These are twisted into yarn. Two or more yarns are then twisted into strands. Several strands are laid together to make rope.

A soft and flexible braided rope, such as sash cord or clothesline, is manufactured of strands of cotton or other material, woven in a usually complicated pattern.

The solid polyethylene rope, although only slightly stronger than hemp, is favored by some canoeists and boatmen both because it is waterproof and because it floats. In the wilderness, though, where rope usually is put to more than one use, many still select manila, even though it is harder on the hands.

KEEPING ROPE IN WORKING CONDITION

The main enemy of hemp is moisture. This rope should be kept as dry as possible, especially when it is stored. The usual wilderness wettings do not harm it, however, if it is allowed to dry before being loosely coiled and hung in a preferably well ventilated spot, away from woodmice, chipmunks, squirrels, porcupines, and other gnawing rodents.

An easy way to coil rope is by grasping one end in the left hand, bending the upper part of the left arm to vertical and wrapping the rope between thumb and

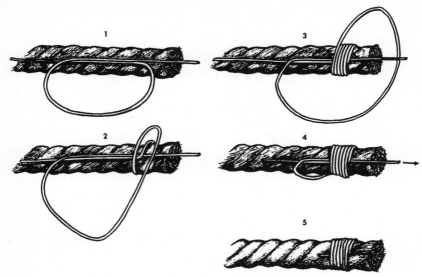

Steps in Whipping Rope

fingers and elbow until all is coiled. Finish off with two snug half hitches (see description under "Two Half Hitches" later in this chapter) around the entire roll.

With rope too long or heavy to coil in this fashion, hold one end in the left hand and hang the rope in loops of the desired size over the left arm. Finish off in the same manner.

Prevention of Raveling

Unless you take special precautions, the ends of your rope will ravel. With materials such as hemp and sisal, a functional procedure is to wrap the ends tightly with either medical or electrical tape. Especially neat is dipping them into about an inch of liquid glue. The ends of synthetic rope can be quickly sealed by melting them with a small flame.

Rope, too, can be whipped. Make a bight in a three-foot length of strong twine, heavy linen thread, or cotton fish line. Lay this a quarter of an inch from the end of the rope. Twine the other end of the cord tightly around the rope, over the bight, until the whipping is as wide as the rope is thick. Push the end of the cord down through the exposed loop of the bight. Pull the loop snugly under the whipping. Cut off the loose end.

Stopper Knot

You may, if you want, splice the end instead. One method of making such a stopper knot is commenced by untwisting about six inches of the rope. Fol-

Stopper Knot

lowing the twist of the rope, turn each of the strands downward to make a loop. Now bring each adjacent free end up through the loop next to it. Pull the knot together tightly and evenly. To give it a finished hardness, put it on the hard ground and roll it for a minute under your boot.

You can reinforce this knot by making several smaller knots, one on top of the other. Or you can finish it off with a crown knot.

Crown Knot

The crown knot can be used by itself to prevent the end of a rope from raveling, or it can be tied on top of the above stopper knot.

You'll need about six inches of untwisted end. Take the center strand and bring the end down toward you against the main part of the rope between the other two strands, to make a bight.

Crown Knot

Crown Splice

Then grasp the left strand. Bring it around the bight to the right, between this and the right strand. This will give you a perpendicular bight and a horizontal loop around that bight.

Take the right strand. Shove it through the bight from right to left without going through the loop. Now each strand is held under one of the others. Pull the strands tight, one by one, to complete the crown knot.

Crown Splice

Most professional of all is the crown splice. Start with a crown knot. Then take one strand and work it down into the main rope by passing it over the nearest rope strand and under the next strand.

Turn the rope a bit and do the same thing with the second loose strand, passing it over the nearest rope strand and under the next one. Do the same thing with the third loose strand. Continue until you have made four complete rounds. Now roll the splice under your foot to round and smooth it, and cut the ends off flush.

THE HANDIEST KNOTS

Square Knot

Basically important is the square knot that, when improperly tied, becomes the disreputable granny knot which commits the double fault of jamming and

Square Knot

slipping. The square knot is used to join two ends of the same size. If the ends are of different diameters, it will slip, and the sheet bend should be tied instead.

To tie the square knot, make a bight in the end of a rope. Bring the other end up through the bight, around the standing parts, and back down through the bight.

Or, more familiarly, cross the two ends, pass the first under the second, reverse the directions of the two ends, and cross the first over the second and down through the bight thus formed.

To untie when the rope or cord is stiff enough, grasp the standing parts on each end of the knot. Move the hands together, forcing the loops apart. When the material is soft, it is loosened by tugging one end so as to turn the knot over, whereupon it will easily slip off the end you pulled.

Surgeon's Knot

This is the same as the square knot, except that in making it by the second method described above, the two ends are given an extra twist around each other at the start. It is used by doctors to prevent the first turn of the knot from slipping. It also is handy in doing up bundles.

Sheet Bend

For joining two ends of rope, particularly when they are wet or frozen or of different sizes or materials, no knot is more efficient than the sheet bend. It

Surgeon's Knot

Sheet Bend

never slips, is simple to tie, doesn't take much rope, and can be quickly un-knotted.

Make a bight in the larger rope. As with the square knot, bring the end of the other rope up through the bight and around the standing parts. Now pass the end of this rope under itself where it comes up through the bight, in such a way that, when tightened, it is held against the outside of the bight.

Two Half Hitches

One is always finding uses for the very simple two half hitches, a particularly useful knot for fastening a rope to a ring, hook, tree, or rail. The only dis-

Two Half Hitches

advantage to this knot is its tendency to jam under heavy strain. This can be complicated by the useless habit some have of making more than a pair of half hitches.

To make a half hitch, pass the rope around a tree, bring the end back around the standing part, and then down through the loop this formed. The other half hitch is formed by bringing the end again around the standing part and down through its own loop. Tighten.

Clove Hitch

The clove hitch, which is merely a pair of half hitches made in opposite directions, is handy for fastening a rope so it will stay up around a tree trunk. It will remain secure, even on a slippery tent pole, inasmuch as the rope pulls against itself. It has the further advantage of not jamming.

Loop the rope end around the tree. Bring it over itself and take it around the tree again at a slant. Finally, slip the end under this last loop, bringing it out in a direction opposite to that of the standing part. Pressure on either end of the rope will not tighten it.

Bowline

The quickly tied and untied bowline, which has raised and lowered tens of thousands of individuals to safety, provides a loop that will neither tighten nor slip. This knot, which will not jam, also is an excellent way to tie the end of a slippery synthetic picket or mooring rope.

Make a small loop in the standing part of a rope. Bring the end up through it, leaving a working loop of the desired size. Now pass the end around the standing part of the rope and back down through the small loop.

A practical way to tie the same type of knot by feel alone, if, for instance, you want to picket a horse by a foreleg at night, is first to make a loop near the end of a rope and then to pull the standing part of the rope through it in a

Clove Hitch

Bowline

Tying a Non-Slipping, Non-Jamming Knot by Feel Alone

second loop, as shown in the drawing, "Tying a Non-Slipping, Non-Jamming Knot by Feel Alone." Hold this second loop in one hand and the rope end in the other. Pass the short end not too snugly below the fetlock just above the hoof. Shove the end into the second loop and, by pulling the second loop back through the first, work the knot into position.

Figure-8 Knot

The self-descriptive and easily untied figure-8 knot, often made in the end of a rope to keep it from raveling or to prevent it from slipping through a block, is a good way to fasten a line or leader to a fishhook. This knot should be pulled as tight as possible.

Inasmuch as monofilament slips more than other common materials, its end should not be cut too short. Too, a knot-holding ball can be made on the free end after the knot is tied and trimmed by touching this lightly with a hot match head.

To tie the figure-8 knot, which has the look of the numeral, make a loop by bringing the end across the standing part. Fasten by shoving the end down through the first loop.

Figure-8 Knot

Handcuff Knot

Handcuff Knot

In addition to other uses, this knot may be used to help immobilize your dog if you ever have to tie him up to get out porcupine quills. The loops can also be slipped over a man's wrists, tightened, and then secured with a square knot. If you have only fishline, secure the prisoner's thumbs behind his back in the same fashion.

The handcuff knot is very simply made by passing a rope back under itself to make a small loop. Make a second loop in similar fashion and lay it over the first. You'll now have four vertical parts in a row. Pull the second of these down through the first loop and the third up through the second loop.

Cat's Paw

The cat's paw affords a simple way of attaching a rope to a hook. Just turn a rope back beside itself to form a bight. Lift the end of the bight back on the bight to make two eyes. Pick up an eye in each hand and give each a complete turn outward from the middle. Loop both eyes over the hook.

Cat's Paw

Timber Hitch

Although the timber hitch is neither a permanent knot nor secure when left slack, it is a useful knot for hauling cabin logs. To lift a log with it, as from a pole tripod, take a half hitch around the end to be first hoisted. Incidentally, the timber hitch is less liable to slip if old rope is used.

To make it, pass the end of the rope around a log. Make a half hitch around the standing part. Then take two or more turns under and around the loop thus formed. Draw tight and maintain a steady pressure.

Sheepshank

A sheepshank, a practical way to shorten rope that is in use, is very simply made by the above principles. Just lay three loops atop one another. Pull one side of the middle loop down through the first loop, and the other side of this center loop up through the third loop. Adjust to your liking and then tighten by pulling on the standing parts.

Hitching Tie

This is a handy knot for tying a pack or saddle animal or a boat painter. The rope is passed around the tree or other object, and then a simple overhand knot is tied around it with the free end, only the doubled rope is pulled in a bight through the loop instead of the end itself. The free end is then used to anchor the knot by being shoved down through the bight, so the hitch cannot become accidentally untied. When this running end is pulled out of the bight and jerked, it will loosen the rope without a lot of working and fumbling.

Timber Hitch

Sheepshank

Hitching Tie

Lashing Shear Legs

When two poles are to be joined to support the ridgepole of a shelter, lay them side by side on the ground, wrap a short rope near their tops several times, and then tie this off with a square knot.

A sturdier job can be done, as when more of a weight is to be supported, by first placing a block between the tops of the two poles to hold them a short distance apart. Make a clove hitch around one pole. Take a half-dozen turns around the two poles, laying these close to one another but not crossing them. Then remove the block and take several very tight turns around the lashings between the poles. Finish off with a clove hitch on the second pole.

Lashing Shear Legs

CHAPTER TWO

BACKPACKING BASICS

Only two packs are really satisfactory for the backpacking vacation. One is the alpine type of frame rucksack, usually with a single large and several smaller fabric compartments built around a strong, light, metal frame to which shoulder straps are fastened. The other is the pack board, basically a rectangular frame over which fabric is so tightly doubled and laced that a bundle lashed to it never touches the hiker's back. Both are obtainable in different sizes.

The best packs in the world for this type of recreation are variations of the pack board made in the United States and available in stores throughout the country.

Light, strong, and durable, such pack boards are made, in the main, of tough aluminum tubing, although such materials as nylon keep all hard surfaces away from the back. Carrying bags, obtainable from the same sources, fit to the frames. The result is utility plus convenience and comfort. Anyone planning to cover very many miles of recreational backpacking would do well, everything else being equal, to make such a pack the nucleus of his outfit. The wrong pack has ruined more such vacations than any other single item.

FRAME RUCKSACK

Whereas the aforementioned packs are in their present forms essentially American, although of course they evolved from the primitive backpacking experience both among the Indians and peoples the world over, the alpine type of frame rucksack is a European development. It largely replaced the pack board in Europe among those interested in packing as a recreation. This has been in part because of fashion, but it's also the result of the low center of gravity provided by such frame rucksacks as the Bergans variety, which makes them particularly adapted to such prime European sports as climbing

Bergan-Meis Frame Pack. A comfortable imported pack originating in Norway. Bag is mounted on a light tubular-steel framework, bow-shaped at the bottom.

and skiing. In recent years, however, the American pack boards have been making increasing inroads in Europe.

Frame rucksacks are, indeed, extremely comfortable with light loads. Their multipocketed sacks, whose utility is widely incorporated in the American packs, are certainly handy when you want to get at various parts of the load without unpacking the whole outfit. Besides dividing the sack into convenient compartments, these partitions also help the sack to keep its functional shape. The rucksacks' design, with the top of the sack hanging away from the back, makes them cool and keeps the point of gravity low.

This latter characteristic becomes a disadvantage, however, when heavy loads are carried. The backward tilt of the sack then becomes a drag on the hips and legs, at the same time pulling the body off balance. Another disadvantage of this pack with heavy loads is its increased tendency to sway, further disrupting the balance.

Lightweight Rucksack for Day Trips. Weighing only 2¼ pounds, this rucksack has a light metal frame and a sack size 12" × 14" × 5"—a typical rucksack adapted to short trips.

Frame rucksacks, then, are functional for ordinary trail carrying only when the loads are relatively light. Lightness, of course, is a relative thing, being largely dependent on an individual's body weight. To sum up, it might be generalized that the Bergans type of frame rucksack is not the best choice for day-after-day trail packing when the load is more than about 25 pounds.

PACK BOARDS

The usual loads carried during backpacking vacations are more comfortably supported along the length of the back, rather than hanging away from it, and with the center of gravity over the hips. A pack frame, either with a convenient sack or with the fabric-wrapped load attached to the frame itself, is therefore recommended. It's true that the ordinary outfit will lighten as you eat your way along the trail. Experience, however, has shown that it is most practical to buy a pack for the heaviest loads that will be carried in it.

The pack board frame, with either a solid backing such as canvas, or with several large fabric bands top and bottom, will hold the properly packed load comfortably the length of the back and not just against the lower part. The best sacks, when one of these is used, are designed so the outfit will be packed

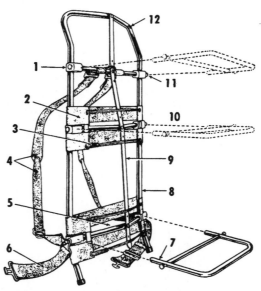

Features of a Modern Pack Frame. This Himalayan Sierra Pak has /1—Magnesium locks /2—Nylon webbing /3—Self-locking laces /4—3-way control harness /5—Double space support /6—Quick release belt /7—Optional loading platform and optional platform locations /8—Titanium-aluminum space saver (frame can carry ½-pint of liquid; crossbars can carry matches, lines, hooks, etc.) /9—Bowrib /10—Nylon webbing /11—Six lash points /12—Smooth frame.

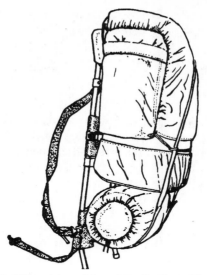

Himalayan Sierra Pak. This pack has a " Summit Bag" and a stuff bag.

Trailwise Pack Bag, featuring a contoured frame and handy patch-type map pocket, is suitable for an extended outing.

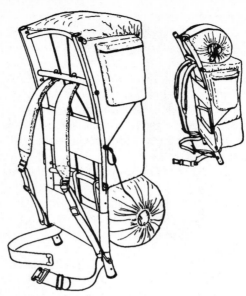

Kelty Mountaineer Pack. A comfortable, energy-conserving posture can be maintained for long-distance heavy packing with this model.

close to the body and high. Then, leaning slightly forward places the center of the weight directly above the hips where it can be balanced with the least physical exertion.

The arrangement of the straps and the other components of this type of pack all combine to keep the weight so centered. However, the pack still must be advantageously packed. With too high a load, you tire yourself in all but the most even of terrain by constantly shifting the muscles to regain balance. A load with the weight too far back will drag backwards on the shoulders.

Alaskan Pack Board

Another type of pack board that has been found eminently satisfactory is the Alaskan variety. The nucleus of this is a rectangular frame of wood or some other rigid material about 15 inches wide by 30 inches long, over which a canvas is doubled and tautly laced. There is about a 2½-inch space between the two expanses of canvas which, because only one surface of canvas rests against the back, ensures a free circulation of air. The effect is exactly as though you were lying on your back on a canvas cot.

There are two cross members to this frame, the top being about 6 inches below the top of the form. To it are attached, closely together, the two broad shoulder straps. These pass through a slit in the canvas on the side toward the back. Their lower ends are fastened to the lower outside corners of the frame.

Your outfit and food are tightly wrapped in a tarpaulin or other covering so a compact bundle is formed, depending on what you have, some 15 inches wide and about 30 inches long. This is lashed to the outside of the pack board. Because the load does not touch the back at all, being held away by the space between the two coverings of canvas, you can pack anything from a sack of fossils to an outboard motor without chafing or bruising.

The pack board should have its shoulder straps so adjusted that it sags just enough to rest some of the weight on the hips. The shoulder straps will then bear straight down on the top of the shoulders instead of pulling them uncomfortably backwards.

The commercial model of this type of pack, known as the Trapper Nelson Pack Board, can be obtained from almost all dealers in camp equipment. Three sizes are now made. The medium size, with a 26-inch by 14½-inch frame, is right for the average hiker. The small size, 24 inches by 13 inches, is excellent for women and youths. There also is a large size for heavy work, 30 inches by 14½ inches.

It can be had with a large canvas dunnage bag that laces to the frame. For lightweight packing with this type of pack, though, it is only extra weight. If you are going to get this sort of pack, it is generally best to obtain it without the bag and to tie your outfit on in a cover that has some other use, such as shelter, and so pays for its weight and bulk.

The Army used a similar pack board for heavy mountain carrying in World War II. This is strongly and substantially made over a fiberboard frame. Some still can be found in surplus stores. Although excellent for the stress of military use, though, these are unnecessarily heavy for backpacking vacations.

Making Your Own Pack Board

If you'd like the fun of a personal project, or if perhaps you have to fit packs to a family and could use the resulting savings elsewhere, it's possible to build your own pack board of this type.

Procure some strips of Sitka spruce, oak, or other strong wood, 2¼ inches wide by ½ inch thick. Cut two strips 28 inches long for the sides of the frame. Round the top ends, but leave the bottom ends square.

Cut two other strips for the crosspieces, one 12 inches long and the other 15½ inches long. Join the two sidepieces by the two crosspieces, making a frame as shown in Fig. 1. The top of the upper cross member should come six inches down from the top ends of the sidepieces. The bottom of the lower cross member should be three inches above the bottom ends of the sidepieces.

The edge of the sidepieces and the flat of the crosspieces face the packer's back. Notice that the crosspieces are flush with the edge of the sidepieces farthest from the packer's back.

The crosspieces must be fastened to the sidepieces very accurately and strongly. Use angle irons with wood screws in each face of the irons. Any

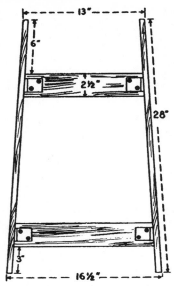

Figure 1. Frame dimensions and layout of homemade pack board.

machinist, or blacksmith, if you happen to live where one is handy, can make these bent pieces of metal in a very few minutes.

The resulting frame will be 13 inches wide at the top, 16½ inches wide at the bottom, 28 inches high, and 2½ inches thick. Using the same proportions, you can design as many different sizes as you need. Children, as well as adults, find these packs very rugged and comfortable. When the youngest member of the family finally outgrows his, so little money will be tied up in it that it can be passed along to some other young hiker without a qualm as to expense.

Over this frame lace a cover of, say, 12-ounce canvas, cut and made as shown in Fig. 2. This is, in this instance, 28 inches wide at the top, 35 inches at the bottom, and 25 inches high. It covers the frame to within 1½ inches of the top and bottom.

Hem it all around and insert seven brass grommets along each side edge to accommodate the lacing. These grommets are obtainable from many sporting goods stores, along with inexpensive tools for inserting them, and from all tent and awning makers. The latter two suppliers, as well as some outfitters, will insert them for a few cents if you prefer. On the side edge, hem the cover with two folds, fastening the grommets through both folds so they won't pull out.

Three and one-half inches down from the center of the top edge there should be a horizontal slit, 8 inches long, strongly reinforced at the edges. This is for the shoulder straps to pass through.

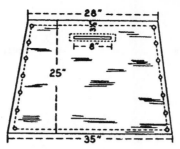

Figure 2. Layout for the pack board cover.

This canvas cover is laced around the frame, drum tight, by means of strong cod line, passed through the grommets. The slit comes on the side toward the packer's back. The lacing is done on the side of the frame where the crosspieces are flush with the edges of the sidepieces (see Fig. 3). The edges with the grommets should not meet by about 2 inches, so the canvas can be laced very tightly.

It should be mentioned in passing that some packers do away with the canvas entirely, lacing these and similar frames with long cord zigzagged back and forth through holes drilled about an inch apart along the sidepieces. This decreases the weight and increases the coolness, but the result is not so stable as canvas and will not hold up under heavier loads.

The upper ends of the shoulder straps are secured around the top crosspiece of the frame at the center. They pass through the slit in the canvas, then around and over the packer's shoulders, and finally are secured to the outside of the sidepieces of the frame 6 inches above the lower ends of these members as shown in Fig. 4. A piece of leather with a 1-inch buckle is screwed to each of the sidepieces for this purpose.

The straps are best made of heavy, chrome-tanned leather, saturated with neat's-foot oil. They should be 2 inches wide at the top and where they go over the shoulders, tapering to an inch wide at the bottom where they are secured to the buckles. Too wide a strap passing through the armpits makes for

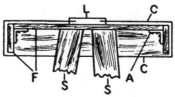

Figure 3. Top cross section of cover installation. *F*-Wooden frame. *A*-Angle iron (or aluminum angle strips for less weight). *C*-Canvas cover. *L*-Lacing. *S*-Shoulder straps.

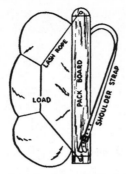

Figure 4. Side view of pack board with shoulder straps installed.

chafing. Holes are punched in the straps to provide for their adjustment in length. If you will install these straps with the smooth side of the leather contacting the shoulders, the pack will be easier to slip on and off.

These days, it should be mentioned, firm wide nylon webbing is available, both in surplus stores and from outfitters, that can be tapered for the installation of buckles. Such webbing is excellent for use as straps. In either event, you will probably appreciate the use of shoulder pads, available so inexpensively that it's hardly worthwhile to bother trying to sew them at home. In a pinch, too, something such as heavy gloves shoved between strap and shoulder will make all the difference.

Putting on the Pack Board

In any event, after the straps have been adjusted for length, they can be slipped over the shoulders most conveniently, just as one puts on coat or suspenders. If you are alone and no elevated surface such as a stump or log is available, merely stand the loaded pack board upright on the ground. Sit down and place your arms through the straps. Run your thumbs under the straps to make sure they snuggle flatly into the shoulders. Then stand up.

Figure 3 shows a section of this pack board as viewed looking down from the top. Figure 4 presents a side view with the shoulder straps in position and with a load lashed on the board. For this last, holes are drilled in the top and bottom of the sidepieces of the frame through which to attach the lashing ropes.

TUMP LINES

Tump lines and backpacking vacations don't really go together. The tump line, whereby part of the weight is supported by the head or forehead by means of a wide band attached by two lines to the load, is common to primitive freighting. In canoe country, too, where the freighting is over portages seldom as long as a mile, the tump line is common (see chapter 11), often supporting one or more tarp-wrapped bundles, or taking part of the weight of a large, frameless pack, such as the Duluth, off the shoulders.

But such a pack heats and galls the back after an hour or more of packing. With head and neck immobilized by tump line, you cannot look around, enjoy the scenery, nor even properly survey the country ahead to pick out the best way. Your eyes are glued to the portage trail, and for the time being you are just a beast of burden with the tump line a tight band over your head.

WAIST BELT

A waist belt, weighing only some three ounces or so, can be welcome when you are starting out with a heavier-than-usual pack, both stabilizing the load and transferring some of the weight from the shoulders to the slope of the buttocks.

OTHER ITEMS

Glasses

If you need prescription lenses to get around, you'll find it only prudent to carry a spare pair in a substantial protective case. You will also be wise to bring along a pair of optically correct and strongly made sunglasses if you expect to find yourself in snow, desert, or high country.

Knife

A knife comes close to being a necessity for carrying on your person or in your kit. The best one is a lastingly sharp, intrinsically rugged sheath knife that you can use for everything from butchering to building a shelter. Ideally, it has a substantial leather case with a handy carborundum sharpening stone in a separate compartment on its front.

Extra Clothing

Care of the feet will be of primary importance. This may well mean the inclusion of at least two extra pairs of functional socks. You may also choose to take along extra light footwear.

Such easily laundered items as underwear and handkerchiefs need not be included in the proportions sometimes witnessed. One always seems to be finding use for a spare woolen shirt, on the other hand.

Cord or Rope

A length of good new rope, perhaps three-eighths-inch manila, may come in handy a lot of different ways if you can manage the extra weight and bulk. If not, at least include a few yards of nylon cord, strong enough to bear your weight in a pinch.

Toilet Kit

This may be where you choose to carry your soap if the supply is to be limited. You'll also likely want a small rough towel that can be regularly washed, toothbrush, dentifrice which may be common baking soda or table salt which will have utility elsewhere, comb, and any small items you may wish such as manicure scissors and safety razor with spare blades.

Flashlight

A flashlight is considered pretty much of a necessity when one is away from power. A conventional two-cell light is generally sufficient, preferably a model with smoothly rounded edges that will not be so likely to wear holes in a pocket.

A spare bulb, protected by cotton batten, can often be carried inside the spring at the end. I've always found it a sound idea, too, to keep a second spare elsewhere in the outfit, in my case softly inside a box of adhesive bandages. If you've the capacity for them, two extra, long-life batteries are also a good idea.

In any event, the batteries will last you considerably longer if you get in the habit of switching on the light only for very brief periods of time, all that will be needed, for example, when you are traveling through the woods at night. To prevent the accidental waste of power, use some tactic such as reversing the batteries, inserting paper between battery post and bulb, or even taping the switch when the flashlight is packed.

Foam Rubber Padding

It is quite easy for even an experienced woodsman to bruise the tissue of the foot. This only requires striking the arch on a ridge or bending the foot in an unnatural way. An injury of this sort can be very painful to walk on. A sheet of quarter-inch foam rubber padding about a foot square, obtainable from your drugstore or a surgical supply house, can be used to cushion fragile articles in the kit, while a section can be easily cut off to fit inside a boot to pad and support the injured foot.

Repair Outfit

You'll have your own needs and ideas for this. Mine, the one I keep in my large survival kit, has changed little over the years after a lot of initial adding and discarding.

The present contents include the following. A small, fine pair of pointed scissors, the best I could find. Small pointed tweezers, also the finest obtainable, valuable for minor repairs and for removing especially pesky slivers and thorns. Two rolls of narrow adhesive tape, valuable for mending as well as for personal uses, particularly if in cold weather it is warmed prior to applying. A roll of dental floss.

Pliers with a fine cutting edge—that could slice through the shank of a fish-hook, for example, if someone in the party is ever unfortunate enough to get one in his body—and with tightly fitting edges that could remove porcupine quills from a dog. Incidentally, such quills will pull out more easily if their tops are first cut off to ease the suction that helps hold their barbed points in place.

Two short, assorted screwdrivers with yellow plastic handles, rugged enough to be held by the pliers. A bit of nylon fishline rolled on some cardboard. Rawhide lacing. An extra coil of light snare wire to keep me in meat if the need ever arises. Recently, I've also been carrying a small, compact, very light clasp knife with two excellent blades, scissors, file, screwdriver, and a can opener.

A small tube, well wrapped, of all-purpose adhesive. A small square of rubber for patching and some rubber cement. A small file for sharpening. Safety pins of several sizes, all pinned to the largest. Some copper rivets. An empty metal toothpaste tube that will serve as emergency solder, along with the pitch from an evergreen tree for flux.

I also carry a small, stoutly constructed can of gun oil and a few cleaning patches. One of these can be tied to the middle of a length of the nylon cord, when you are ready for it, and thus worked back and forth through the barrel, without the need of a cleaning rod which would be bulky even when disjointed.

Finally, I have a small sewing roll that can be shifted to my pocket when I am traveling too light for the entire repair kit. This contains strong thread, wax for further strengthening it, assorted needles, and a couple of cards that I've wound with darning wool for sock repair. There are only several buttons, as these latter can be easily improvised from leather, bone, or wood.

Camping Checklist

___plastic sheet

___pack

___tent

___tarp

___sleeping bag, foam pad

___cord or rope

___food, extra rations

___cooking equipment

___grill

___dish scrubber and soap

___rain gear

___clothing, extra clothing

___first-aid kit

___toilet kit

___whistle

___candles

Optional:

___ax

___saw

___hatchet

___ice ax

___snow knife

___gun and ammo

___pre-assembled emergency kit

—matches, waterproof case   —mirror

—map, map case   —flares

—compass   —wire

—knife and carborundum   —snakebite kit

—glasses   —watch

—sunglasses   —repair outfit

—suntan lotion   —camera and film

—insect repellent   —binoculars

—flashlight, extra batteries   —fishing outfit

—water purification tablets   —paper and pen

A Basic Backpack Checklist

Pack	3 lbs. 12 oz.
Plastic tarp and poncho	1 lb. 5 oz.
Sleeping bag	3 lbs. 8 oz.
Cooking utensils*	1 lb. 12 oz.
First aid kit*	4 oz.
Underwear and socks	12 oz.
Wool shirt, jacket, or sweater	1 lb. 8 oz.
Toilet articles	8 oz.
Knife, whetstone	8 oz.
Flashlight	15 oz.
Needles, thread, buttons, personals	4 oz.
Total weight, without food	15 lbs.

In a party of two or more, these articles will be used in common, each individual carrying his share. Add a plate, cup, and spoon to cooking utensils for each additional hiker.

HOW TO STOW THE GEAR FOR BACKPACKING

With loads changing constantly as food is used, packing is a matter of day-by-day ingenuity. It should be emphasized that backpacking always remains pretty much an individual affair. In other words, experiment until you find out what arrangement suits you best.

There are certain general fundamentals, however, that may serve as a basis for your trials. These differ somewhat, depending on the country. For example, too high a load will work against you in two ways if you have to do much climbing. First, it's easy to overbalance in strenuous going, and such a load under these circumstances will leave you tired out just from trying to keep it balanced. Secondly, when a load is packed high under such circumstances, it's difficult to get your head back to see where you're going.

The ideal, again, is to keep the weight tight to the body and comparatively high. The light sleeping bag, then, will probably go at the bottom, either in the sack or wrapped separately below it. The lighter objects will graduate up from the bottom and will be placed at the front of the pack to press the heavier impediments toward your back.

That's really about all there is to it. Personal trials will do the rest. A couple more things. The load should ordinarily be packed so that it's narrow enough not to interfere with the natural swing of the arms. And flat objects should be placed at the very back, so that parts of the load will not prod the spine.

A husky man fresh out of the cement jungles can, without particular difficulty, shoulder about 75 pounds at a stretch over short portages, and he can take his time in making several such trips. He should not usually pack more than 35 pounds, of which 20 pounds may reasonably be food, when hiking day after day for pleasure over high country.

CHAPTER THREE

OUTFITTING FOR THE OUTDOORS

When you outfit in any part for the outdoors, you'll be
well advised not necessarily to get the most expensive, but
certainly to buy the best.
—Bradford Angier
Survival with Style

FOOTWEAR

Warm Feet

If your feet are cold, clap on your hat. This may sound jocose, but to those who realize how the human body functions in a cold environment it is a simple statement of fact.

The human body is actually a machine, continuously producing heat through the burning of food or food-storing tissues and then losing this heat so as to maintain a constant temperature within itself.

One way this heat loss is regulated is by the reduction, in ratio to the outer cold, of the blood supply to both skin and extremities. Because the head has such an abundant blood supply, and because it is the only part of the body where this flow is not reduced in frigid weather to conserve the available warmth for the vital organs, it is the major radiator for excess body heat.

If you want to shunt this heat down to the feet, you must make certain it is not lost through the head and, incidentally, through the unmittened hands. Therefore, you put on your hat if your feet are chilly. In this regard, a parka hood is more effective than even a stocking hat because of the way it also protects the neck.

Breaking in Footwear

The boot, where the woodsman and the wilderness meet, is of course the most important part of the clothing. What about breaking them in?

New footwear should, if at all possible, be well broken in before you take to the woods. Even with something like low rubber boots, which need no breaking in as such, there will be pressure points that you'll want to toughen.

There are two eminently practical ways of breaking in new leather boots. You can stand in four inches of water for fifteen minutes, then hike until the shoes dry on your feet, a procedure that is far less uncomfortable than it sounds. Or you can go at it more gradually by hiking two miles the first day, three the second, and so on up to five miles, by which time the process should be completed.

Buying the Right Size

Too many individuals wear wilderness footwear that is too tight. There's a simple formula that will keep you on the right track. For use with one pair of thin- or medium-weight woolen socks, get your boots one size longer and one size wider than your correct fit in city shoes.

For heavy socks, buy them one and one-half sizes longer and wider. If half sizes are not obtainable, get the next full size larger. For the extra pair of socks you may find most comfortable in a severely cold environment, experiment to achieve the same easy fit.

The shoe size you wear on pavement is all right for two or three miles of walking, but beware of this size for a daily tramp of eight or more miles over woodlands, particularly if they are hilly.

Just one such trip in city-size footwear will almost surely lay you low with blisters and bruises. After three or four miles of hiking over rugged terrain, your feet swell markedly because of the repeated and varying pressures. The footwear you select must be sufficiently big to remain comfortable when your feet are in this enlarged condition.

Waterproofing Footwear

Boots, particularly in this day of silicones, are usually nearly waterproof when new. After a day of hiking, some water may seep through at the seams. During continued wet travel, a bit of water will work through the leather.

If wax, preferably that containing silicone, is then worked into the seams, wrinkles, stitchings, and where the uppers meet the lowers, they will once more be fairly waterproof until the compound wears off. Leather footwear should be waxed this way about once a week when you're using it. Treating it more often than this can make the leather too soft.

In any event, the dubbin will go on more easily and satisfactorily if the leather is slightly warm.

That leather footwear is seldom entirely waterproof is usually all to the good, for otherwise the boots would make your feet more uncomfortably wet than would leather still able to breathe.

What About High Boots?

High tops nearly always wrinkle and when they are softened, sag at the ankle. The trouble is that this can bring pressure on the Achilles tendon, the body's largest, at the back of your ankle. This may become negligible in the case of well-broken-in boots. Too, it can be offset with even rubber tops by the insertion of some stiffener such as a strip of bark or of some pad such as a folded handkerchief.

Unless there is an important reason for high tops, however, the point remains that such unrelieved pressure can set up a painful inflammation of the sheath through which this tendon runs. This is known medically as synovitis, and the only remedy in the bush is ten days off the feet.

Then there is the matter of weight. A boot with a ten-inch top will weigh some eight ounces more than one six inches high. This is an additional half-pound to be lifted three inches high and to be carried twenty-eight inches ahead about twenty-five hundred times every mile. This extra expenditure of energy really builds up on a long trek back to civilization.

Canvas Sneakers

These are light, easy to stow, and are far better than city shoes along reasonably smooth trails when the weather is not too cold. For adequate ankle protection and support, buy them with approximately six-inch tops. For woods use, the rubber soles should be cleated or roughly corrugated. Sneakers are best worn with one pair of medium-weight woolen socks.

Sneakers will soon wet through in rain, in swamps, and even in heavy morning dew. With the woolen socks this is not uncomfortable, however, and once the going improves they'll dry out rapidly without stiffening.

Innersoles

Plastic mesh insoles, which tend to ventilate the soles of the feet and which are both nonabsorbent and nonmatting, are an excellent choice.

Not liking the flat feel of the usual boot, however, I personally compromise with a multilayered leather insole with a steel arch support which can be adjusted with the fingers. In cold weather, I use the same type of insole but with a soft, closely clipped lambskin surface next to the feet.

Felt insoles are common, and before they become damp are indeed warmer than the ideal plastic mesh variety. Laden with moisture, however, they become excellent conductors of heat. You can get around this by carrying a dry pair, but at best this is a nuisance.

Socks

Three closely fitting pairs of good woolen socks are not as warm as two more loosely fitting pairs. Aside from the fact that the feet's already poor circulation is further impeded by such a tight fit, the resulting compression of the woolen fibers cuts down on the insulative dead air space. Here again, thickness means warmth.

The simple but vital formula for the most efficient wilderness walking is heavy socks and big shoes. Regardless of cold or heat, wetness or dryness, only good woolen socks are suitable for a long hike. Nylon stitching, augmenting the strength of heels and toes, may serve to lengthen their usefulness. These socks may vary from thin to medium during the growing seasons and from medium to heavy in the chilly months.

Throughout the year, nevertheless, try to wear only the best quality, painstakingly processed, and well-made woolens. Have nothing to do with shoddy products in this category. Poor woolens mat, soon losing much of their insulative quality. They contain impurities that irritate the all-too-vulnerable feet. As for loosely and skimpily knit socks, these are abominable from the first time you don them.

If you are one of the rare individuals whose feet seem allergic to wool, try wearing thin socks of some other material beneath the wool. These may be of well-knit cotton, but not the thin, stretchy products that frequently appear on the market. Or you may select nylon, which surely has longevity but which, for many of us, is much too slippery unless either worn too tightly or gartered in some way, neither of which fits in the outdoor routine.

Do your best to start out with well-fitting and reasonably new socks with no harsh seams or unduly rough darns. Wash both the feet and the socks, if at all possible, when you stop to camp for the night. When the going is rough and not too cold, it is refreshing to stop several times during the day and bathe the feet. At this time, if you can, change to a fresh pair of socks, hanging the damp ones on the outside of your pack or looped through your belt in back where they can dry.

Making Moccasins

If you have animal skins and the time, you'll find it a comparatively simple matter to fashion moccasins. Soft, tanned hides afford a lightly comfortable, easily worked material for moccasins and mukluks, but wet or rough going soon wears holes in them. In those parts of the North where such footwear is common, the practice is to protect the feet with larger, exterior moccasins, store-purchased rubbers or overshoes, and often both. You can travel warmly all day in the cold snow with such a combination.

Especially under survival conditions when no outer shell of thick rubber or plastic is at hand, it is best to use for your moccasins as tough a flexible hide as is available. In readying the raw skin, if you start with that, you should not attempt to soften it in any way. The hair or fur can be left warmly inward. Not only is it best not to tan such a skin, but it should be scraped only enough to level off any irregularities that might otherwise hurt the feet.

A moccasin pattern that is as functional as it is simple is shown in the accompanying drawing. To fit the pattern to your feet, stand on a corner of the

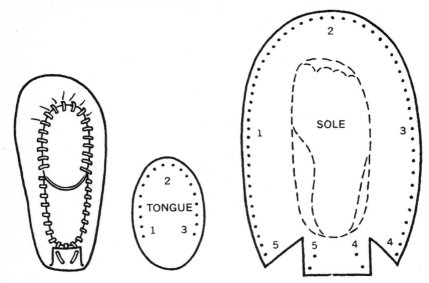

By using this pattern, you can fashion moccasins from animal skins.

hide you will be using or, if possible, on a more manageable cloth sample that can later be utilized as a liner. Draw an oval around the feet. Do not try to trace closely about the toes but allow space for easy movement.

Then add at least three inches all around for the moccasin sides. If you have ample leather, it's even better to bring these high above the ankles and shins in two broad flaps that can later be tied with three or four turns of lacing.

As soon as the two parts of the moccasin are cut, slit or punch holes around the edges as indicated. Rawhide or leather laces can easily be made from odd bits of hide by cutting them around and around, as we'll consider next. These thongs, or some other lacing, should be run through the holes to join the two moccasin parts as marked.

Cutting the Lacing

A lace or thong can be swiftly and simply cut from an old shoe top or a random piece of rawhide. If you have a sharp knife, just find a smooth log with a branch stub sticking up for use as a guide. Or whittle out, then drive in, a wooden peg for this purpose.

If you want your lacing a functional quarter-inch in width, first round any square corners from the leather. Second, start the lace freehand, beginning a strip two or three inches long.

Then tap your knife point-first into the log so that the blade, facing away from you, is approximately one-fourth inch from the projection or peg. Next,

Cutting rawhide lacing for moccasins.

place the already started lace between this guide and the knife edge. By pulling the lace and turning the leather, you will be able to cut around and around, making as long a thong as you have material.

CLOTHING

The Layer System

In extremely cold weather you can freeze very rapidly in wet clothing. It is therefore imperative under such circumstances to keep from sweating. This you can accomplish by shedding layers of clothing as you warm up, thereby always staying moderately cool. This ability to gauge and maintain a comfortable body temperature increases with experience.

This is a major reason why the layer system is best. In the chill of the morning many like to start with everything on. Whether you are on a winter desert or high in mountains realms, the practice is to continue shedding layers as the sun soars higher.

There is one thing to watch out for with such a system, and that is not to carry it too far. In the thin dry air of the upper altitudes, the sun burns deeply, even through a basic tan. The shoulders and back are particularly vulnerable.

It is always best to anticipate personal warmth variations and to open clothing before you'd otherwise begin to sweat and to close it again before you actually feel chilly.

No matter what you wear, the garments as a whole must be sufficient to give you an average thickness that will be adequate according to both temperature and your particular rate of metabolism. With correctly designed clothing and proper underwear, you can wear your maximum insulation throughout the day and ventilate any excess heat out from inside it.

Clothing Ideals

Always make certain that no part of your garb is too tight or restrictive. Knees especially should work freely.

A side point is that many woodsmen choose to have their debris-collecting trouser cuffs removed and the legs stagged some three inches shorter than city garments. Otherwise, the trouser legs, particularly if they are at all full, have the dangerous tendency to catch on snags and trip you.

Picking out clothing with fast, bright colors is to be recommended for several reasons. It's much easier to spot in a wilderness terrain, especially from the air. You are less likely to break camp and leave some article behind, drying on a bush. Too, there is the very important factor of safety if you are abroad during the hunting seasons.

What Underwear to Choose

The primary principle to remember is the need to prevent the always-present body moisture from entering the clothing. It will not do this if it can escape an easier way. Therefore, the basic requirement is an air space around your body so that the moisture can evaporate immediately after it is formed by insensible perspiration and perhaps a little sweating, as when you first start out in the morning before you settle down to the even pace of the trail. Then, if you leave an ample neck opening, the vapor-heavied air can move harmlessly out.

You can set the stage for all this by wearing one of the many brands of net underwear, preferably with a three-eighths inch or larger square mesh, about one-eighth inch thick and entirely open like a fishnet. Much smaller holes, as well as the familiar waffle-weave undersuits, do not permit the necessary evaporation to take place.

The neatest supplemental trick for cold country comfort lies in some of the recently developed insulative underwear, such as Polarfleece and Polypropalene, which wicks moisture away from your body. If you begin to perspire heavily, you should first slacken your activity if possible, or remove the bottom, the top, or both parts of your insulated undergarments. These can be stowed in a pack, actual or improvised, until you stop. Then put them back on until bedtime. One of the secrets of sleeping warm is going to bed warm.

You have to be careful what you buy, however. Underwear made of some synthetics entraps perspiration as tightly as rubber. In weather that is at all warm, you might as well be journeying in a portable steam bath. In really cold going, much more than just discomfort is at stake. Some trapped body moisture freezes, and if you continue trying to bull it through, so may you. Again, better to go with those synthetics that wick moisture away from your body.

Pockets in Your Clothing

Although most belongings can be carried more comfortably in the packsack, pockets are still handy on a hiking trip; so special attention should be paid to their deepness and ruggedness when you buy clothing for a trip. Because of the danger of losing your already limited essentials, it is well to get most or all of these with fasteners.

No compromise should be made with shirt pockets. Flap closures, buttoned or otherwise secured, are best. But if you have an old shirt that you plan to wear out on a trip and it has open pockets, install flaps or at the very least snaps. With the latter arrangement, you'll have to secure the contents further—as with a handkerchief wadded across the top of the opening.

The side trouser pockets should not be loaded (as is often done) in such a way that they interfere with free leg motion. As for pockets low on the legs, the feature of some older military surplus clothing, experiments have shown that it is three times more tiring to carry anything here than on the back.

Wool

For a cold or even a chilly environment, all but the underclothing and what you are wearing in the way of down or otherwise insulated garb should be lightweight wool throughout. Wool also gets wet from perspiration, but if you are dressed properly most of this moisture passes directly through it to be evaporated on the outside.

Furthermore, wet wool does not feel particularly cold. It does not chill in the same way as, for example, wet cotton unless there is a brisk wind. Under these conditions, a closely woven but still porous outside jacket of tight cotton or thin nylon should be carried for use as a windbreaker.

Wool is warm because of the insulative effect of inert air retained in the minute spaces among its innumerable fibers. A pair of light wool garments are warmer than a single heavy one of the same total weight because of the additional dead air retained between them.

Cotton

Cotton jeans are the worst things you can wear in the bush, if only because of the chilly way in which they absorb water. Then there is the nationally used heat loss test. Four cans were filled with 110°F. water; three were covered, each with a different fabric, then they were left out in the wind and rain to demonstrate body heat loss through conduction and convection.

After four hours, the water temperature in the can with a wet cotton covering fell to 61°F., and that in the can without any covering dropped to 72°F. The water in the can with a wet woolen covering showed an 83°F. water temperature, and the wool-covered can protected with a plastic cover stayed at 96°F.

Incidentally, a sock doll test illustrates that when floating wool is partially inundated in water, it remains absolutely dry above the water line. Cotton, on the other hand, absorbs water like a wick and soon becomes soaked. If even a half-inch of a cotton sweatshirt is exposed below your raingear on a wet day, water will be soaked up through the cotton until the entire garment is sopping.

Kerchiefs

One or two large bandana kerchiefs always come in handy. In really hot going, some hikers carry one in the belt to wipe off accumulating perspiration. Some twist one around the forehead to keep perspiration out of the eyes. In cold weather the bandana can be worn around one's neck as a barrier against rising body warmth. They can also be used where needed as pads or to ease chafing. In an emergency they can serve as triangular bandages or a sling. They also afford a certain amount of wind, sun, and insect protection.

Gloves or Mitts?

If warmth is an important part of your hand protection, mittens will be more satisfactory than gloves. Because of the paradoxical effect of curvature, the first layers of insulation you add to your hands actually increase the heat loss. This is particularly true of the fingers, and if your gloves fit tightly, you are doing more harm than good as far as warmth is concerned until you reach one-quarter inch of thickness.

Therefore, everyday gloves, even foam-insulated ski gloves, do not provide effective insulation. Most of these latter are made with straight-tailored fingers which, cramped around a ski pole, stretch so tightly over the knuckles that just where you need thick insulation you have thin spots.

Although everyone likes the unrestricted action of gloves, a thick pair of mitts where the loose fingers can warm one another will vastly prolong the comfort span, particularly if when your hands get cold, you bare and warm them next to the body, perhaps under your opposite armpits. You will thus make every effort to keep the fingers from freezing.

PART TWO
THE ALL-IMPORTANT SURVIVAL ESSENTIALS:
FIRE, SHELTER, WATER

CHAPTER FOUR

FIRE AND FIREMAKING

What remain most fondly in our mind after a wilderness hike are the campfires.
—Bradford Angier
Home in Your Pack

The campfire, cheery and companionable, is the backwoodsman's most fundamental necessity. The average tenderfoot, when he becomes turned around in the woods, immediately begins fearing starvation, death from thirst, and peril from dangerous animals. There is almost never any reason for the first, seldom any for the second, and none on this continent for the third aside from rabidity, and the occasional polar bear or grizzly. Exposure, on the other hand, can kill you in a few minutes.

With a campfire, though, we can warm and dry ourselves, relish a night in comfort and safety, cook the meals which we'll consider later to be of nearly limitless scope and, if necessary, signal for help. None of us, therefore, should travel through or over the wild places anywhere at any time without the knowledge and means of building an emergency fire in the course of daily living.

When you are alone or with a small party, the making of campfires should be approached with due thought and preparation, not blithely, casually, and desultorily—the way one sees too many nincompoops tackling the problem. For instance, what is the most common reason for accidental death in the Far North? It is not cold, but fire. One doesn't even have to look that far afield. Consider the outdoor conflagrations of civilization, some of them started by natural causes, such as lightning, or by some reasonably unavoidable accident. But far too many life-and-property-destroying blazes are begun by fools. Never take any chances.

The way to be ready for that possible crisis in the backwoods, when a successful campfire may make the difference between comfort and misery or even life and death, is to go about lighting every fire as if you have only one match. In New Brunswick, a required-by-law guide who got lost when we were hunting apart in unfamiliar country nearly froze to death the stormy night he was out, not because he did not have several matches and an unlimited quantity of good tinder and fuel, but because he was in the habit of having a large quantity of paper and matches at hand when it became time to start the campfire. He had come to regard fire-making as a triviality.

The Boy Scout requirement for learning to start a campfire with no more than two matches and only natural fuel is a sound one, and was what probably made me serious about being able to start a blaze in every situation, no matter what the conditions. I don't think this can be overemphasized even today.

Such certain and sure firemaking often takes a lot more time than many individuals are inclined to give it, but this is one aspect of good woodsmanship that should never be hurried. What keeps the average person from developing this skill is that campfires are usually easily handled and that, if one falls short of matches, the other fellow generally has plenty.

The hardest time I ever had in starting and retaining a campfire was after a Northeast week of drizzly, windy, frosty weather, when rain was falling and constantly adding to the coating of ice that seemed to sheathe every twig. Wet and miserable, I had been out a week in unfamiliar country on my own, and I had only two matches left in my waterproof match case. What to do? I was in my teens and had a lot to learn, as I still do.

Well, at least I was in softwood country where spruce, interspersed with occasional birch, were so plentiful that today I wouldn't give the matter a second thought. Incidentally, I had belted to my waist the best six-inch sheath knife with attached sharpening stone that I could afford, even though at that time one of these was regarded by all too many as the sign of a tenderfoot.

There wasn't a dry foot of ground anywhere on which it was reasonable to make a fire, so the first thing I did was to strip large sheets of birch bark from some living trees—this being utter wilderness—to floor a space in front of a thickly needled young fir into which I had stripped a niche in which to sit. I put a sheet of bark to sit on in here, too, where at least it wouldn't get any wetter.

I then cut a third sheet of bark from another birch, which incidentally wouldn't kill the tree, and divided this into thin, dry, paperlike scraps which, filled with oil as they were, could be depended on to burst into flame, giving off a heavy, sweet, black smoke when—facing the wind so that the fire would eat down the stick—I applied one of my hand-and-body-shielded matches to it. I stored these bits of bark beneath the largest curling sheet.

On the bottoms of all thick, small evergreens there are masses of tiny dead twigs that are full of resin. These could be counted on to ignite from the tiny scraps of birch bark. In turn, they would start burning the larger limbs of well-protected and fairly dry spruce that I collected and turned into what I knew as fuzzsticks: one-foot lengths of straight-grained wood on which I cut curl after dry curl, detaching as few as possible and saving these for additional tinder.

But softwood won't hold a fire, so I found a standing dead poplar, broke several heavy limbs from it by my weight, reduced these by levering them be-

Dry, dead, resinous twigs and branches on the lower trunks of all evergreens make good kindling.

tween two rocks, scraped the ice from them, and then made them into kindling with my boots. Some old, upright, softwood stubs of trunks were about, remains of an ancient fire. They were pretty well rotted, but I kicked enough of them apart to get a number of tough, resin-rich knots.

I made and covered with birch bark a square-foot space in front of the niche where I intended to retreat. Then on the heavy birch bark which, incidentally, is flammable even though wet, I carefully piled my wisps of birch bark. I added in turn the closely amassed twigs, and, in a well-ventilated wigwam, the fuzzsticks, the poplar kindling, and finally a few of the resinous knots. This, I figured, would make a fire hot enough to dry out and burn the large, standing, dead poplar limbs that I heaped loosely over everything.

Fuzzsticks

Then I applied one of my two precious matches to the shielded little nest of birch wisps. It caught. It worked.

I broiled my tenderloin venison kabobs on a sharpened green willow while comfortable on my water-impervious seat within the cavity whose back was toward the wind. I suspended my large can of tea water by its wire bail from another green willow limb, pressed into the ground at one end and held at the proper height at the other end by a forked green stick. Warm, sated, and re-

"B'iling" the Kettle

freshed, I continued with my packboard load of deer meat to my river camp and canoe, well ahead of the advancing winter.

PRINCIPLES OF FIREMAKING

Although campfires can be built in innumerable ways, the principles of firemaking are always the same. The fire proceeds from spark, to tinder, to fuel. It is in these three essentials that the differences lie. An understanding of the fundamentals will add to your ability to kindle a fire under every practical circumstance.

For one thing, firewood itself does not burn directly. It is a combustible gas, driven from the fuel in sufficient quantities by heat, that combines with enough oxygen in the air to give you your warmth.

The starting fire, in sequence, must be hot and long-lived enough to light more and more gas from progressively larger amounts of fuel. In other words, firemaking under extreme conditions is much more likely to be successful if it is approached deliberately and with thoughtful concern, not haphazardly and helter-skelter—the way you see too many individuals trying to light their blazes.

Have the fuel ready and everything else set to go before you bare your hand. If the fire does not catch with the first match, warm your hand before proceeding further, perhaps by shoving it under an armpit or inside the shirt. As soon as enough stiffness has left the fingers, the attempt can be made once more as swiftly and surely as possible.

Although a hatchet, knife, or other cutting tool will be an asset in gathering firewood, it's easy enough to make small sticks out of big ones by the hands alone. You can break them over a knee, by wedging one end against rocks or roots and pulling or pushing or by bridging two high points with a dead branch and dropping a stone on its middle.

It's a whole lot easier, though, to burn the large sticks in two. Another backwoods stratagem is to place the ends in the blaze, continuing to push them further in until they are consumed.

Gathering Tinder: A Critical Step to Firemaking Success

Tinder is highly combustible substance in which a spark can be blown to flame. Innumerable materials of this sort have been popular in different localities ever since man came groping out of the cold of fireless eons. Many of these tinders were carried, and some still are, in special containers such as tinderboxes, pouches, horns, and other such receptacles.

Birch bark can be detached in the thinnest of layers and shredded to make tinder. The barks of some of the cedars can be similarly utilized. Dry moss, lichen, grass, and dead evergreen needles are among the additional substances pulverized for tinder. Other suitable dry materials so used are obtained from abandoned nests.

The dry fuzz from pussy willows is a well-known tinder. So is wood which has dry-rotted and can be rubbed to a powder. A number of mushrooms and other fungi are dehydrated for such a purpose. The dessicated pith from the inside of elderberry shoots was employed by some Indians. So was the down from milkweed, fireweed, and like vegetation.

A handful of very dry pine needles often works. You can use the fluff of the so-called cotton grass, that of cattails, and the downy heads of such flowers as mature goldenrod. Many dry vegetable fibers serve as tinder. So do the powdery dry droppings of bats. So does the down found in some nests and on the undersides of certain birds.

Birch bark is so inflammable that it will light even after being freshly dipped in water. But even in the deep woods, there is no need to scar a birch tree. To start your fire, just a handful of the wisps that are fluttering on all birches will do.

It will pay you to make fuzzsticks, firesticks, feathersticks, or whatever you want to call them. These are surer and more effective than just bare kindling, and with practice you'll be able to manufacture three or four of them in half as many minutes. In the North I use them every morning to start the fire in my log cabin stove.

The fuzzstick is made by shaving a stick of dry kindling again and again, leaving the ribbons of wood attached so that they curl away from the parent stick in a sort of fan. You'll need at least three of these, and if conditions are drastic I commonly add another one to start the blaze with even more sure swiftness.

You can lay your fire with the fuzzsticks at the bottom, angling these upward for better draft and so that you can get the match under them. Atop of these will be progressively larger fuel, crisscrossed or peaked so that plenty of oxygen can reach the upward-licking flames. This way takes a little more time, but it is a surer method, and the heaped firewood also serves to protect the light against the wind although, it should be noted, it is generally most satisfactory to light your fire from the windward side.

Or, if you are in a bit more of a hurry and are an old hand, have the fire materials at hand. Light one, then another of the fuzzsticks, and lay them in a well-ventilated pile, building the fire as it is burning with larger and larger fuel. This way, too, you can control the starting fire better.

Keeping Your Tinder Dry

The tinder must be absolutely dry. This property is not always easy to find, as tinder is prone to absorb moisture readily from the atmosphere. It is a good idea in humid country to carry a supply of tinder on your person, in such a manner that it will not be dampened.

For this purpose, I use a little rawhide bag with a leather drawstring, originally intended to encase a fishing reel.

Dry evergreen needles, twigs, birch bark, wood shavings, and fuzzsticks provide tinder for speedy firemaking.

Which Wood to Use

The numerous softwoods, particularly when time is taken to split them, will quickly laugh into a cheery campfire, not good for most cooking but satisfactory for boiling a kettle and for rapid toasting or grilling.

For steadier and less flamboyant heat, the hardwoods are more long-lived. Coals are best for most cooking, and for a glowingly enduring bed you'll likely select such wood as oak, ash, and hickory whenever possible. Split green birch, which burns with such a sweet black smoke that it is sometimes used in the tanning of leather, is particularly effective.

The difference between hardwoods and softwoods is a matter of botany, not of hardness, some of the softwoods being markedly more solid than some of the so-called hardwoods. Softwoods, such as the familiar evergreens, have different sorts of scales or needles rather than flat leaves.

The resinous softwoods, if they are dry, make the quicker kindling. However, they are short-lived, smoky, and prone to snap sparks. The dry hardwoods, as well as a few living hardwoods like the ash and birch, make a slower, longer, and steadier fire. These serve best for your night fire, for instance. Too, these fall apart into the glowing expanses of red coals that are best for most cooking.

Sparking can be a danger, particularly at night. The worst culprits include both softwoods and hardwoods. In order, they are: white cedar, red cedar, alder, hemlock, balsam, the spruces, the softer pines, basswood, box elder, chestnut, tulip, sassafras, and the ubiquitous willow.

You often have to use one of the above woods because no other is readily available. Then don't make the mistake of adding fresh fuel to the fire in front of your bivouac and leaving the scene even for a couple of minutes. Sparks don't usually do more than char a tiny circle of canvas, so if you have a pack cover or tarpaulin, throw it over your precious sleeping bag. In windy weather be careful that a spark does not start a quickly leaping grass or forest fire.

Hickory is the leader among North American woods in heat-generating properties. Oak is a close second. Beech follows, succeeded by the birches and hard maples, the sap and inner bark of both of which are valuable foods as well. Ash is favored by many. Likewise is elm. Then trail locust and cherry.

The above woods are fifty percent again as effective as short-leaf pine, western hemlock, red gum, Douglas fir, sycamore, and soft maple. They are twice as hot as cedar, redwood, poplar, catalpa, cypress, basswood, spruce, and the decorative white pine.

Many of the barks, such as that from the hemlock, are notable for the steady warmth they will impart. Others, particularly the birch, excel at starting the fire.

Even when there is no birch, if there are softwoods in the vicinity, you are still well away. The small, dead twigs that characterize the bottoms of all spruce, pine, balsam, fir, and the like are filled with resin and will burn like torches. Just gather a handful of the smallest, straightest stuff, snapping it off with the fingers. Light this and shove it beneath a pile of heavier, equally pitchy dead branches. Then, unless you want just a brief hot fire, you'll probably add some hardwood limbs.

Experimenting with whatever fuel is at hand is often wisest, especially as some species vary among themselves in different parts of the continent because of the prevalent soil and atmosphere. Too, there are numerous separate varieties in every family group, each with its own individual characteristics.

There is a general rule that you can use in selecting firewood if you don't know the various species of trees. The heavier a wood is, the more heat it will throw. This works with green woods, too, an excellent reason for mixing green wood with dry, particularly when you want a long-lasting fire such as at night.

Standing Deadwood

You'll ordinarily want dry fuel. For this reason, you'll normally avoid fallen wood except during prolonged dry spells because it has absorbed too much moisture from the ground. If you have a choice, you'll ordinarily only use this when you want to hold a fire and when excessive heat is not important, as with the night fire in mild weather or with the cooking fire you wish to hold, buried, until you return to camp in the later part of the day.

Standing deadwood is generally the choice, although there are exceptions. Dead birch, for example, rapidly loses most of its heat-generating qualities if the bark has remained around it to hold in its abundant moisture. Such easily toppling dead birch can even be a hazard, and should be pushed over if you are making your camp nearby. The bark will still be good.

A rotten stump is generally of no use except to hold a fire. Again there are exceptions, and a decayed softwood stump may kick apart into tough knots or a hard pitchy core that will burn as if saturated with oil, as indeed they are.

Fuel Where No Trees Grow

Driftwood is often the best fuel in country where no trees are growing. Above the timber line, you can usually find sufficient bush to make your small fire, perhaps in a heel dent to protect it from the wind. On this continent's great central plains, you'll find yourself using small brush such as the traveling tumbleweed, roots of plants such as the mesquite, knotted clumps of grass, and the dry cattle droppings which are to the modern wayfarer what the buffalo chip was to the earlier frontiersman.

In parts of the far north where driftwood is not at hand, dried chunks of fuel from the great northern muskegs, which are actually peat bogs in the making, are sometimes available. There is also fully developed peat and even coal which, as I can attest, burns with a fine hot flame. In the continental northwest, there are also vast quantities of oil-rich shale and oil sand which burn with a heavy black smoke.

In the Arctic, too, brush and roots are often yours for the collecting. Moss and the numerous lichens can be used for fuel. The small heatherlike evergreen known as Cassiope is so resinous that it will burn while green and wet. If necessary, all these can be secured from beneath the snow.

Fuel in some deserts is so rare that when you find suitable plant growth you'll find yourself utilizing all twigs, leaves, stems, and underground roots. Dry animal dung gives a very hot flame.

No matter where you are, when fuel is scarce, it is sound practice to gather a supply whenever you can.

Foresight

Even if fuel and tinder are so easily available that you need not gather them as you proceed, it is always a good idea to keep an extra supply of both dry in case of storm. Stow this under cover in a handy place near the fire. Once the fire is going well, dead wood that is wet only on the outside will burn readily.

The most desperate condition you'll likely ever come across in wooded country is when every twig, branch, and trunk is sheathed with ice. The solution? Start your fire with birch bark or the dead evergreen stubs that usually remain dry in the bottoms of all softwoods.

Split logs always burn better, and it is interesting to note that you can split many a log with no tool of civilization other than a small knife. Not even that is absolutely necessary. You can utilize a sharp stone, instead. For the splitting, whittle hardwood wedges. Start a division with knife or stone. Then keep driving the wedges into the crack with a rock or club.

Matches

The easiest way to light a fire is with a match, and it follows that it is only sensible to keep a supply in a waterproof and unbreakable container whenever you are in the unfrequented places. Even though you may momentarily have sufficient matches, it is still best to get in the habit of making that first match count. Such gradually acquired skill may one day mark the difference between a snugly, warm camp and a miserable, damp, and chilly one.

If you can carry them, common wooden, strike-anywhere matches are best. The trick is to hold them so that the fire can feed down the wood. You'll do this in the most practical method of the moment. For example, you may face the breeze with your hands cupped before the lighted match. You may kneel between the wind and your methodically piled wood with your body serving as a shield. You may use your coat or any other convenient thing to guard the first wavering flames.

If possible, you should carry an unbreakable waterproof case kept filled preferably with substantial wooden matches whenever you are in the farther places. At the very least, you should have such a container filled with safety matches and a strip on which to strike them.

The match case I carry has a top ring by which it can be pinned inside a pocket. In deep wilderness, too, I consider it inexpensive insurance to carry a second filled case. For everyday use, so that you don't have to disturb the emergency supply, it's a convenient idea to scatter other matches throughout your clothing, most safely one to a pocket with the strike-anywhere variety.

If you find that your loose matches are damp, rub them through your hair. If your hair, too, is wet at the moment, rub the match to and fro between the palms of the hands with its head protruding slightly.

With any container filled with strike-anywhere matches, you have to be careful not to light a match accidentally and thus set off the whole batch. Always close the container gently and carefully. It's a smart dodge, too, to pack the matches with their heads about half and half in both directions. That way you can stow away more, besides.

Paper matches are not reliable enough to depend on for emergency use, although you may have several folders distributed among your pockets for casual use, particularly if you are a smoker. If you ever find yourself in a situation where your life may depend on your ability to light fires and you've nothing more dependable with you than a folder of paper matches, do everything you can to protect it from dampness, whether this is from rain, melting snow, or perspiration. Wrapping the pack in foil or a convenient bit of plastic to keep the heads and stems dry, in addition to the vulnerable striking surface, is sound procedure.

One ingenious invention that will start a very great number of fires without matches and will remain intact despite most survival hardships is the metal match. A metal match may be purchased inexpensively and should be a part of every survival kit. Just scrape a twinkling of the dark metal into the tinder, hold the short metallic stick against it, and strike it briskly with your knife.

Lighting a Fire with Water

If the water is frozen, find a clear piece of ice. Experiment with shaving this with your knife, then finally smoothing it in the warm hands, until you have a lens capable of pinpointing the sun. This method works surprisingly well.

If the weather is warm, you're still not beaten. Hold the curved crystals of two watches of similar size, or even such compass crystals, back to back. It does not matter if these are made of unbreakable plastic instead of glass so long as they are clear. Fill the space between the crystals with clear water. Then hold this contrived enlarging lens so as to converge the sun's rays in a point hot enough to start tinder glowing. Blow the glowing tinder into fire in both cases, and you're in business.

Fire from Glass

Forest fires are occasionally started by the sun's shining through a discarded bottle, especially if this has been partially filled with rain or melting snow, and from broken segments of such a bottle, particularly the ends. It follows that you can often find in your outfit such a bottle to use with clear water, or a bottle whose sides or base contain sufficient distortions to pinpoint the brightly shining sun.

Lenses taken from binoculars, telescopes, telescopic rifle sights, and cameras are excellent for magnifying the sun to produce fire. A little pocket magnifying lens will also turn the trick. Even with somewhat clouded sunlight this starts a fire in short order. It is thin, light, flat, and unbreakable, making it a likely candidate for a personal survival kit.

Flint and Steel

The flint and steel of buckskin years still work today. The spark may be made by striking the back of your knife against a piece of flint, perhaps the top or bottom of a match case. If there is no recognizable flint in your vicinity, experiment with other hard stones. Quartzite, jasper, nephrite, obsidian, iron pyrite, jadite, and agate are among the rocks that will work.

You don't even need a knife, of course. Any steel or iron will work. Holding your hands closely over your dry tinder, strike flatly with your knife blade or other small piece of satisfactory metal with a sharp, downward scraping motion so that sparks will skitter into the middle of the tinder.

Sparks from Two Rocks

The Eskimo in northern Canada often carries two fist-sized chunks of fool's gold. This iron pyrite is easily recognizable because it looks more like flecks of gold than many a piece of gold-bearing quartz itself. To get a spark, just strike the two rocks together.

If no fool's gold is at hand, try to find two other rocks that will give sparks when briskly stroked together. Many have this property.

The Bow and Drill Technique

Fire can also be started by friction as with the bow and drill technique or the fire thong, although these are the most difficult methods of all. But you may be in a spot sometimes when you have to rely on a bow and drill to save your life.

Make a strong bow, strung loosely with a shoelace, thong, or string. Use this to spin a soft, dry shaft in an easily handled block of hardwood. This will produce a powdery black dust which eventually will catch a spark. When smoke begins to rise, you should have enough spark to light your fire. Then lift the block, add tinder, and begin blowing on it. Sound easy? Then let's consider the details that are important to success.

In North America, both the drill and the fire board are often made of one of the following woods: fir, balsam, cottonwood, white or red cedar, linden, tamarack, cypress, basswood, yucca, poplar, and willow.

The drill can be a straight and well-seasoned stick about one-half inch thick and about twelve to fifteen inches long. A longer drill is too difficult to press effectively into position for twirling by bow alone.

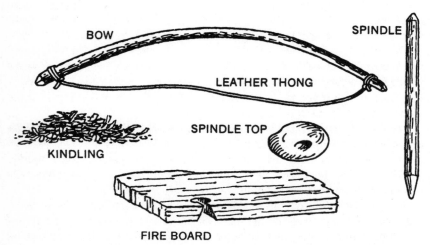

Implements of the bow and drill method of firemaking.

Using the bow and drill technique to start a fire.

The top end of the drill should be as smoothly rounded as possible so that it will turn in the socket with the least possible friction. On the other hand, a maximum of friction is desirable at the other end. This end consequently will be blunter.

It is interesting to note that a longer drill, perhaps one three feet in length, is sometimes used when it is to be rotated between the palms rather than by a bow. The hands, pressing downward as much as possible, are rubbed rapidly to and fro over the drill so as to spin it with the utmost strength and speed. If you are ever in a position where you cannot somehow fashion a thong, if only from your clothing, this method is one to remember. But it is less effective than the technique with bow and socket.

The sole function of the socket is to hold the top of the turning drill. Inasmuch as it is grasped with one hand, it may be an easily held knot of wood with a hollow formed in its underneath. It may also be a block made for that very purpose. Or if you are near water, it is often possible to find a slick stone with a smooth depression eroded in one side.

The socket may be oiled or waxed with native materials such as animal fat or bayberries to permit the drill to rotate more freely.

The bow may be made from a limber stick which, if strung more tightly, could be used to shoot arrows or darts. More often, however, you would use a substantial segment of branch with a natural crook already in it.

One end of the bow may have a natural crotch or branch stub that will make securing the thong easier. Or the bow can be notched for this purpose. If you are using one to experiment with by the fireplace, a heavier stick can be drilled to allow the insertion of the then-knotted cord.

The bowstring, which may be anything from a shoelace to tightly braided strips of clothing fabric, is tied at both ends with enough slack remaining to permit it to be wound once about the drill.

This works well with rawhide, but when cord, especially that of nylon, is used, the cord mostly slips on the drill. A second loop of the cord around the drill makes the bow want to twist out of position. A solution might be to use two cords, one tied to the drill at the top and one at the bottom, wound on the drill to meet in the middle.

The fire board can be split out of a dry log and then split again, and may be whatever size you can handle easily. You'll want it to be long enough to be held under one of your feet.

Using a knife, hatchet, ax, or even a sharp stone, begin a hole some three-fourths of an inch in from the edge of the fire board. Round out this hole, at the same time fitting it to the end of the drill, by turning the drill with the bow.

Finally, cut a notch through to this cup from the edge of the board. The sides of this slot generally slant so that it is noticeably wider at the bottom, permitting the hot black powder that is produced by the drilling to fall as rapidly as possible into the tinder that is laid at the base of the notch.

Tinder is massed beneath the slot in the fire board. If you are righthanded, kneel on your right knee and put your left foot as securely as possible on one end of the fire board. Take the bow in your right hand. Loop the string once around the drill or perhaps, as suggested above, use two cords to avoid slippage. Place the drill in the concavity made in the fire board.

Hold the drill in position with the socket which you grasp in your left hand. You'll likely discover that you can maintain more steady pressure on the drill by hugging your left leg with your left arm, keeping your wrist against your shin. Press on the drill, not enough however to retard it, when you begin spinning it to and fro with the bow.

Draw the bow back and forth in smooth sweeps, making these as long as the string will conveniently allow. At this stage you might try dropping a few grains of sand in the hole to build up the friction. In any event, the hole will eventually start to smoke. Spin the bow even more rapidly now, never ceasing the swift, even motion. Press down more determinedly on the drill.

Hot black powder will start to spill into the tinder. Continue drilling, for the stouter a spark you can start reddening there, the more speedily you'll be able to blow it into fire.

Everything finally will seem ready. Then carefully remove the drill. Blow gently into the slot until you can see a glow. Then lift both tinder and fire board if that is easiest. Press the tinder easily about the gleam. When the spark finally begins spreading, lift the board out of the way so you can fan and blow on the heat more freely. Gently continue feeding air to the area until the tinder bursts into flame.

Fire Thong

The thong can be a strip of dry rattan, preferably about one-fourth inch in diameter and some two feet in length. You'll also need a dry stick.

Prop the stick off the ground on a log or rock. Split the elevated end of the stick, holding this open with a wedge. Place a small wad of tinder in the split, leaving enough room behind it to insert the thong. Then, securing the stick with your foot or knees, work the thong rapidly back and forth until the tinder starts to glow, whereupon it will be possible to blow it into the flames.

Distracting the Smoke

Ever notice how smoke seems to follow you around a campfire? Matter of fact, it actually does follow you. The reason for this is that smoke is pulled into the partial vacuum made by any nearby object. The way out is to create a larger attraction than that of your person. One method of doing this is by building the fire against a boulder or sandy bank. Or locate some other bulk or surface nearby but at a safe distance.

Reflector

If you have an ax and the time, an excellent reflector can be made by leaning green logs against several stout stakes, driven into the ground at an outward slant. If you keep your blaze going long enough, these logs will eventually burn, furnishing more heat. The reflector, too, can be a safe ledge or bank. If the weather is extremely cold, situate yourself between the fire and the reflector.

Starting a fire with a thong.

For extra warmth sleep between your fire and a reflector.

In Snow

The only provision you normally have to make in snow is to scrape or stamp out a depression large enough for your blaze. In extremely deep snow, though, it may be necessary to provide a loose platform of green logs. Snow ordinarily makes things even easier, for you can stop and build your fire wherever there's fuel, at the same time obtaining your water for soup, tea, and such by melting undisturbed snow.

In the Mountains

Here the problem is often a combination of sparse fuel and howling wind. Make a small depression in the ground, narrow enough so that your cooking container will bridge it. Build your little fire in the bottom of the shallow hole. This way you'll be using all the heat with the utmost efficiency.

Safety

The ideal place for your campfire is on mineral soil or solid rock. The hazard of fire is always present with campfires on pine needles, muskeg, dry grass, leaves, or even dead roots.

Even after you've extinguished your campfire, a subterranean root can still be burning. This smoldering can continue slowly underground all winter, to burst into flame and possibly a devastating forest fire in the hot days of spring. Roots will sometimes continue to burn in this fashion even if you've kindled your blaze in snow near the bottom of a wind-scoured tree.

When you break camp, make sure your fire is dead out if there is the slightest chance that it may spread. Drown it with water if possible, stir the coals, and drown it again. Pay particular attention to the vicinity where sparks may be glowing.

It is a good idea to break matches once they are used. If they're cold enough to be handled this way, they are safe.

Speaking of safety, open fires are prohibited in some regions during the dry season. If there is a lookout your campfire may be spotted and individuals, who'll be your rescuers, dispatched to the scene.

NIGHT FIRE

If you are camping in the open and desire a fire for warmth as well as for companionship, the trick is to build one as long as your body and sleep between the fire and some reflector such as a large rock. At the same time, the fire itself should be reflected by some such arrangement as a slanting wall of green logs, held up by poles or stakes. This is a technique that determines at a glance the difference between a cheechako and a sourdough. No matter how large you make your fire, seldom will it last the night. The best procedure is to gather a large pile of firewood by your head so that you must only lean up on one elbow to lay fresh fuel into place.

Unless you were utterly exhausted when you retired, the encroaching cold will awaken you for this chore. In the morning, if you have planned well, a glowing bed of coals will remain for cooking your breakfast.

Far from being hardships, these occasional rousings in the peaceful intensity of darkness, serene and mysterious as from the sources of life, are memorable respites. Perhaps the timber wolves, no danger to any man except on the very, very rare occasions when one is rabid, are howling with all the beautiful, sweet intensity denied those who elect to remain behind in the cities. A pair of owls may enliven the peacefulness with their hoo-hoo-hooing. Sparks soar straight up toward Orion's belted brightness, and perhaps you mark the position of Polaris so that in the daylight you can check your compass's local declination. Then almost instantly you are back asleep.

CHAPTER FIVE

SHELTER

I for one, unless circumstances intervene, don't go into the deep wilderness to shut myself away from the some two thousand stars we can see with the naked eyes, from the spacious view, nor to miss the joy of a campfire—and the memorable luxury of hunching up in the morning and getting breakfast started, with the glory of the east, whenever possible, and the country I am going to hunt, fish, prospect, or explore that day quickening before me.
—Bradford Angier
The Master Backwoodsman

Holding to the truth that exposure is the backwoods' surest and swiftest killer, we must concede that shelter is second only to fire in importance. This shelter need not be at all elaborate, depending of course on the adequacy of your clothing and your sleeping provisions.

"A comfortable home was once made here almost entirely of such materials as Nature furnished," Henry David Thoreau noted more than a century ago. "Consider how slight a shelter is absolutely necessary."

Although this is still very true, invading civilization has opened so many tracts of what we once considered to be wilderness that only a portion is left of what the mountain men, trappers, early prospectors, and timber cruisers once considered to be virgin territory. Yet millions of unspoiled acres remain, in prime pockets here and there and in immense stretches along the roof of the continent where, as the saying goes, the hand of man has seldom set foot.

Here we can still go and build lean-tos, make browse beds, and sit at night by a lone campfire with the yips of coyotes our only companions. This is the country for the canoeist, the backpacker, the individual who's handy with a diamond hitch, and the pilot of a small plane with pontoons.

We can no longer fell trees, feed night fires, or blaze a trail in much of the former wilderness that is now the domain of the paid guide, the snowmobile, the outboard motor, and the four-wheel-drive vehicle. But the modern adventurer who wants to escape the concrete chasms and the asphalt jungles and to depend entirely on his own God-given abilities can—with determination and a bit of hard work at first, before he settles into the ease of the true woodsman who has already tasted the joys of roughing it and is now smoothing the way for himself well back of beyond—find the real backwoods that we are considering in this volume. Thereafter, what may have seemed hardships on the fringes of the settled places will, beyond the domain of the snowmobile and the trail bike, be to him merely a moderate amount of vacationing exercise.

The niche in a Christmas tree is so simple to contrive that I often make one in perhaps five minutes for nestling in while boiling the kettle at noon on a stormy day. It is perfectly adequate for an overnight shelter if you sit on a warm browse bed on the side opposite the wind with your back to the trunk, strip or cut off no more than enough additional boughs to contain yourself snugly, and build a small campfire in front, with sufficient dead, dry wood within easy reaching distance to keep it burning all night.

Security from wind and cold can be intensified, in other words, if you intersperse the living boughs with others shoved in from other trees. First, of course, shake such an evergreen free of snow if necessary. To keep out further moisture in stormy weather, roof the opening with something such as birch bark. For years I have carried an eight-by-ten-foot sheet of plastic that is so thin it can handily be folded into a breast pocket of my shirt and is always available to solve any such roofing problems.

THE INDIAN CAMP

"The simplest and most primitive of all camps is the 'Indian Camp,' " Colonel Townsend Whelen's old friend Nessmuk—George W. Sears—wrote nearly a century ago. "It is easily and quickly made, is warm and comfortable, and stands a pretty heavy rain when properly put up. This is how it is made.

"Let us say you are out and have slightly missed your way. The coming gloom warns you that night is shutting down. You are no tenderfoot. You know that a place to rest is essential to health and comfort through the long, cold November night. You dive down the first little hollow until you strike a rill of water, for water is a prime necessity. As you draw your hatchet you take in the whole situation at a glance.

"The little stream is gurgling in a half choked frozen way. There is a huge soddened hemlock lying across it. One clip of the hatchet showed that it will peel. There is plenty of small timber standing about . . . long, slim poles, with a tuft of foliage on top. Five minutes suffices to drop one of these, cut a twelve-foot pole from it, sharpen the pole at each end, jam one end into the ground and the other into the rough bark of a scraggly hemlock, and there is your ridgepole.

"Now go—with your hatchet—for the bushiest and most promising young hemlocks within reach. Drop them and draw them to camp rapidly. Next, you need a fire. There are fifty hard, resinous limbs sticking up from the prone hemlock; lop off a few of these and split the largest into match timber; reduce the splinters to shavings, scrape the wet leaves from your prospective fireplace, and strike a match on the balloon part of your trousers. If you are a woodsman, you will strike but one.

"Feed the fire slowly at first; it will gain fast. When you have a blaze ten feet high, look at your watch. It is six P.M. You don't want to turn in before ten o'clock, and you have four hours to kill before bedtime. Now, tackle the old hemlock; take off every dry limb, and then peel the bark and bring it to camp. You will find this takes an hour or more.

"Next, strip every limb from your young hemlocks; and shingle them onto your ridgepole. This will make a sort of bear den, very well calculated to give you a comfortable night's rest. The bright fire will soon dry the ground that is to be your bed, and you will have plenty of time to drop another small hemlock and make a bed of browse a foot high. You do it.

"Then you make your pillow. . . . It is half a yard of muslin, sewed up as a bag, and filled with moss or hemlock browse. You can empty it and put it in your pocket, where it takes up about as much room as a handkerchief. You will have other little muslin bags—an' you be wise. One holds a couple of ounces of good tea; another, sugar; another is kept to put your loose duffle in: money, match safe, pocketknife. You have a pat of butter and a bit of pork, with a liberal slice of brown bread, and before turning in, you make a cup of tea, broil a slice of pork, and indulge in a lunch.

"Ten o'clock comes. The time has not passed tediously. You are warm, dry, and well-fed. Your old friends, the owls, come near the firelight and salute you with their strange wild notes; a distant fox sets up for himself with his odd, barking cry, and you turn in. Not ready to sleep just yet.

"But you drop off; and it is two bells in the morning watch when you waken with a sense of chill and darkness. The fire has burned low, and snow is falling. The owls have left, and a deep silence broods over the cold, still forest. You rouse the fire, and, as the bright light shines in the furthest recesses of your forest den, get out the little pipe, and reduce a bit of heavy plug to its lowest denomination. The smoke curls lazily upward; the fire makes you warm and drowsy, and again you lie down—to again awaken with a sense of chilliness— to find the fire burned low and daylight breaking. You have slept better than you would in your own room at home. You have slept in an 'Indian Camp'!

"You have also learned the difference between such a simple shelter and an open-air bivouac under a tree or beside an old log."

Nessmuk's *Woodcraft,* for all its charm, dates back about eighty-five years, and Kephart's *Camping and Woodcraft* about sixty years. Lots of water has gone over the dam since then.

"Except for a ten-day trip in Michigan some ninety years ago," Colonel Whelen told me, "the only backpacking that George W. Sears (Nessmuk) ever did was across short carries between lakes in the Adirondacks. I met Nessmuk when I was a small boy, came on him in a small cabin on Eagle Lake in the Adirondacks one day. I remember him as a very friendly old man.

"Kephart I knew personally and corresponded with a lot. A very fine man indeed! His was long the best book on its subject, but it is weak in parts, and Kephart did not have extended field experience. In fact, all his experience was confined to the Great Smoky Mountains in North Carolina and to some of the swampy country on the Mississippi River below St. Louis, in neither of which place could he have acquired much information on backpacking, for instance. Kephart was well read, but there were relatively few books by specialists in outdoor living in his day. In Sears's time there were practically none."

As each of us observes the world from a different trail, it is only natural that points of view will vary. Take for example, three sportsmen approaching a water hole. One will see only the disappearing cubs. Another will see the large bear hurrying nearer. The third will see both cubs and mother. I do not, for a moment, suppose that my ways are the only ways, but at least it may be helpful to know the other fellow's points. Here is what I have learned from a lifetime in the farther places about building a lean-to.

The Lean-To

There are so many common sense variations that lean-tos are suitable for almost any country. For instance, one or both ends of the horizontal top pole can be tied to or notched to standing trees, laid in the crotches of trees, in the crotches of other poles that are leaned against trees for support, or in tripods made by lashing three poles together at the top. Other variations, as for example those employing rocks, will readily come to mind, depending on the terrain in your location.

Once the top pole is in place, the framework can be rapidly completed by leaning other poles short distances apart along the back. These are often supplemented by horizontal poles laid in crotches or tied in position.

How long should the ridgepole be? How high should it be erected? At what angle should the back extend to the ground? The following facts may act as your guides.

First of all, the lean-to should be as long as your body. This is because you'll be most comfortable sleeping beside a fire that is as long as you are tall. Even when you have a companion, the two of you will be snugger sleeping lengthwise to the fire than with either your head or feet facing it.

Ideally, the lean-to should be high enough to stand in. On the other hand, a low lean-to will reflect heat more conservatively and is easier to build. For a satisfactory compromise, make the emergency lean-to just high enough so that the occupants can sit comfortably in its mouth.

The steeper the roof, the better the structure will both shed precipitation and reflect heat. A forty-five-degree slope is usually considered a suitable compromise between water-shedding efficacy and available interior space. If you have a sleeping bag, of course make the shelter wide enough to accommodate it.

The fourth basic variable has to do with the wind. The fundamental rule is to have the opening on the side away from the wind. In open snow terrain, however, drifts may form in that lee. Then the most satisfactory compromise is to make the entrance crosswise to the wind. This is also the thing to do when you are camped in a canyon beside a mountain stream or in some other location where the thermal air currents alternate with the time of day, in fair weather flowing downward in the early morning and then back upwards toward evening.

Suppose you may be stranded in relatively flat country for an extended period? Then you'll be influenced by the prevailing wind rather than by any momentary breezes. This prevailing wind will be indicated by such natural signs as leaning trees and the direction of the majority of the downfall.

An ax will make this job simple, a hatchet easy, and just a light, small knife feasible. In a pinch, you can get by with your bare hands. Let's assume that you have at least a good sheath knife.

Roof a lean-to with evergreen boughs.

You want a shelter seven feet long, to accommodate you lengthwise in its mouth. So you cut and trim a slim poplar sapling, say, at least two feet longer. Place this ridgepole four feet high in the crotches between limbs and trunks of two trees.

At each end, you slant a roughly trimmed sapling in a forty-five-degree angle toward the back. You'll want three or more additional poles the length of the ridgepole. There are enough stubs of branches on the first two saplings to support these poles, parallel to the ridge, evenly spaced from the ground up. Now your framework is complete.

You'll want walls at least six inches thick. One foot would be even better. The back wall is the only problem. You bush in the ends by leaning there several thickly needled young fir.

A large quantity of fir boughs will cover your shed roof. Start with the bottom layer, just as if you were shingling a house roof. Hang the boughs close together over the pole nearest the ground. The next row will overlap these, and so on, until you have a substantial roof that will shed a fair amount of precipitation. The boughs are laid upside down, with the butts uppermost, then overlapped and covered by the tops of the next row.

Extend your campfire until it is as long as your body, and lay in a towering pile of firewood so you will be able to replenish it during the long night without leaving your bed.

Birch bark makes your lean-to practically waterproof.

There are innumerable other types of lean-tos, all made in the same general fashion by shingling a pole framework. For example, you might make a bivouac seven feet wide and five feet high in front by laying the crotches of two poles together. Hold this angle upright by leaning a ten-foot pole, which will serve as your ridge, from these crotches to the ground in back. Thatch this with available browse, preferably softwood boughs, or just lean a quantity of small leafy trees against it. Moss, bark, vines, reeds, grass, and other outdoor materials may be used, too. For that final master touch you might curl rolls of birch bark entirely across the top, extending down atop the shingled browse on both sides, to make the bivouac practically waterproof. This will make a fine den for the night.

The companionable way to put up a pair of lean-tos, when the party is large enough, is face to face with a cheery campfire between. Unfortunately, such a setup is as impractical as it is charming. No matter how you arrange things, the fire will tend to fill one of the shelters with smoke. You may have everything going along happily for an hour, and then a changing caprice of breeze will cause trouble.

One large lean-to, built so that all occupants will be sleeping parallel to its front and to the long fire, or two smaller ones side by side, will handily solve the problem.

Drainage

You may wish to protect your shelter with a small but functional drainage ditch. Of course, if you are bivouacking on a ridge where moisture sinks almost at once into the forest floor, or if you are camping on sand, no such ditching will be necessary.

A furrow a couple of inches wide and deep can be quickly scratched with a sharp dead stick when no more likely tool is at hand. In front where this indentation is in the way of traffic, and also where the soil is such that it falls in readily, fill it loosely with pebbles.

Such a drain should be placed so that it will bear away any water cascading down the walls. If you are bivouacing on an incline, moisture will have to be turned away only from the upper portions of the shelter.

Fallen Tree

A fallen tree may be your answer in a number of ways, and some of my most comfortable shelters have been constructed around them. The roots of a toppled forest giant often provide a solid vertical bulwark against which, in the clearing left by the roots themselves, several poles can be set at a conservative forty-five-degree angle and a bough roof laced to them. One of the shelters I so fashioned nearly three decades ago, in one of my favorite hunting territories in the Canadian Rockies, is still habitable.

The boughs of a fallen titan often come close in their natural state to providing shelter, in front of which a body-long fire can be kindled. Often all that's necessary is to cut away several of the blocking boughs. These and others from the same tree can be used to thatch the roof and ends. Be careful,

Even a fallen tree can provide comfortable shelter.

however, not to cut any of the underneath limbs that may be helping to support the tree in its new position.

SIMPLE SHELTER SOLUTIONS

A Handy Poncho

A fifteen-ounce poncho, 5½ by 7½ feet, which folds into a pocket-sized wad, will keep even the backpacker's knees dry in wet going in the open, and will ward off chilly wind along the ridges. It will also quickly waterproof a makeshift lean-to shelter. On nights when you prefer to sleep beneath the stars, this poncho will protect your sleeping bag from damp ground. (Take a light mosquito bar into country where you may need one.)

A Sheet of Plastic

The simplest form of shelter is merely a large sheet of plastic which, if it is of light material, will fold and stow handily in a breast pocket. These are so convenient to carry, as a matter of fact, that I always have one with me when I go into the woods. With such protection, even in a downpour you can boil the kettle and have lunch while remaining comfortable and dry. It is easy, too, to improvise a sleeping shelter. A plastic sheet quickly waterproofs a pile of equipment, and protects it from the heavy dews often encountered even on fair nights.

Where these plastic tarps are most handy is in forested wilderness. There you can quickly and easily throw up a shelter with boughs, but you may have trouble making it waterproof. Here the plastic can be sandwiched in the roof in between the layers of boughs. Along the main, heavily frequented trails, such shelters should never be built except in an emergency, because they involve defacing the trees.

In these areas the plastic can be used to waterproof the roof of a lean-to framed of forest litter. Or it can be pitched as a tent. One way to do this is by stretching it over a rope or pole extended between two trees, then weighing down the back, and also the sides if it's that big, with rocks or other poles. A large one pitched as a canopy really makes cooking and eating a pleasure on a stormy day.

Any plastic sheeting will do. However, reinforced plastic tarps are made especially for this type of packsack camping, with nylon threads woven into them and with well-spaced grommets.

Plastic tubing provides a way to have a shelter for just a few pennies that's light to carry and quick to pitch. Just get a piece of plastic tubing about eight feet long, available at many outfitters. Put it up by running a rope through it as a ridge and tying the rope several feet high between two trees. No pegs are necessary, for the weight of the occupant anchors the tube. Such tubing can also be obtained in longer lengths, say fifteen feet, so that one camper can sleep at each opening and still have room for his duffle. An efficient insect de-

Shelter made with plastic tubing.

fense can be fashioned at each opening from a few draped yards of bobbinet or cheesecloth. Dark netting is suggested for two reasons: it's easier to see out through, and the darker colors attract fewer mosquitoes and flies.

Tarpaulin

Tarpaulins are generally conveniently large in size, while being light in weight. They are inexpensive and may be used in a number of different ways. The disadvantages on a hiking trip are that they are apt to involve more fabric, and therefore more weight, than a specially cut small tent.

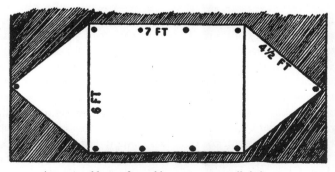

A suggested layout for making your own small shelter tarp.

One answer to that problem is the economical shelter tarp shown here, made in any size desired, either of light waterproof fabric or of durable plastic sheeting. This type cuts out a lot of excess material.

Even this small a lean-to bivouac provides comfort and an enjoyable convenience. You profit to the fullest reasonable degree from your fire while you sleep, when it's cold enough to keep a blaze going and when you are where you can do this. And when you awake in the morning, there is the sky to study for weather hints and the surrounding country to scan.

When you are sitting in front of your small cooking fire preparing your meals, you will have plenty of room for food and utensils on either side. When you lean back to relax after supper, you can enjoy the color and hearty warmth of your fire.

Such a shelter, with triangular wings forming side walls when it is erected, can be easily put up in a few minutes. I usually look for a tree to support one end of the ridgepole and use a couple of poles tied together like shears at the other end. The top of the shelter ties to this ridge.

For the back, it's often handiest to locate a fair-sized pole and stake it in position, then tie the lower part of the rear wall to this instead of bothering with stakes. Not only is this practice generally faster and easier, but it makes a more substantial job that keeps out furtive drafts. In really cold weather, when you can do it, imitate the trapper and choose a cubbyhole for your camp site—a sheltered spot among thickly spreading spruce, or perhaps a tiny clearing in a thick fir grove.

Incidentally, both the necessary grommets and grommet-setting kits are available inexpensively from many sporting goods stores and from the equipment companies that sell fabrics.

TENTS

Tents are very nearly necessities in the frequented places, if only for privacy. In the real backwoods it is a different matter, except when you're spending cold nights above timberline. Otherwise, not even flies or mosquitoes will make one a necessity, as you can travel with a mosquito canopy to pitch over your bed that is light enough for carrying and for good ventilation but has a mesh small enough to withstand the intrusion of even the pesky no-see-ums which appear mainly at dawn and at dusk.

The tent's principal characteristics should include resistance to storm, wind, heat or cold and—with today's usually tough, long-lived, lightweight fabrics—condensation, an especially important consideration when you realize that an individual of average size and weight emits close to 45 cubic inches of moisture per night through breathing and perspiration. For this reason, a breathable inner fabric covered with a waterproof outer fly will create a dead-air space that is several degrees warmer than the outside air, so that vaporized water from within the tent proper will escape through the walls before condensing. This is done most effectively today with a breathing inner tent and an outside waterproofed fly.

Cotton fabrics have been found to present too many problems, including weight, weakness, mildew, and rot. Nearly all quality lightweight tents today are made of nylon in two general weaves: a taffeta with a smooth texture that, being more abrasion-resistant, is suitable for flooring when it is finished with a heavy application of durable, waterproof urethane; and a breathable ripstop fabric reinforced with extra thread to help stop tearing. This is suitable as is for the usual tent proper and, when treated with the waterproof urethane, for the waterproof flies.

. Such a combination tent, which functionally should be fire-resistant if only so that a spark from the campfire will not burn it—as happened all too frequently with the old, paraffin-waterproofed cottons—should have seams that are well overlapped, conscientiously sewn, and reinforced in the stress areas. A sound thread is dacron for strength, covered with a cotton that will swell when wet to fill and waterproof otherwise vulnerable needle holes. Finally, it should have a fine nylon mesh front and back for thorough ventilation and to keep out the smallest insects. This should be as darkly colored as possible, both because it makes for easier visibility and because it attracts fewer bugs. The zippers should be the ruggedest, most troublefree available.

In extreme conditions, even the best tents are plagued with two shortcomings which, fortunately, can be handily solved. In severe cold, even tunnel vents are not sufficient to handle moisture which is always being expelled by the body and which tends to freeze upon contact. A breathable, cotton, inner frost lining can be added and removed daily for shaking out the frozen moisture, while the most substantial nylon zippers are a great improvement over the old, weaker, colder metal zippers which tended to freeze. Secondly, above the tree line you'll need implements for erecting the tent, such as poles, frames, pegs, etc. These should be light but robust aircraft-alloy aluminum pieces with extra-strength center sections to insure their reliability against heavy snow and wind.

Such a total combination, easily sleeping two individuals and rugged enough to withstand heavy weather, can be obtained in models weighing less than eight pounds. As for expense, I've proved to myself over the years that the aptest policy is to buy what, although not always the most costly by a long way, is the best. The best safeguard for the uninformed is to deal with a reputable, experienced, and trustworthy dealer. The best proof of this is that I am still using the everyday equipment that I bought when I first took to the woods.

Pitching Your Tent

When pitching your tent, look for a dry, smooth, level spot with, preferably, a good view. Halfway down the lee side of a slope will be the warmest. Get as near a good water source as practical without subjecting yourself, in season, to too much humidity and too many insects. Respect, of course, the usual safety factors.

Getting the floor of the tent square and not too taut is well worth the extra time and trouble it will take. As you proceed, put a little tension evenly on the guy ropes. If you are using a fly, make sure that this does not sag and rub on the tent itself, as this can cause leakage and wear. Naturally, keep the highly vulnerable fabric free from sharp or abrasive objects. Finally, sponging the fabric with warm water and mild soap and wiping the pegs and such clean will make for a longer and more pleasant tent life.

The Whelen Lean-to Tent

Since I have always loved the primitive wilderness for itself, I do not like to shut myself away from it in a closed tent. For that reason, when traveling back of beyond where weight is not a factor, as by canoe or horse, I have always used a so-called Whelen Lean-to Tent, designed by my late writing companion and successor to Nessmuk and Kephart, Colonel Townsend Whelen. As a result of such Army assignments as Director of Research and Development at the Springfield Armory, commanding officer at the Frankfort Arsenal, and ordnance representative in the Infantry Board, experimentation in attaining maximum performance came to be second nature to my friend, who thought up what he modestly called a Hunter's Lean-to Tent.

The Whelen Lean-to has a canopy under which you can cook in a rainstorm. The sides are ideally suited for heat reflection and additional room, for they angle outward and forward at the bottom some two feet from where a weighted cord would touch the ground if suspended from the ends of the six-foot-wide ridge. With this, the walls angle at such a pitch that, besides reflecting heat and light into the shelter, the frontal extension hinders wind and breezes from making the front sanctuary chilly while at the same time affording storage room for personal belongings near the head of the sleeping bag. The cooking gear and foodstuffs can be stored at the foot. Because there is only a single slanting wall in back, both the expense and the difficulty of construction is lessened, while pitching is made easier. Additional room for storage is also provided, usually even when two individuals sleep side-by-side and parallel to the front.

Loops extend above the six-foot tape ridge to hold the ridgepole. Under this tape ridge are two additional loops to hold a short pole on which clothing can be hung for convenience or for drying. An awning is sewn to the ridge. Although it is easiest to toss this backward over the ridgepole in warm fair weather, it can be extended forward and downward to provide additional shelter in front, to help prevent a storm from hurling itself into the tent, and to create a covered area under which to sit and cook.

Troublesome guy ropes over which one is always tripping are unnecessary. Instead, sharpen both ends of a pair of poles some six feet long. Extend one

Whelen Lean-to Tent.

end of each through the big grommet at each outer end of the awning. Implant the other end at the head and foot of the sleeping bag, thus maintaining the awning taut some four feet above the forest floor where warmth and illumination from the long fire in front will beat snugly under it.

For pitching the Whelen Lean-to Tent, merely cut and trim a slim ridgepole perhaps a dozen feet in length, long enough to extend between the branches of handy trees or to be held some six feet high by shear poles. Then just stake down the sides and backs, and your shelter is ready.

The sides, splayed as suggested, will do a great deal to keep smoke from being drawn inside the shelter and, indeed, will do away with this annoyance almost completely if you build your fire against a large rock or safe ledge or slant a tier of back logs at least a foot high against green poles behind the blaze. This will make the tent the coziest living quarters available back of beyond. With an adequate sleeping bag you'll need no night fire except for the cheery blaze you'll want to dream in front of until it's time to turn in; without even getting out of your bag, you can have tinder, kindling, and wood available for building the morning fire for breakfast and for getting the kinks out of your muscles.

If flying pests are around, merely pitch on small poles above your head an easily available, inexpensive mosquito bar, small-meshed enough to prevent even the intrusion of no-see-ums. And before you leave its sanctuary, douse yourself with a good repellent. In really cold weather, insulate the air or foam mattress beneath you with browse, then keep a rousing fire going all night.

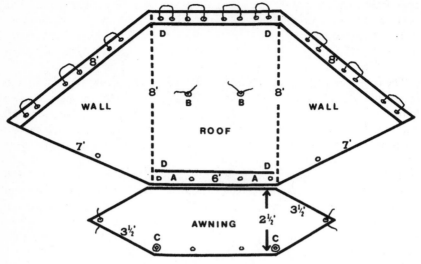

Pattern for Whelen Lean-to Tent.

Colonel Whelen gave me permission to pass along his long-proved design if you'd like the easy and pleasurable adventure of building such a shelter yourself for the fun of it, for economy, and perhaps because such a commercial tent may no longer be easily available.

The Comfortable Forester Tent

One of the most pleasant parts of any hiking vacation should be the camps. For these—especially if you want to build your own tent and at the same time cut weight and costs—the Forester Tent is a good solution if you are going to be traveling in wooded country. It is one of the best tents ever devised for a chronic outdoorsman, particularly for one who objects to spending any of his outdoor hours confined in a closed canvas cell.

The Forester Tent is the cheapest of all tents, in ratio to size and convenience, to make yourself. It is the easiest and quickest to pitch. Considering its weight and bulk, it is the most comfortable in which to live and do your few camp chores. With the exception of some of the special lean-to tents such as the Whelen, it is the easiest to warm with a campfire out in front.

The one weak point of the Forester—at first glance, anyway—is that if you try to mosquitoproof it, you ruin its inexpensiveness and functional simplicity. But in bug time it is an easy matter to secure a light mosquito bar for a dollar or two and hang or stake this net enclosure over your bed.

The Forester Tent is triangular in shape. The tent can be built in any size of course. But the smallest really comfortable dimensions for one backpacker, or for two who do not mind a bit of crowding, are about seven feet wide at the open front, three feet at the back, and seven feet deep from front to rear. The peak of such a model should stand about six feet above the ground in front, while the triangular rear will be about three feet high. With the entire tent open to the fire in front, the angle will be such that heat and light will be reflected throughout the sheltered area.

The tent is usually pitched with three poles and eight sticks procured at the camp site. The ridgepole should be long enough to extend from the peak and to pass down and out through the hole at the top of the back wall at such a tilt that it will rest on the ground about three feet behind the tent. The two shorter poles are arranged at the front like shears and, holding the ridge pole at their apex, run from the front corners to the peak.

You pitch this tent with its back to the prevailing wind. But if the wind shifts around to the front, and brings rain or snow with it, the front of the tent and the more exposed parts of the bedding can get wet. This is why some makers sew a hood or flap to the front of the shelter that can be stretched out protectively in case of storm. A poncho or any small piece of canvas or plastic can also be used to close the top of the open space.

In any event, the entire front should not be closed all the way to the ground. If only the top part is shut, or if in ordinary cases a flap is extended outward, moisture will be kept out. It will be possible, at the same time, to cook comfortably during a storm. Another advantage inherent with this particular type of tent is that one is so easy to handle that only a very few minutes will be required to strike and then erect it again with its back to the new wind direction. Made in this small size, from one of the light water-repellent tent fabrics, such a tent need not weigh more than three pounds or so.

The pattern for making a Forester Tent, passed along to me by Colonel Townsend Whelen, is shown here. Colonel Whelen's directions were: "This tent is for one or two campers, with beds arranged along the side walls. Cut

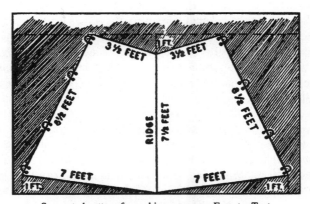

Suggested pattern for making your own Forester Tent.

and sew to the dimensions shown, allowing one inch all around the edges for hemming.

"Note how the bottom of the sides is set back one foot to make the tent sit right on the ground. To manage this, cut the pattern from rectangular fabric as shown, then angle the front and back. The rear wall—an isosceles triangle three feet high, with a three-foot base and three-and-one-half-foot sides, not including the one-inch allowance for hemming—is cut off square at the top. When this portion is sewed to the main body of the tent at the rear, it leaves a hole at the top of the rear through which the ridgepole is stuck. It makes about the most comfortable camp imaginable."

CAMPING ON ROCK AND SAND

If you're thinking of camping on the summit of a high mountain, try to pitch your tent a bit below the exposed peak on the side away from the prevailing winds. Above the sheltering treeline, try to find a reasonably flat place among the rocks where there is at least two-sided protection for your sleeping bags or small tent.

It's especially unwise to make camp on an exposed mountaintop in regions where thunderstorms are common. You'd be an invitation to lightning. For the same reason, don't set up near lone trees or a fire tower. They're often struck during such a storm.

If high winds are common in the area, tie your tent down in every way possible. On a rocky mountaintop it's often impossible to stake down a tent in the usual way, but you may be able to tie it to bushes, clumps of vegetation, or small boulders. Failing that, drive a stake in a ledge crack and rope off to that, or jam the guys into such cracks, or use heavy slabs to weigh down the tent corners.

A mountain tent, desirable for its lightness, is generally small, making it comparatively easy to erect. Several types of such tents are supported by inside or outside frames of fiberglass rods, which can be carried with little difficulty. These tents can be lifted about even when fully pitched and make ideal shelters where staking is difficult. However, if you can lift such a tent, so can a strong wind. Flat rocks inside, or outside on the corners, may solve the problem. If a bad storm is on the way, it may be advisable to drop your tent flat to save it from possible wind damage. It's amazing, however, how a small tent, pitched low to the ground and anchored solidly, will ride out all but the highest gales.

Keep campfires small and sheltered from high winds. Gusts have a habit of blowing sparks that can lodge in ledge cracks and start a blaze after you've left. Fuel may be difficult to locate above timberline, but look about the ledges or between the rocks where wind-strewn branches from below may have lodged. Too, there is dried brush and vegetation. Any live trees found near the peak of a mountain, if you're allowed to cut them, may be tough to

Ideal tentsite for mountain camping should have shelter from wind.

chop because of their stunted, twisted grain. It's better to scout around for fallen dead stuff. This, too, may be hard to sever. Probably the best bet is to try breaking it by jamming one end into a crack and putting your weight on the other end.

When taking to the mountains, be sure your sleeping bag will keep you warm down close to freezing temperatures. Even in summer, mountain nights can be mighty chilly. A short air mattress will be well worth its weight if you sleep on sandy or rocky soil. An inexpensive beach float of plastic will be of great value under the bag even if it supports you only down to the knees. Longer mattresses are more comfortable, but this must be balanced against the weight they put on sagging shoulders. Many camping-goods dealers carry short mattresses especially for mountain campers, and they are obtainable by mail from one of the big catalog-issuing concerns.

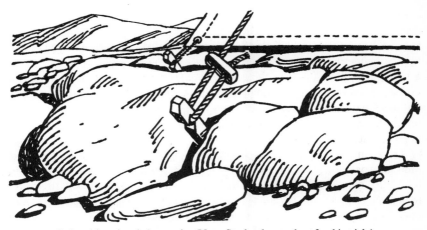

Stakes driven into ledge cracks. (Note: Steel stakes are best for this trick.)

Every summer you read of inexperienced hikers and campers who are caught on a summit or high trail by sudden cold, sleet, or snow. This often results in rescuers being called out at great personal risk. So even if you feel positive that the skies will remain clear, carry adequate clothing for cold weather and at least a lightweight tarpaulin for emergency shelter. The experienced mountaineer watches the weather continually and is seldom caught unready. To venture into high country unprepared is not only a mark of the rankest greenhorn, but it's downright dangerous.

On such a camping trip, unless you're an old-timer bent on exploring or perhaps prospecting, stick to marked trails as much as possible. The walking will be easier. There will be a better chance of finding water, shelter, and emergency help. And you'll run little risk of getting lost.

Do not camp on, near, or under what might be a slide area—slopes of loose rock slabs or round stones that could easily start dusting downgrade. Such traps can be especially perilous during a thaw or prolonged rain.

Keep your pack light, rest often while climbing and descending, and mountain camping will be an exciting adventure. The clear air, the pulsating immensities, and the smoldering solitude of the sunrise alone are worth the effort.

Those who partake of desert camping will find it an engrossing challenge. You'll discover a multitude of new sights and sounds, as well as a few special problems. For example, staking a tent may present a fresh hurdle. The ground may be too soft to hold ordinary stakes securely. If the sand is really fine, anchor shields may be needed on your stakes. These are broad metal disks that slip over metal and plastic stakes to present a wider surface to the ground, thus reducing the proclivity of a stake to pull loose.

If you don't care to buy shields, try longer stakes. Or hitch the guy ropes to logs or crossed sticks buried in the sand. Some campers on desert and beach have found that cheap tin plates make good anchors. Just punch a hole in the center of the plate, run a rope through, anchor it with a large knot or a cross stick, and then bury the plate a foot or so beneath the sand. If your tent guys have slides, it will be wise to rig each plate with a short piece of rope and a hook to catch the loop that's normally thrown around a peg. A practical substitute for a tin-plate anchor is a short length of wide board having a hole in the middle. When camping in the desert, even close to the civilized bustle of a highway, do not make the mistake of pitching your tent on the luringly level bottom of a dry gulch or riverbed. A faraway storm, of which you may not even be aware, can send a flash flood roaring down such a declivity with hardly a moment's warning, sweeping everything in front of it. Just keep to high ground and you'll be safe, but make certain that the area is on the same side of the gulch or dry river as your car is parked. High ground will afford a better possibility of an energizing breeze, too. But beware of high winds that may mean sand and dust storms.

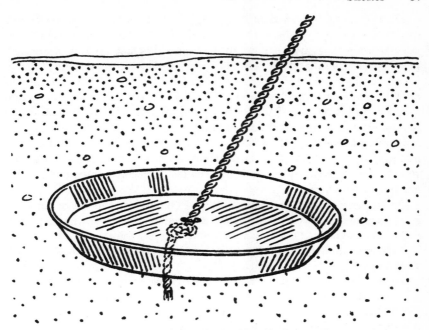

Tent anchor made from tin plate buried in the ground.

In sandy country all such precision equipment as cameras, firearms, and binoculars should be kept in their cases when not in use. A sudden whirlwind or dust devil may spring up to fill your tent with swirling clouds of abrasive clutter. This can penetrate all but the tightest cases. A tarpaulin thrown over such gear when a dust cloud approaches may be of some help. If your car is nearby, this equipment will be safe inside with the windows rolled up tight.

There may be plenty of fuel in desert country. Sagebrush builds a hot fire, and there may be other kinds of dry growth about your site. Dried cattle refuse, akin to the buffalo chips of the pioneers, makes a low hot fire. When poking about low brush, though, keep your eyes alert. It's unlikely, but you might spot a lizard or snake. The best defense against snakes is to avoid known snake country and to use a tight tent with a sewn-in floor; or to sleep in a car or station wagon.

Of far greater potential peril to desert campers, though, is scarcity of water. Keep to well-known roads or trails, and never enter desert country without plenty of water, far more than it seems likely you'll ever need. Never wander off into the open desert without ample water and a compass, and then only if you've had considerable desert experience. The wind-rippled sands can be dangerous for the stranger to solitude.

Don't be misled by hot days. The chill of desert nights can cut through to your bones. Have warm duds along for donning after sundown. An eiderdown jacket or woolen sweater will be most welcome, and your sleeping bag should be heavy enough to keep you warm down around the forties or lower.

Shelter in the Desert

A trench three feet deep, running east and west to avoid as much sunlight as possible, can result in a difference of as much as one hundred degrees in temperature between its shadowy bottom and ground level. Scooping out such a shelter for daytime use, when no natural shade is to be found, may save your life. Of course, always leave some sort of signal, such as a brightly colored shirt, so that rescuers can spot you.

If a sandstorm should blow up, take shelter at the earliest possible moment. Mark your direction with an arrow of stones perhaps, lie down with your back to the gale, cover your nose and mouth with a cloth, and sleep out the storm. If possible, seek shelter in the lee of a hill. Don't worry about being buried by the sand.

In fact, it's recommended that you get some protection from the sun in exposed conditions by covering your body with sand. Burrowing in the sand also reduces water loss. Some desert survivors report that the pressure of sand affords valuable physical relief to tired muscles.

If you have a parachute or other suitable fabric, dig out a depression and cover it, always leaving some clear signal outside. In rocky regions or where desert shrub, thorn shrub, or tufted grass hummocks grow, drape a parachute, blanket, or sheet of plastic over the protuberances.

Also make use of natural desert features such as a tree, a rock cairn, or a tall clump of cacti for shelter or shade. The overhanging back of a dry stream may offer a retreat, although after even a distant cloudburst your home may be abruptly flooded. Banks of valleys, dry rivers, and ravines are especially good places to look for caves, and maybe you'll find a deserted native shelter.

If you are unaccustomed to desert travel, a rule of thumb is to multiply your estimates of distance by three, as both the clear, dry air and the absence of land features are apt to make underestimation likely. The main objective in the desert during the hot seasons will be to keep cool and thus conserve as much body moisture as possible, so traveling at night and bivouacking during the day may be the best answer.

Shelters in the Snow

Snow is a good insulator. Shelters during cold weather are, therefore, many times more easily achieved than during more temperate months. I have bivouacked during the snowy season along northern Canada's Peace River more easily than I've been able to do this at other times of the year.

Here, as on many wilderness rivers, there is a scattering of huge boulders interspersed with driftwood of all sizes. Whereas during the warmer months it is understandably drafty among these rocks, snow had closed the crannies. It proved necessary only to find several such boulders with a reasonably level place between, roof the wider end by piling several young spruce across it, and build a fire in the narrower portion. Driftwood kept this easily fueled all night. All in all, the experimental camp was an unusually agreeable one, even though I found out later that the temperature had dipped more than forty degrees below zero during the darkness.

You need neither boulders nor drifted snags to enjoy such a snug shelter in deep snow. Just open a rough hole from the top down, by tramping, by digging with snowshoes or gloved hands, or by a combination of both. The result may be in the form of a crude triangle. Floor the wider end with evergreen boughs. Roof it with more boughs or with whole small trees. Kindle a small fire in the apex, so that it will be reflected about you as you lie or sit in secure comfort.

If the snow is deep and firm enough, you can also find warmth and shelter by tunneling into it, being careful to do this at right angles to the wind to avoid drifting.

Dangers of Drifting

Always take care to keep from situating your snow camp where there are perils from overhangs, slides, or dangerously amassing drifts.

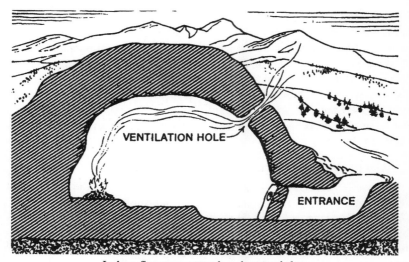

In deep, firm snow a tunnel can be your shelter.

Beware in open country of fashioning a snow shelter on a slope that is shielded from the wind. This is a precaution diametrically opposed to the way you'd proceed in a forest. It is important to heed, nevertheless, because in open terrain such sheltered sides collect drifts that could bury and suffocate you.

Sleeping on Snow

Although snow is an excellent insulator, you should never sleep or even sit directly on it, as snow is then too prone to melt. Wet clothing, so susceptible to freezing and so difficult to dry at subzero temperatures, is one of the major dangers in snow country under survival conditions. As slight a substance as a thin sheet of plastic or a strip of bark should be used between body and snow.

The Snow House

Building a snow house is another survival stratagem that harks back to the instinctive play of childhood. It is none the less effective for all that.

All you need to do when the weather is cold and you require shelter is to pile a mound of snow a bit larger than the bivouac you wish. Tamp down the surface. If water is available scatter it over the mound until you have an icy glaze. Otherwise, allow the pile to compact as hard as it will in the air for upwards of a half hour.

Then, cutting an entrance at right angles to the wind, tunnel into the mound. Continue to scoop out snow until you have a shell, making any repairs that may be necessary by smoothing and pressing fresh snow in place.

Finally, kindle a tiny fire inside the snow house. Any meltage, you'll find, will be quickly absorbed by the remaining snow. When the fire has burned down, carefully cut and then shove out a ventilation hole in the roof, close the entrance with browse or even a large snowball, and leave the shelter to ice.

You won't credit, until you try it yourself, how small a blaze within will, supported by the heat of your body, keep you snug. As a matter of fact, you'll likely discover that the tendency is to overheat. Of vital importance, because of the smoke and the carbon monoxide fumes that would otherwise accumulate in such an impervious shelter, is the establishment and maintenance of good ventilation.

CARBON MONOXIDE

There may be times—as when you're mountain climbing above timberline, sleeping and cooking in a closed tent where mosquitoes are thick enough to kill anyone unprotected from them, camping in such cold that it would take too long to accumulate the wood for a body-length fire and you're using instead perhaps a Sims folding stove, or when in deep wilderness you come across an abandoned prospector's or trapper's shack that is too handy to pass by—when you should take into account carbon monoxide, which is a peril in any closed space where there is combustion of any kind, even the motor vehicle which is carrying you to the jumping-off spot.

Carbon monoxide, the always existing and vital carbon dioxide with a single atom of oxygen missing, is the everyday byproduct of incomplete combustion. Carbon monoxide is so avid for that absent particle of oxygen that it will seize it at the earliest possible moment from whatever is at hand. If this is the blood, it can be lethal. Carbon monoxide is especially hazardous because it is both invisible and impossible to smell and, even more insidiously, because its effects build up in the body until just one more breath can overcome the victim. Like scurvy, it has killed more outdoorsmen than will ever be known.

In the woods, carbon monoxide commonly becomes fatal before one is aware of it. There is no difficulty in breathing. In an enclosed place, one may become alerted by the fact that a candle or lantern starts to lose its brightness, but what generally happens is that the victim is so suddenly stricken that before he comprehends that something is awry, he is almost, if not entirely, immobile. In a closed tent whose fabric is sealed by waterproofing or by frost, rain, or snow, a heater as tiny as a primus stove can, and on numerous unrealized occasions has, killed the occupants.

Symptoms of carbon monoxide poisoning, if one becomes alerted to them as one may be in a cumulative situation, start with tautness across the forehead, headache, and a redness in the complexion. The headache becomes increasingly annoying with continued exposure to the gas. Then comes debility, giddiness, failing sight, indigestion and possible vomiting, and finally helplessness and unconsciousness.

If one is alone, the only possible remedy is somehow to get fresh air, as by slitting a canvas, breaking a window, or crawling into the open. If the weather is cold, there will be the added danger of freezing unless one can somehow manage to drag a sleeping bag with him. Rest is the rule to decrease ordinary oxygen requirements in breathing and warmth to lessen the amount of oxygen needed by the tissues.

If there is help, begin mouth-to-mouth resuscitation at once. This is preferable to other personal methods of forced breathing because of the small amount of carbon dioxide in the breath. In fact, if several unaffected individuals will take deep breaths, exhale into a container, such as a plastic bag, and have the patient take similarly deep breaths of the stored air, the effects of the carbon monoxide impregnation may be cured in half an hour rather than the several hours otherwise necessary.

An unconscious camper who has been exposed to the gas as in fires and smoke, and whose skin, tongue and interior of the mouth, and tissue under the fingernails are bright red, may be assumed to be a victim of carbon monoxide poisoning. To prevent it, make certain of adequate circulation of fresh air at all times, no matter where you may be.

GOOD CAMP KEEPING

To begin with, a well-kept campsite looks good. It's free of scrap paper and cigarette butts. There's nothing to trip over or run into. All edged tools are safely sheathed or placed handily so that they won't cause any trouble. Firewood is neatly stacked so it's convenient to the fire. Incidentally, it's smart camping to keep some extra kindling covered with an old piece of oilcloth, tarp, or under a tent fly or overhanging ledge in case of rain.

If you get pitch on the tent or other gear, gasoline from the stove or lantern or nailpolish remover will take it off, but it will possibly remove the waterproofing, too. It's best to let the pitch dry, then to scrape it carefully off with a dull knife. The same applies to cooking grease, although many such stains can be removed with soapy water or by gentle rubbing with a hard-fiber soap pad.

After a downpour, the bottom of your tent will probably be spattered with mud. This may be flushed off with clear water before it dries. Or, if water is scarce, let the mud dry and whisk it off with a stiff brush. Some campers carry a small broom for such uses.

Any dirt in the tent should be swept out daily. If your trousers have cuffs, and in the woods it's better that they don't, you'll be bound to bring in a fine assortment of twigs, leaf bits, small pebbles, and other forest debris to be spilled out when you shuck off your clothes at night.

Mud should be kept out, especially if the tent has a sewn-in floor. One trick is to put an old blanket inside the tent where you walk most. This can be carefully borne out and shaken free of dirt each day, thus saving the floor from stains and wear. If the tent has a floor and can be easily dismantled and erected again, it's often not a bad idea to strike it every few days, turn it inside out, and shake and brush it clear.

If the weather is continually damp, keep an old pair of boots or moccasins just inside the door to change into before entering, or leave your rubbers outside when you come in. Few things can make a tent more uninviting than a wet, dirty floor in rainy weather.

The gear kept inside the tent should have specific places. Each member of a party should have a duffle bag or other container for his belongings. This is particularly important if there are small fry along. Don't just unzip the tent door and toss your gear inside, figuring to put it away later. You may want it quickly. Community items such as first aid kit, ax, and lanterns should be in a handy spot where they can be reached and replaced easily and quickly.

One of the most glaring evidences of poor camp keeping is dirty dishes. While you're eating, be heating the water for dishwashing. Attend to this chore the minute the meal is finished, before lassitude sets in. Do not make the mistake of sitting down first for a little relaxation. Better complete the job while you're about it. You will appreciate leisure so much more afterward.

Scrape the dishes as clean as possible before washing them. That dirty fry-pan set on the heat with water and a few grease-cutting wood ashes will get the job started. Wash the cleanest pieces and the silverware first, saving the pots and pans for the last. Many campers prefer to keep part of the dishwater good and hot and to use it strictly for rinsing. That way drying chores are cut to a minimum. Once the dishes are washed and dried, get them under the cover of at least a mosquito netting to keep off flies and other insects.

Assuming that you have a supply of pure drinking water, store it so that it will stay pure. Keep containers covered tightly, using either a fitted cover or netting attached with clips or weights. If there are pets in camp, keep your water containers where they can't reach them.

There's a fairly simple gimmick that'll take the place of clothespins in the woods and still keep your stuff from blowing all over the place, as it can if you merely lay it over a line. Use a double clothesline. That is, fasten both lines between two supports, first twisting the ropes together, several times to each foot. Then merely slip corners of each garment between twists in the line.

The sleeping bag or blankets should be aired frequently over a line, bush, or rock when the sun is out and preferably a brisk, dry wind is blowing. Either open the sleeping bag flat or turn it inside out.

A veteran camper leaves his campsite as it was when he came upon it. Fill any dug holes. Be sure all clotheslines and other ropes are removed, and make certain that all scrap paper and rubbish is burned or packed out. Finally, be sure the fire is dead out, so that the ashes can be stirred deep down with your bare hand.

Stack leftover firewood so it can dry out after rain and be easy to find. Otherwise, scatter it so that it will decay naturally.

CHAPTER SIX

WATER: THE ESSENCE OF LIFE

Water is a necessity no matter where you are. With other
conditions being favorable, you can live for a month or
more without food, but you'd be lucky to stay alive much
more than a week without water.
—Bradford Angier
The Master Backwoodsman

The average adult, whose body is some 80 percent water, needs about three quarts of water daily depending on such factors as activity, heat, and wind. Half of this is lost through body wastes, another third through the lungs in humidifying the air we breathe, and the final sixth in perspiration evaporated to keep the body at an even temperature.

In a pinch, you can get along with two cups a day, but what you lack now you'll have to make up for later. Dehydration of from 6 to 10 percent of the body weight will result progressively in dizziness, headache, difficulty in breathing, and a tingling in the extremities. The body takes on a bluish hue, speech is difficult, and finally the individual finds himself unable to walk. Unless water becomes available, death follows. On the other hand, the man who has collapsed from dehydration can be restored in a very brief time by the gradual intake of water.

Fortunately, water is obtainable nearly everywhere, even on the desert.

IS IT PURE?

Although you'll generally be able to get along awhile longer without a drink, just one drop of impure water may so weaken you that at the very least you'll be unable to travel. It follows that you should take every reasonable care to make sure that the water you are drinking is not contaminated.

How can you tell, then, if water is pure? Short of laboratory tests, you can't. Even when a mountain rill bubbles through sheer alpine fastnesses, the putrefying carcass of a winter-killed animal may be lying a few yards upstream.

The folklore that any water a dog will drink is pure enough for his master is unfortunately as baseless as it is charming, as even the fondest master must testify upon recalling a few of the potions his pet has assimilated with impunity. The more reasonable assumption that anything your horse will drink is safe for humans is likewise at fault. Pollution may be entirely odorless, whereas a horse's basis for rejection or acceptance is familiarity of smell.

The fact that natives may assert a water source is pure may mean, instead, that either they have built up a certain degree of immunity or that, because of familiarity, they cannot believe that water is tainted. A domestic water supply used by the inhabitants and guests of a Montana ranch for some twenty years was found to have been infecting not only present but previous owners with tularemia. The germs of this, incidentally, can be carried to water by pets such as dogs, and by domestic animals such as pigs, even though they themselves may seem perfectly healthy.

Even the loneliest wild stream can be infected with this so-called rabbit fever by such wild animals as muskrat and beaver. Yet taking a chance with drinking water in a well-settled community is, in one sense, a lot less dangerous than laying yourself open to a small fraction of similar risk in wilderness where medical help may be hours and perhaps days away. The safest principle in any event is to assume all water is impure until it has been proved otherwise, positively and recently.

Knowing how wild animals can infect wilderness water with tularemia, far beyond the pollution of man, I've long been cautious about what I drink in the

Boiling drinking water is an important wilderness precaution.

farther places. The importance of all this care was emphasized about a dozen years ago when I was boiling the noonday kettle in a remote little canyon on the headwaters of the Peace River, where I was probably the first human within the past fifty years to set foot.

I simmered the water my usual (at that elevation) seven minutes for tea, toasted my sandwiches, and was soon continuing my explorations. A quarter mile inland, the canyon so narrowed that to proceed I had to wade the brook. Another few steps and I came upon the half-submerged, decomposing carcass of a moose which had evidently fallen in from above. Needless to say, my water-boiling precaution no longer seemed a waste of time.

BEST WAYS TO PURIFY WATER

The safest way to purify water before using it for drinking, cooking, dish washing, and for such intimate tasks as brushing the teeth is first to boil it for five minutes at sea level and one more minute for each additional thousand feet of elevation.

If you are going to use the water hot, you're well away. If you plan to carry it in a canteen for drinking later, it'll taste flat because of the driving off of the air content. This can be restored by pouring the liquid back and forth a number of times between two containers. Or, as I usually do, you may be philosophical about the whole thing. When you're thirsty, you'll scarcely notice the lack of taste.

Formerly, one could do a pretty safe job in the North with Halazone tablets, and we still can if we want to spend, at this writing, something like three dollars for what used to be a forty-cent bottle of the tiny chlorine-releasing pellets. Iodine water purification tablets, necessary in warm and tropical climates for similar use, cost even more.

It's too bad, for both are easy to use. A pair of Halazone tablets can ordinarily be depended upon in temperate climates to make a quart of water pure enough for human consumption in half an hour. If the water seems particularly dangerous or if it's muddy, use four Halazone tablets and leave them in for an hour.

All parts of the container with which the water will later come in contact must, of course also be sterilized. Say you're using a one-quart canteen. Fill it, drop in the Halazone, cap loosely, and wait for five minutes. Then shake the contents so vigorously that some of the water will splash over the top, lid, and lips of the canteen. Tighten the cap and let stand for the desirable time.

The U.S. Government found out a few years ago that compounds that release chlorine gas cannot be relied upon for water purification in hot country. Necessary in such regions is something such as the iodine water purification tablets manufactured as Globaline by WTS Pharmaceuticals, Division of Wallace and Tiernan, Inc., Rochester, New York 14625. Any drugstore can secure these for you, although most pharmacists will probably have to do some looking.

Like Halazone, these tablets must be kept dry. The container, therefore, should be tightly capped as soon as possible after opening. Directions for use are:

1. Add one tablet to a quart of clear water in container with cap, two tablets if not clear;
2. Replace cap loosely and wait five minutes;
3. Shake well, allowing a little water to leak out to disinfect the screw threads before tightening container cap;
4. Wait ten minutes before using for any purpose and, if the water is very cold, wait ten more minutes.

By the way, don't heed the hopefuls anywhere who assert that a high-proof alcoholic beverage will automatically make the accompanying water and ice harmless.

Aside from the present prices, additional disadvantages of Halazone are slow solubility and a short life of five months when stored in temperatures as warm as 89.6°F. At the higher temperatures to be anticipated when left in your automobile's glove compartment on a summer day, up to 122°F, the effectiveness is cut fifty percent. Furthermore, Halazone loses three-fourths of its activity when exposed to air for two days, which gives you some idea of what happens during the frequent opening and closing of the container to get tablets.

Globaline, which is more stable, still loses one-fifth of its power when kept in sealed bottles for half a year at 167°F. Its initial potency lessens one-third when exposed to the air for four days.

The best, and at the same time least costly, method of chemically disinfecting camp water is with iodine. Eight drops of reasonably fresh two percent tincture of iodine, used as the tablets above, will replace Globaline adequately and won't break your budget. Only individuals with a definite sensitivity to iodine will risk any ill effects. If you have ever been treated for hyperthyroidism, get your physician's approval before using any such water disinfectant.

In extreme cases in remote regions anywhere, boiling, not chlorination, is the answer. The problem of the traveler is different from that of the municipality where, with constant testing, so-called breakpoint chlorination can be practiced where the addition of sufficient chlorine to the supply binds with its organic materials while leaving a sufficient residue of free chlorine. Even in such a renowned world capital as Paris, where breakthrough chlorination was not practiced, enteroviruses were found in the chlorinated public water. Infectious hepatitis, for example, is then a threat.

The use of crystals of elemental iodine, obtainable from your pharmacist, is the most palatable and effective way to disinfect, important because most

streams in even the remotest parts of this country are now known to be polluted. The sole equipment needed for iodination with crystalline iodine is a
one-ounce clear glass bottle with a leak-proof bakelite cap, containing a small
quantity of USP grade resublimed iodine, I_2.

The bottle is filled with water, capped, shaken hard for about a minute, then
held upright to allow the heavy iodine crystals to drop to the bottom. These
crystals are not to be used directly. Disinfection is effected at 77° by the addition of 2.5 teaspoonfuls of the near-saturated iodine solution to one quart of
water for fifteen minutes. The action can be safely repeated almost a thousand
times without exhausting the iodine crystals, and the shelf life of crystalline
iodine is limitless. Under usual conditions, a teaspoonful of the iodine solution to a quart of water, allowed to stand for forty minutes, will provide satisfactory taste and effective disinfection. If the water is murky, particularly
cold, or suspected of being heavily contaminated, the concentration of the iodine solution may be increased to four teaspoonfuls with a contact time of
twenty minutes.

A clear glass bottle is suggested for the procedure to allow observation of
the iodine crystals. Any plastic bottles I have used have eventually taken on a
brown stain. Plastic bottles are prone to leak as one climbs to high altitudes,
then to distort and crack as one descends toward sea level.

Iodine Water Purification Tablets

Chlorine-releasing compounds cannot be depended upon in semi-tropical
and tropical regions. And, incidentally, it's erroneous to assume that the presence of a strong alcoholic beverage will render the water and any ice harmless. Water in these areas should either be boiled or treated with something
such as iodine water purification tablets.

Containing the active ingredient tetraglycine hydroperiodide, these small
tablets have proved effective against all common water-borne bacteria, as
well as the cysts of *Entamoeba histolytica,* which cause dysentery, and the
larvae of the parasitic fluke, *Schistosoma.* Added to water, each tablet frees
eight milligrams of iodine which act as the purification factor. One tablet will
purify one quart of clear water.

These tablets must be kept dry. The bottle should be immediately and
tightly recapped after being opened.

Using Iodine Directly

You can use tincture of iodine from your first aid kit instead of the iodine
water purification tablets. Eight drops of reasonably fresh, 2½ percent tincture
of iodine, used as the above tablets, will purify a quart of water in ten minutes. It is a good idea to let it stand twenty minutes if the water, as it may be in
the mountains, is extremely cold.

Only individuals with a definite sensitivity to iodine will risk any ill effects. If you have ever been treated for hyperthyroidism, or if you are pregnant, get your physician's approval before using any such water disinfectant.

Poisonous Water Holes

There are no known sources of deadly poisonous water in the wilds of Canada. In the southwestern deserts of this continent, on the other hand, a very few water holes contain dissolved poisons such as arsenic. You'll generally be able to recognize such water easily, both from the presence of bones of unwary animals and from the lack of green vegetation. A good general rule, therefore, is to avoid any water holes around which green plants are not flourishing.

SOFTENING HARD WATER

The water in some regions on this continent is what you might consider to be so *hard* that, until you get used to it, indigestion may result unless you drink only small amounts at one time. Here is another instance in which boiling can be of assistance, as some of the hardening compounds are then solidified and thus avoided, the reason for heavily encrusted teakettles in such areas. Or use rainwater or melted snow when possible.

CLEARING MUDDY WATER

In numerous wilderness areas, principally where cutbanks are being eroded, the water is so muddy as to be unpleasant. There the solution by river-

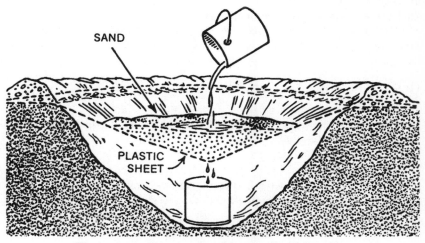

Filtering water will remove vegetable matter, but not impurities.

men, where bulk and weight are not problems, is to carry a barrel of clear water. There are also several other ways around the problem.

If the muddy water is left standing in a container, gravity may clear it. Another method is to pour the water into a container through sand held in a cloth. In the South, a handy portable filter is easily contrived by first stuffing one end of a three-foot section of bamboo with fresh grass, then filling the remainder of the hollow with sand. The easiest solution, and one that works more often than not, is to scoop a hole several feet back from the body of water and dip from it the water that seeps in. A sandy beach, where available, is best for this process. It must be realized, of course, that such filters will not do away with any dissolved minerals or impurities. As for the latter, the water should still be purified. Incidentally, water that a resident finds harmless may not be such for the unaccustomed newcomer.

WATERBAGS

In a hot climate, water can be cooled to a more pleasant temperature by using one of the waterbags that is porous enough for a little fluid to seep out and wet the outside, where it evaporates and so lowers the inner temperature. The water can be purified at the same time by adding the necessary iodination.

BOILING SNOW WATER

While boiling the kettle at noon in snow country, special caution must be exercised not to burn the utensil. Snow acts like a blotter. It is not enough to scoop a can full of snow and hang it over the campfire. Small amounts should be melted at first, while stirring with a clean stick, until a safe several inches of fluid protects the bottom of the container. Then begin filling the can with the snow necessary to fill your container.

You will quickly learn to break off any bits of available crust or to use the more concentrated granular snow from former storms. Best is ice or the grain-like snow found in permanent drifts in high country.

HOW TO SWEETEN WATER

Even when it has been purified, slough, muskeg, and swamp water may have an unpleasant odor and taste. It will be convenient to sweeten and purify the liquid in one operation.

Just drop several fragments of charred hardwood from the campfire into the boiling pot. Keep the water bubbling for at least fifteen minutes. Skim away the majority of the foreign matter. You can then either strain the water through a clean cloth or, if you're not short on either time or utensils, just allow it to settle.

WHERE WATER IS FOUND

Water flows downhill, of course, eroding canyons and other declivities as it goes and encouraging a ribbon of bright vegetation, especially such telltale growth as willow and alder. You'll find water atop mountains, too, and glaciers and permanent snowbanks may also be there to refresh you.

Water also lies near the base of elevations, where it can often be distinguished by the presence of prolific vegetation. In some country, in fact, the major problem is not so much in locating water but in discovering an easy way to it.

When country is flat and open, long winding tangles of green brush tell their important stories.

In rocky areas, search for springs and seepages. Limestones and lavas have more and larger springs than any other rocks. Springs of icy water are safest, by the way. Warm water, except where there may be hot springs, has been recently at the surface and is prone to be polluted.

Limestones are soluble, and ground water erodes channels and caverns in them. Look in these caverns, both large and small, for springs, but be careful. If you venture into a large series of caves beyond the sight of the entrance, make absolutely certain that you do not become lost.

Most lava rocks are filled with billions of bubble holes through which ground water may seep. Also look for springs along the walls of valleys that cross the rough hard flow. Some lava has no characteristic bubble holes, but, on the other hand, is marked with so-called organ-pipe joints—vertical cracks that dissect the rocks into spectacular columns a foot or more thick and often two dozen feet or more high. At the feet of such joints, you may find water bubbling out as seepage or gushing forth in springs.

Search for seepage where a dry canyon barrels through a layer of porous sandstone. As for other common rocks, like granite, water is contained only in irregular cracks. Scan hillsides for swaths where the grass is lush and green. Then scoop out a ditch at the base of the verdancy and wait for water to seep in.

Water is more abundant and easier to find in loose sediments than in rocks themselves. Look for springs along valley floors and down across their sloping sides. Even in the Southwest when streams are dry, the flat benches or terraces about the meandering river valleys ordinarily yield springs and seepages about their bases. In low forests, along the seashore, and in river plains the water table is close to the surface. Very little digging generally yields an ample supply.

Percentages are so much against success, that you shouldn't waste time and energy digging in a locality where there are no favorable signs. On the other hand, you're apt to find water by digging in the floor of a valley under an abrupt slope, particularly if the bluff is cut into a terrace. Or dig out a lush green patch where there's been a spring or pocket of water during the wet season.

Water seeps slowly through clay, but a large number of clays contain sandy strips which may yield springs. Look for a wet spot on the surface of a clay bluff and try scooping it out. Try wet places at the bluff's foot.

In mud flats, during the dry season, you may be able to locate wet mud at a low point. Wring this out in a piece of cloth to get water, but do not drink it if it's salty or if it is soapy tasting.

Dew

Dew can be collected on clear nights by using your handkerchief as a sponge. During a heavy dew you may be able to collect as much as a quart an hour.

You may also scoop out a hole, line the bottom with a piece of canvas or plastic, and fill this improvised basin with cool clean pebbles taken from a foot or more beneath the surface. Dew may collect on the rocks and trickle down onto the waterproof fabric. Collect the water in the early morning.

Dew also sometimes collects on exposed metal surfaces such as aircraft parts and the cover of tin cans, as well as on stones and small desert plants such as lupine. Drain this into a cup, gently shake it onto a sheet of plastic, or mop it up with a cloth.

Water in the Desert

Water seeks the lowest levels it can reach, and in the deserts that comprise one-fifth of the world's surface these may be underground. If you're walking out instead of camping and signalling, if there seems to be no especial direction to head, and if you can see hills, start toward them, inasmuch as the likeliest spot to obtain water will be at their bottoms.

Perhaps you'll wander across the cramped, narrow bed of a stream. Even though this may be dry, water may very well be running beneath the surface. Hunt for the lowest point on the outside of a bend in the channel and dig. The same general principle may be followed if you encounter a dry lake bottom. If the presence of water is not directly indicated by damp sand, pick the lowest point and dig.

Collect dew in a sheet of waterproof fabric suspended over a hole and filled with pebbles.

If you come across a palm, you can rely on water's being within several feet of the base of the tree. Reed grass is another good sign that moisture is near. Cattails, greasewoods, willows, elderberry bushes, rushes, and salt grass grow only where ground water is near the surface. Purify all water from any frequented pools you may discover. Incidentally, small water holes in dried-out stream channels and low places, known to the natives, are often covered. Search carefully for them.

The presence of other vegetation does not always mean that surface water is available. But the sound of birds in a semiarid brush country often means that water is near at hand. In very dry deserts, birds will circle over a water hole. Places where animals have scratched or where flies are hovering indicate recent surface water and are good indications for digging.

In the desert your life will depend on your water supply. In hot sandy wastes, for example, you'll need a minimum of a gallon of water a day. If you rest during the day in some shaded spot, even if it's only the previously suggested east-west trench, and travel only during the cool desert night, you can put some twenty miles behind you to the daily gallon. If you do your walking in the daytime sun and heat, you'll be lucky to get half that distance on the same amount of water, and you'll be in far worse shape when you stop. But whether you sit out your desert ordeal or walk back to civilization, you'll need water.

CONSERVING WATER

There are a number of ways to conserve the water you already have. Importantly, though, a major survival factor is to drink your available water until your thirst is sated, rather than to retain it in an attempt to conserve the supply. Pinpoint your energies, instead, on retaining as much as you can of the water already in your system.

By eating less, you'll cut down on the amount of water demanded by the kidneys to rid the body of waste. The general rule for survival when water is not available, or in very short supply, is to eat nothing. The amount of food that can be eaten increases in direct proportion to the amount of drinking water available.

In any event, don't eat dehydrated foods and other dry victuals. Carbohydrates are best, one gram when assimilated by the body yielding four calories of heat energy plus water.

By doing less, you'll both reduce perspiration and also cut down on the loss of water through the otherwise exerted lungs. Too, keep heat out of your body by keeping your clothes on. You may feel more comfortable in the desert without a shirt and trousers. This is because your sweat will evaporate faster. But it takes more sweat.

Slow and steady does it in a hot desert. If you must move about in the heat, you'll last longer on less water if you take it easy. Stay in the shade as much as possible during the day. Sit or lie a few inches above the actual ground if this is at all possible. The reason is that it can be thirty or forty degrees cooler a foot above the ground. That difference in temperature can save a lot of sweat.

SOLAR WATER STILL

The same piece of plastic which may be folded and borne in a breast pocket for shelter and other everyday uses can help save you from dying of thirst in the desert or at sea.

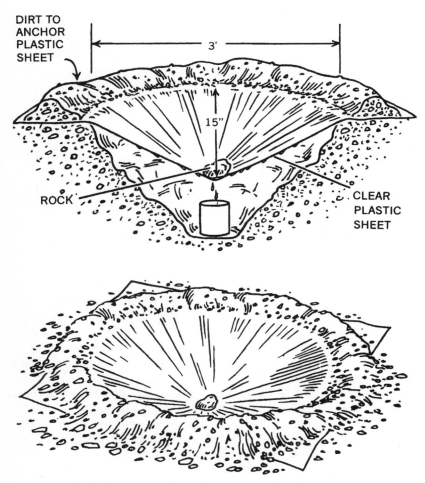

In the desert a solar still provides up to three pints of water a day.

In the deserts of the world, with a plastic sheet six feet square, up to three pints of water a day can be extracted from a bowl-shaped cavity some twenty-inches deep and forty inches across. Place a cup, can, upturned hat, or other receptacle in the center of the hole. Anchor the plastic all the way around the top of the opening with dirt or stones. Set a fist-sized rock in the center of the sheet so that the plastic will sag in a point directly over the container.

Heat from the sun shines through the plastic and is absorbed by the sand, causing the evaporation of the moisture already in the earth. The vapor is almost immediately condensed on the cooler underneath side of the plastic, the drops flowing down the underside of the steeply angled sheet and dripping into the ready container. Capillary action causes more water to be attracted to the surface of the sand to replace that which has gone, and the process will go on.

Two such stills will, when operating well, keep a man going in the desert, for even when the production lessens after a day or two, it is a simple matter to move the still. Production will even continue at night at about half the rate of the daytime flow.

Varying with the condition of the soil, the amount of water you can expect to extract in a twenty-four-hour day will be from somewhat less than a pint to three pints. But you can help the process along, particularly if you have selected a hollow or dry wash for your location.

You'll get even more fluid by cutting cacti and other water-holding desert plants into pieces and dropping them under the plastic. The rate of output can thus be increased up to nearly three times that of the sand alone. Even contaminated water such as urine, seawater, and radiator fluid not diluted with such a highly volatile substance as antifreeze can be purified if poured into the hole and allowed to vaporize and drip in the heat.

Seawater in the bottom of a boat can be vaporized and condensed in pure drinkable form by this same method. Incidentally, no matter where you conduct this operation, remove the plastic as seldom as possible, as it takes half an hour or more for the air to become resaturated and the production of water to start once more.

WATER FROM VEGETATION

The possibilities of obtaining water from vegetation are many, including the discovery of trapped rain. In the American tropics, for example, the branches of large trees often support air plants, relatives of the toothsome pineapple, whose thickly growing and frequently overlapping leaves catch and retain rain. It is a good idea to strain this through a clean piece of cloth to eliminate blown or fallen debris and insects. Be wary when climbing, too, to avoid such critters as ants and snakes.

In the temperate and northern regions of this continent, the sap from such trees as the maple and birch is both refreshing and nourishing. The Indians

Sap drawn from maple and birch trees helps satisfy thirst in an emergency.

used to gash V-shaped cuts in the lower trunks of these and similar trees, such as the hickory, and insert in their points spouts which they fashioned by pushing the poisonous pith out of elderberry limbs.

Vines are good sources of water in the tropics, although unless you know what you're doing, you should never drink from a vine whose sap is milky. Otherwise, choose a large vine and lop off an easily handled length, perhaps as long as you are tall. Make the first cut at the top, as you'll already have done. Sharpen the lower end and hold your mouth or a container under it. The water will be pure and fresh.

An even easier method is to cut a deep notch in a vine as high as you can reach, sever the vine close to the ground, and let the water drip into your

First Step in Obtaining Water from a Barrel Cactus

Crushed pulp from the barrel cactus yields thirst-quenching juice.

mouth or a container. When the water stops flowing, cut another section off the top, repeating this until the supply of fluid is exhausted.

Bamboo shoots also often have water in their hollow joints. Try shaking the stems of old, yellowish bamboo. If you detect a gurgling, cut a notch at the base of each joint and catch the water.

Only in a very genuine emergency, look to the disappearing barrel cactus of the Southwest for water. To secure this, lop off the top of the cactus and macerate the pulp in the standing portion as thoroughly as possible. Again, don't do this for an experiment or for the fun of it, for the day may come when it may save someone's life. A barrel cactus some four feet tall will give five pints of refreshing, milky juice. It is preferable to scoop and press this out. You might also suck the juice from a hole cut in the plant as low as you can reach with your mouth or a container. When traveling, you can also cut the pulp into chunks and take them along to suck on when it may again prove necessary.

No cactus is poisonous, so other cacti may also give emergency drinking water if you squeeze and mash parts of them. But, again, don't try this except in a dire emergency.

The Coconut Palm

The coconut palm, so abundant in tropical America, furnishes both water and food. In an emergency, you may even use for sustenance the large terminal bud of the palm, usually referred to as the cabbage because of size, appearance, and shape. This delicacy, which is delicious raw or cooked, has been called Millionaire's Salad because its removal kills that particular tree.

Fallen coconuts germinate where they lie. In these, both milk and meat are consumed in the process, but the cavity is filled with a spongy mass which is

RIPE COCONUT

HUSK

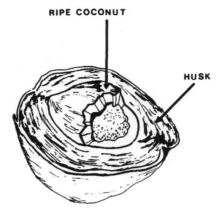

Cross-Section of Coconut

called the bread. This is very sustaining either raw or roasted over the camp-fire, with the shell itself the handiest of containers. Even the little sprouts can be enjoyed like celery.

The young coconuts grow in clusters near the top of the palm, but the slim and slippery trunk may be very difficult to climb. The answer to this problem can be a so-called climbing bandage—a dependable belt or rope that is a bit longer than the circumference of the tree. Fix this around the trunk, leaving enough room so that you can step on it with both feet. The loop on the other side of the trunk will support your weight as you reach up and grasp the trunk with both arms. Pull yourself along, doubling your knees and sliding the bandage up to a higher position with your feet. Then straighten, resting your weight on the loop while achieving a higher position. By repeating this process, you can climb to any height.

When you get them down, you'll find the nut is encased in a husk composed of a smooth exterior except for a matting of tough fibers. When you have an ax, machete, hatchet, or heavy knife, you need not remove the husk of the green coconut to drink the liquid. Whittle the husk at the top, not the stem end, to a rough point. Then cut off the point and the top of the nut inside.

If you haven't a tool, drive into the ground a stake three or four feet long so that it slants slightly away from you. Give the top of this stake a crude, wedge-shaped edge so that it can pierce the longitudinal fibers of the husk. Stand about a foot from the stake, trying to judge a point of entry that will clear the nut within the husk. Then press the whole firmly downward against the sharpened stake with both hands, giving the coconut a twisting motion to pry off a small part of the husk. By repeating this procedure, you can remove the entire husk from either a green or a mature nut.

How to Husk a Coconut

Once the coconut is free of the husk, the problem becomes one of breaking through the hard shell. To open a nut, hold it in one hand so that the stem-end eyes are uppermost. Using the master hand, strike it sharply just below each eye with a stone or with the point of a mature nut. The shell will crack, whereupon it will be possible to pick off the top of the nut without spilling the milk. Green coconuts give more milk than ripe ones. With a mature nut, just poke out the eyes and drink the liquid.

Incidentally, be careful not to drink more than three or four cups of ripe coconut juice a day, as it is a drastic laxative. You get over a quart of cool fluid from one young nut, especially at the jelly stage when the meat is soft. A ripe nut will gurgle when you shake it, but do not drink from very young or very old nuts.

The Banana Trunk

The banana or plantain trunk of tropical and subtropical America can be made into an excellent source of water with a few cuts from a knife, machete, hatchet, or ax. Cut down the tree, leaving approximately three inches of the trunk protruding from the ground. Hollow out a bowl-like basin in this section of trunk.

Water will immediately flow into this reservoir from the roots. This fluid will taste bitter, but if the bowl is allowed to fill and is then scooped empty three times, the fourth inundation will be palatable and a continuing source. The same trunk can be used for up to four days, after which you can make another such reservoir. It's a good idea to keep the basin covered with something like a banana leaf to keep out insects and debris.

BEFORE WATER IS SCARCE

If you have plenty of water at the moment but may have little or none later, drink as much as you possibly can, short of making yourself sick, before leaving the source of supply. You should sate your thirst, for instance, if you have the chance to do so before abandoning a ship or plane. In dry country, start drinking as soon as you reach a safe water hole and keep it up until you leave.

All efforts should be concentrated on taking what water you can, even at the cost of leaving other things behind, before quitting what may be an isolated supply. Don't ration the supply later on. In opposition to the now-outmoded ration practices of past centuries, you should drink until you have reasonably satisfied your thirst. Carrying a round, clean pebble or button in your mouth will help decrease the later sensation of thirst.

PART THREE
STAYING FOUND: KNOWING WHERE YOU ARE
AND HOW TO GET BACK TO CIVILIZATION

CHAPTER SEVEN

ALWAYS KNOWING WHERE YOU ARE

---

*Just as cold is the lack of heat and darkness no more
than the absence of light, so is getting lost an entirely negative state of affairs.
We become lost not because of anything we do, but because of what we leave undone.*
—Bradford Angier
Living Off the Country

One lost man I found in the New England woods, when I was still pretty much of a tenderfoot myself, had started running when he first realized he didn't know his whereabouts and hadn't stopped until he fell, exhausted, breaking a leg. Another for whom I joined the search in arid mountains just west of the soaring Grand Tetons years later had donned light moccasins to go down to the creek for water, missed camp on his way back with brimming pail, and had walked what turned out to be forty-two miles in a nearly straight line before being located, dehydrated and dead, coiled in a small cave, his feet actually worn through to the bones.

I've talked to other individuals who were found safe after being mislaid for one or two days, and they said it is the emptiest, bleakest, loneliest feeling in the world. Here's how to make sure its terrors never overtake you.

FREEDOM IN THE WILDS

You'll never feel utterly free in the wilderness until you're able to tell, anywhere at any time, almost exactly where you are. Far from being complicated, the procedure necessary for this is positive and permanent, an ever-intriguing problem of angles and distances. Even a youngster can learn it—often better

113

than the typical native who is proceeding by knowledge of his territory and not by any instinct, which science has proved does not exist in man—from the simple details considered in this chapter.

The principal part of the procedure started about five thousand years ago when some Mongol, probably, found that if a longish chunk of a certain rock—magnetic, although he didn't know what this meant—was laid on a piece of wood large enough to keep it floating on still water, it would finally come to rest with one end pointing almost exactly along the shadow cast by the sun at midday. Or perhaps he even hung this length of magnetic rock on a thong, as Kubla Khan did years later.

THE NORTH STAR AND THE SOUTHERN CROSS

From this discovery, in any event, evolved the compass, now usually a light, slim length of magnetized steel so balanced that it will pivot freely. Previously, man had traveled by the sun or, more accurately, by the night stars. Primitive man finally understood that this early compass, for that is what he now had, pointed nearly precisely toward a certain star that we now know as Polaris or the North Star.

He learned that in the Northern Hemisphere this star, not as bright as many but having the peculiar characteristic of staying almost stationary in the

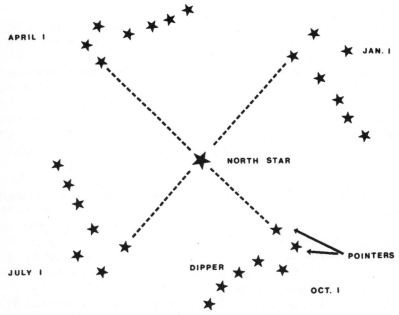

North Star and Big Dipper, Showing Pointers

heavens, could be recognized on clear nights by what we now call the Big Dipper (also known as the Big Bear). An imaginary line joining from bottom to top the two stars forming the outer side of the bowl, if extended some five times its length, will end near the North Star. This guiding star, so important to early mariners, is about the same brightness as the two pointers, and there are no bright stars in between. The pointers are about five degrees apart. And so it came about that the north end of these first crude compasses was important. If enterprising civilization had started and continued more assertively in the southern half of the world, it would have been the wavering sunward end of the early magnetic ones that would have become the more important, and the arrows and importantly marked ends of today's compasses would point south instead of north.

When one travels south, the same sort of celestial navigation comes into being. There, as primitive man finally observed, what we now know as the Southern Cross is the most distinctive constellation in the Southern Hemisphere, coming into view shortly before the Big Dipper drops below the horizon behind us as we journey southward. An imaginary line carried through the longer axis of the Southern Cross points toward the South Pole. A pair of the four stars of the Southern Cross, also called the Crux, are among the most vivid in the night skies. These two are on the southern and eastern arms. The former, at the foot of the Cross, is known as Alpis Crusis and, when viewed through a telescope, turns out to be a magnificent double star. Those on the northern and western arms, while bright, are smaller.

Although the Southern Cross is the most celebrated of the constellations of the far south, it looks more like a kite than a cross and, so, is a disappointment to many world travelers when they view it for the first time. However, the fact that it lies nearer the South Pole than any other well-defined constellation gives it an importance, despite its smallness, comparable to that of the Big Dipper in the Northern Hemisphere. There is no star above the South Pole to correspond with our North Star. As a matter of fact, where such a star would gleam there exists a region which to the naked eye seems void of stars. This pear-shaped hole in the midst of an otherwise brilliant section of the Milky Way, like an island in its stream, is so dark that early sailors called it the Coal Sack, a name so apt that it has remained.

Also known as the True Cross, the Southern Cross should not be confused with the False Cross which has five stars, including the one in its center. The drawing shows the Southern Cross and, to its west, the False Cross. You may care to hold the book over your head for realism. Then note the two very bright stars just to the east of the Southern Cross. With them and the latter constellation as guides, you will be able to locate the point within the Coal Sack which is precisely over the South Pole.

First, extend an imaginary line along the long axis of the Southern Cross to the south. Then join the two bright stars to the east of the Southern Cross with

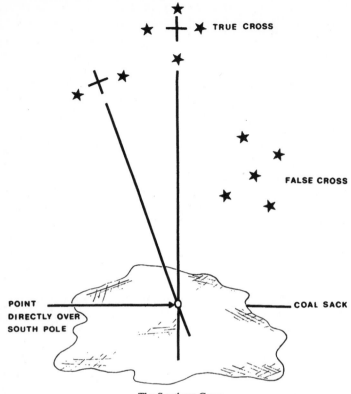

The Southern Cross

another imaginary line. Bisect this latter line with one at right angles. The intersection of this latter line with the line through the Southern Cross is above the approximate position of the South Pole.

OTHER STARS IN THE NORTH

You can check the North Star by the fact that Polaris is the bright star at the free end of the handle of the far dimmer Little Dipper, which the Ancients called Ursa Minor, or Little Bear. This arrangement of stars, not as easily found as the Big Dipper and easily missed when the stars are obscured by even scant cloud cover or the brilliance of moonlight or the northern lights, pours its imaginary contents into the Big Dipper and vice versa.

Too, the constellation known as Cassiopeia—the large W or M in the northern heavens, its shape depending on the time when it is seen—is always the same angle away from Polaris, as shown by the drawings. In the event that the

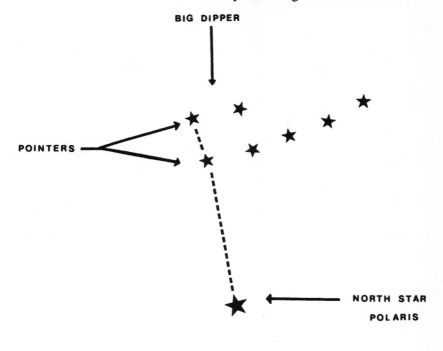

Relation of Big Dipper and Cassiopeia to North Star

Big Dipper is obscured and you want to know exactly where you are, it may be a sound procedure to memorize this relationship.

TELLING DIRECTION BY ANY STAR

Stars, because of the earth's rotation, seem to swing across the heavens in great east-to-west arcs, like the moon and sun. The way in which any star at all is moving at the moment can, therefore, give you a fairly accurate

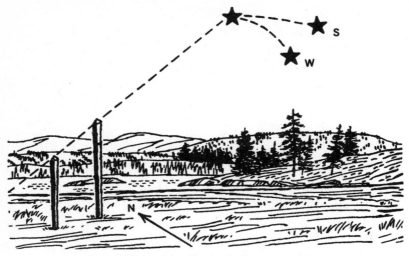

Determining direction by the stars.

indication of direction. This can be important if the sky is nearly clouded over, and only a few stars are visible.

Begin by taking a sight on any star. The brighter ones will be easier to follow. The orb's movement will be too slow, of course, for anyone to detect just by glancing at the sky. You'll need two fixed points over which to look. These may be two pegs, driven into the ground for the purpose, their tips lined up accurately. If you watch a star over these markers for several minutes, it will seem to be falling, rising, or swinging left to right.

If your star appears to be falling, it is situated just about west of you. If the star gives the appearance of looping flatly toward your right, you are facing approximately south.

If it appears to be rising, you're heading just about east. If it gives the importance of swinging flatly toward your right, then you are facing north.

Make your check with several stars if you want to be sure. Then mark north with a slanting stick or scratched line so that you can head in the right direction in the morning.

THE OUTDOORSMAN'S COMPASS

Every circle can be divided into 360 degrees. It is this way, too, with the compass. Compass degrees can be most easily pictured in your mind as 360 possible paths extending like the spokes of a wheel from where you chance to be. Compass degrees are ordinarily numbered clockwise, beginning at north.

East is one-quarter of the way around the dial. In degrees, in other words, east is regarded as 90 degrees. The distance between each of the four cardinal

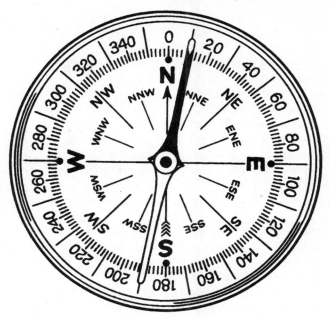

Your compass is one of your most valuable survival tools.

points—north, east, south, and west—is likewise 90 degrees apart. Therefore, south is often thought of as 180 degrees and west as 270 degrees.

Halfway between north and east is northeast. In degrees, therefore, northeast is half the distance between 0 degrees and 90 degrees or 45 degrees.

There will be times when you'll want to designate directions even more closely. You can do this by splitting the already determined eight points, giving you sixteen in all. Named with equal logic, halfway between north and northeast is north-northeast. The nearest of the four cardinal points always comes first in the nomenclature. Halfway between west and southwest, for example, is west-southwest.

Some compass dials are broken down into thirty-two points. Halfway between north-northeast and northeast, for example, becomes northeast by north, and so on.

A compass needn't be expensive, but it should be rugged enough to withstand ordinary hard usage if necessary. By all odds, it should have a luminous dial. If not, the night may sometime come when you have to waste unnecessary time and matches to keep located. I like a small compass that pins on so that the face is horizontal, always ready for a quick check. Too, this sort of compass has the advantage of being attached to the clothing and thus being less easily lost or mislaid.

Despite the preponderance of natural direction signs, it is always assuring in sheer wilderness to have a second compass with you, perhaps as mine is, in the hilt of your knife. A spare compass may prove almost as vital under survival conditions as an extra waterproof case filled with matches. Both are worth far more than their cost in reassurance alone.

The time may come, too, when you seriously question the accuracy of one of your compasses. Then place or hold both compasses level. Keep them well apart and as far as reasonably possible from any metallic objects. See to it that the needle or dial of each is wavering freely on its point.

If there should be any marked difference between the two, travel by the instrument whose indicator quivers more freely, in gradually shortening arcs, before oscillating to a stop. If you still have doubts, pinpoint north to your own satisfaction by one of the methods discussed later, and compare that to the compasses.

In winter particularly, ample time must be allowed for the needle to complete its swing. It will do this slowly and sluggishly, but taking a bearing can not be hurried if it is to be accurate. If you'll keep the compass warm, this will speed the taking of bearings.

An important point to remember, though, is always to make sure that no iron or electrical field, such as a gun or transistor radio, is close to your compass. Iron ore, too, can throw you off. You can check this by observing whether the distance from compass to rock will change your compass reading.

Which North?

There are two norths, true north and magnetic north, the first situated at the North Pole and the second located at the magnetic pole some fourteen hundred miles away near the shallow Northwest Passage. We're interested in true north, but our compasses point to magnetic north.

This problem is further complicated by the fact that the magnetic north isn't stable but is drifting all the time. Yet for all purposes of everyday travel in the unmarked places, an ordinary little compass is entirely sufficient. The only allowance you usually have to make is to allow for the difference between the two norths in a particular region, so as to follow more easily the maps of that locality. This declination is generally noted on the map itself.

Despite the fact that the above is not technically accurate, it is exact enough for day by day travel. As a matter of fact, the whole whirling earth is magnetized, causing the compass variation to differ at various localities. In some spots this magnetic shift may be as much as twenty-five degrees from the declination shown on your everyday map.

In northern latitudes the horizontal magnetic field is weaker than it is farther south. For this reason, it is most important to make certain that the compass is not affected by the iron mass in the ground, by nearby equipment, or by magnetic objects in the observer such as a battery-operated watch.

Checking Your Compass

Only in a narrow strip that passes through the Great Lakes does the compass point to true north, yet allowing for this declination when reading a map is simple in the extreme. Just lay the map flat on the ground or other flat surface. Orient the map roughly by placing your compass on it, then turn it until the north-south grid lines are parallel to the compass needle and north coincides with compass north.

Finally, turn the map again until the needle on the compass indicates the amount of magnetic declination for the area. For example, if the declination is fifteen degrees east, true north is not where the needle is indicating but fifteen degrees to the right of the needle.

It's easy enough to find the compass declination at night by seeing how closely the dial or needle points toward the North Star. If your compass does not have a luminous dial, point the way from you to the North Star with a scratched line or an angled stick. Then in the morning make your comparisons. If your compass is working reliably, the difference between the North Star and where your compass indicates will be the local magnetic variation.

It is a good idea to note this variation and to check it with the declination indicated on your map. If the difference is less than three degrees, check again before noting the change on the map. If even a small difference of slightly more than one degree is constant, however, it will be a good idea to adjust your reading of the local map to correspond with your observations.

Checking magnetic declination can be very important to the traveler who's suddenly stranded in the wilderness, especially if he has been covering vast distances by plane. Much of North America, particularly in the Far North, has

Note the difference between true north and magnetic north.

Using the North Star to check magnetic declination.

not been accurately mapped magnetically. Small local variations that would not mean much to a swiftly flying pilot can be of great concern to the man traveling twenty-five miles a day on foot.

If you're neither using a printed map nor paying any particular attention to such natural signs as the sun, it's entirely feasible to travel all day from the direct readings of the compass, not taking declination into account. If you head out by compass north from a river, for example, you'll return by compass south, although for practical reasons you'll like to return either slightly west or east of south so that when you reach the river you'll know precisely which way to turn.

FINDING NORTH ANOTHER WAY

You've no compass. You've no watch. The sun is bright. You want to find out exactly where true north lies.

Push a short pole into the ground, making sure that it is vertical by holding a weighted string beside it. Then loop the string, lace, thong, vine, etc. around the base of the pole.

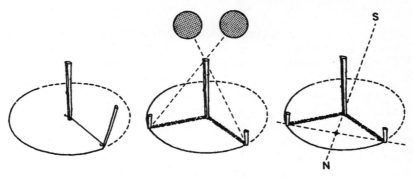

It's easy to find north with no compass or watch.

Holding this taut, measure the length of the pole's present shadow. Then tie or hold a sharp stick to the line at this precise point. Draw a half circle, either starting at the tip of the present shadow or marking this point with a stake.

The shadow of the pole will shorten until it is noon by local standard time. Then it will commence lengthening again. Watch for the moment it once more meets the arc. Mark this point with a second stake.

A line connecting the pole with a point halfway between the first and second marks will run north and south. South, of course, will be toward the sun.

USING THE SHADOWS ONE MORE WAY

Again sometime before midday drive a rod vertically into the ground, checking the alignment of the stick with a makeshift plumb bob. Mark the end of the present shadow with a peg or stone.

Keep on doing this while the shadows shorten, then begin lengthening again. The shortest shadow will run north and south. It should be noted, however, that even with this method you often have to compromise and find your north-south line by selecting a point halfway between two shadows of equal length.

WHERE IS WEST?

There is an even swifter method of telling direction from shadows. All you need is sunlight or moonlight strong enough to cast a shadow. Press or drive your pole or stake into the ground as before.

Mark the top of the shadow, perhaps with a pebble or twig. Five or ten minutes afterward, mark the tip of the new shadow. A line joining the second mark with the first will, in the Northern Hemisphere, point generally west.

With the sun this method is surprisingly accurate during the middle of the day. The line runs a bit south of west in the morning. Afternoons it tends somewhat north of west. During a day of travel by this method, however, these inaccuracies will average themselves out.

SETTING YOUR WATCH

You can do this in the wilderness, although unless you know where you are in any of the fifteen-degree time zones and do a little figuring, the time you get will be the sun time rather than Greenwich. But, even at the extreme, it won't be far off.

It's easy to set a watch in this manner if you have a compass, which must be accurate when you are telling time. Therefore, local magnetic declinations must be reckoned with. If your maps do not give this, you can use the North Star as previously considered.

If you are in British Columbia or Wisconsin, for example, and want to set your watch, find due south with your compass. Then, using a twig and shadow to keep the hour hand of your watch pointed toward the sun, turn the hands until south is midway between the shadow and twelve along the shorter arc. Your watch will then be set to within a few minutes of the local standard time.

If you are stranded in the bush with your watch but no compass, you can still proceed in the above fashion by previously determining south, either by one of the previously described shadow methods or from the North Star.

NATURAL SIGNS SHOWING DIRECTION

In open country, snow and sand drifts are usually on the lee or downwind side of protruding objects like knolls, high banks, rocks, trees, or clumps of willow. If you know in which direction the wind was blowing when the drifts

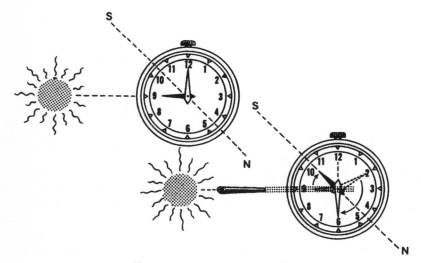

Use your compass to set your watch.

The compass plant's leaves point north and south.

were formed, you'll have a direction-indicator directly in front of you as you travel. In any event, the angle at which you continue to cross drifts will serve as a checkpoint in maintaining a course.

The snow on the south side of knolls, ridges, and the like tends to be more granular than on the north. You can thus maintain your direction by the sun even when it is not shining, if no new snow has fallen since it shone last.

Snowdrifts and sand dunes also accumulate in such a way that they are lower and narrower to windward. This, too, will help to orient you if you know the direction of the prevailing wind. Even if you don't, this phenomenon can keep you traveling in a straight line.

Knowing the direction of the prevailing wind can also be valuable in country where there is considerable deadfall, perhaps after a lightning-started or manmade fire. You have to take into account, though, the results of unusual storms and the air deviations caused by hills, gorges, and the like.

In the barrens and semi-barren lands of eastern Canada, wind-blown trees point to the southeast because of the prevailing wind. The prevailing wind will also blow away the snow at the bases of drifts to give these anvil-like shapes. These snow anvils point to the northwest.

There is the compass plant, sometimes called pilotweed or rosinweed, whose alternate leaves, attached directly at their bases instead of by stems to stalks five to twelve feet high, hold their edges vertical, generally pointing north and south. The yellow flower heads, several inches across, resemble those of a wild sunflower.

Willows, poplars, and alders tend to lean toward the south unless, of course, the prevailing winds turn them in another direction. Similarly, the tops of such trees as pines and hemlocks naturally point to the east.

The age rings revealed in standing stumps are generally widest on the southern side if, as under ideal conditions, this has been the sunniest side. To make sure of your direction, it is wise to select several stumps of trees so situated that they would have been in the full warmth of the noonday sun and to average the results.

Too, pines, spruces, hemlocks, and other softwoods tend to be bushiest in the south side. Look for single coniferous trees growing apart from others.

The bark of poplar trees is whitest on the south side and darkest on the north side.

Anthills are always found on the warm south side of trees and other objects.

All vegetation also tells its own tale, growing larger and more open on northern slopes, and smaller and therefore denser on a southern exposure.

Then there is the story told by moss. It does, indeed, thrive most thickly on the shadiest side of trees which, if these are sufficiently in the open where the sunlight can touch them all day, will be on the north. However, certain lichens somewhat resembling moss to anyone who does not examine them closely grow best on the sunniest portions and could cross you up.

WHY EVERYONE NEEDS A COMPASS

Too many find their way through a certain area by familiarity. This is too restrictive a practice to be sensible unless one plans to stay in his own neighborhood all his life. Even then there will be occasions, as when a storm blots out surroundings, when at the very least a compass can save a lot of time, not to mention its benefits when one strays beyond his own locality.

Furthermore, as has happened to me, you may find yourself out later than you'd planned. On one occasion I recall, the overcast night was no more than thirty minutes away. From a knoll in back of our new cabin, I could see chimney smoke drifting upward from where I knew Vena had a moose mulligan simmering, perhaps a mile and a half away through a series of spruce swamps. Not taking declination into account, I could see that the familiar spot on the river was due south. So by continually checking my compass, I reached there in a straight line while I could still see obstructions such as eye-threatening branches ahead of me. This would not have been possible during the remaining dusk without a compass.

Too, I once climbed an almost sheer peak in the sheep country of the Liard River, where the only way of descent without ropes was precisely northwest. This was easy enough to see at the moment, and the time was midday. But before I could get around to climbing down, clouds of a fast-approaching weather front closed out all but immediate visibility. With my compass I cautiously and safely reached the mountain lake below where my outfit and horses, their leader belled, were waiting.

Who needs a compass? Everyone! This instrument need not be expensive, but it should be rugged enough to withstand moisture and hard usage. It should have a luminous dial, especially if there is some way of having this luminosity periodically renewed. Otherwise a cloudy night may lessen the effectiveness of your compass. This nearly happened once to me in the mountains of Idaho, when I had to get back to camp within a few hours to make necessary connections. Without a luminous compass, I'd have had to waste both time and otherwise-needed matches to keep located.

I prefer a small compass such as the recently developed luminous, lightweight Williams Guide Line Compass, inexpensively obtainable if not yet stocked by your dealer from the catalog-issuing Williams Gun Sight Company [Davison, Michigan 48423]. This compass is waterproof, shockproof, so light that it floats, and filled with a liquid that won't freeze. Pinned to the outer clothing, it has the advantage of being less easily mislaid or lost. Best of all, the floating face remains always horizontal, ready for a quick check at any time.

Despite the usual preponderance of natural direction signs, both celestial and terrestrial, you may agree with me that in the real backwoods it is reassuring to always have a second compass. Mine is in the hilt of my Randall knife which W. D. Randall, Jr., [P.O. Box 1988, Orlando, Florida 32802] made for me after extensive personal consultations and was kind enough to name the Bradford Angier Survival Knife, although I have never had any financial connection with him or it. Under extreme conditions, as in sheer wilderness, a spare compass proves to be as reassuring as the extra waterproof, unbreakable case carefully filled with strike-anywhere wooden matches that I always carry.

METHODICAL USE OF THE COMPASS

Too many people today look upon a compass as being something magic. They think that all they have to do is look at it and it will automatically tell them how to get back to camp. This it will do, but only if it is used correctly. It must be so used from the moment you first leave your campfire.

If you are not using a printed map or paying any particular attention to such natural signs as the sun—a very bad habit to get into—it's entirely feasible to travel all day from the direct readings of your compass, not taking declination into account. If you head out in the morning by compass north from a compass east-west river, you can return by compass south. For practical reasons, however, as we'll consider in a moment, you had better return either slightly east or west of compass south so that when you reach the river you'll know which way to turn to reach camp.

First of all, whenever possible, you should camp by a long line that cannot be reasonably missed and whose general direction and length you have

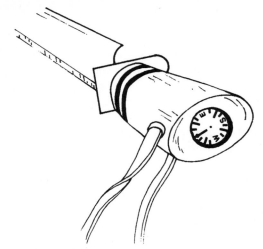

Bradford Angier Survival Knife

ascertained. This can be a large river (not a brook, where you may become confused by coming on a branch or similar stream); a road such as the Alaska Highway (one you definitely know does not come to an end within a few miles and one you will not sanely cross in a heavy snowstorm); the foot of a well-defined mountain range rising abruptly from a flat; a power line; or something of this sort.

Let us take the example I know best, the Peace River, a 2,200-mile-long wilderness thoroughfare which begins west of the Canadian Rockies where the Finlay River flows south along the Continental Trough and the Parsnip River runs north, meeting just below what was Finlay Forks and abruptly becoming the Peace River. The river follows, with some name changes, east into Great Slave Lake, from whence it slips as the notable Mackenzie River to the Arctic Ocean. The headwaters of this system have unfortunately been altered by the political damming of the Peace at Rocky Mountain Canyon. Where the dam extends is fourteen miles in a straight line from Hudson Hope, British Columbia, making a huge log-clogged lake that backs up both the Finlay and the Parsnip but which does not alter the direction-locating potential of the watercourse.

We originally built our log cabin on the sunny north shore of Rocky Mountain Canyon, five miles above the then tiny log-cabin settlement of Hudson Hope. No matter where we were, unless we managed by boat or ice to cross the broad river, we could always be sure of finding the cabin by hiking south to meet the watercourse and then, if we were not too exhausted, by following it to our cabin. In practice, because of the vastness of the distances involved, we had to pinpoint the cabin. In this lay the first shortcut of finding our way alone in the bush.

THE INITIAL SHORTCUT IN FINDING YOUR WAY

We are camped, for purposes of illustration, on the middle north shore of the unsettled Wapoose River somewhere in the grizzly country of the Continental Northwest. We have reached our tent site by boat. The Wapoose, we know from the map we have, runs some 100 miles from a fairly large mountain lake and is the only river of any size nearby. It runs from west to east, and we are about 50 miles from where it rushes into the Liard—certainly a long line at which to aim.

We are each proceeding on our own, you hunting and I prospecting, although of course I'll gladly help you bring back any meat, and if you want the head and pelt, after you get it. But the first morning in this wilderness, absolutely strange to each of us, we each set out alone—you with your scope-sighted .30-06 Winchester Model 70 rifle which, with the 220-grain cartridges you are using, is big enough to bring down safely and surely any big game on this continent with an anchoring and killing shot one-third of the way down the foreshoulder of the animal, or in front halfway between the eyes and slightly high.

You set out north from our tent, across wind, at daybreak, which here is about 6 A.M. You want to be back by a safe 6:30 P.M. Thus by boiling the kettle for half an hour at noon, toasting your sandwiches and sipping your tea, you effectively divide the day in half. You don't know how far you have traveled north, but you can be sure that by returning at about the same pace during the remaining daylight you should safely reach camp by dusk.

Not having a detailed map, you draw one as you go, frequently turning to check the look of your back trail. This is flattish, wooded country. The prevailing wind continues to blow across you, which is good for all-day hunting. Checking your compass occasionally, you continue to travel in a fairly straight line by keeping two specific trees, and then two more, lined up most of the time ahead of you. You realize, of course, that with downfalls to skirt and small creeks to cross where comfortable, there is no such thing as a straight line in the forest. But by consulting your compass and allowing for zigs with corresponding zags, you keep traveling in a generally northerly direction.

Lunch over soon after noon, it's time to start campward. You know this lies generally south, but to hit it on the nose would be either a matter of luck or would have taken from the first a lot more reckoning than you had time for. By walking generally south by compass at the same pace you'll reach the Wapoose close to dinnertime, true. But then, not knowing the country, would you head up or down the river? Here's where that all-important shortcut comes into play to make your orientation simple.

You want to hit the river definitely a bit west or east of our tent. Because that very important hunting wind is still blowing from the west and because the going looks just as promising that way, you decide to reach the river upstream from our outfit. So you head south-southwest (see Map A). This will take a little longer, so you hasten your stride a trifle. You reach the broad Wapoose at 6:15 P.M. If you'd knocked over a grizzly and stopped to open him up, you'd have quickened your pace even more to allow for the delay. But you know for sure that camp lies a bit downriver. All is well.

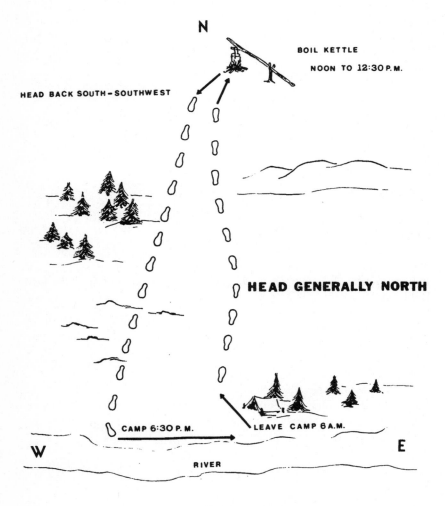

Map A

REACHING A TRAIL GOING DIRECTLY AWAY

The preceding plan, whenever it will work, is the foremost stratagem for staying found in the wilderness anywhere. I have also used it a number of times—in Maine, Quebec, and British Columbia—for locating a trail leading directly away from me. The last occasion remains most vivid in my mind, so let us refer to it.

This took place across the Peace River from our cabin where, for several weeks earlier in the year, I'd been ferrying an acquaintance, George Waugh, and his survey crew for preliminary work in laying out some Crown Land for logging by a local friend, Earl Pollan. George and his men had bushed out several miles of the generally north-south Peace River Block Line, and I followed this on my look for a fat buck to help fill our cabin's meat cache for the coming cold weather.

I found my tender muley spikehorn unexpectedly in a sapling-filled field beside a fallen-in cabin. Neither of us had realized the other was nearby, and I dropped it with a brain side halfway between eye and ear openings from the side. I butchered and skinned it, enclosing the meat in a protective fabric sheath where it was safe from blowflies and Canada jays. I hung it in a shady, breezy spot until I could return in the cool of the evening to carry it, draped over my shoulders, to the boat.

By ten o'clock that morning I was continuing on my travels, it being much too fine a day to spend behind a typewriter. By far the easiest and quietest way to traverse this heavily overgrown and generally fallen-in country was along the brushed Block Line. So I continued to follow that slowly and comfortably for another two hours, using my binoculars and Leica frequently, until I reached a grassy spot, long ago cleared by fire set by the Moberly Lake Indians to bring in game, where there was a spring. Here I boiled the kettle. Bullhead Mountain, although across the river, was close to my northwest; ahead, to my south, was a small unknown lake which I figured I had time to reach and explore before commencing my homeward journey.

There was no longer any evidence of the Block Line on the now south slope, but I thought little of this because of an inch of tracking snow as, by compass and sun, I continued southward.

The sun was hot, and the west wind chinooky. When the time came to head back to the Block Line, no semblance of my back trail remained, for the snow had melted. To save myself a lot of trouble in getting back through that jackpot on the side down to the Peace, and in order to pick up the spikehorn without backtracking, I had to locate that narrow Block Line.

I could have headed due north by compass, sun, and wind with the hope of hitting the Line on the nose. Too much chance! I could have continued north to the crest, then started zigzagging northwest and northeast in widening traverses until I reached the trail. Not enough daylight! So, continuing to hunt for bear crosswind, I traveled a safe hour north-northwest through the erratic jumble of jackpot (see Map B), which by no means ended smoothly in an east-west direction. By the time I was sure the elusive Block Line was a short distance east, I headed that way. My pattern worked.

THE SECOND BIG SECRET OF ORIENTATION

We are prospecting, this time moving our outfit with saddle and pack horses, in unknown, unexplored, and unmarked country three days east of the Alaska

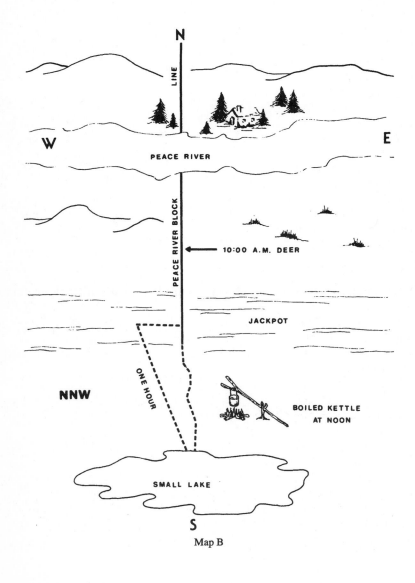

Map B

Highway. We have camped for a week in a meadow by one of several small streams, where the graze is particularly good, and we've hobbled and belled our half-dozen cayuses. It is flat, forested country without landmarks. How do we leave camp each morning with the certainty of returning safely by nightfall? Again the solution is a positive one. We keep from getting lost by staying found.

Our method takes time, but it will save considerable time and worry in the end. Carefully considering compass declination, which we check with the North Star, and using camp as the central point, we blaze four lines—north, east, south, and west—each some two miles long. To save additional time in such cases, the method I use is to put the higher of the two opposite blazes on the side of the tree nearer camp (*h* for *high* and for *home*). Such blazing, in effect, gives us a giant spoked wheel at which to aim. It isn't difficult to keep close enough tabs on our whereabouts during the day to be able to return to this blazed landmark toward evening.

This, of course, is a method that does not allow for many mistakes, or the course would be to head west for the Alaska Highway, in the meantime putting our companion through a great deal of work and worry. So we have arranged two things. If for some reason we are delayed one afternoon so that we might not return to the critical area while there is still enough light to find the blazes, then the only safe and sane procedure is to make an overnight camp wherever we might be and proceed the next morning. Furthermore, if one of us is ever in any difficulty and needs help, he is to fire three shots one minute apart, the answer to which is to be a single shot. Incidentally, we never have had to do either.

FOLLOWING A STREAM

This usually works in well-settled country if you take the very important precaution of skirting any swamps on the upwater side. You'll usually find that you can travel more swiftly and with greater ease if you keep to the better going instead of holding to each curve and crook of the stream, following the water's progress as well as you can with your eyes and cutting back occasionally to check it.

In sheer wilderness, though, following even one of the larger streams can take you through some mighty rough going, particularly in country where such running water digs almost impassable gorges, only to bring you to a desolate lake or muskeg miles from any habitation.

As a matter of fact, using any but well-mapped water for landmarks in strange country should be only part of the process of establishing one's whereabouts. Small streams in particular loop around so much that you're apt to come upon them flowing in apparently the wrong direction and read the wrong story. Or a similar stream may parallel the first before flowing into it. I spent a confused hour one late afternoon when unwittingly I cut directly across a stream that had gone underground for a mile or so.

STAYING FOUND

You stay found by keeping track of approximately where you are. Far from being complicated in practice, this becomes, instead, an ever intriguing problem of angles and distances. Anyone can do it.

At the very least, you can stay located by means of a map, compass, and pencil. Every quarter hour, or whenever you change your direction, will not at first be too often to bring that map up to the moment. You don't have a map? Then sketch one as you proceed.

This is the entire secret. As you gain in experience, you'll do more and more of this mapping in your head.

HOW TO MEASURE DISTANCE

A watch is of particular value in the wilderness, especially under survival conditions, not only because you can tell direction with its help but because it affords the best method of measuring distance. Any watch adjusted to a reasonable speed will do for this latter purpose, although if you wish to be in closer ratio with the sun in determining direction, you can set the watch by one of the previously suggested shadow methods.

Miles as such mean little by themselves in wilderness travel, for a stretch may be across open level country, or it may wind and twist the same distance up and down gorges and through downfall.

Suppose a prospector sets you right one early morning after you've been wandering aimlessly. Where you stand, two trails lead to the road where you're camped.

You ask how far it is along either trail to your camp. His laconic answer, "Ten miles apiece," still leaves you at a loss. If he says instead, "The left trail is an easy three hours. I suppose you could get there along the right path by nightfall if you rustled right along," you'd know precisely what to expect.

Suppose you are stranded on a river shore after a plane crash and decide to stay with the aircraft and its supplies until you find a sure way out. Leaving a note telling exactly what you are going to do, you head generally north for four hours, marking the trail as you go. You probably won't know how many miles you have traversed. But you can be certain that the return trip over the same ground at the same general pace will take another four hours.

THE VALUE OF TELLING WHERE YOU'LL BE

It's a common thing to come across where a lost man has been camped a night or two before, only to find no indication of his present whereabouts. Anyone who's lost or stranded should always leave behind him, before quitting any camp or wreck, the exact information of where he's headed and what he has in mind. The more explicit this data, the better. But even an indicative arrow scratched beside the remains of a campfire may save your life.

The only way to keep from becoming lost is, as we've already considered, to stay found. One preliminary safeguard in the wilderness anywhere is never to go anywhere without making your plans known to someone else or, if you are camping alone, by at least a marker indicating where you are heading. Members of hunting groups would get into trouble far less often if they just observed this primary precaution before leaving camp en masse in all directions each morning.

Even if you park your automobile along a wilderness road for an hour's fishing, it's a sound idea to leave a note under the windshield telling of your plans.

HOW TO FIND A LOST HUNTER

The most practical advice that I have ever seen on this subject was written by Leon L. Bean.

"In case one of your party does not show up at camp when night falls, as has previously been his custom, do not get excited and do not do a thing until 6 P.M. If you started signaling before 6:00 P.M. other hunters, who have not gotten into camp, are likely to butt in and make it very misleading.

"Eat your supper and see that the lantern is full of oil. Then go outside with rifle, lantern and flashlight. At exactly 6:00 P.M. fire two shots. Listen a moment for a reply. Not hearing any, walk about one-quarter mile and repeat your signal. If you get a reply, see a fire or note any odor of smoke, continue the signals, always walking in the general direction that you believe your man is located.

"In the meantime what is the 'lost' hunter to do? If, in the late afternoon, he realizes that he is lost or so far from camp that he cannot get in, he selects a sheltered spot where dry wood is handy, starts a fire, and collects a lot of wood before dark. At exactly 6:00 P.M. he listens for a signal. On hearing it, he answers and the signals continue, the same as in daytime. Hearing no signal, he wastes none of his shells but pounds a signal at regular intervals with a club on a sound, dead tree. If there is no dead tree available, select a live tree and peel off a spot of bark where he wants to pound.

"In the morning, if not sure of the direction to camp, he is not to leave the spot or to shoot except to answer his party's signals. Keep a smoke going and pound out a few signals about every ten minutes.

"The party at camp should not stay out too late. Notify a Game Warden or Sheriff during the night and continue the search at daybreak.

"By following these simple rules the lost hunter or his party have nothing to worry about."

THE BIGGEST SECRET IN GETTING BACK

There are, as with every other pursuit, various time-saving shortcuts. The biggest one involving finding one's way back to camp has to do with knowing exactly which way to turn when you reach a broadside such as a road, river, lake, mountain range, etc.

Let's take an example. You're camped, say, on the south shore of a wilderness river which flows from west to east through the backbone of the Canadian Rockies. Such a broadside, incidentally, is the place where under normal conditions you should always try to camp. Then even in a heavy snowstorm you'll be able to find your way safely back.

You take your camera and telescopic fishing rod and walk generally south for four hours. Straight lines, of course, are only a figure of speech in the bush. But by compensating for swings around such obstacles as beaver ponds and by occasionally checking your compass, you can keep traveling in a single direction.

If you return generally north for four hours at the same speed, you know you'll be close to your river. Then camp will be only a short distance away. Perhaps you're acquainted enough with your surroundings to head in the right direction without any delay. But suppose you've never been in this country before. Darkness is filling the swamps and coulees, and you want to be back in camp before there's the danger of walking over a cut bank or getting a dead stick in an eye. What do you do?

The correct procedure of return starts back at your noon campfire. You look over the country. To the west are open poplar benches. To the east are the occasional muskeg and spruce swamp. So you decide to bear west. By heading slightly west of north, say north northwest, you will still reach the river in slightly more than the same four hours. But now you know that camp definitely lies downriver to the east a short distance.

STAYING ON A TRAIL

There are trails and trails. Even game trails can be useful to a lost man, making for easier going if nothing else. In dry country, such trails may lead to water. In areas where water is no problem, deepening and widening game trails usually lead around comparatively impassable sections. If you're lost, therefore, you'll do best to take the fullest possible advantage of the often centuries-old game routes when they're going in the same general direction you wish to travel, then to leave them when they divert.

A blazed trail is very apt to go somewhere, even if only to a distant trapper's cabin, and will be well worth following if one is lost and wandering aimlessly. When these cuts are old, you'll have to pay particular attention to which marks are indeed blazes and which are made by antler-shining deer, eating moose, or spring bear hungry for the laxative bark of the spruce.

You can often feel the flatness of even a burned ax cut, while in some the telltale flap of bark still remains at the bottom. Also, a trail is ordinarily blazed both going and coming, and you'll be able to check a blaze by the presence of a companion blaze on the other side of the tree.

If you ever find yourself off the trail, be sure to mark the starting point of your search to regain it. Then circle or zigzag out from that particular spot. That way you'll never wander very far from the trail.

When a blazed trail seems to stop, stand still and look forward and backward. Usually you can find the blaze again by determining where you'd have gone if you had been blazing the trail in the first place.

STARTING POINT

When you do not know where you are, establish a starting point from which to begin your search. This may be an oddly shaped boulder or tree, or it may be just a branch or bush that you break on the spot.

This way when you suddenly realize you are lost, you can stay, by retracing your footsteps to this new starting point whenever necessary, within the same general area which usually is not too far from where you are supposed to be. Too many lost individuals walk right out of the country that is being searched.

If your starting point is in totally unknown country, as when you are walking away from a crashed plane, you'll at least be able to keep track of your new position and thus proceed with some method.

LOST NEAR CIVILIZATION

In settled country, where traveling in any one direction, usually downhill and around the upper sides of swamps and such, will bring one out, the lost individual who keeps his head seldom has much of a problem. If he has a compass, he's well equipped even though he may have to camp out overnight. If he has no compass, he can keep going straight by always keeping two trees or other objects lined up ahead. In mountainous country, all he may have to do is keep a certain peak at his back.

Sound may play a part: a distant locomotive whistle, factory siren, car horn, or even a man chopping wood. As the weather becomes colder, so proportionately does the hearing range increase.

As cold intensifies, one is able to see farther, too. In such regions distant smoke, perhaps viewed from a hilltop or safely climbed tree, with one's keeping as close to the trunk as possible for additional security, will usually mean habitation.

When you're lost, don't make the all too common and often fatal mistake of rejecting a road or power line just because it doesn't seem to be the one you're seeking.

THE IMPORTANCE OF MAPS

You can't travel intelligently for any distance in the wilderness without a map, even though this map may be one you're sketching as you go or, if you are more of an old woodsman, are keeping mentally.

Most traveled parts of North America have been mapped. If you are on an extended hike, you should be armed with a contour or topographic map. These are usually available from the major camping outfitters, or from the Map Information Office, U.S. Geological Survey in Washington, D.C.

Before entering sheer wilderness anywhere, it's profitable practice, even when you have what seems to be a good map, to have some old-timer correct and supplement it, particularly if you're in one of the vast northern areas where even the most diligent and ambitious surveying crew can do only a sketchy job in the short summer season when they can work.

AERIAL PHOTOS

Not even the best aerial photograph can take the place of even a sketchy map. Used together, though, they can make an excellent combination. When a map is both general and selective, the photo truly reveals all that can be seen from the air.

An aerial map, essentially, differs from a snapshot you take of wild country only because it is photographed straight downward, or nearly so, from a higher spot. Because of the accuracy thus obtained, wild recesses throughout much of North America have been mapped and opened to the master outdoorsman. Simple to use, such maps enable more precise journey-planning, then on the spot attain even more importance in that with care they can be read immediately in terms of the actual country, showing exactly what to expect around the next bend. The regular map is still needed for exact orientation and, of course, for explanatory names and scale. Then, too, excessive bush and forestation often hide vital details such as trails, trappers' and prospectors' cabins, and such, a shortcoming that any cloud cover will exaggerate.

Aerial maps are available in groups. The flyer generally works from west or east, thus keeping all shadows in the same direction. After he has thus worked one edge of the desired area, he makes a half turn and shoots his series of pictures to show a corresponding and adjacent series from the opposite direction. This pattern is followed until the complete target area is covered. Or it should be.

Each photograph is then numbered with three designations: the mission identification, then the flight line, and finally the individual nine-by-nine contract print number. By using the compiled index, you can find the exact area or areas in which you are interested. Plane and exposure speeds are diligently controlled to get a sixty percent overlap on successive photographs, at the same time sidelapping by approximately half that distance to prevent gaps in any direction.

Scale, of course, depends on the height of the flight and the focal length of the particular lens and is generally noted in the index. As with any maps, the larger the scale the more detail and the smaller the region covered in each particular print. But, depending of course on your purpose, the added information is usually worth the extra expense of more prints.

Incidentally, check the filled order upon its receipt to make sure you have acquired what you want, best verified by first lining up the prints in sequence. Using a large flat area such as a bare floor, find key points in each picture and use these, always watching the shadows for maintaining precision and allowing for the handy overlaps, to number each print plainly for your future identification. A river, for instance, may help with this. Using a large sheet of transparent paper, perhaps made by several sheets joined with transparent tape, make your own detailed, photo-numbered map for future reference. When the time comes to store the prints, arrange them in sequence, place between two heavy pieces of cardboard (perhaps cut from a box), and put away in some place where there will be no extremes in humidity and warmth, keeping a large book or some sort of heavy object on them to combat the natural tendency to curl.

The way geologists and surveyors work is by using two sets of identical photographs with a legged stereoscope which, consisting of two lenses, directs each eye to a separate print, giving a three-dimensional effect.

Always line up the photos with the shadows of trees, cliffs, and such pointing toward you so that the result will not seem to be upside down. Use a key point such as a prominent crag to get lined up, moving the uppermost picture back and forth so that the pinpointed feature appears to drift together. Then, when the prints are correctly aligned some 2½ inches apart and the normal converging of the eyes conquered, the three-dimensional effect will abruptly come into being. This may take anywhere from a second to several minutes, although vision defects in some individuals preclude their ever achieving a stereo effect.

Relative to the image's position as regards the edge of the photograph, some curling upward, out of the way, of the uppermost print may have to be resorted to. This is apt to result in some confusion and manipulation until all is coordinated. Therefore, it's usually best to experiment first with your table stereoscope and a pair of familiar scenes. But the results, when you master the technique, will be astonishing, if perhaps overemphasized, until you get used to the overall effect.

You'll be better able to judge distances, too, once you've worked with a pair of familiar scenes. For instance, two lakes six inches apart on a pair of photographs with a scale of 1:12,000 would be a trifle more than a mile from one another, six times the scale of 12,000 inches or 72,000 inches. Transposed into feet by dividing by 12 inches, this gives 6,000 feet. A mile, as you know, is 5,280 feet. But you must always realize that only at the photo's center is the scale approximately correct. It all takes experience, but what it adds to the knowledge of unfamiliar country is infinite.

CHAPTER EIGHT

GETTING OUT AND GETTING HELP

WALKING OUT

Five basic requirements should be met before you try to travel out of a survival situation. If any of these can not be fulfilled in regards to your particular emergency, then camp and signal.

1. Know approximately where you are and where safety lies. If you are relatively uncertain about either your present whereabouts or about the way out, do not start.

2. Are you physically up to the trip? Perhaps you are already exhausted and in a weakened condition. Perhaps there is waist-deep snow or tough muskeg country. Be extremely cautious when you are assaying your stamina and if you are at all in doubt, stay where you are. The chief factor in exposure death is exhaustion.

3. Have a definite means of both setting and maintaining direction. If you have a compass and understand the simple essentials of its use, then you can count on keeping to a planned course. If not, then there are the stars, the sun and moon, and the several basic shadow methods of telling direction, not to forget the numerous natural signs. But if you are still hazy about determining and keeping a heading, stay put.

4. Do you have adequate clothing? Whereas you can get by with insufficient garb and especially poor footwear when you have to go no farther from your campfire than to pick up more firewood and secure food, trying to travel when you are improperly protected is an entirely different matter and could end in disaster. In warm weather there will be the masses of insects that a smudge fire would have kept at bay. Even wet socks, when you have no spares, may eventually incapacitate you. So unless your clothing is sufficient to protect you from all the hardships of the trail, remain by your bivouac.

5. Food, fuel, shelter, and the ability to signal for help at a moment's notice, as when a search plane is heard, must all be considered from the view-

point of traveling. If you cannot depend on living off the country to at least a strength-maintaining degree, you'll do better to fit your activities more closely to your caloric intake by staying put.

Fuel may be no problem, but if you have to cross barren country, particularly in winter, then your life may depend on your carrying sufficient fire-making materials. Unless you can readily make yourself some of the bivouacs considered in this book, you'd better settle for one where you are. And unless you know you can signal instantly from the trail as with fire or flashes, you'll do better to sit tight.

Make Your Own Map

It's a good idea to keep a sketch map of your journey showing landmarks, distances covered, and direction. No matter where you may be, this will help to keep you on a direct course, show your progress, and enable you to get back the fastest to the starting point. And once you return to civilization, you'll know enough about keeping track of yourself that you'll never get lost in the woods again.

Travel Hints

Save your strength and minimize the possibilities of accidents by always choosing the easiest and safest way even though it may sometimes be the longest. Don't spend a morning clambering through a fallen-down burn when you can walk around it in an hour.

Don't go straight up a steep slope. Instead, climb at a slant as animals do, zigzagging back and forth to save energy. Try to maintain your height, going around the edges of gullies and canyons rather than descending and climbing up again. Don't tackle a muskeg, morass, or wet mud flat if you can proceed around it.

Take it easy. Maintain a steady, mile-eating pace which you can keep up all day if necessary. When you're traveling with others, adjust everyone's pace to that of the slowest individual. You'll go farther with a minimum of wear and tear if you occasionally rest for brief periods. Trying to bull it through at top speed, then taking prolonged breathing spells, is a good way to stiffen up early in the journey.

Especially in the exhilaration of going down a steep slope, always control your center of gravity so that if you do fall, it will be backwards in a maneuverable sitting position. In fact, anywhere in the wilderness, particularly in the stress of trying to survive, it is always wisest to expect to fall at any time, as when the bark on a dead log slips or when there is a sudden glaze of ice, and to be ready to do this in as safe a position as possible.

The only reasonable rule in the farther places anywhere is not to take unnecessary chances, weighing always the possible loss against the potential gain and going about your affairs with as wide a safety margin as practical.

A good traveling formula that I still find myself repeating whenever I have a lot of ground to cover is: Never step on anything you can step over, and never step over anything you can step around.

Maintaining a Straight Line

A good way to follow a straight course is to choose two easily visible points, such as trees or rocks, which are exactly on the line you wish to follow and as far apart as feasible. Then hike, keeping the two points in line. Before coming to the far point, select a third point in the same line ahead and continue the method.

Check your back course occasionally. Doing this will not only assure that you are traveling in a straight line, but it will also give you a back view of landscape features which will help you to recognize them if you have to backtrack.

When resting, face the direction in which you are traveling, or make a pointer of stones, twigs, or scratches on the ground.

Among the Peaks

Travel in mountains and other high country can be both dangerous and confusing unless you take heed of a few tricks. What looks like a single ridge from a distance may be a series of ranges and valleys.

In extremely high mountains, a snowfield or glacier that appears to be continuous and easy to travel over may cover a sheer drop of hundreds of feet.

Follow valleys or ridges in mountainous terrain. If your route leads to a hidden gorge with walls almost straight up and down, search for a bypass.

To save time and energy during mountain walking, keep the weight of your body directly over your feet by placing the soles of your shoes flat on the ground. If you take small steps and move slowly but steadily, this is not difficult.

When you ascend hard ground, lock your knees briefly at the end of each step in order to rest your leg muscles. As you zigzag up steep slopes, turn at the end of each traverse by stepping off in the new direction with your uphill foot. This will prevent crossing your feet and losing your balance.

When you descend hard ground, come straight down without traversing. Keep your back straight and your knees bent so that they take up the shock of each step. Keep your weight directly over your feet by placing the full sole on the ground at each step.

Survival Skills

You may have to go up or down a steep slope and cliff. Before you start, do your best to pick your route carefully, making sure it has places for hand- or footholds from top to bottom. Try out every hold before you put all your weight on it, and distribute your weight.

If possible, do not climb on loose rock. Move continually, using your legs to lift your weight and your hands to keep your balance. Be sure you can go in either direction without danger at any time. In climbing down, face out from the slope as long as possible, as this is the best position from which to choose your routes and holds. As you travel *down* a grade, be on the lookout for slopes of loose, relatively fine rock. Such slopes can aid your movement. Turn slightly sideways, keeping your body relaxed, and descend diagonally in long jumps or steps.

If the slope consists of large rocks, move slowly and carefully to prevent a boulder from rolling under your weight. Always step squarely on the top of a rock to prevent it from throwing you off balance.

Traveling Snowfields and Glaciers

The quickest way to descend a steep snowfield is by sliding down on your feet, using a stout pole some five feet long as a brace and to dig into the snow to stop your fall if you should stumble. You can also use this pole to probe for the deadly crevasses that may extend beneath innocent-looking snow. If you must cross one of these, find the strongest part by poking with your staff, then distribute your weight by crawling.

If you are crossing a glacier, you must expect to find such cracks in the ice, usually at right angles to the direction of the flow. It is generally possible to go around them, inasmuch as they seldom extend completely across the river of ice. If snow carpets the scene, the greatest of caution must be exercised. It is a good idea when you have companions to tie yourselves together.

In any event, heavily crevassed areas should be avoided whenever possible. Unless you are already experienced in glacier travel or unless you can locate no other route, you should avoid this ice which is so dangerous for the untrained.

Travel up or across a steep slope covered with snow will be easier if you kick steps into it as you move diagonally across it. Always be on the alert for avalanches, especially during a spring thaw or after new snowfall.

If you must move where there is the peril of avalanches, stay out of the valley at the base of the incline. If you have to cross the slope, do this as high as reasonably possible. If you must climb the slope, ascend straight up.

Anyone caught in a snowslide, however, has a good chance to survive it, particularly if he can keep on top of the swirling, billowing, sweeping avalanche. One way to accomplish this is by swimming. The backstroke, especially effective if you can manage it, has saved many lives in such emergencies.

Another hazard when traveling mountainous snowfields is the cornices which will not support your weight. These often spectacular projections are formed by the snow's blowing from the windward side of a ridge. You can generally spot them from the leeward side. From windward, though, you may see only a gently rounded, snow-whitened ridge. The best practice is to follow ridges on the windward side well below the cornice line.

When crossing snow slopes in warm weather, it is less perilous to traverse them early in the morning when they have a hard crust. By the same criterion, in the spring especially, ford mountain streams in the early morning, thus avoiding the heaviest flow which takes place when the sun is melting the snow.

Making Your Own Snowshoes

You'll use much less energy walking on top of the snow than struggling through it. Therefore, throughout much of the winter wilderness, you should have some sort of snowshoes even if they are but light wide evergreen boughs attached to the feet.

The oval bear-paw snowshoe will be the easiest to construct and wear and will work fine when obstructions are not too thick. When you have to go through thicker woods, a narrowed and longer web may be necessary.

For the frames, cut down substantial live saplings, let them thaw in front of your campfire if necessary, and bend them into the desired shape. Strips of rawhide will make adequate webbing. Make these heaviest beneath the foot. In hilly going, leaving on the hair and facing it outwards will help to cut down on slippage. If you have wire, string it on the frame and twist the rawhide around it.

You can also use rope in a pinch, but it has the disadvantage of stretching in cold going and shrinking in slushy travel. In the first instance, you will likely have to stop and tighten it, whereas if you don't loosen it when it is wet, it will be apt to break the frames. Rawhide is also a nuisance when the weather warms, sagging as it does when wet. The wire nucleus will do away with this trouble.

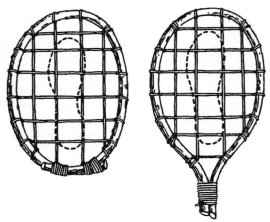

If you must walk through deep snow, you'll conserve energy by wearing a pair of simply made snowshoes.

The snowshoes should be as small and as light as you can wear and still get across the snow you have to traverse. In soft snow they'll have to be larger, with the webbing strung closer together. Naturally, you'll do the best you can, and this should be enough to get you out.

You'll want to attach the webs so that the front of the shoe will swing up and out of the way under its own weight when the foot is raised. Even with regular webs, though, some sourdoughs help themselves along in rough going by tying a rope to the end of each web and then assisting its swing with their hands.

What About Arctic Survival Travel?

Travel in the Arctic is difficult, dangerous, and in too many instances useless. Journeys in winter or summer should ordinarily be limited to movement from an undesirable to a more advantageous place, as from an unsafe to a safe location or from a frigid valley to a less extreme position on a hillside. Energy for the most part should be expended in shelter building, in putting out highly visible signals, and in getting food.

In any event, do not travel in a blizzard or in bitterly cold wind. Make camp and conserve your strength until the gale lets up. Unless absolutely necessary, do not travel in poor visibility even when the wind is quiet.

If you must be on the move, head for a coast, a major river, or a known point of habitation. Most settlements are near the coast or close to large junctions, lake outlets, points of land, and mouths of streams. Travel downstream, and in summer use a raft if possible. In winter, the rivers generally make broad highways, but carry a long pole and beware of thin ice. Travel is sometimes easiest on the ridges, especially in summer when the low land is wet. Watch out for ice overhang.

Hindrances to summer travel are surprisingly dense vegetation, rough terrain, insects, soft ground, swamps, lakes, and unfordable large rivers. In winter, the major obstacles are soft deep snow, dangerous river ice, overflows where long stretches of fresh water from the still-flowing river are covered if at all only by a thin layer of snow or ice, severe weather, and a scarcity of food.

On all glaciers and in all snow-covered terrain in spring, travel from midnight to noon to avoid run-off streams. Surfaces are better for journeying at night, and rest periods are more comfortable during the warmer day. On valley glaciers, watch out for falling rocks early in the evening.

Cross glacier-fed streams early in the morning when the water level is scantest. When floating down a northern stream anywhere, watch out for and avoid sweepers—trees that lean out horizontally across the current and which may brush you and your outfit off the raft.

In traveling, too, remember that you will be likely to misjudge distances because of the clear polar air and the lack of familiar scale such as that furnished by trees and other landmarks. Underestimates of distances are more common than overestimates. Mirages are common in the Arctic.

When the sky is overcast and the ground is covered with snow, the lack of contrast makes it difficult to judge the nature of the terrain. In these conditions, men have walked over cliffs without seeing them. Do not travel in these white-out conditions, or if you must, at least keep probing ahead of you and on all sides with a long, dry stick.

The Broad Highways

Frozen streams and rivers are often the great highways of the North, opening country sometimes impassable during the temperate seasons. Always carry a light dry pole, long enough to bridge a gap where the ice suddenly lets go. Avoid places where such weak ice may be formed.

Stay away from rocks and partially submerged deadfall, since freezing in these areas will have been retarded by eddies. Travel on the inside of curves, inasmuch as on the outside the river current will have had an eroding effect on the underneath of the icy pavement. Travel on the bank or on the opposite side of the stream at the juncture of two streams, as the currents from both hold up, by turbulence, the formation of ice. Finally, stay on bare ice whenever possible. A deep covering of snow will insulate the water and retard freezing, perhaps leaving only a snow bridge.

If You Fall Through the Ice

A lifesaving article to have where you can quickly grab it, during ice travel anywhere, is a good sheath knife. Then if you do crack through, and because of pressure holes and varying thicknesses this is possible everywhere, you can drive it into the usually solid ice nearby and with its aid roll yourself out and away.

Another way of gaining immediate traction in such an emergency is, as quick as a breath, to reach out as far as possible with your arms and to lay your wet sleeves and mitts against the remaining ice where, if temperatures are frosty enough, they will freeze nearly instantaneously.

When the weather is warmer, you may have to break away fragile ice with your hands so as to reach an expanse thick enough to support you. However, it is generally possible in the meantime to keep yourself above the surface by resting a hand or arm flatly on even thin ice. Then if there seems to be no likelier way, get as much of your shoulders as you can over the edge, bring your body as horizontal as possible with perhaps a scissoring motion with the feet, get a leg over, and roll to safety.

Watch out in the spring for candle ice, so treacherous that you can step on an apparently solid stretch and sink through it as if it were slush. What happens is that ice up to several feet in thickness decomposes into long vertical needles, among which your pole can be driven in a single thrust.

This, then, is the way of testing ice that becomes all the more important as seasonal thawing progresses. Candle ice is best avoided completely, especially because of the difficulty in reaching safety again once you've encountered it.

How Dangerous are Quagmires?

You sometimes come upon quagmires where mud, decomposing vegetation, and sometimes both are mixed so much with water that they won't support your weight. That's all there is to it. No suction lies within to suck you downward. Nothing operates but gravity, perhaps speeded by unwise struggling; if you attempt to withdraw one unmired foot while putting all your weight on the other, the action will force this second foot deeper.

At the worst, when you get very deep into the mire, your body will likely be lighter than the semisolid it is displacing, and you'll cease sinking. You'll not become more deeply entrapped, that is, unless you writhe and twist your way downward in trying ineffectually to escape.

The thing to do is to present as much body area to the surface of the quagmire as may be necessary and to do this with the least possible delay. If when you feel the ground quiver beneath you, you run to solid ground, you'll be safe. If you cannot run, fall to your knees, for you'll usually be able to crawl out.

If you are still descending, look around speedily to see if there isn't some bush or branch you can grasp. Or you may have a pack or jacket to help support your weight. If not, flatten yourself on your stomach, with your arms and legs as far apart as feasible, and worm your way out.

You'll find quagmires in all sorts of country. Areas where water stays on the surface, and especially where water has so glittered in the immediate past, can be treacherous. You should watch out, then, for tidal flats, marshes, swamps, old game licks which tremble beneath a flooring of dried mud, and definitely for muskegs.

About Quicksand

Quicksand is similar to quagmire, being sand that is suspended in varying proportions of water. It may sink you considerably more rapidly, but methods of survival are alike. You do not have such a span of time, however, and unless you keep your cool you're in more potential danger.

If there is no help at hand and no support to grasp, you may succeed in throwing yourself instantly full length and either crawling or swimming to safety. You may have to duck under the surface to loosen your feet, digging them out with your hands and perhaps sacrificing your footwear. Outside of that, you'll want to avoid as far as possible all abrupt movements that will only serve to shove you deeper.

Rest, but never give up; for quagmires and quicksands often occupy a hole no bigger than a refrigerator. Another inch or two of progress may very well bring your hands either to solidness or to where you can toss over a bush a belt or a rope made of clothing.

The Best Ways of Fording

Unless you are traveling in the desert, there is a good possibility that you will have to ford a stream or river. The water obstacle may range from a small, ankle-deep brook to a tumultuous, snow or ice-fed river. If you know how to get by such an obstacle, you can often use the roughest of waters to your advantage.

However, before you enter the water, check its temperature. If it is bitingly cold and if a shallow fording spot can not be located, it will not be advisable to cross by fording. The cold water may easily cause a severe shock which could temporarily paralyze you. In this case, try to make an improvised bridge by felling a tree across the course, or build a simple raft.

Before you attempt to ford, move to high ground and examine the river for level stretches where it may break into a number of channels. Look for obstacles on the other side that might hinder your progress. Pick a spot on the opposite bank, if you can, where travel will be easier and safer. Watch out for a ledge or rocks that crosses the river, indicating the presence of rapids or other turbulence. Avoid heavy timber growths. These show where the channel is deepest.

When you select your fording site, keep the following points in mind. When possible, choose a course leading across the current at about a forty-five-degree angle downstream. Never try to ford a stream directly above or close to a deep or rapid waterfall or abrupt channel. Instead, always ford where you would be carried to a shallow bank or sandbar should you lose your footing.

Avoid rocky places, since a fall could cause serious injury at a time when you can't afford any such handicap. However, an occasional rock that breaks the current can be a help. Remember, except in still water the most shallow part is generally where the current is widest. Too, sheer banks are apt to continue their steepness beneath the water, while a gradual bank suggests the possibility of shoals.

A stout pole will be useful during the actual wading, both as a support against the tugging current and as an implement with which potholes can be avoided. Any pack, of course, you will want to hold loosely enough so that it can be rapidly shed if necessary.

If there is much of a flow, the most comfortable process will be to strip with the idea of holding the clothing high and thus keeping it dry. In all but the easiest going, though, you'll be wise to protect your feet by putting your boots back on. Wiped out when you're safely on the other side, they'll then be only briefly uncomfortable when put back on over dry socks.

Rafts

You will save strength, time, and rations by rafting down a stream whenever possible. However, everything is relative, and raft travel is normally slow, so still don't try to hurry. Rivers are the vast highways of many great wilderness areas.

Three long logs will make, for one man, a raft that can be poled or paddled with reasonable ease. A raft for three men, on the other hand, should be about twelve feet long and six feet wide, depending of course on the size of the logs available. Ideally, the logs should be from twelve to fourteen inches in diameter and well matched in size so that the notches you make in them will be level once the crosspieces are driven into place.

A knife and hatchet will complete the job which an ax will make even easier. Build the raft on two skid logs, placed so that they slope downward to the bank. Smooth these logs so that the raft timbers will lie evenly across them.

Cut two sets of slightly offset, inverted notches one in the top and bottom of both ends of each log. Make each of these notches broader at the base than on the outer edge of the log. Use a small pole with straight edges, or a taut string, to mark the notches. A three-sided wooden crosspiece, about a foot longer than the total width of the raft, is to be driven through each of the four sets of notches.

Complete the notches on the tops of all logs. Turn the logs over and drive a three-sided crosspiece through both sets of notches on the underside of the raft. Then finish the top sets of additional notches and drive through them the two extra crosspieces.

If you have the materials, you can lash together the outjutting ends of the pair of crosspieces at each end of the raft, giving the whole contrivance added

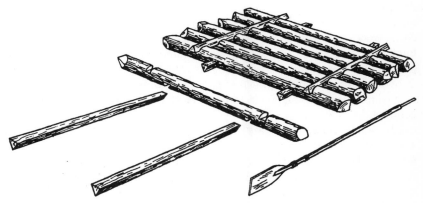

With just a knife, hatchet, and a few sturdy logs, you can build a raft to speed your travel.

Lash together the pair of crosspieces at each end to give your raft added strength.

strength. When the contraption is immersed in the water the crosspieces will swell and tightly bind the raft together even without this lashing.

However, if the crosspieces are found to be fitting too loosely, wedge them with thin, boardlike pieces of wood you have split from a dry log. When the raft is in the water, these will swell, fastening the cross members tightly and staunchly.

To keep the packs, the other gear, and your feet dry, make a deck of light poles on top of the raft. Now cut yourself a sweep, or, for shallow water, a pole.

Swimming

The breast-, back-, and sidestrokes will prove less exhausting than other swimming techniques and will permit you to carry small bundles of clothing and equipment. If possible, remove clothing and gear and float it across the river. Wade out until the water is chest deep before you commence swimming. If the stream is too deep to wade, jump in feet first with your body straight, keeping your legs together and your hands at your sides. In deep, swift water, swim diagonally across the stream with the current.

If you are unable to swim, try to find a dead log or other floating aid. Test it before you set out.

If you have something like a down sleeping bag, that will be highly buoyant. Otherwise, take off your trousers in the water. Knot each leg and fasten the fly. Grasp the waistband and swing the trousers over your head, from back to front, so that the waist opening is brought down hard on the surface. Air will be trapped in each leg. Or hold the trousers in front of you and jump into the water. Either of these methods provides a serviceable pair of water wings.

In an emergency, your trousers can serve as water wings.

Swimming in rapids or swift water is not as much of a problem as you may think. In shallow rapids, get on your back with your feet pointing downstream. Keep your body horizontal and your hands alongside your hips. Flap your hands much as a seal moves his flippers. In deep rapids, swim on your stomach and aim for shore whenever possible. Watch for converging currents whose swirls might suck you under.

SITTING IT OUT AND SIGNALLING

There are innumerable occasions when sitting out an emergency, as among three widely spaced signal fires on a subzero day, is preferable to trying to make it out on your own. But your chances of getting help will be markedly decreased, sometimes nearly to the point of nonexistence, if you don't make adequate signals.

If people know you're lost and generally where you are, a major trouble with trying to walk out—unless you're absolutely sure of both your direction and your capabilities—is that you may hike completely out of the search area.

If food or especially water is in short quantity, to boot, you'll do well to conserve your energy by moving about as little as possible. And if the weather is excessively hot or cold, you'll be best advised to stick to an improvised shelter, unless adequately clothed for the situation, and to set up signals.

If you're with a stranded automobile or downed plane, unless you're sure it is only a short distance to a frequented route or populated area, you should always stay with the vehicle. It's much easier to locate an airplane or automobile than an individual on foot.

Even then you'll need to signal, as is borne out by the frequency with which private planes in the United States and Canada, downed in winter usually in the mountains, are often not located until spring. An aircraft that has crashed or been forced to land will be easier to spot if highly reflecting or brightly colored objects are placed about it. Remember that any unusual sign or color contrast is visible from the air, even the tracks of one man in the snow.

Signalling with Fire

Three fires, or groups of three signals such as those possible with smoke, are international distress calls. As a matter of fact, if you are in one of the many forested areas where regular watches are maintained from towers and observation aircraft through most of the year, just a large fire, smoky in daylight, will bring aid in an emergency.

Otherwise, make your three signal fires at least one hundred feet apart if possible, either in a straight line or, for easier maintenance, in a rough triangle. If you are in trouble beside a pond or lake, though, it may be eminently

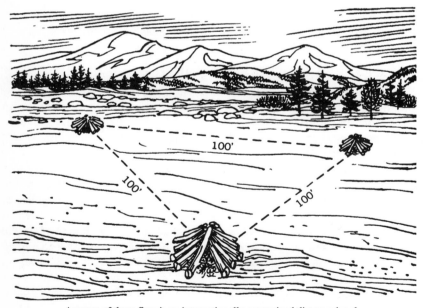

A group of three fires is an internationally recognized distress signal.

successful to build a raft and to have a fire ready to light on it whenever the sounds of aircraft manifest themselves.

The smoke from a signal fire can be invaluable for showing wind direction to the pilot of a rescue craft.

If there is any scarcity of fuel, or if because of a dwindling food supply you are husbanding your strength, it may be preferable to keep only your own small campfire going for warmth and companionship and to have three signal pyres, protected if necessary by bark from any rain or snow, ready for the torch.

If there is a thin cloud area, night fires will be diffused and not so readily visible from the air. But it will still be advisable to keep fires, as large as practical, burning.

Smoke

Fire making and the maintenance of fires have been considered at length in the section on that subject, but there is still the matter of smoke, so conspicuous during daylight hours if the weather is at all clear. If a low inversion above keeps the smoke in layers close to the ground, it is frequently possible when fuel is plentiful to get the smoke above it by kindling a larger fire than usual before adding the smoke-producing material.

Cut plenty of green boughs if they're available; when burning, they make a lot of smoke and a good signal. Evergreens are particularly efficacious in this respect, crackling readily and rapidly into black-smoking flame. A longer lasting smudge, effective against any biting insects as well, can be made by covering hot coals with wet dead leaves, damp green foliage, moist decayed wood, damp plane matting, slowly burning green wood, damp animal dung, and like materials.

Voluminous black smoke can be produced in a hurry with the oil from a disabled plane, cruiser, or even a small motorboat. This is one of the important reasons for a plane's oil to be drained in a cold environment before it congeals. It will then burn even when frozen.

Although with care oil can be thrown on a burning fire, this is not possible with gasoline, which ignites with such explosive fury that extreme caution must be exercised with it at all times. Even when it drenches an unlighted signal pyre with no live coals glowing nearby, at the moment of your tossing in a burning stick from what seems to be a safe distance you should stand upwind and turn your face away. Gasoline will burst violently into a sheet of flame, emitting intense black smoke. Burning rubber, too, either from tires or electrical insulation, gives off heavy black smoke. When water is used with discretion it will give you a white smoke.

With an ordinary single conflagration, not one powered with gasoline, you can still send up three puffs of smoke by momentarily cutting off the column, Indian fashion, by briefly holding a wet blanket over it.

You'll always make sure, of course, that you don't unintentionally start a forest fire; or on the plains, a grass fire.

Distress Signals

When you are signalling for help, no matter what your predicament, the most universally recognized distress signals are based on the number three; three fires, three smokes, three flashes; even to the three dots, three dashes, and three dots of the familiar SOS.

The international Morse code, most widely used throughout the world, follows. A knowledge of it, or just the plain following of this chart, will make it possible to send and receive messages by mirror, flashlight, whistle, smoke, flag, radio, and innumerable other contrivances including the primitive thumping of a hollow tree.

If you undertake to learn this code, and there are less productive ways of putting in time while husbanding your strength beside a campfire and waiting for help, you'll save time by thinking directly in terms of dahs and dits; that is, longs and shorts. The other way you'll hear two dahs, for example, and have to visualize two dashes before you identify it as the letter M. You'll save this intermediate step by learning directly the sounds of the various symbols.

International Morse Code

Intervals	Letters	Flag
short-long	A	right-left
long-short-short-short	B	left-right-right-right
long-short-long-short	C	left-right-left-right
long-short-short	D	left-right-right
short	E	right
short-short-long-short	F	right-right-left-right
long-long-short	G	left-left-right
short-short-short-short	H	right-right-right-right
short-short	I	right-right
short-long-long-long	J	right-left-left-left
long-short-long	K	left-right-left
short-long-short-short	L	right-left-right-right
long-long	M	left-left
long-short	N	left-right
long-long-long	O	left-left-left
short-long-long-short	P	right-left-left-right
lont-long-short-long	Q	left-left-right-left
short-long-short	R	right-left-right

short-short-short	S	right-right-right
long	T	left
short-short-long	U	right-right-left
short-short-short-long	V	right-right-right-left
short-long-long	W	right-left-left
long-short-short-long	X	left-right-right-left
long-short-long-short	Y	left-right-left-right
long-long-short-short	Z	left-left-right-right

Wigwag

Such signals can be identified for miles under good conditions, especially if the sender spots himself in a clear location, preferably against a contrasting background.

Your flag may be a white or brightly colored shirt, for instance, tied to the end of a light pole about six feet long. This can be most easily maneuvered if you'll hold the heavier end of the stick in a palm at waist level, then grip it some twelve to fourteen inches higher with your master hand.

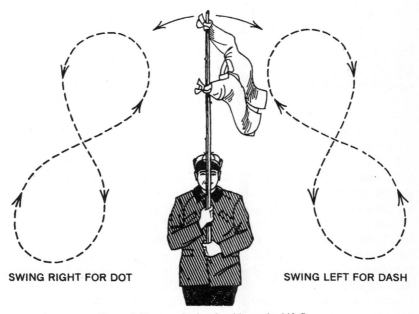

SWING RIGHT FOR DOT   **SWING LEFT FOR DASH**

Transmit Morse code signals with a makeshift flag.

Body Signals Recognized by Airmen. (1) Medical aid urgently needed. (2) Everything all right; don't wait. (3) Can proceed shortly; wait if possible. (4) Mechanical help or parts needed. (5) Pick me up. (6) Don't land here. (7) Land at spot pointed to. (8) Have working radio. (9) Affirmative signal.

All letters begin with the flag held straight upward. The dot is made by swinging the flag down to the right, then back up again. One way to remember this is that "right" has a dot over its *i*.

The dash is accomplished by swinging the flag in a similar arc to the left. You'll always want to keep the flag as flat as possible for better visibility, and the simplest way of doing this is to move it in tight loops. To send the letter *A*, for example, swing right and back to upright, then left and back to upright, in what is a narrow figure 8.

Always hold the flag upright for a moment to end any letter. Lower, then raise it, in front of you to end a word. Swinging left-right, left-right several times shows that the message is concluded. Common sense, not correctness of form, is the important factor in emergency signalling, of course. Just space your letters reasonably, and the receiver will make out enough of your message at least to understand it.

Mirrors

By using contrasting long and short flashes, the international Morse code can be sent by mirror. This, however, is not the mirror's most important function in an emergency. Limited only by the curvature of the earth, its flash is visible for miles.

A substantial mirror is a valuable asset to keep on your person whenever you're in the farther places. An armed forces emergency signalling mirror, still occasionally to be found for a few cents at surplus stores and obtainable around air bases, is rugged enough to be especially useful to keep in a pocket. Instructions for its use, if you forget them, are printed on the back. A small open cross or aperture in a screened target area facilitates aiming.

When you're trying to get the attention of the occupants of a plane that is no more than a right angle away from the sun, for example, hold a double-surfaced mirror three to six inches from your face and sight at the aircraft through the hole in the center of the mirror. Continuing to look at the plane through the center aperture, adjust the mirror until the spot of sunlight reflected from your face in the back mirror coincides with the mirror hole and disappears. The reflected light will now be accurately aimed at the plane. When the angle between aircraft and sun is more than ninety degrees, adjust the angle of the mirror until the reflection of the light spot on your hand behind the mirror coincides with the hole and disappears.

Stop flashing once an aircraft has definitely acknowledged your presence, except for an occasional flash if this seems necessary as a guide. From that point on, continued flashing may blind the pilot.

On hazy days a flier and his observer can often see the flash of a mirror before the survivors can spot the plane. So signal this way in the direction of any plane you can hear even when you cannot see it.

By reflecting a flashlight, such a signal can even be sent at night.

Substitute Mirrors

A reflecting surface of any sort whatsoever, even if it's only a peeled slab that is bright with moisture, can be used instead of a mirror. This is important, for such heliograph signals have probably effected more rescues than any other method. Some raft paddles and oars are coated with material that will reflect such a light in the darkness.

A flattened tin can, or even the shiny end of one, will provide an excellent substitute for a mirror. So will a sheet of foil. Just punch a small aiming hole in the center of either, while it's lying on a flat surface, use as instructed for a regular mirror, and you'll be well away.

Whistle

A metal or plastic whistle, the louder the better, is especially handy for signalling in far country. Mothers can do worse than hang police whistles around the necks of the younger members of the family. Even the venerable Hudson's Bay Company includes two such whistles in their survival kits.

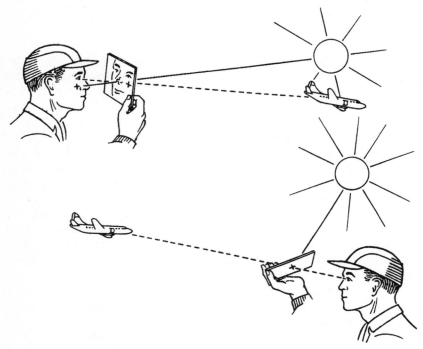

A mirror's flash can be seen by the occupants of a plane miles away.

PART FOUR
WEATHER OR NOT: NATURE'S WEATHER SIGNS AND COPING WITH EXTREMES

CHAPTER NINE

LEARNING NATURE'S WEATHER SIGNS

Knowing what nature and the woods are saying about the weather is a skill essential to feeling and staying at home in the wilds.

Despite the innumerable legends that have built up around them over the centuries, animals are worthless as long-term weather forecasters. Their actions, however, often give a clue to the immediate climate.

Spiders show a most delicate apprehension of what weather conditions will be within the next few hours. When the day is to be fair and comparatively windless, they will spin long filaments over which they scout persistently. When precipitation is imminent, they shorten and tighten their snares and drowse dully in their centers. One of the best fair-weather signs is the familiar profusion of fresh webs over grass and shrubbery.

Insects are especially annoying before a storm. At such times they also cling vexingly to shelter canvas and to the screened windows of log cabins.

Insects also do not fly as high as usual when bad weather is breeding, a fact you can verify by the heights at which the birds that feed on them soar. Swallows are especially good indicators.

If bees are swarming, fair weather will continue for at least the next half-day.

CLUES FROM ANIMAL BEHAVIOR

Elk particularly have built-in barometers. In the fall they will migrate suddenly out of high country just before heavy snows cover their feed and block the passes.

In moose and deer country, you can tell when a big storm is on the way by the unusually heavy feeding activity. The animals then lie up in cover until the bad weather is nearly over, whereupon they again feed vigorously.

In the snowy north, the wilderness becomes alive with tracks, and both wild and domestic animals become youthfully frisky before a chinook, the hot, dry west wind that sometimes lifts temperatures close to 100° within an hour and which the Indians call "snow eater."

161

But long-term weather proverbs involving the animal kingdom are just so much fiction. Goose bones or, for that matter, the thickness of hickory shells, have no bearing on what the weather will be. As far as that goes, neither does the thickness of fur. The depth of a bear's den means nothing weatherwise. And when bruin emerges earlier than usual in the spring, only to return to his bed, it doesn't indicate more wintry weather, but merely that there is not yet enough food to satisfy his huge appetite.

If the groundhog does not see his shadow on February 2, winter is not necessarily over. When squirrels lay in heavy caches of food, it does not follow that a severe winter will ensue.

Night birds call every night, although it is true that their sound carries farther just before a storm. Other birds, such as waterfowl, cannot sense the weather more than a few hours ahead, or so many thousands would not be entrapped and killed by storms or by returning north too far in advance of the tardy spring.

OTHER NATURAL SIGNS

There are certain time-tested and accurate signs by which the woodsman, especially when he balances one against another, can forecast the immediate weather. However, two companion proverbs should always be considered. In dry weather all signs fail. In wet weather it rains without half trying.

When campfire or cabin smoke, after lifting a short distance with the heated air, beats downward, it is a sign of approaching storm. On the other hand, steadily rising smoke prognosticates fair weather.

A red sun or sky in the morning indicates nearing rain. When forest fires are burning, this effect can be deceptive because of smoke. The redness, however, is still deepened by the telltale presence of excessive moisture in the atmosphere.

A red evening sky shows that the air contains so little moisture that rain within the next twenty-four hours is highly improbable.

A gray, overcast evening sky shows that the moisture-carrying dust particles in the atmosphere have become so overloaded with water that conditions favor rain.

A gray morning sky, implying dry air above the haze caused by the collection of dew on the dust in the lower atmosphere, justifies the expectation of a fair day.

When sudden green light slants from the late afternoon sun as it sinks behind a clear horizon, fair weather is probable for at least the next twenty-four hours.

A rainbow late in the afternoon indicates fair weather ahead. However, rainbow in the morning, woodsman, take warning.

A corona is the circle that appears around the sun or moon when either shines through clouds. When this corona grows larger and larger, it shows that the drops of water in the atmosphere are evaporating and that the weather probably will be clear. When a corona shrinks by the hour, it means that the water drops in the clouds are becoming so large that rain is almost sure to fall.

When the breeze is such that leaves show their undersides, a storm is in the offing.

When you are in the mountains, the sight of morning mist rising from ravines is an excellent sign of clear weather.

In fair weather, as any hunter can tell you, air currents flow down streams and hillsides in the early morning. They start drifting back towards sunset. Any reversal of these directions warns of a nearing storm.

The higher the clouds, the better the weather. Prospects are even finer when scattered clouds, preferably decreasing in numbers, are separated by brilliant clear blue. The combining of clouds, especially in a milky sky, does not augur so well.

A night sky alive with stars is a good sign. Except near the coast where fog may give a deceptive picture, when only a few stars gleam the clear weather is about over.

When thin but tight cloud cover slowly blankets the moon, the spell of fair weather is coming to an end.

Dew and frost occur abundantly only when the atmosphere is such that rain and snow can scarcely fall. On calm nights, one or the other, depending on the season, fails to form only when conditions favor precipitation.

Anyone who has a touch of rheumatism can forecast approaching bad weather by the onset of increasing discomfort.

When sound travels more distinctly, and you are able to hear distant noises such as woodchopping more clearly, stormy weather is coming.

You also can smell an approaching storm in that ground, swamp, muskeg, and tideland smells become more noticeable.

Another sign of the approaching storm is the increase of high wind and its gradual extension to lower and lower air, causing the forest to murmur and the mountains to roar.

As the air grows damper and stormy weather comes nearer, canvas, hemp rope, and ax heads tighten; camp salt picks up moisture; and curly hair, whether in humans or animals, becomes more unruly.

Clouds

When moist air is cooled, water molecules condense on dust and other particles in the atmosphere. As more and more of these molecules collect, they form drops of water. When enough of these drops float together, they combine into a cloud.

Still other clouds, massing together at subfreezing heights, are made up of ice.

Clouds provide the most accurate signposts for wilderness weather forecasting. It is necessary to keep watching them, however. Even more important than momentarily predominant cloud formations is the way they change.

Cumulus

Cumulus clouds are fair weather clouds. Clear nights usually follow days when cumulus clouds drift dramatically and picturesquely through the sky.

Cumulus clouds, which grow as warmed air soars skyward until its water vapor cools into drops of moisture, heap themselves into flat-bottomed piles. Towards evening, when this process slows, they become small or even non-existent. At their heights, they measure from about a thousand feet to more than a mile thick from puffy tops to flattened bases.

Fractocumulus

Being formed when strong overhead gales blow the fluffy cumulus clouds into shreds that hurtle across the heavens, fractocumulus clouds indicate the presence of high wind. Their speed helps distinguish them from younger clouds that have not yet reached maturity. In late afternoon when the winds die with the setting of the sun, fractocumulus formations also ebb away to leave a clear fair sky.

Stratocumulus

Although light showers may slant down from stratocumulus clouds, these formations generally thin to cumulus or fractocumulus by the middle afternoon and later disappear entirely, leaving a clear night sky. They also form at sunset when cumulus clouds blend into one another before dissipating. Spreading in irregular patches or layers, stratocumulus clouds are not as fluffy as cumulus.

Stratus

Stratus clouds of themselves often bring light drizzle but seldom rain. When thin stratus clouds form during the night to cover the morning sun, they usually mean a warm clear day.

Stratus clouds are layers of water particles, flat on top as well as bottom. When one approaches, its edge appears to be nearly straight and almost equally thick throughout. Although some are small, others cover all that can be seen of the sky. Thickness varies, too, from almost a quarter of a mile to a few, sun-filtered feet.

The high coastal fogs of California, Maine, and Newfoundland, made by the mixture of cold and of warm moist air above the mingling ocean currents, are stratus clouds that form close to a thousand feet above the surface of the Earth and thicken downward. Such fogs customarily dissipate in sunlit skies.

However, pure stratus is the predominant cloud when the center of a low-pressure area is approaching. When this is the case, the stratus generally gives way to the denser nimbostratus, which is characterized by rain or snow. When the low is passing, the nimbostratus may revert again to stratus or to the wind-churned fractostratus. This latter usually disappears to leave a clear sky alive with cirrus tufts.

Nimbostratus

Nimbostratus clouds in three out of four instances indicate rain or snow within four or five hours. The duration of such storms varies, but in winter snow often lines down from them for about eight hours.

Cumulus Cloud

Fractocumulus Clouds

Stratocumulus Clouds

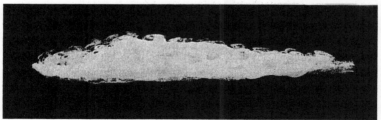

Stratus Cloud

These layers of gray rain or snow clouds, darkening the day, many times sheet the sky for miles. Although their average height is about 3,500 feet, some almost scrape the treetops, while others soar nearly three miles high. Rags of clouds that move beneath them, dangling like torn remnants, are known as scud.

Cirrus

When the sky is brilliantly blue above cirrus, the clouds will probably dissipate during the morning, leaving clear skies. This happens when the heat of the forenoon sun, attacking the floating ice of these clouds which form some five to seven miles above the earth, changes them again to vapor.

Cirrus clouds resemble thin curls and wisps of soft hair. Some are straightened by the wind except for a twirl at one end, while others are filigreed in silvery nets that nearly enclose the sky. Those that are blown into wispy streaks are called mares' tails.

Cirrostratus

When the sky is grayish above cirrus, the clouds likely will thicken to cirrostratus, as rain or snow is probably on the move. Cirrostratus clouds almost always indicate that a storm is no more than a day away.

Cirrostratus clouds, which are made up of ice particles, look like white veils, often decorated with milky streaks and patches. Shining hazily through them, both the sun and moon form misty rings of light known as halos. These clouds may float as high as the loftiest cirrus, but the biggest and densest of them usually are no more than about 18,000 feet above the ground.

Altostratus

As the storm area approaches, the cirrostratus clouds thicken and lower to altostratus which either completely hide the sun and moon or let their light through in shapeless blobs. Altostratus clouds look like gray or dull blue haze, banded or spotted with thick streaks or patches. The rain or snow that usually follows generally is steady but not very hard. These clouds range in height from some two to three and one half miles.

Cirrocumulus

Cirrocumulus clouds are almost always a sign of fair weather. They commonly appear the first or second morning following a storm, usually dissolving that forenoon to leave a flawless, deeply azure sky.

So-called mackerel skies, resembling the patterns on this fish's back, are the result of floating rows of cirrocumulus. Being made of ice, inasmuch as they form at heights of from three to five miles, cirrocumulus clouds are about midway between puffy cumulus and wispy cirrus. They are seen near cirrus and cirrostratus. They are so thin and shadowless that diffused sunlight beams through them cheerily.

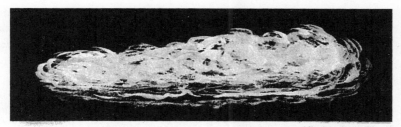

Nimbostratus Cloud

Cirrus Cloud

Cirrostratus Cloud

Altocumulus

The altocumulus is another fair weather cloud, usually showing itself on the first day following a storm or forming above the breaking stratus. However, when these clouds take on the aspect of towers and castles, they generally mean that showers will be arriving in eight hours.

These small, high, white clouds often tag one another so closely that the sky seems packed with tightly massed white mounds. Floating from one to four miles high, they are sometimes assailed by up-and-down currents that divide them into flakes resembling those of a mackerel sky. The lower portions of these clouds often are gray, however, and the larger ones run their shadows across the ground.

Cumulonimbus

These towering piles of rain clouds, usually forming on moist hot days, often cause hail as well as rain. Since they contain lightning and thunder as well, they are commonly called thunderheads, even when they do not result in precipitation.

Thunderheads start out as puffy cumulus clouds some 2,000 feet above the earth, piling and towering into dramatically ominous heaps up to seven miles high. When these gleaming white masses are toward the southwest, they can be expected to approach steadily, darkening to blue, purple, and even green, as they do so. Sheets of rain often can be seen in the distance. Then the day suddenly chills and darkens.

Afterwards, the precipitation abruptly slackens. The thunder again becomes a distant rumble. Fresh wind, cool and invigorating, blows out of the west.

Being in the wilderness during the height of the most spectacular thunder storm of the season is far less dangerous than driving downtown to the store. Taking certain precautions will lessen even this very small amount of peril.

Although it is natural to seek shelter from the rain, the worst refuge you can pick is a tall, isolated tree. Small evergreen growth offers much better, as well as comparatively safe, protection. So does a cave or a niche among overhanging rocks. If you come upon a barn, stay out of it, as the mass of dry, warm air within invites the passage of electrical bolts. It is best to lay down such natural lightning rods as metal fishing rods. If you are caught in the open, your safest procedure will be to lie flat.

HOW TO READ A BAROMETER

A small aneroid (without fluid) barometer, whose rising needle is so handy for prognosticating the best fishing days, can be of considerable help in weather forecasting when you are away from newspapers and radios.

Unless you are traveling particularly light, a good one is a wise addition to most wilderness outfits. The following facts will help you read it in the United States and Canada.

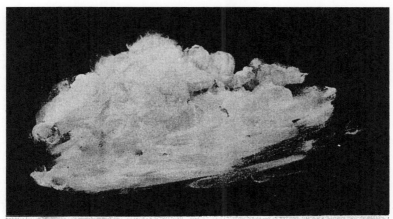

Altostratus Cloud

Cirrocumulus Clouds

Altocumulus Cloud

Cumulonimbus Cloud

Barometer	Wind	Weather
High, steady	S.W. to N.W.	Fair with little temperature change for one to two days
High, rising rapidly	S.W. to N.W.	Fair with warmer weather and rain within two days
High, falling rapidly	E. to N.E.	Summer: rain in 12 to 24 hrs. Winter: snow or rain with increasing wind
Very high, falling slowly	S.W. to N.W.	Fair, with slowly rising temperatures, for two days
High, falling rapidly	S. to S.E.	Rain, with increasing wind, in 12 to 24 hrs.
High, falling slowly	S. to S.E.	Rain within 24 hrs.

High, falling slowly	E. to N.E.	Summer: light winds, fair Winter: precipitation in 24 hrs.
High, falling slowly	S.W. to N.W.	Rain within 24 to 36 hrs.
Low, rising rapidly	Shifting to W.	Colder and clearing
Low, rising slowly	S. to S.W.	Clearing soon and fair for several days
Low, falling slowly	S.E. to N.E.	Rain for one or two more days
Low, falling rapidly	E. to N.	Northeast winds with heavy rain or snow, followed in winter by cold

GAUGING WIND SPEED

The wind, the moisture content of the air, and the sun all make weather. Of these, the wind is many times the most interesting, especially in the wilderness. When you are bucking it in a canoe or trying to keep out of the way of toppling branches, you often wonder exactly how fast it is blowing. The following table will then be of use:

Beaufort Scale	Wind Velocity (mph)	Air	Signs
0	0–1	Calm	Smoke rises straight up
1	1–3	Light air	Wind direction shown by drifting smoke, but not by waves
2	4–7	Slight breeze	Wind felt on face, leaves rustle, ordinary waves moved by wind
3	7–12	Gentle breeze	Leaves and twigs move constantly, flag extends
4	13–18	Moderate breeze	Dust and small branches are moved
5	19–24	Fresh breeze	Small-leafed trees start to sway
6	25–31	Strong breeze	Large branches move
7	32–38	Moderate gale	Whole trees in motion
8	39–46	Fresh gale	Twigs break off; hard to walk
9	47–54	Strong gale	Slight structural damage occurs
10	55–63	Whole gale	Trees uprooted, considerable structural damage
11	64–72	Storm	Widespread damage, very rarely experienced
12	73 up	Hurricane	Devastation occurs

CHAPTER TEN

COPING WITH HEAT AND COLD

Staying warm or keeping cool, whichever difficulty besets you at the moment, is the third most important challenge in successfully living, which includes enjoying yourself, in any remote region. Once you have proved to your own inner satisfaction that you can take, with the barest possible minimum of gear, whatever the elements have to offer, you come to realize—the wiser you are the quicker—that the real requirement is learning to smooth it. After all, we get it rough enough in the ever tightening tentacles of civilization.

COLD-WEATHER CAMPING

When wraiths of mist, which the Hudson's Bay Company men call the ghosts of departed voyageurs, began coursing down the Peace River the first winter I stayed in the Subarctic Forest, I was ready for hibernation. Oatmeal sacks, both for my pack dog and myself, bulged plumply in the newly readied cache by my log cabin. Moose quarters, marbled with fat, promised many a steak and savory roast. Glancing through the whiteness at stacks of split poplar and lodgepole pine, I stirred my cookstove fire with more satisfaction than ever.

I wasn't planning to get very far outdoors in weather so frigid that an individual's spittle was reputed to congeal between mouth and ground and if, when lost, you stopped walking around a tree all night, they'd have to sharpen your frozen body to drive it into the earth to bury it. Besides, what about drinking water? Everything would be thick with snow, and I'd heard that snow is something a thirsty man should shy away from for, besides making him more parched than ever, it's for some reason downright hazardous to eat in cold weather.

Of course, I didn't go for that frozen saliva legend. This would require more than a 60° temperature drop between lips and the ground. As for the other things, well, like most of us, I'd been hearing them all my life, along with what passes as other cold-weather lore. Such as how to thaw a frostbitten

172

ear by rubbing it with snow, and about shoving a frozen foot into some cold liquid like kerosene that's been kept outdoors. And about bundling up in lots of heavy clothing to stay alive when the colored alcohol in the thermometer falls an inch or more below zero; and how if you fall asleep on a log in such cold, you're not going to awaken this side of paradise.

Dangerous is something cold-weather camping very definitely is not. This kind of venture is in many ways actually the most comfortable and pleasant you can enjoy. There are no troublesome insects, and the litterbugs and ribbon clerks are back where the steam heat is sizzling.

The wilderness is wide open. There's a wonderfully lonesome wail to the wind. You can see everything that's going on around you during this marvelously unobstructed time of year. Not only that, but at your feet is tracked the record of what has happened not long before. To have a good time, though, you've got to go at it the right way, but that's easy. Let's have a look at some of the honest facts.

Snow

One of the very real luxuries of the winter outdoors is that a drink of water is as near as your hand. As you prospect, track, or progress along, you can at any time scoop up a handful of snow. The only precaution that need be taken is to treat it like ice cream and not put down too much when you're overheated or chilled. Aside from that, clean snow can be safely eaten whenever you are thirsty in the bush.

Dangerous? Why? Wilderness snows, after all, afford in flake form the purest of distilled water from the atmosphere. The only disadvantage is that it takes a lot to equal even a small amount of water. This drawback is more than made up for, though, by the fact that snowfall makes water quickly available through the wild places, an invaluable advantage inasmuch as we need a lot more water in freezing weather than one might suppose—at least two quarts a day—for the kidneys then have to take over much of the process of eliminating waste materials otherwise handled by the sweat glands. Snow used for drinking water, far from being harmful, is therefore an extremely healthful convenience.

Frostbite

The same sort of good judgment can be applied to the widely reiterated nonsense that the way to thaw a frozen ear is to rub it with snow. First of all, thawing frozen flesh by friction is apt to compound the damage by tearing the sensitized area. Second, rubbing the ear with snow under such conditions is like reaching up right now and scrubbing it with gravel.

To thaw a frozen ear on the trail, press a warm hand over it. To thaw a frostbitten finger, shove it under a warm armpit. To thaw a foot that has started to freeze, usually a totally unnecessary emergency, build a fire if you can do so quickly. Otherwise, keeping as well covered as you can, hold it against a warm part of the body, such as directly against the bare thigh. If a companion is with you, the thing to do, if he will agree, is to thrust it against his bare abdomen. The warm body cavity of a freshly killed animal can also afford a solution.

Don't ever make the terrible error of trying to thaw a part of the body by immersing it in a liquid such as oil or gasoline that has been stored at subzero temperatures. Although far colder than 32°F., these and other fluids have sometimes been used in the disastrous belief that because they were not frozen, they were just the things to use to painlessly thaw something else.

Freezing, like every potential danger in the wilderness, isn't actually much of a threat to an experienced individual except as it may result from accidents. Against these we habitually take simple but ample precautions. Our own in-bred ingenuity and resourcefulness, stimulated by the instinct for survival, care for the rest. Besides, as has been said, a man sits as many risks as he runs.

Among the many prospectors, trappers, sportsmen, outfitters, loggers, and other outdoorsmen among whom I've lived for years, often in primitive wilderness where the population averages less than one human for every dozen square miles and where temperatures fall 100°F. below freezing, no one I know personally has ever been incapacitated or even seriously bothered by freezing. Do you know what's really the greatest cause of accidental death in the snowy regions? Another case of opposites: it's not cold at all, but fire.

Keeping Warm

"Bundle up in lots of heavy clothes. It's cold outside," may be good advice for the city, but it's another thing that can kill you in the Far North. An error to avoid, no matter what, is the extremely common mistake on the part of the newcomer of dressing too warmly in subzero weather. Excessive sweating should be avoided by every reasonable means during the northern frigidity, if only because it undermines insulation efficiency. The amount of sweating that goes on at all times is heightened by clothing that is warmer than necessary. If the garments do not allow sufficient ease of movement and if they are not un-restricting enough to permit the escape of this dampness, the perspiration can freeze inside the garb in subzero weather. The consequences will be, at the very least, uncomfortable; at worst, it can lessen the amount of insulation enough to kill you.

It is therefore imperative that on those days when one needs a twelve-inch thermometer with zero at the top, he should avoid sweating too profusely. All this is a major reason why, for the typical outdoorsman, the layer system is best in cold country. In the morning chill, which actually deepens at sunrise because of the breezes stirred by the lifting of the sun, many like to leave camp wearing everything reasonable. Whether on the tundra or high in the mountains, the practice is to continue shedding layers of clothing as the sun soars higher and storing them in a packsack. It is always best to anticipate personal warmth variations, to open clothing before you'd otherwise begin to sweat, and to close it again before you actually feel chilly.

The neatest undercover trick for cold-country comfort lies in some of the recently developed insulative underwear. You should still don net underwear next to your skin, however; ideally, this should be ⅜ of an inch or larger square mesh, about ⅛ inch thick, and entirely open like a fishnet. Much smaller holes, as well as the familiar waffle-weave undersuits, do not permit the necessary evaporation to take place.

No matter what you wear, the garments as a whole should be sufficient to give you an average thickness that will be adequate according to both temperature and your particular rate of metabolism. With correctly designed cold-weather clothing and the best of the new down or synthetic underwear, you can wear your maximum thickness throughout the day and ventilate any excess heat from inside it.

When you find that you are wearing too much at the moment, uncover that most efficient heat radiator you have, your head. If this isn't enough, open your neck and, if necessary, your front to let out the heat accumulating at the torso. The wrists and hands are next on the ventilating scale. The veins that are closest to the surface on the underneath of your wrist make these effective radiators. In addition, by permitting air to move up the arms, you are cooling the armpits which are one of the foremost heat-producing regions of the human system.

The final source of ventilation is the legs. The general practice, often necessary because of deep snow, is to leave them very lightly insulated. Although this generally works, it increases the tendency toward cold feet by dropping the blood temperature as it travels down the exposed limbs—the solution to which may be two sets of heavy woolen socks and a pair of lightweight thermal boots.

Falling Asleep and Freezing

One of the commonest and most dangerous of the many false notions surrounding the subject of cold-weather camping is the persistent notion that if caught out overnight in very cold weather, you shouldn't let yourself fall asleep, or you'll freeze and never awaken.

That chestnut, which a good many people took the trouble to pass along when they heard I was going to live in the North Woods, had me so apprehensive for awhile that I found myself not caring even to relax too comfortably on a log during the day for more than a couple of minutes. When you stop to think it over, however, you'll see as I did, and as I went to the trouble of personally proving for the good of my soul, that the precise opposite is true.

To put it briefly, passing over the obvious effects to be expected from excessive perspiring and from exhaustion, the only way the human system can

manufacture the warmth needed to offset cold is by burning calories. The reserve of these energy units readily available for this need will be greatly lessened if, as many advise, we consume them by aimlessly hiking around a tree all night.

The ideal, if you are caught out unprepared, is to get a campfire going and then to lie on something waterproof between it and its reflected warmth. The next best procedure is to hole up while dry and fresh in as sheltered a spot as you can find, to curl or hunch on something such as bark or boughs, and to relax.

If you do fall asleep, the increasing coldness will finally awaken you. You may stir around just enough to get warm, which is frequently all one does at home, and then relax again and maybe grab another strength-conserving nap. From a perspiration-chilled sleep of exhaustion that too many times is the result of trying to keep going, there is often no awakening.

Cold-weather camping lives longer in our memories than most done in the milder seasons, as I confirmed that first northern year and reaffirmed during many afterward.

DESERT ACCLIMATIZATION

The low humidity in desert country is an advantage in that it makes the body seem cooler by evaporating the moisture that is always being excreted through your pores, even when you do not seem to be perspiring. It is a disadvantage in that you need more water to continue this function and, even though you do not seem to be thirsty, you should continue to drink small amounts of water frequently.

To keep body heat at its lowest and thus conserve this water, wear loose, light-colored clothing, which will reflect the heat better, and a wide-brimmed hat, preferably with a chin strap so that it will not be blown off and dangerously lost. Again, a light-colored hat reflects the heat more efficiently. A high crown, not fashionably dented, provides functional air space. Ventilation, provided by air holes in the crown near the top, is very helpful. Although a straw hat passes the test for ventilation, it will give no protection from wind and infrequent rain, nor will it long withstand the necessary rigors to which it must be subjected. In any event, keep the head covered from the bludgeoning sun, even if this covering is only fabric or extra clothing held in place as securely as necessary by a lace or cord.

It has been proved that a fully clothed individual will remain cooler than one who is only partially clothed. This may be extended to sleeves, although, like everything else, they should be loose and as well ventilated as possible. Avoid, too, coming into any more contact than necessary with hot objects and seek shade whenever possible.

As the U.S. Air Force recommends, "Take a lesson from the Arab. He is not *surviving* on the desert. He lives there and likes it. He isn't lazy. He's just living in slow motion, the way the desert makes him live." Slow and steady, in other words, does it on a hot desert. When you move about in the heat, you'll last longer on less water if you take it easy.

It is the custom among desert inhabitants to keep their tents open on all sides during the light of the day to permit free circulation of air. Sit or lie a few inches above the rocks and sand if this is at all possible, for it can be 30° to 40° cooler above the desert floor.

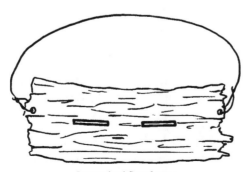

Improvised Sunglasses

Sunglasses in the Desert

Sunglasses are such a necessity against the glare that, in a pinch, you should make substitutes by slitting bark or fabric and holding them in place by a cord around the temples and the back of the head. As far as seeing is concerned, if you are unaccustomed to desert travel, triple your estimates of distance, as both the clear dry air and the relative absence of terrain features are apt to make underestimations probable.

Desert Footwear

Although you will be avoiding loose sand and rough terrain whenever possible, which requires following the hard valleys or ridges among sand dunes, care of your feet is essential. In a pinch, you can cross sand dunes barefoot in cool weather, but during the summer the sand will burn your feet.

Dependable low boots with composition soles, the same that are recommended for general travel, are a necessity. Hard leather is slippery on the rocky desert and, as if this were not enough, wears out too quickly. For short excursions only, rubber-soled sneakers, preferably one of the ankle-supporting and -protecting varieties, will do. So, too, will the rubber-soled leather boot when laced loosely so that the air will squish in and out. The usual high-heeled western cowboy boots are, among other shortcomings, too slippery.

Sandstorm Protection

If a sandstorm should blow up, take shelter at the earliest possible moment. Mark your direction with an arrow of stones, lie down with your back to the gale, cover your nose and mouth with a cloth, and try to sleep through the spectacle.

If possible, seek shelter in the lee of a hill. Don't worry about being buried by the sand. In fact, it's recommended that when necessary you get some protection from the sun by covering your body with sand. Burrowing in the sand also reduces water loss, while its pressure affords valuable physical relief to tired muscles.

In extreme situations, if at all possible scoop out an east-west trench several feet deep, as the temperature at the bottom of this may be as much as a dramatic 100° lower than that on the desert floor. A shovel should be in your outfit for desert travel.

Gloves in the Desert

Because nearly everything on the desert is sharp, pointed, thorny, rough, dusty, or hot, a pair of heavy, flexible, and preferably leather gloves that are stout enough to withstand cacti are pretty much a must.

Cold on the Desert

Especially on the high North American deserts, it can get downright cold when the sun goes below the horizon, and a fleecy woolen shirt or, preferably, a lightweight down jacket will be needed. If goose down encased in nylon is selected, the garment will be both more versatile and warmer in relation to weight.

Elastic knit cuffs are effective to seal off the wrist openings, and a hooded top, even when the hood is not used, is warmer about the neck. Without it, I would substitute a small woolen scarf. For utmost efficiency in warmth, use a waist belt.

Lightweight nylon fabrics and metal snaps tend to tear loose. Although I formerly was a staunch supporter of snaps on all outdoor wear, I have used one of the improved nylon zippers on my Gerry jacket for several years. Each half of the zipper is made of a single strand of heavy-gauge monofilament, making it virtually impossible for a tooth to break or for the material to be torn if it is accidentally caught in the mechanism.

PART FIVE
CANOE TRIPS AND PACK TRAINS: WILDERNESS TRAVEL ON YOUR OWN

CHAPTER ELEVEN

PADDLING YOUR OWN CANOE

There is a heady elixir smoking from this bottle. Sniff it? Smells like balsam,
doesn't it? And a river. Hear the wind? It swishes in the pines. See the fire embers
glow. The sleeping bag is warm. Hear the rapids gurgle. They will sing all night long.
—Bradford Angier and Zack Taylor
Introduction to Canoeing

"To have commanded the paddle, tasted the wind, and challenged the river—one
would have believed that the splendor of God's wilderness is reserved for the canoeist.
My own load, including canoe, extra clothing, blanket-bed, two days' rations,
rod and knapsack, never exceeded 76 pounds, and I went prepared to camp out any
and every night. . . . My canoe is my yacht, as it would be if I were a millionaire."
—George Washington Sears, 1888
(The legendary "Nessmuk")

With a light canoe and outfit, one or two individuals can today go far back of
beyond for several months at a time by living largely off the land with rod,
gun (where one is legal), and edible wild fruits and vegetables.

So it goes. Man dueling with nature, taming mighty streams. More than
that, triumph! There is something in everybody that cries out for the chance to
pit brains and brawn against what can be merciless and deadly. That's what
canoeing is all about.

Is the medicine taking? Want to try it? Here's how, told as one will travel
out there—lean and spare.

WHICH CANOE?

This continent's Indians developed bark canoes, the forerunners of the
present water craft which have never been equalled in their universal efficiency for stream and lake travel, by using chestnut, elm, cedar, spruce, hickory and birch barks. The toughness, pliability, and lightness of birch bark
soon proved it best for the purpose.

183

Today the elegant, responsive, relatively safe and rugged, and easily maintained aluminum canoe merits the satisfaction that keeps it outselling all other canoes in the United States by five to one. Most popular in Canada, though, and accounting there for four out of every five sales, is the canvas-covered, cedar-strip canoe. And then there's fiberglass. All the exciting new canoe shapes—slimmer, lower freeboard, faster, easier to control in wind, sleek, and beautiful—are fiberglass.

If you want durability, buy aluminum. For speed and easy handling, get the competitively priced plastic craft, always wary of so-called *budget* canoes. For tradition and beauty, the canvas-and-wood crafts are supreme. In any event, purchase only the best, as a good canoe never depreciates more than about fifty percent. And so the debate goes on, but whatever choice the American or Canadian finally makes, one thing is certain—the North American backwoods are filled with canoeing waters to satisfy every taste!

WHICH PADDLE?

It all starts with the painstakingly selected canoe, by means of which we can invade the deep wilderness for weeks at a time with more of an outfit than it would be possible to carry any other way than by pack animal. Second comes the paddle.

In all active sports, the difference between a good and an inept performance often starts with the choice of the specific tool that is essential to the activity. With canoeing, it's the paddle that is all-important, particularly since during the usual day of cruising the ordinary North American outdoorsman will average about a stroke every two seconds, 30 a minute, 1,000 an hour, and close to 15,000 during a bracing day. This works out to something less than 500 strokes an average mile.

There is one beguiling fact, gleaned from the Indians. A short, quick stroke covers more miles with less effort than the more customary pace of some 25 to 30 strokes a minute. Try increasing the stroke to more like one every 1½ seconds. Accomplishing this, the Indian centers his power in the first portion of the stroke. The strength he exerts falls off rapidly once the paddle is opposite his side, and he ends the stroke quickly after this point is passed. Actually, with a sufficiently limber paddle, the swing of the blade and shaft will do much to shoot the paddle forward for the next stroke, and there should be a short surge of renewed power immediately before the blade leaves the water.

No matter what the technique, the paddle balance, shape, grip, weight, material, finish and, particularly, length are especially important. Initially, the paddle should fit the job, whether for bow or for stern. For work forward in the canoe, where little if any steering will ordinarily be done, the paddle should reach from the floor to the chin when the standing canoeist holds it upright. The stern paddle should be at least eye high. There are those, too, who like this master paddle in particular to be a couple of inches longer than standard depending largely on the lines of the specific canoe.

The most important thing about a canoe paddle is seldom mentioned. That is, the paddle should be long enough so that the user does not have to curve his back downward for the stroke. Basic canoe paddling is done by swinging the hips and shoulders so that the big muscles of the legs and back do the work smoothly. What is not wanted is hunching at every stroke. If you paddle kneeling, the correct paddle length for you will be different than if you stroke from a seat.

A third paddle for possible emergency use in every two-man canoe, a second if you are alone, should be included. It's easy to lose a paddle and possible to break one, and this spare should be carried handily under the load lashings where it may be grasped in an instant. If two individuals are about the same height, the length of the spare can well be a compromise between chin and eye measurements.

The canoe will travel faster and answer steerage demands quicker with a wide paddle. Conversely, it takes more power and endurance to draw a wide paddle through the water than it does to handle the often sufficient narrow blade. The actual widths in the stores today generally run between 5½ and 8 inches. By the way, if one of the blades selected is wider than the other, it should be in the stern paddle. When it comes to handling a paddle, much will depend on your own muscles and physical condition. The American Indians preferred the less tiring narrow blades.

Because of potential slipperiness and blisters, it's a sound idea to take any finish off the grips and shafts with sandpaper and if necessary a hardware-store solvent, leaving the original varnish to protect the blade. Thoroughly soak the wood that has been bared so as to raise the grain. This should then be sanded smooth. Continue until the wood remains smooth after soaking. Once everything is again dry, slick the hands with linseed oil and rub this into the shaft and grip. Backwoodsmen to whom this may not be readily available sometimes use bear oil instead, but the drawback to this is that it makes the wood more appetizing to gnawing porcupines, mice, and their compadres.

CANOEING BASICS

Most people fear the possibility of capsizing in a canoe, and it can certainly happen. In the normal sitting position, on the seats, the center of gravity is probably higher than in any other boat and, of course, the canoe shape with its roundness can go over easily.

However, if the paddler sits on the bottom as in C1 and C2 canoes and kayaks as well as in the tiniest canoes, the center of gravity will go well below where the center-point of the roll is located and stability will be increased remarkably. This teaches one fast lesson. In any rough water or weather, get off

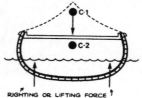

LOW CENTER OF GRAVITY
KNEELING — PADDLING
C-1 IS CENTER OF GRAVITY
C-2 IS THE CENTER OF LATERAL STABILITY
SINCE THE TWO ARE CLOSE IT IS HARD TO CAPSIZE
BOAT.

RIGHTING OR LIFTING FORCE

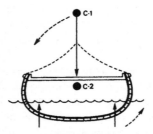

HIGH CENTER OF GRAVITY
WHEN MAN SITS ON SEAT
CENTER OF GRAVITY RISES,
DISTANCE OF TURNING
"FULCRUM" IS GREATER.

WITH LONGER "FULCRUM"
IT IS EASIER TO GET
GRAVITY PULL OVERCOMING
CENTER OF STABILITIES
RIGHTING ACTION.

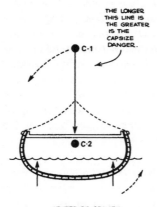

THE LONGER
THIS LINE IS
THE GREATER
IS THE
CAPSIZE
DANGER.

CENTER OF GRAVITY
STANDING UP IT'S ALMOST
IMPOSSIBLE TO KEEP CENTER
OF STABILITY IN LINE WITH
CENTER OF GRAVITY.

How the canoe's stability is affected by location of load and center of gravity.

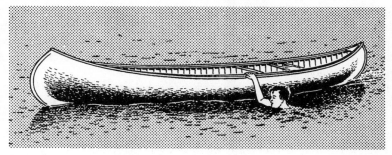

Swimming a canoe. Before doing any extensive canoeing, it's wise to have some practice doing this.

the seat and down on the canoe bottom, either sitting or kneeling there. In heavy weather or water, too, it is best to try to center the load and weight, leaving the ends light and free to rise in waves and, if necessary, to spin toward smoother water.

It's important that youths especially should, by predetermined plan and not accident, try swimming with a canoe. This way they can learn about its submerged stability. Too, everyone who uses a canoe should know how to right it and empty it; should become really familiar with it. Learn how to stand up and paddle, even to stand on the gunwales and thus get the fear of tipping over licked once and for all.

All the tricky basics should be learned firsthand, although it should be realized that it's impossible to empty even an unloaded canoe if there is any kind of wave action running. Then as much water will splash in as the canoeist is able to splash out. What experts consider to be the other most fundamental mistakes are these:

1. Greenhorns especially do not realize how cold most of the canoeing waters on this continent are and how very quickly the immersed individual loses the ability to function. This happens all the time to inexperienced canoeists who are in mountain streams in the summer. The day is hot, the stream at 45°F. or so, and early while shooting a rapids they go overboard, try to swim the rest of the way through while holding to the stern or bow, and become so numb they can't even hold on at the other end. It's been in their minds that because it is July or August the water will be warm.

2. Most, too, don't appreciate how frail a canoe can become in big water when the wind starts to blow. If one has a banana boat or a decked canoe, he can last through a hurricane. In an open canoe that's well loaded down, trouble starts when the waves get as little as a foot high. Quickly there is a bailing situation, at the same time all-out attention is needed just to handle the craft.

There is a sea adage that is smart as heck although most people don't fully comprehend it. This is that the time to take all precaution for the safety of the ship is when one *can* take precaution. This is particularly applicable to canoes, their being essentially such fragile crafts. It isn't going to take much in the way of difficulty before one loses the ability to do anything except maybe bail or pray. Canoeists in general shouldn't attempt to cross big water but rather should skirt the edges.

In other words, when canoeing one has to anticipate a potentially bad situation far in advance. By the time the rapids or storm has gripped the craft, it's too late. There's then not much the inexperienced individual can do. Taking precautions means looking well into the future and avoiding risky situations. The canoe is a magnificent craft, but it isn't very forgiving.

Righting a Canoe

To right a capsized canoe that is still floating, press down on one gunwale until the craft slowly rolls over. Then, though filled with water, it will stay afloat while the occupants climb back aboard, careful not to roll it under again. They can then sit or kneel on the bottom and paddle ashore, using just the hands if necessary.

Many times, however, the occupants are lurched overboard from a rolling canoe which then rights itself, despite shipping water, before eventually going entirely over. Then, especially in rapids or in wind, it must be regained before it moves beyond reach. If a shore is close, the canoe can be swum back to land.

Otherwise, one swimmer steadies either the bow or the stern with both hands. The other swimmer makes his way amidships, grips the nearer gunwale, brings his body as nearly horizontal as possible in the water at right angles to the canoe, then kicks and pulls himself forward into the canoe, grasping the farther gunwale and bringing his body across both gunwales. From this position, particularly with the second man continuing to steady the canoe, it is a simple matter to roll fully aboard.

There the occupant steadies the canoe to the best of his ability, one hand on each gunwale, while the second swimmer boards in the same manner.

Surviving a capsize in open water, two canoeists. Step 1—Return to canoe, empty most of water by rocking it.

Step 2—While one steadies bow (or stern), other canoeist prepares to scramble aboard.

If the canoe has shipped a lot of water, this can be first emptied to a large extent by the swimmers, who first press one end as far down as possible so as to empty a large portion of the water; then move amidships and rock the canoe so as to slosh out a good part of the remainder.

The Storm Hazard

Canoes can survive in big waves raised by storms. After all, kids are using them like surfboards in ocean breakers. Cruising canoeists get into trouble

Step 3—Kicking water to raise his feet and grasping the opposite gunwale, the one canoeist works aboard.

Last step—The canoeist aboard now shifts his weight to stabilize canoe while his partner scrambles aboard.

when storm winds raise big waves because the bow is not powerful enough to lift the canoe over the waves. The prow sticks into the wave ahead and, of course, the boat is swamped. For this reason, the main heavy-wind-and-wave tactic is evasion; that is, turning and running before the sea.

Since the canoe's speed is allowing the stern to remain in the wave surge a slight time longer than it would otherwise, there is more of a chance for the stern to lift. Also, in such a situation, there is the possibility of stuffing the gear astern, or if necessary in the bow, to create a sort of deck that will throw the water off the sides. Here again, one usually has to anticipate the need for this. By the time wind or waves get bad enough to demand it, the canoeist likely cannot dare to put his weight far enough aft or forward to accomplish it.

The white-water enthusiasts usually use a cover over their open canoes and, in addition, stuff the ends with something such as inflated beach balls for extra flotation.

Overloading

The most common cause of boat accidents is overloading, and this applies in particular to canoes.

Incidentally, on long cruises where heavy loads are nearly unavoidable, especially when one starts out, both weight and bulk can be cut by substituting freeze-dried foods for canned grub, by taking along only the usually adequate tarpaulin or lightweight tent for shelter, and by steadfastly eliminating equipment which is not essential. As with all travel, the more skilled and experienced the canoeist, the lighter his gear.

Kneeling

Seats are fine for calm water, or for the usual canoe trip. In rough or white water, however, kneeling on the canoe bottom is more safe and efficient. A cushion, folded down jacket, or knee pads make the kneeling position easier to hold for an extended period of time.

Standing

The best way when afloat to make a quick survey of the rapids one is about to shoot is by standing. This is also the most satisfactory procedure for spotting obstructions in shallow water. Canoe fishermen can get added distance and accuracy in their casts if they are erect. Too, standing in a canoe is almost a necessity when one is poling. For enchanting, relaxing pleasure while paddling along an intriguingly placid shore, try it standing.

In other words, the often-repeated axiom that one should never stand in a canoe is heard only from individuals not experienced with the craft.

Changing Position

The stern paddler and the bowman can change positions afloat if proper deference is paid to balance, but why bother? The usual canoe paddles almost equally well in either direction. All that is necessary for a shift in position, in other words, is just to face about. In fact, the best rule is never change places in a floating canoe.

Boarding

The same sort of overcaution as not standing is seen among tyros when it comes to boarding the canoe, and this sometimes makes for a loss of balance. Be careful, yes, but get aboard with more confidence than precision. In other

Procedure for boarding canoe at dock; use reverse technique for disembarking at dock.

words, with a loaded canoe especially, it is not necessary to make a long step directly over the keel, then to ease cautiously into position.

First of all, the canoe should be completely afloat. Then the stern man, being the captain, steadies it while any passengers step aboard and settle themselves on the floor, followed by the bowman. The latter then takes on the job of steadying, perhaps holding to a wharf or bank or shoving his paddle firmly against the bottom while the stern man gets into position.

When landing, the succession is reversed. The stern paddler gets the canoe into position, then steps out, perhaps into the water, and holds the craft for the bowman to disembark. Both hold the canoe while the passenger gets off.

Again, to stress the point, the canoe should be afloat before it is boarded. When the canoe is drawn up on shore with most of the boat in the water, for example, it is most capsizable. This unsteadiness is increased by anyone's sitting on the seat rather than standing on the floor. The reason is the same as when tending that aft outboard. One becomes balanced on the round part of the bottom. The flat section of the bottom that is in the water is severely reduced, and the occupant is, in effect, trying to balance himself on the bottom half of a round ball.

Incidentally, when embarking from sand or gravel, it will protect the finish of the canoe if one first washes the soles of his shoes before making that last step from land.

Needed—A Painter

Every canoe should have a painter, a short tethering rope about 25 feet long, fastened to the prow. When the canoe goes ashore, this painter should be tied to something solid such as a rock or tree. Otherwise, a rise of water might very well float the craft loose, or a gust of wind might blow it adrift. Canoes are so light, especially in relation to their broad sail-like surfaces, that this danger is a very real one, and more than one canoeist has suddenly looked over his campfire to find himself marooned.

Landing

It is unduly rough on both the paint and the structure of a canoe bottom to beach it prow first, as is commonly done on sand and even gravel. Instead, whether landing at a beach or a pier, come directly in, slowly enough that at the last moment the stern man swings the canoe to his master side, usually the right, and the bowman backs up the action, bringing the craft in parallel. Then be ready to step off into shallow water if necessary, or perhaps to a ledge or rock, with the canoe still fully afloat.

The exception is the landing made in heavy weather, particularly when it is not possible to reach quiet water. Again, come in directly, at right angles to the rock shelf, for instance. Instead of then trying to come around parallel, the stern man steps off into the water, preferably before any contact is made. He

Approach procedure when not landing and disembarking from a canoe on sandy or gravel shoreline.

Bow man disembarks first while stern paddler holds canoe steady. Same procedure can be used for boarding canoe from a shoreline.

Illustrating method of disembarking (or boarding) canoe when it is not landed on gravel or sandy shoreline.

then steadies the canoe while the bowman steps into the water. Both steady the boat while any passenger disembarks. Then both move on opposite sides to the middle of the craft, there grasping the gunwales and half-lifting and half-floating the craft, move it in beyond the turbulence.

Loading

Ideally, the canoe should be in the water when loaded, but practically it can be partially beached, yet not so much that it will not be easy to lift its beached end and ease this back into the water.

If the load is not too bulky, a stratagem to keep it drier will be to lay first several poles on the bottom. Such a practice also tends to make bailing easier.

The heavier items go down first, everything behind balanced so that the canoe will lie evenly in the water with the bow slightly higher than the stern. The exceptions to this last is that an evenly trimmed canoe proceeds best downwind on lakes, while a lighter stern makes for increased maneuverability in rapids. If at all possible, when the crew and duffle are all aboard there should be at least six inches of freeboard—the distance between the top of the lowest gunwale and the water.

Storm Techniques

If one has to drive into big seas, it is usually wisest not to hit them straight on. Instead, meet them at a slight angle so that more of the bow, and consequently more lifting surface, is presented to the wave. Then as the canoe rises it will kind of roll over the wave, tilting away from it at first, then leaning toward the wave's direction as the surge of water passes underneath.

This is the time for short, swift strokes. When there are two paddlers, these strokes need not even be in rhythm. In fact, alternate efforts may even keep the canoe on a more stable course. With heavy gusts catching the bow, both may paddle on the quieter side to balance the wind pressure.

One thing to avoid, a mistake that's far too easy to make when the travelers are heading for a lee shore, is not to force the canoe too hard against incoming combers. This way it may nose-dive into each wave, shipping too much water. Let the bow lift. Then keep the canoe under firm control once it is balanced on the crest, as the tendency will be for it to swerve downwind into the forward trough with the resultant risk of capsizing. The stern man should power the craft straight ahead. The bowman should paddle into the wind.

Once the balance of the canoe slides over the crest, the stern in turn will lift. Then too much paddle will plunge the bow into the next wave instead of over it. In such a situation, the first objective will be to lift over each wave, glide through its crest, and then descend the farther side without shipping more water than one has time to handle. The second objective will be to make headway.

If possible, practice beforehand near a safe shore wearing life jackets and preferably bathing suits. The bowman in particular is important in such a

LIGHTEST GEAR
LIGHTER GEAR
HEAVY GEAR

Loading gear into canoe—two-man outfit.

When trying to proceed against big seas, paddle at a slight angle to them, not into them.

situation, where a major problem will be to lift the bow over each oncoming surge of water. At the decisive instant, the bowman can help by actually lifting himself on flexed thighs, at the same time thrusting downward into the wave with the flat of his paddle. All this must be accomplished so smoothly that the canoe is not veered and so that he'll be once more in paddling position as soon as the canoe glides over the top of the wave.

Suppose the paddler is alone? Then, kneeling as far amidships as will be necessary to balance the craft, he should drive the canoe into wind and waves at such an angle that he can do all his paddling on the lee side. The wind pressure will then bear more strongly on the stern, itself assisting the canoe to remain on course.

Subnormal Body Temperature—A Deadly Hazard

A personal flotation device that will float the individual to start with can be expected to sustain him for an indefinite period. However, water temperature and exposure will likely have the first detrimental effects and these are measured in minutes and hours.

Immersion hypothermia, subnormal body temperature, involves the loss of body heat to the water. It is assumed that an individual will succumb if his normal temperature, about 98.6°F., falls as much as twenty degrees. In water warmer than 70°F., heat production may be expected to keep pace with heat loss. Then fatigue, leading to ultimate exhaustion, is the limiting factor.

The following chart shows the effect of exposure:

Water Temperature (°F.)	Unconsciousness or Exhaustion	Expected Survival Time
32.5°	Under 15 min.	Under 15–45 min.
32.5°–40°	15–30 min.	30–90 min.
40°–50°	30–60 min.	1–3 hr.
50°–60°	1–2 hr.	1–6 hr.
60°–70°	2–7 hr.	2–40 hr.
70°–80°	3–12 hr.	3–indef.
80° Plus	Indef.	Indef.

The Weather Hazard

It is *wind* that is the danger. Rain, though perhaps disagreeable, isn't dangerous. Squalls are very hazardous. The worst are cold fronts that appear as a long black line. But a thunderstorm can generate winds up to about 60 miles per hour. Getting caught on open water in one is too often an invitation to the undertakers.

High steady winds create big waves. Often in lakes, though, especially the island-studded Canadian lakes, one can find a lee shore and make progress.

Many of the reservoir lakes in the Southwest hold a danger in that the desert heat creates thermals, which are channeled by the hills and manifest themselves as savage wind gusts. These don't last long and usually don't build up big waves. But they may hit the canoe at 90 mph. If the canoeist sees one coming—noting the oncoming streaks on the water—he should get his weight down as low as possible and head into it.

Lightning is an overrated danger, as only 600 Americans are killed by it annually. But the sound and sight of the bolts are often terrifying. One is much safer on land than on water. If caught in a thunderstorm, the best procedure will be to take the canoe ashore in a group of trees all about the same height. Avoid heights, as well as single trees in the open. Turning the canoe over and getting under it will give shelter as well as an increased feeling of security.

PADDLING TECHNIQUES

Everyone knows how to hold a paddle, one hand on the grip at the end and the other partway down the shaft near the throat where this widens into the blade. The lower hand should be high enough to remain out of the water. This grip is shifted so that the left hand is atop when paddling on the right and the right hand is above when one changes to the left side of the craft.

The blade, of course, is held at right angles to the canoe. Then reaching forward only as far as is comfortable, bring the blade down into the water and draw it back, sending the canoe ahead. The upper hand continues to push while the lower hand, held at least temporarily extended, serves as a pivot to the lever action. For the utmost impact, both arms should be straight. Many find such practice tiring, however, and let the arms bend naturally as they paddle.

Bring the blade back nearly vertically until it reaches a spot opposite the hip. Do this by pushing with the upper arm, not pulling with the lower arm. Then lift the paddle out with the lower hand, at the same time dropping the upper hand toward the waist so that the blade floats upward and leaves the water.

All-important now that the stroke is completed is to relax both arms, an action so restful that it will be possible with a little practice to paddle all day without becoming more than pleasantly tired.

Bring the blade back for another stroke, turning it parallel to the canoe so as to minimize air and any water resistance. Complete all this with the hands and paddle close to, but not scraping, the gunwale or side of the canoe.

All this should be accomplished smoothly and comfortably, with the entire body contributing to the easy and thus enduring power—something that will come naturally with practice.

Basic Stroke

When two individuals are paddling, each works on a different side of the canoe, the canoeist in the stern ordinarily adapting his position to that of the bow paddler. The man in the stern, though, is captain and may direct the bowman with voiced commands, especially when running rapids.

With two paddlers each working from a different side, the direction of the canoe tends to equalize itself. However, the stern paddler usually has to make a special effort to keep it straight. This he does by giving a twist to the blade when it is opposite his hip, turning the inside edge of the blade backwards and bringing the entire flatness parallel to the canoe. The paddle thus serves as a rudder, and it is an easy matter to give it a final push to one side or the other to keep the craft on the desired course.

When one is paddling alone, this basic stroke will keep the canoe smoothly and continuously going in the desired direction no matter on which side the canoeist paddles.

Guide Stroke

Again driving the canoe ahead by stroking smoothly parallel to the craft, not being distracted by the curve of the gunwale, the guide stroke varies from the basic stroke in that at the end the blade is brought back feathered underwater—that is, held parallel to the side of the canoe—to a point opposite the hip, where it is withdrawn. Thus, again, the paddle works like a rudder.

This stroke varies among different canoeists; one practice, that sacrifices a certain amount of impetus, is to hold the blade at a slight angle during the entire sweep, then to make the final correction during the quick upward flip at the end. The gunwale may serve as the support from which this final bit of

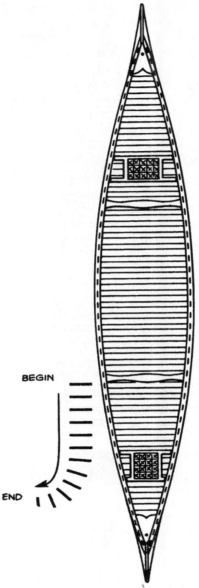

BEGIN

END

The J stroke, a basic steering stroke.

pressure is exerted. Both variations, although they take practice at first, can be maintained for hours without undue tiring.

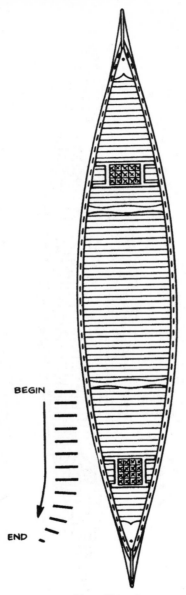

BEGIN

END

The guide stroke.

Backing Stroke

The fundamental forward strokes should be mastered first, for they will be used most during the pleasant hour upon hour of canoe travel. When the time comes to halt, slow, or go backwards, merely reverse the cruising stroke.

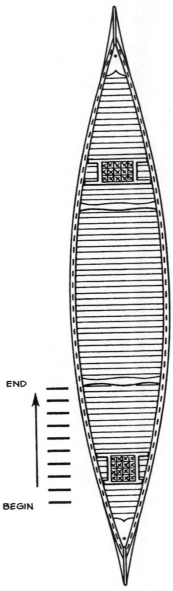

The backing stroke.

Jam Stroke

To stop suddenly, plunge the blade vertically into the water at right angles to the canoe. It will be easier to hold it there if one hunches forward over the shaft, pressing this tightly against the side of the canoe with the lower hand.

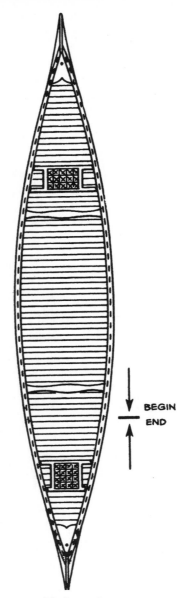

BEGIN

END

The jam stroke.

When two individuals are paddling the one canoe, for the utmost efficiency and balance this jam stroke should be applied simultaneously on signal.

Sweep Strokes

The most difficult stroke to master is the one used for ordinary cruising. This stroke makes good sense throughout, however, whatever variation is used, and skill will come with practice. The other strokes depend on common sense, too, and even the untutored canoeman will find himself practicing most of them without any prior instruction when he needs, for example, to swerve or to turn. Yet it is best to know the best timesaving techniques, for in such a situation as rock-frothing rapids waste motions could be disastrous.

To turn the canoe, swing the paddle like an oar out from and back to the gunwale in a circular sweep. Performed on the left side of the canoe, this will turn the craft to the right. The same thing can be accomplished by a full reverse sweep on the right-hand side. The reverse sweep, of course, starts in back of the canoeist and completes itself in a half circle in front of him.

There are so-called half-sweeps and quarter-sweeps when the turn to be made is less abrupt or where there is more time in which to accomplish it. These are merely shorter sweeps.

When there are two paddlers and each completes a full forward sweep on the same side of the canoe, the craft will swing widely away from the paddles. To pivot a canoe within its own length, the stern paddler should execute a forward sweep and the bowman a reverse sweep on opposite sides.

Draw and Push Strokes

The draw stroke, applied to move a canoe broadside, is executed by reaching straight out from the side, with the blade at right angles to the craft, and drawing the paddle straight back towards one. Two paddlers doing this from opposite sides will pivot the canoe sharply.

The push stroke is merely the reverse of this, starting from the paddler's side and pushing straight outward. The same result, of course, can be accomplished with a draw stroke on the opposite side, but there is not always time to shift sides. Again, two canoeists executing a push stroke on opposite sides will rotate the craft.

The push stroke is most effective, abruptly setting over either a bow or a stern depending on which of two paddlers applies it, when the shaft is held against the gunwale and the top pulled strongly and swiftly inward. Such a drastic stroke, which can break an inferior paddle, is usually reserved for white water.

POLING AND POLING TECHNIQUES

The use of a setting pole is greatly restricted by the kind of water in which it is employed. One works best on a shallow, rocky stream like the sprawling Half Moon of New Brunswick's Southwest Miramichi River where, as the stage of water lowers, it becomes increasingly difficult to paddle.

On streams much over four feet deep, such as British Columbia's Peace River, the depth of water is too much. Here except along some of the upper

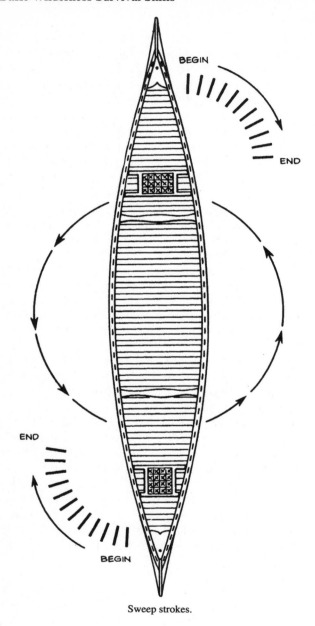

Sweep strokes.

stretches, pulling a pole in and out becomes too cumbersome. On the other hand, on the streams of New England, especially Maine's, poling conditions are just about perfect.

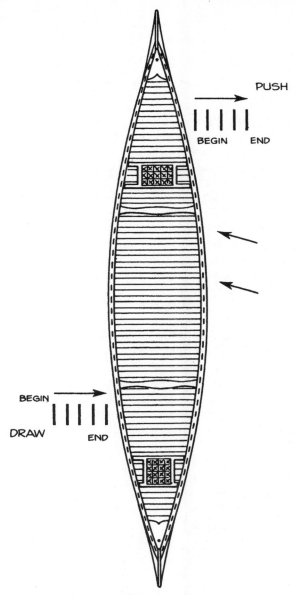

PUSH

BEGIN   END

BEGIN

DRAW   END

Push and draw strokes.

An advantage poling has over paddling is in upstream work where, even with one man, there is nearly continuous power. The only time one loses control of the canoe is for the instant it takes to reset the pole. With two individuals there really can be continuous power.

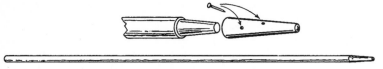

Canoe pole, illustrating poling shoe.

The reason why poling is not more widely practiced, aside from its being hard work, is probably due to the fact that many streams have soft bottoms. However, one can rig a fork of branches at the end of his regular pole for this sort of going. Too, an opening iron shoe, which closes upon being lifted, is available commercially for the pole point.

One can cut his own pole, although logger's pickpoles, usually of some tough wood such as hickory or ash, may be purchased. The pole should be some 12 to 14 feet long, with an average taper of about 1½ inches.

Poling techniques are best learned by practice. Pick a shallow stream, up which the canoe otherwise would perhaps have to be lined or portaged, and pole up it. Or first get the feel of the pole along a shallow lakeshore.

Although some handicapped individuals pole from a sitting position, by far the most popular stance is standing in the stern for one man and in both the stern and bow with two canoeists. The canoe should be balanced with the bow riding only a bit higher than the stern. To accomplish this, the lone poler may have to stand near the center of the craft, one leg braced against a thwart. Otherwise, the lead poler should stand slightly off center in the stern with the back leg braced against the seat or rear thwart.

Although, as in paddling, one can pole from both sides, the more powerful thrusts are when the right or master leg is advanced. Stand facing forward with the feet comfortably apart and parallel to the keel. As in riding, there

Poling upstream.

should be give in the knees, which should be partially relaxed, but still springy.

Start in this position by holding the pole with the master hand near the top and with the other hand about a foot and a half below it. Set the pole, close to the canoe, just back of the rear foot. Then, being sure to be well braced and balanced, push. As the canoe moves forward, continue the thrust by climbing the pole hand over hand. When reaching the top of the pole, give a final firm push so as to maintain the momentum while shifting the hands back down toward the middle and resetting the point in the waterway's bottom.

Direction is controlled by push, itself, not by the later resistance of the pole to the water, as might be presumed by paddling techniques. In fact, the pole should be lifted completely clear of the water before being replanted.

Rhythm is important, and this will come with practice. Keep the bow pointed into the current, the canoe parallel to the shore, and in shallow enough water that the bottom can be easily reached. Seek the quietest water where there will be the least pressure from the current. Often, in fact, it will be possible to find backwaters where the water is actually swirling upstream.

Sometimes the pole will be caught between two rocks. Then try to jerk it free. Failing, release the pole before capsizing, and return to it by paddle or by wading.

That's all there is to poling. But it's hard work, although usually not as hard as portaging the canoe and duffle as might have to be done otherwise. Skill comes with practice, and it is encouraging to note that it is usually more easily achieved than mastery of paddling!

The Pole in Snubbing Use

Downstream progress is more a matter of control. Then the pole is used to slow and direct the current-propelled canoe. As in paddling, one still has to select a channel. Again, on strange rapids this is best done from land beforehand.

Although one will probably start the canoe downstream with a soft forward thrust, the rest of the passage will be mostly the hand-over-hand technique in reverse. Try to keep the speed no faster than that of the current itself. Snub the craft frequently by setting the pole ahead and resisting the current. One can even come to a complete stop before setting the canoe over sideways to avoid an obstruction. It is best to keep the canoe parallel to the current.

To snub the canoe, thus slowing or stopping it, reach ahead with the pole to a point about amidship and as close to the gunwale as possible. Upon feeling the pressure, lean into this as much as may be necessary. Several such snubs may be necessary, as in fast white water, to bring the canoe under full control. Practice until mastering this basic technique.

All in all, poling either upstream or down will open new waters to the canoeman.

RIVER RUNNING

Respect White Water

The fact is, the novice canoeist should approach any white water worthy of the name with the same respect he would allot to a climb up a sheer rock wall. Yet the rock wall is somewhat self-regulatory. Hard effort, crumbling footholds, and the dizzy look down soon put the novice mountain climber in full awareness of the situation.

The budding but bungling white-water canoeist can expect no such built-in protection. Once he is committed, escape from a white-water nightmare is open only to experts. The amateur soon loses all control over his boat. The river takes charge, throwing its vast armament of rocks, ledges, waterfalls, and fallen trees with impersonal fury at its terrified and helpless victim. The result is dismally predictable and at best yields a sunken canoe, equipment scattered and ruined, and occupants soaked, sodden, bruised, and chastened.

At the worst, disaster awaits. Even on sunny summer days, river waters run cold. All canoeists should get out of the ice-cold deep water as soon as possible, even sacrificing the canoe if need be. Even when he is out of the water, be wary of a soaked victim's assurances that he is all right. His strength is being sapped faster than he realizes. No time must be spared in getting him into dry clothes. If anyone must enter cold water, let him strip so that he can come back and let the dry clothes warm him.

Just as ignorance masks the danger of cold water, it fails to calculate the staggering forces of hydraulics. Engineers estimate the thrust of an average-sized canoe immersed crossways in a ten-mile-an-hour current as more than *three tons!* Even when one is standing thigh-deep in such current, a weight of more than 300 pounds forces itself against the wader's legs. (Rapids faster than 10 mph do exist, but they are rare.)

The much more frequent river-killer is all the more sinister because it strikes without warning and instantaneously. A dancing rapids is attempted. The canoe grounds on a rock, swings sideways, capsizes. Several occupants are swept downstream, getting nothing but a wetting for their pains. Another is not so lucky. He is spilled ahead of the canoe which the current forces against a rock, pinning the individual. If his head is above water, there is a chance for life. If not, picture the situation.

Those who know of the mishap, being swept downstream themselves, may not even notice the victim's absence until too late. If they do, fighting their way to shore and back upstream may take too long. Boats following may or may not see what has occurred, and if they do, they are probably fighting for survival themselves. Or—the pinned person may be in an unapproachable area.

It is a deadly web of coincidental but interconnected circumstances—so much so that canoe clubs will send their best team down bad stretches to take post on rocks or ashore so accidents can be spotted, reported, and rescue efforts instituted at once.

None of this has to be, of course. Skill, equipment, training and experience enable members of white-water canoe clubs to conquer the toughest rapids in the country with ease and in complete safety. The novice approaches this as all else in stages, a step at a time, carefully learning to balance the challenge of the singing waters with his own mastery over them.

Reading the River

Just as every popular canoeing river in the country is mapped and charted, most of the rapids in them are also ranked according to the degree of difficulty they pose. The American White Water Association rates them as follows:

Difficulty Rating

Class 1. Occasional small rapids with low regular waves not over one foot high. Course easily determined. Rescue spots all along. Shallow.

Class 2. More frequent rapids. Eddies and whirlpools offer no trouble. Ledges not over three feet high with a direct uncomplicated chute. Course easily determined. Waves up to three feet high but avoidable. Water more than three feet deep.

Class 3. Long rapids, maneuvering required. Course not easily recognizable. Waves up to five feet high, mostly regular, avoidable; strong cross currents; a good rescue spot after each rapid.

Class 4. Long rapids, intricate maneuvering. Course hard to determine, waves high (up to five feet) irregular, avoidable; or medium (up to three feet) and unavoidable; strong cross currents, eddies.

Class 5. Long continuous rapids, tortuous; requires frequent scouting. Extremely complex course. Waves large, irregular, unavoidable. Large-scale eddies and cross currents. Rescue spots few and far off. Special equipment; decking, life jackets.

Class 6. Long continuous rapids without letup. Very tortuous, always scout. Waves very high (above five feet), irregular, unavoidable; powerful cross currents. Special equipment; limit of canoeability, involves risk of life.

What makes the problem more difficult is that rivers and rapids change as water volume increases or declines. The average river in spring flood stage can offer many rapids in the Class 4 and 5 stage; in mountainous areas, add a few Class 6s to it. Yet when summer water levels do go down, the river is far gentler, the Class 4s and 5s being tamed into 1s and 2s.

How does one tell at what stage a river is? Observing it is no good unless the river is known in all its phases. However, it can be taken for granted that plenty of people are keeping close tabs on any river in the land. The Corps of Engineers has jurisdiction over many. Game wardens patrol others daily. Any fishing-tackle store owner knows the condition of local streams, and most can offer constructive advice on the dangers involved in running them at any given time.

Special White-Water Equipment

The cardinal rule every novice should burn into his mind is never to run dangerous stretches alone. Always proceed in company with other canoes and with a plan of rescue action decided upon before any trouble arises. For this reason, special safety equipment should be added to any canoe heading into white water. Each boat should be equipped with 50 feet of ¼-inch rope. A high visibility blue or yellow polypropylene is best as it floats and can be readily spotted even in white foam. To one end attach an 18-inch throwing ring. This can be of light plastic, and in a pinch a preserver cushion is better than nothing. (Tie it through both straps.)

Another special item is a spare paddle. White-water lurches and shoves can easily snap canoe paddles, and unless another is available instantly the canoeist is helpless. The paddle should be lashed in with string sufficient to keep it in place in case of an upset, but light enough so a frantic pull can instantly tear it free.

Life preservers that can turn an unconscious person upright are another sensible precaution. Since in any dangerous rapids the proper technique is for both paddlers to be kneeling, knee pads can be used. If water is cold, heavy clothing should be worn. A skin diver's wet suit keeps the body warm even in freezing water.

A canoe for white water should be without a keel or, at most, with only a "shoe" keel. It should have a pronounced bottom curve or "rocker." This enables the ends to turn quickly, and the lack of keel makes it possible for the boat to be moved bodily sideways by powerful draw or push strokes.

Reading the Rapids

It is a river characteristic that while rapids may contain boils and raging waves of such intensity no boat can live through them, adjacent to such places, often only feet away, can be found a path of smooth water. The trick is: first, finding the smooth path and, second, having the technical ability to position the canoe in it despite strong, often unexpected currents.

Any dangerous rapids should be scouted. The canoeist should walk the length of it, marking in his mind (and even in a sketchbook) where the hazards are and the exact route to follow to miss them. This may mean crossing at such and such a point, backwatering into a rest area, etc. He should figure where to dodge rocks and decide what "haystacks" can be met squarely and which must be skirted. Canoeists of great skill and experience can do this almost by instinct as they speed down an unfamiliar rapids. But note that the AWWA ratings contain advice as to whether a given rapids should be scouted. It is a safe bet the experts study the bad ones carefully before plunging into them.

While coming down the rapids, the river ahead must be read from the small height the kneeling or sitting position allows. The skipper must know at all times at what point on his "chart" he is, not so easy in a long rapids. More important, the safe path ahead must be continually plotted and the canoe directed toward it. No words can substitute for on-stream reading lessons. However, there are some generalities.

Up & Down Vs

Vs with their point upcurrent, pointing toward the downrushing canoe, are the enemy. Vs where the wide angle of the V is upriver open their arms for the canoe to glide through and are friends.

A rock above water parts the water, making a white wave on either side that extends back past the rock in an ever widening V like the wave of a ship. If the rock is below the surface, the V of the wake still shows. The deeper the rock, the farther back from it is the apex of the V.

Time and experience tell the canoeist where and how deep a rock is by the tiniest of signals. Does the water bulge slightly in front of the V? There is probably sufficient water to float the canoe over it. Is the bow wave a slow rumble that indicates deep water or an angry froth that means the rock looms close to the surface? Currents of varying intensities add to the difficulties of reading. A rock with 10 inches of water over it will give one signal in a current of 5 mph; another when the river flows at 10 mph; no signal at all if the current is nonexistent.

Conversely, while the captain of the canoe (he can be bowman or stern man, although usually the stern man is in command) avoids upstream Vs, he seeks out downstream Vs. Most rapids are a series of obstacles that obstruct the flow of water in a chain of haphazard, inefficient dams. Water will start flowing for the dam opening well upstream of it, gradually constricting until it reaches the opening. The telltale V upstream sweeps the canoe into the deep safe slot.

"Haystacks" are large standing waves that form where water suddenly rushes from a shallow section into a much deeper area. These waves do not change position like ocean waves but froth and boil in the same spot constantly. There is usually good deep water under them. They pose problems only when they reach such size and intensity that the canoe cannot plow through them without taking on an undue amount of water.

However, at times the waves become so big that they simply overpower any canoe not equipped with white-water decks. The boat hits a solid wall of water and scoops itself full even though it charges through the wave. Here again, time and experience are the teachers. Although it is easiest to hit the haystack dead center (because the current there is swiftest), those that pose threats must be taken on the edge, the canoe scraping past the rocks along the side if necessary to avoid the water wall.

Currents

Most novices assume the current flows straight downstream, but nothing could be further from the truth. Any stretch of fast water contains side and back currents that the canoeist must recognize and use to his purpose. A back eddy makes a perfect spot to shoot *upstream* to safety. Yes, upstream.

In fact, safety much more often lies up a raging rapids than down. The reason is because every stretch of bad water automatically creates eddies behind it. These currents swing around toward shore, then upstream in a circle back to the main stream, and can readily be utilized to seek haven.

How to Acquire River Know-How

The stream in spring is a most benevolent teacher, if the aspirant picks a gentle stream, and a most pleasant one. The hours spent observing the play of the bottom on the surface in ever bolder versions surely are the least wasted of all. Is there a rapids by a road nearby? The budding canoeist could do worse than observe it through four seasons; in his canoe in gentle season, from his car if weather and water turn unwelcome.

White-Water Canoe Control

Once the white-water canoeist learns to see and identify the hazards so swiftly being served up to him, he must then have the skill to avoid them. The great risk is the canoe's grounding on a rock on one end or the other. If the stern section of the boat grounds, the results are not so instantly disastrous. The bow merely swings in line with the current, destroying whatever control was in effect or whatever maneuver was underway.

However, if the bow grounds, the effect is immediate. Instantly the stern swings sideways to the current, even 180°. In such an event, novice canoeists should swap positions. Both should turn in their seats, the bowman becoming

If the bow of a canoe grounds in white water, the stern will start swinging sideways immediately. In the process, the hull may catch on some second obstruction.

In going through white water, keep tight control over the canoe's course at all times.

sternman, but still in the bow. Such a maneuver will lift eyebrows among experts, but is far safer than attempting another 180° sweep to restore order.

Seldom is a river benign enough to permit such wild contortions without penalty. More often the canoe grounded at the bow never reaches the 180° turn. A rock or obstruction catches it somewhere along its length. The current then pins the boat strongly against the obstructions. Ofttimes the boat capsizes somewhere in the process.

If it does not, what happens next depends on the particular situation. If the water is shallow enough, it's probably best for one man to get out and try to free the boat. If the water is deep, the boat can sometimes be pried off the rocks with paddles. In extreme cases, lines may have to be taken ashore, and with sunken canoes especially it is not uncommon for a boat to be pinned so strongly that such additional help will be needed to free it.

Iron control over the craft at all times is the method of avoiding such a gamut of horrors. At no time should the boat be allowed to take charge. It should be kept pointed straight up and down in the current, cocked never more than 30° from the straight line in the fast current during turns, draws, or sets.

The lone canoeist, of course, relies on his own assessment of the water and handles the boat as need be, usually from a kneeling position slightly aft of amidships. But two-man maneuvers require teamwork. Both paddlers must coordinate their efforts, often at split-second intervals. For this reason a set of commands should be agreed on before skills are put to the test. These need not be complicated: simple shouts of "back," "draw right," "set left" are sufficient if they clearly convey the skipper's intention and put two strong backs working to the same purpose.

Holding Course to Clear an Obstacle

Since the canoe seldom shoots straight down a stream, naturally it is some-times difficult to determine exactly what course the boat is on and whether it will or will not clear an obstacle ahead. The way to tell quickly is to line the obstacle up with a mark on shore. If the mark and hazard stay aligned, the boat is on a collision course. If the two positions "open," the canoe will miss the hazard without effort on the part of the occupants.

Hazards and Evasive Tactics

Essentially, three basic tactics are utilized to avoid hazards. The first is ob-viously to steer the canoe around them. Oddly enough, this is not as easy as it sounds. In flat water a canoe steers well enough if the boat has fair speed through the water. A paddle used as a rudder turns it. But, immediately, this poses a problem in fast water.

While it is sometimes profitable for the canoe to careen down a rapids with the bowman paddling frantically to gain boat speed through the water so the stern man has steerage way, usually the reverse is desired. More often, the need is to slow the boat so the safe road ahead can be plotted and the boat positioned with care. Moreover, a canoe paddling down a current in a turn does not go in the direction it is pointed. At every moment the current is car-rying it down while the effort is steering it sideways. The actual course then is a crabbed sweep, with the boat at an angle the whole time and, as such, al-ways vulnerable to grasping underwater obstructions.

More useful are paddle strokes that will move or turn the boat when it is dead in the water. The draw or a combination of draw and push strokes are the most valuable. In these, both paddlers lean out, shove their paddles down as far right as they can, and pull toward the canoe with all their might. The effect is to jump the boat sideways a foot or two.

The push stroke, using the paddle as lever against the gunwale, is such an extremely powerful stroke that care must be taken not to snap the paddle. A series of draws and pushes by experts can make a canoe accelerate sideways with eye-opening speed.

How this works should be obvious. Either with both paddlers seeing obsta-cles or with one calling commands, the boat is moved sideways into safe paths. As an example, suppose an upstream V offers deep water, but immedi-ately below the V slot is a rock. The boat shoots the slot. As it starts down, the stern man shouts, "Draw left."

Both men lean out and in, and three swift strong strokes simply move the canoe sideways far enough to shoot past the rock. Sounds easy, doesn't it? Yet play the scenario with variations. Suppose one man has no idea what the draw stroke is? How about if no one takes command and one man draws left, the other right? What if neither knows how to draw stroke, and the stern man tries to steer around the rock in the fast current? In all such cases, a canoe "horse-shoed" around the rock can be forecasted.

"Setting" is a third evasive tactic. More than that, it is an escape route. It is the way the knowing canoeist lands or rests in fast water. Essentially, it employs frantic backing on the part of bow or stern man. But it is difficult to back a canoe in a straight line (try it in calm water sometime), so a long easy turn is the usual setting course. The maneuver is most effective when coordinated with a back eddy.

Let's say a particularly bad stretch has in its middle a huge rock. Water races around the rock, but behind it there is a quiet eddy. To race through the channel and attempt to turn the boat bow first into the eddy would be nearly impossible since much of the turning would have to be done in the fast water which would carry the boat far downstream. Look how setting solves the problem.

As the rock is approached, both paddlers frantically reverse, slowing the boat. The second the rock is past, the stern man backs and pushes or draws the boat's stern into the quiet water. The instant his paddle reaches that quiet water, the power of the current is vanquished. Since the distance between current rushing at 10 mph and dead quiet, or even turning slowly upstream is often measured in feet, sometimes inches, the set is extremely effective.

Most serious obstructions in a river offer quiet water havens behind them. Usually there is a circular current set up from water being drawn back upstream. In these the draw is used to yank the canoe out of the fast water. Caught in the upstream current, it is a simple matter to set the boat in toward the haven or shore stern first.

Fending Off

It is too much to expect that every rock can be missed. It is permissible (albeit poor form, like end swapping) to use the paddle to fend off rocks that should have been avoided by maneuvering. The bowman gets this assignment. There is no special art to it. He just sticks the blade against a point on the rock where he thinks it won't slip and throws his weight on the haft. The stern man should respond with a push or draw to move the whole boat in the direction away from the shove.

Grabbing branches is another common maneuver of dubious value. It greatly heightens the center of gravity because of the usual upward pull. A capsize here is hard to avoid. In any case, the stern man should always do the grabbing. If the bowman holds, the boat will certainly swing.

Line and Portage

Lining a canoe means to draw or guide the craft less its passengers either up- or downstream by the use of a line or lines—one usually attached low at the prow, the other at the stern. A canoe might have to be "lined" up or down a stretch of very shallow water, for instance. No hard and fast rule can be laid

Fending off during white-water passage. In fast water this calls for alertness at all times because there is usually only one right moment to fend off properly from each obstruction.

down about when to line and/or portage. Everything depends so much on the individual situation. Some rivers are very difficult to line because of high banks. Others are easy. A portage consumes time, and always extracts some cost in discomfort, insect attack, and so forth.

Certainly, the rule for novices should be never to enter any rapids above Class 2 which has not been scouted in advance. If on the scouting party he feels any hesitation, opt for the safer route. Similarly if there is much at stake, much equipment, small children, unusual hazards, the safer path should be adopted.

Spills and Other Dangers

One of the most important white-water rules the beginning canoeist should always remember is to resist the normal urge—when the boat is sweeping down sideways against a rock—to lean the boat on the upstream side. It invariably appears that hitting the rock will tip the boat by stopping the bottom and that the inertia of the boat's movement will then capsize it. This ignores the current, of course, which is the determining factor.

But tipping the upstream side merely increases the boat's underwater area and thus increases the current's push against it, pinning the boat strongly and often capsizing it. However, if the canoe is tipped *toward* the approaching rock, the effect will be to send the current under the boat as it pushes the upstream side even higher, decreasing its force. Thus the current lifts the boat, often freeing it without further effort by the occupants.

Waterfalls are such obvious danger points that it is a wonder that every year canoes continue to get swept over them. The "boil" beneath the falls and in certain other deep spots in rivers, may trap swimmers by drawing them down time and again by the circular current.

Here, as when being swept against a rock, the swimmer should go against his instincts and dive instead of struggling for the top. The strongest currents sweep the bottom and will shoot him into the clear. Simple scouting or reading a map of the river reveals waterfalls well in advance, of course. The boat should be landed well upcurrent and the falls portaged.

Trees fallen across a stream pose a greater problem than most canoeists realize, for several reasons. Unlike rapids or falls, they do not advertise their presence by sound. Nor do they obstruct stream flow. If they topple into a fast stretch, the stretch stays just as fast. This obstruction neither slows the current, nor often offers any place to dodge. Finally, trees may fall at any time and are seldom mapped. The canoeist rounds a bend and is surprised.

Defense depends on the situation. Perhaps the boat can sneak under a spot or over a submerged portion. Often a quick set to land is required, followed by some ax work.

Capsizes and Swamping

The vital rule to remember is that if the canoe does capsize, never get downstream in front of it. Duck under it or hold position so it goes past.

Also, swimmers are safer to stay with a swamped canoe than to abandon it. The accepted procedure is to grab the stern and ride the boat down through the rapids as if swimming a horse, holding the stern to keep the boat straight.

Oddly, because of its now greater depth, the boat directed this way will in uncanny fashion seek the deeper water and often glide through bad stretches with amazing ease. If the canoe cannot be reached, swimmers should face downstream on their backs, feet first, treading water until a calm is reached.

Often canoes become trapped against rocks and must be man-handled off. Small saplings can be cut to serve as levers. Ropes may be tied together and to a tree, and a Spanish windlass set up. Usually, several individuals heaving at one end will jockey the boat around enough so that the current's grip is broken.

TRANSPORTING AND PORTAGING

Cartopping the Canoe

With two people there isn't any problem in putting a canoe on car racks. They just lift and slide it on.

One man may have a problem, though. A stern outboard bracket is an assist. This, because of its flat surface, allows one end of the canoe to be picked up without the craft's pivoting on its sharp point at bow or stern.

Very important in cartopping singlehanded is a roll bar. This is a bar that connects the front and rear rack. One lifts one end up on the bar, then hoists the other end, slides the canoe about halfway at a 90° angle to the way the

The average canoe can easily be put up on cartop bars by two people.

boat will finally ride, and then swings the end around so that the canoe lies fore and aft on horizontal racks. Reverse to unload.

If the after-crossbar is located far enough toward the rear of the car, one can put one end of the canoe on it, then go around, pick up the other end, and slide the boat forward into position. The thing about the roll bar is that one only has to pick up one-half the canoe at a time. And one always maintains control, which can be important if the wind is blowing. Say the canoe weighs 130 pounds. Then with the roll bar the packer lifts only 65 pounds or less at a time because one end of the boat is always supported on either the ground or the roll bar.

Two-canoe rigs are easy on a car. One can even sandwich a third canoe on top of the pair, using life-preserver cushions to cradle the boat. Beforehand, though, both racks must be lengthened.

Plenty of canoes, too, are carried on cars without racks. Most of these travelers just rest them on cushions and lash down. This is risky, though, as the wind is always lifting and lightening that boat, and the cushions can then easily blow away, whereupon the roof of the car catches it. Still, many travel this way.

Canoes should be lashed to the racks and additionally secured by ropes fore and aft to the bumpers. The front line is the more important, as the wind gets under the bow and tends to lift it. Canoe beams are around 40 inches, incidentally, and standard racks a comfortable 60 inches, so the load is an easy one.

Lashing the Canoe Down

In addition to having well-secured bow and stern lines, any canoe loaded for cartopping must be solidly secured to the carrying bars (or cartop), a requirement usually adequately met by fastening two strong web straps across the canoe bottom, their ends anchored to the carrying bars. There is much room for improvisation here, it being relatively easy to rig quick-detachable/ attachable fastenings which make canoe tie-down and dismounting a swift and simple job, particularly appreciated by those who cartop their craft frequently. In lieu of using heavy-duty straps—and few of the carrying bar kits contain straps of desirable strength and width—the canoe can be merely lashed down securely. Some canoeists employ a crisscross X lashing. A good way of getting lines like this secure is to tie a bowline in one end, then to use that loop like a pulley to pull the line tight. Then with the rope pinched around the loop to maintain tension, throw a half hitch in the free end. One can pinch the loop and bring the hitch up snug before any slackening occurs.

Whether a canoe has been well tied down or not will quickly become apparent upon traversing a stretch of washboard road.

Portaging

When it comes to portaging, discretion continues to be the better part of valor, especially when one is more or less a greenhorn in this new canoeing world. Particularly when a trail around rapids seems to be well traveled, it will be well to heed such eloquent counsel.

On most canoe trips of any length, one or more portages will be necessary, perhaps a carry from one lake to another or an overland route around a stretch of white water. If it is not exceptionally windy and one is traveling, as he should be, light, then the work will not be too strenuous, even when one is alone. In fact, it often feels good to get out and stretch one's legs.

Ideally, it will be possible to complete a portage in two carries. On the first trip over, carry the packs. At that time, armed with an ax, it will be possible to scout out the trail and to clear away any obstructions. Finally, come through with the canoe itself.

Perhaps the carry will come at tea time. Then build the lone bright fire at the other end. It is both a psychological and physiological mistake to rest *before* a portage. For one thing, muscles stiffen. For another, the task looms all the more formidable. To boil the kettle is all the more gratifying when all that remains to be done, first making sure that every last spark is extinguished, is to board the portaged and repacked canoe and set forth once more.

If one is traveling with a map, portages will be marked. Otherwise, stop and look for them at the sound of white water. The portage trail, if any, will be along the line of easiest going. It may, of course, be on either side of the stream, especially if that is on the inside of a bend. A landing place is usually obvious, perhaps because of tracks, or clearing, or dead fires, or even litter.

In crossing overland from one lake to another, look for a dip in the hills. The earliest individuals to use such a portage wanted to make it as easy as possible. In the old days, such portages were frequently marked by blazes or by lopping off the higher branches of a conspicuously high tree, some of which still stand.

Shoulder Protection

The most arduous portage begins with one step; and even that will be more comfortable to take when some provision is made for padding between the canoe and the shoulders. This may be only the flats of the lashed paddles, plus a folded extra shirt.

Stores and outfitters also sell aluminum, plastic, and hardwood yokes to ease portaging problems. These go on the inside of the canoe in the center, so that on balance the bow will lift a bit higher than the stern. But they are one more item to carry.

With most canoes one can make his own yoke by lashing two paddles between the thwarts, preferably so that the flat portion of the blade will rest against the shoulders on balance, the stern again slightly lower than the prow, making it handier to lift the forward end for better vision. When there is a center thwart, this is no problem. If the paddles must be secured instead to bow and stern thwarts, it may be the slim parts of the paddles that will meet the shoulders, in which case one will want plenty of padding.

In any event, the yoke should be well secured. Any slipping would not only be uncomfortable, but it could be downright hazardous. Caution should be exercised on all carries so as to avoid falls and sprains. Incidentally, bugs may be a bother when one is occupied in keeping the canoe balanced on his shoulders. During fly seasons, apply plenty of repellent, for few things are more distracting than mosquitoes whining in the enclosed stuffiness directly over the imprisoned head.

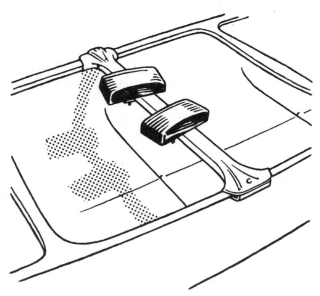

Commercial-type yoke for canoe portage use.

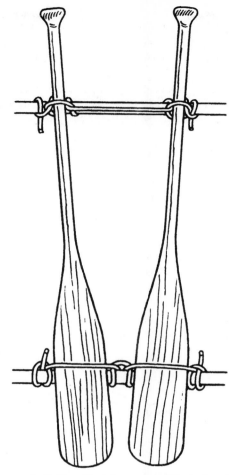

Portage yoke fashioned by tying canoe paddles to thwarts.

On short carries with light canoes that have a central thwart, the voyageur frequently does not bother with any yoke, merely upturning the craft over his head and resting the thwart against his neck.

As for tiny canoes, these can be transported under an arm.

On short carries, too, the lightweights are sometimes carried upright and unpacked by two men, the keel resting on the shoulders. It then becomes all the more important for the partners to maintain the same rhythm in walking, usually a process that requires considerable concentration because of the unevenness of the ground. A good waltzer has more luck in carrying a canoe, as

Lifting canoe in preparation for portage—one man.

a gliding walk rather than a bouncy stride helps keep the weight from continually jabbing into the neck and shoulders.

Lifting

The secret lies in tossing instead of pressing. With one man, roll the emptied and upright canoe away from one's self on one side and take hold of the

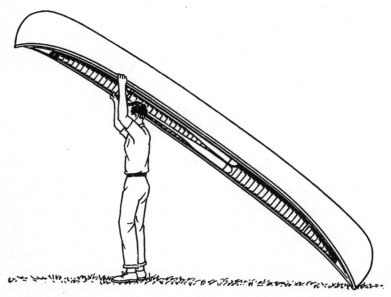

Lifting canoe when readying to load on car top or to put in portage carry position.

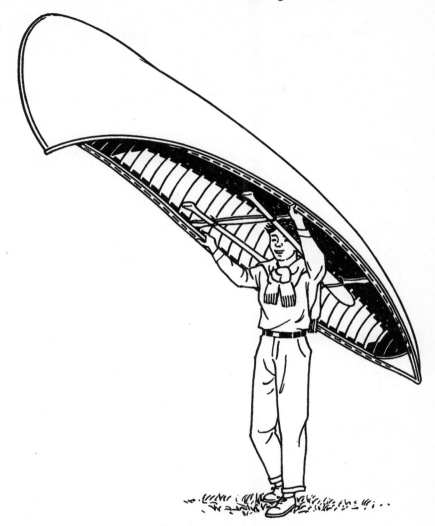

Portaging—one-man carry.

yoke or the center thwart. With an upward jerk of the arm and a forward shove of the knees, toss the craft up and around. The knees support the bulge of the canoe briefly when it is halfway up. Then when the craft is tossed and bounced nearly upside down, duck the head beneath into its position in front of the yoke or center thwart. This way, the two hands and the knees will get the canoe up without straining or even overexerting the back and arms.

When two partners are involved, the lift is easy. Again, the canoe is started right side-up. The bowman stands slightly ahead of the front seat, the stern man a bit ahead of the rear seat. Each bends down and grips the gunwales. Then, on signal, they lift together, rolling the canoe over as it is hoisted. The seats themselves can then become the carrying yokes.

The greenhorn working by himself can, until he gains experience, instead prop the bow against a rock or tree, get in position under the thus half-raised canoe, and easily bring it in balance across his shoulders and neck. When one man will be carrying the canoe, the other the duffle, then the second canoeist himself can half-lift the craft for his partner.

With a carry longer than 50 yards, some sort of padding will make things a lot easier. Many a canoeist just puts on his down jacket.

CHAPTER TWELVE

HANDLING YOUR OWN PACK TRAIN

You're at the jumping-off place.

Maybe this is a fog-sodden wharf in Alaska. Perhaps it is somewhere along the Alaska Highway in British Columbia or the Yukon. Possibly it is where a dirt road halts against a mountain. Or the place may be a remote western airport almost anywhere. A loose-limbed fellow with a grin stretching his freckles begins ambling your way.

"I take it you're the hombres who've had me hitched to a ballpoint pen?" the outfitter asks. "Well, your horses are itching to hit the trail. What fishing gear did you finally bring?"

It's been your lifelong ambition to fish a camp in the horse country of the continental West. Here most of the really fine backwoods lie at least several days and usually farther from the closest steel or the nearest four-wheel drive or wagon road, and although planes are taking over to a certain extent these days, the cheapest and most common method of transport on any extended trip is with pack animals. These can be arranged for beforehand, for hire or even purchase. Well, by tomorrow, you'll finally be forking that saddle.

At the base camp where they are preparing for another trip, this one with guides, you shake hands with the wrangler. You swap the busy cook a hello for his grunt. You take a doubtful look at the salt-licking buckskin who's going to be both your transportation and your companion for the next few weeks.

Somewhere in the midst of a confab that builds between the outfitter and the wrangler about the best way to get within photographing distance of that grizzly they've glassed a few hours away, the sizzle of steaks begins asserting itself. The cook lets go with a heartfelt whoop. As you and the others turn toward the billowing cook tent, your saddle horse surprises you with a velvet-nosed nuzzle.

All of a sudden you realize that this trip that you and a companion have been planning for so long is really going to be something. You hope that you can pull your own weight. If only you knew a little bit more about what lies ahead. . . .

The outdoorsman who finally gets around to that long-awaited pack trip has almost invariably picked up plenty of wilderness savvy along the way. He's generally a top backwoodsman, to boot. The only things he hasn't had much chance to become familiar with beforehand are western horses and gear. The following observations may help to acquaint this otherwise experienced outdoorsman with what the pack animal journey holds for him.

PACK ANIMALS

A large pack mule will freight more than a horse unless it happens not to be in the mood. Pound for pound, so will a burro. But among the disadvantages to be met with both mules and burros is that it becomes nigh impossible to make many of them ford rivers and even fair-sized creeks, or to cover really boggy and muskegy country. The result is that their use is confined almost exclusively to desert and high, arid regions.

For general transportation, the more amenable horse is commonly used. How much one of these can pack day after day depends on a combination of details and approximations having to do with terrain, weather, type of load, gear, food, skill of the human packers, and the aptitude and temperament of the individual animal.

An average grass-fed horse, to generalize, can be expected to pack about 140 to 180 pounds for weeks at a time along the steep trails to be found in high country. Many times this minimum can be increased. To load an animal beyond its usual limit for very long, however, makes for all kinds of trouble, including incapacitating sore backs. This limiting figure, whatever it may be, will suggest the number of pack animals called for to handle a particular outfit. There is this, too. Food supplies are apt to lessen as the pack train progresses, although you may also be picking up additional weight, as in the form of ore samples.

Along reasonably decent going, the usual pack horse or mule can average about 15 miles a day, starting about 10 A.M. and stopping about 4 P.M. Burros are much slower. The location of good graze and water is what ordinarily determines the picking of the camping areas and, therefore, the duration of the day's journey.

Plenty of water and graze exists throughout much of the western reaches. This is all to the good, for otherwise the animals, even though hobbled and belled, will stray for miles in search of nourishment. Where there is ample fodder, it is reasonable even in the wilder regions to take a pack string through almost any area where steep cliffs, very heavy forest, and downfall do not bar the way. Almost all the western forests, except those on the thick southern sides of some mountains and where jackpots resulting from Indian or lightning-set fires require that you ax your way, are open enough to ride through freely nearly everywhere. Even where you do not see an open trail, your animal will many times find one, particularly if it is in familiar country.

LEARNING TO RIDE

The prospective rider who has not previously journeyed with a pack string should understand certain details about the horse and his load, as well as some of the procedures of traveling and camping. These vary somewhat in different localities and among various outfits. Basically, however, they're hitched to the proposition that keeping the livestock in good condition is the primary essential. For the purposes of this book, we'll mainly consider the problems of one or two outdoorsmen who are fairly well experienced with the ways of the wilderness although not necessarily with livestock.

That's the way I started out, and because I suppose that my particular problems were rather characteristic, let us consider them. For one thing, except for riding farm animals on my Grandfather Adams's farm in western Massachusetts and later excursions on English saddles along Boston bridle paths, I knew nothing about riding. Nevertheless, once we had built our log cabin at Hudson Hope, British Columbia, my wife and I bought a couple of well-broken local cayuses, selected a flat open stretch downwind and downstream of our wilderness home, and put up a pole corral for them. I took the more unruly of the two for myself.

Riding the first few times as instructed by the horses' former owner made us stiff and sore, and there were areas where it removed skin, too.

"My knees feel it most," Vena said.

"So do mine, but they'll get toughened."

"I suppose it's the western saddles," my wife said. "I have to use my knees so much, along with my ankles, to take up the shock and to keep from bouncing."

"We'll get used to that," I said. "I'm not worried about that at all."

"There are places where I don't have any hide left," Vena said, "like the inside of both knees."

"It'll all work out," I said, "when we get the rhythm of it. That's it, I suppose, the rhythm."

"I don't know about Chinook," Vena said, "but Cloud has a lot of different rhythms, and when he isn't on a trail he adds a few more. It's not just a matter of keeping time the right way. I wish someone was around who could really teach us how to ride correctly."

"I don't think they know themselves what they do," I said. "They just grew up riding, and they never thought much of anything about it, just as we never thought about walking. We just tried, I suppose, and kept on trying until we were getting around."

"I suppose so, but that doesn't help much now."

"There may be a way," I told her. "King Gething told me that the best way to learn to ride naturally is to go on a trip for several days. By the time you're through, he said, you've learned in self-defense to stop irritating the sore spots you shouldn't have been making sore, anyway."

"Why don't we do it?"

"All right," I said. "Now that I've sent off that article on wild foods and the Chinaman Lake trip, let's accept King's invitation and ride up to his mine and back. It's not too rough cross-country, he said, and we'll come up against a lot of different kinds of terrain. Then we can get in some extra riding while we're staying there."

She didn't say anything for a moment. Then she smiled.

"When do we leave?" she asked.

"How about the day after tomorrow? There's something I want to do first."

"Where are you going now?"

"Riding," I said. "I'd like to go alone this one time if you don't mind. And would you keep the dog in, please?"

"You'll be all right?" she asked.

"If I can't handle Chinook when Cloud isn't along," I said, "it's time I was finding out."

Chinook was docile enough when I saddled her, although, as usual, she danced some when I was tightening the latigo and trying to get the bit past her teeth. She kept jerking her head toward Cloud while I was untying the halter shank, coiling it, and fastening it with a rawhide lace to the front of the saddle. Then, when I got the reins in my left hand, the saddle horn in my right, with my back to her head and my left foot awkwardly in the stirrup, she started before I was ready.

"Whoa," I was saying, "whoa!"

It was all right, though, because the forward impetus swung me into the seat. Then my off toe was groping for the iron stirrup which kept banging me on the ankle, and I was trying to turn her and to keep my balance, all at the same time. Cloud was whinnying. When Chinook crooked her head to answer, I managed to keep her head turned until she was going in the direction I wanted.

She had her mind made up that she was traveling to town and that, in any event, if she had to leave the grey gelding behind, she certainly wasn't going into the woods and upriver. By digging my heels into her ribs, I finally got her up past the cabin. Vena waved, and I heard her telling the Irish wolfhound to be quiet. Then we reached a loop of Bull Creek that Chinook decided she wasn't going to cross.

"How's about a drink," I said, as if we were both in this thing together and I wanted to be agreeable about everything. "Go ahead and have a drink."

I loosened the reins. She ducked her head several times, but the creek bed here was steep and narrow. She tried bending her front legs. She gave this up, though, when her bare hoofs slipped. Then she wanted to go back.

I turned her three or four times, bringing her again to the creek. She wouldn't cross it, although the water was no more than three feet wide, and the whole terrain was perfectly safe. When I went back down the trail a ways and then ran her for it, she reared at the last moment and stood there quivering.

There didn't seem to be any use in having a horse and not being able to manage her. The trouble, of course, was that I wasn't sure of myself and that I didn't know anything about riding. Well, I decided, it was about time I learned what I could. Settling myself as solidly as possible, I reached up and broke off a poplar branch.

Just the motion set Chinook off, and she was across the brook in a single leap. The impetus shoved me hard against the stirrups, then slammed me into the cantle. I was thinking how she'd be reassured now that she'd found I'd been right and that there was nothing at all to the crossing. Then I was just thinking about how to stay on.

Chinook was running through the woods. Whenever an obstruction such as a log appeared in the way, she leaped it. Every few stops she bucked. If she had twisted at all, I would have been off after the first lunge or two. As it was, whenever I left the saddle, I always found it there to receive me again.

I was hammering against the leather so hard that my back ached. At first, I clung to Chinook with my thighs and knees while managing to keep enough spring in them and my ankles to take up some of the shock. I kept turning and ducking in an effort not to be swept off. Then I realized the strength was leaving my leg muscles. The pain knifing down from my hips to my shins didn't bother me too much because I didn't have time to think about it. But when all tension left my legs, leaving them limp, all I could do was grab for the saddle horn and hold on with all my might.

It was then that I learned something about balance. My body must have been equalizing itself automatically, for now that I was gripping the horn I was no longer an instinctively centering weight but, instead, a loosening sack attached to a peg. I tried to hold myself down in the saddle. Young poplars were flashing across me. A black stump loomed up in their midst. Chinook veered, and suddenly there was no longer anything beneath me but atmosphere.

I was yelling something. Then I was on my back in a patch of bunchberries. It wasn't any worse than being tackled hard in football, only I wondered why I wasn't just relaxing there instead of shouting and scrambling up. Then I realized I was yelling, "Whoa!"

Chinook was standing there, the two black reins trailing on the ground in front of her. She was breathing hard, and when she backed away from me and stepped on a rein, the resulting tug caused her to rear.

"Easy," I said, forcing my voice low and keeping my motions gradual. I didn't want her galloping back to the cabin riderless and frightening Vena. For that matter, maybe she wouldn't even stop at the cabin; saddled and bridled, she could get hung up somewhere. "Easy, now. Whoa."

Then my foot was on a rein. When she jerked back again, the tightening leather fairly straightened into my hand. I've wondered afterward why I tried again, alone out there in the woods. I suppose if I hadn't been alone, though, I wouldn't have had the temerity to risk making a spectacle of myself, although what I did seemed to be the only thing there was to do.

The second time was infinitely worse. My legs gave out sooner, not that the pain made much difference any more, but I couldn't make them grip or take up any of the jar. I was bounced so high against the thumping saddle that it was difficult to maintain my seat.

I had very little control over my body any longer, and I had far less over Chinook. It wasn't that she was a bad horse in any sense, for she could have easily wiped me off by going under a low limb, while if she had put any twists in her straightforward bucking, I wouldn't have lasted a minute. It was more as if she'd been accustomed to being on her own and making her own decisions, and now she'd worked herself into such a state that she couldn't quit any more than I could.

She was running now through an old burn, and I could see the short, charred ends of poplar saplings like spears below me. That was when I grabbed leather again. The realization came to me, too, that she was pounding along the edge of the cliff which, with the way the Peace River kept undermining the shale, was treacherous at best.

I pulled on both reins, then sawed on them and eventually got her neck twisted so far that she began veering in a wide circle. That was something, at least, although her wildly plunging pace didn't slacken. When I tried to halt her by steering her into a great fallen spruce, fearful all the while of the crash that might result, she just disregarded the direction in which her head was being hauled.

What halted her finally, I don't know. I suppose the fact that I'd fortunately secured a stout bridle enabled me to tire out her neck muscles. She began turning in such a tight circle that she could no longer run, although when I thought I had her at enough of a standstill so I could descend safely, she gave a final pitch that sent me sprawling. This time, however, I kept hold of the reins.

My aching legs were trembling, but I noticed that she was quivering, too. Her heaving body was so white with sweat in places that, despite everything, I was sorry for her. But it was no time to think of that.

This time when I got into the saddle, I grasped the cheek of the bridle as firmly as I could and somehow found my right stirrup in a single, shaky motion. Then I tried to forget about Chinook's mouth as I held her head as high as I could. She didn't seem to be able to get started running again, and each time she tried to pitch, I tugged her head higher.

Then, grimly, I turned her the way we'd come. She balked once more at the creek, and then she wanted to leap it, but partly because I was afraid I'd never survive another plunge, I made her walk across. Then I turned her and walked her back. I walked her back and forth through the water until she was doing it automatically.

Then, not relaxing the pressure of my left hand on the reins, I broke off another poplar branch. Scarcely daring not to leave well enough alone, I waved it back and forth by her head. Nothing happened. I brought it down easily against her flank the way I'd meant to that first time. Muscles twitched, but the only other effect was that she obediently picked up her pace. I took her back and forth across the stream again, and then, hot and exhausted, I headed her homeward.

Cloud whinnied as we approached, but Chinook gave no heed. She stood, head down, while I tied her halter rope, then pulled off bridle, saddle, and saddle blanket. She was so wet that on second thought, although I was sore and shaken enough not to feel much like it, I got an old piece of blanket and rubbed her until she was glossy. She just stood there, never moving while I worked all around her.

When I was finished, I stroked her gleaming neck. She turned her velvet nose and, to my surprise, softly nuzzled me.

"Did you have a good ride?" Vena asked when I went in.

"Yes, it was quite a ride."

She was looking at me with an intent expression, but I guess she could see I didn't want to talk about it, for she turned back to the stockings she was darning. She must have been worrying, I thought, because it usually took some sort of cataclysmic occurrence before she could get herself to do any darning.

"I had an idea that you might be back early," she said. "It looks so much like rain."

It wasn't that I made a practice of keeping anything from her. It was just that I didn't want her to worry. She didn't say any more about it, although just from the condition of my legs, which were raw in places and had stuck to my trousers, she could certainly tell that something had happened.

Then I realized that she'd concern herself needlessly if I kept silent, and that this worry would so spread to other things that she'd become afraid I might be concealing things from her if only for her own peace of mind. I told her then, and it didn't seem important any more.

"It might be just as well if you ride only Cloud for awhile," I said. "Not that I think I'm any better a rider than you, but I just don't want you getting hurt."

"I don't want you getting hurt, either," she said, "especially not alone out in the woods somewhere."

"I think Chinook and I understand each other now," I said. "I don't think she'll ever be any more trouble."

"I hope not," Vena said, putting down her work and coming toward me. "I think it's easy for me to understand Chinook a little bit, too."

DUTIES OF THE WRANGLER

You're already in the wilderness, say, with your partner and a saddle cayuse and two pack horses apiece. You're going to break camp and travel on this day. At the first quickening of dawn, the one whose turn it is to be wrangler starts out to find and drive in the animals which you turned loose the afternoon before to feed. All of them, probably, have hobbles strapping their front legs rather closely together. The bells buckled around the necks of the leaders and any recalcitrants will clang, bong, and peal the melody of their whereabouts.

Nevertheless, the horses may be feeding anywhere from a few yards to maybe a half mile from camp, although the experienced wrangler usually keeps an ear open. If before dark they start to drift too far, he'll often edge around and whoop them back. His own horse, if he can manage it, is staked nearby in a lush stand of grass at the end of a picket rope.

Trouble comes when the animals are not all out of the same bunch. Then they may be scattered in several groups. It can take a good half of the morning before both partners have located them all. Every once in a while delays of this kind must be expected. If a particular knothead becomes too much of a nuisance, though, it may be tied short to a tree all one night so it will keep so busy eating the next night that it won't have time to wander. When the wrangler drives the horses into camp, he ties them up by their respective saddles.

DUTIES OF THE COOK

In the meantime, the partner whose turn it is to be cook starts dishing out breakfast. Then he sees to it that both he and his sidekick get their lunches, in many cases put up the night before. After washing and drying the dishes, he packs the kitchen and the food panniers, making sure that what he needs for the next meal is where he can get at it. He then turns to with his partner to roll up the tent and finish getting the outfit ready to travel.

PANNIERS

There is no standard size for panniers. Most of them, the better ones, measure on the outside about 22 inches long, 15 inches high, and 9 inches wide from front to back. Packers in country where it matters prefer the bottom angled inward so the pannier will not stick out on the animal and bump into trees. A lower portion 6 inches wide will be functional.

The top, bottom, and sides can be made of ⅜- or ½-inch waterproof plywood, and the ends of ⅞-inch pine or spruce. To prevent mice and chipmunks from getting at the contents when they are vulnerable, the food panniers can be lined with metal or with copper screening. Notches on the front edges are made for the lash ropes that secure the pannier on the sawbuck saddle. Hinges and fasteners can be either metal or leather.

Various camp outfitters sell panniers, or kyacks as they are also called, made of fiberboard and plywood. If you cannot easily rent them, you also can build them yourself, as most bushmen do. Some are made of the heaviest canvas. Especially picturesque, although not as practical as the wooden variation, are those made of tough, untanned cowhide laced together with the hair outside.

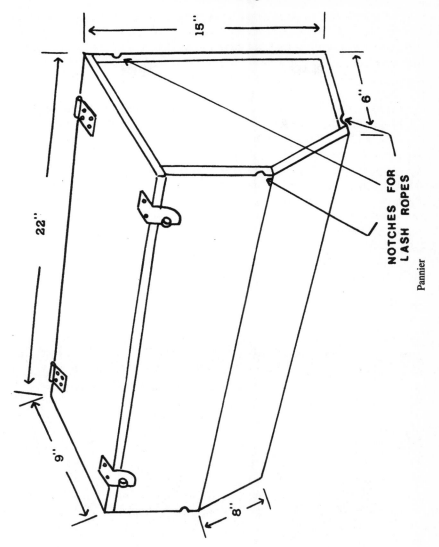

15"

6"

NOTCHES FOR
LASH ROPES

Pannier

22"

9"

8"

SADDLEBAGS

Camera equipment is usually carried on the riding horse. So are binoculars. Saddlebags are handy for this purpose in open country. If you're sidling around among trees, though, anything fragile is better wrapped in your extra shirt or down jacket and tied securely behind the pommel.

Watch it, too, when you stop, for a lot of cayuses have a habit of occasionally rolling while still saddled.

Fishing rods can be a problem. Some stow them in or by stiff rifle scabbards slung from the side of the riding saddle. Often the best idea is to have a stout aluminum or fiber case for them and to trust them to the most reliable pack horse.

TARPAULIN

Sleeping bag and air or foam mattresses may be rolled in a tarpaulin about eight foot square, which later may serve as a ground cloth, and tied with a rope. Such a bundle will measure about three feet by a foot and a half. Often flat rather than round, it will be some seven or eight inches thick. It can, therefore, be conveniently laid atop the saddle and panniers. The pack cloth of heavy waterproofed canvas, spread over each packhorse load before the crosstree diamond, one-man diamond, squaw, or other hitch is thrown, will protect the equipment from moisture and from snagging in the brush.

Be sure that the ax in the sheath goes where it is both safe and readily accessible. On a pack horse, it generally can be shoved under the lashings with the handle angling backward and with the sheath strapped over a rope as an additional precaution against loss.

Ordinarily, you should place the most often used articles at the top of their particular panniers which, along with the pack saddles, should be numbered to avoid confusion. Shirts and such can be used to wrap breakables. Tie possessions which dampness can ruin, such as camera equipment, securely within slightly inflated waterproofs. The oilskin variety was popular when I first took to the woods, but now lighter and far more secure plastic containers are cheaper and less bulky.

Equal weights must, as nearly as possible, be placed in each member of a pair of panniers so that the two will balance on the animal. It isn't a bad idea to carry a small bathroom scale for this purpose, as the panniers should be within two or three pounds of each other. Desirable maximum weights vary according to the animal. Fifty pounds is sometimes the limit.

Immediately after breakfast, then, each rider packs his own gear and bundles up his bedroll. He makes sure that he has on his person whatever he'll want during the day. He checks to see if his camera and extra clothing, including maybe a waterproof poncho, are ready to secure on his riding saddle.

PACKING LOADS ON HORSES

Two experienced individuals working together will pack a horse in about ten minutes when everything is at hand, and you soon become experienced. From this, you can figure approximately how long it takes you to get on the trail after the animals arrive. Every outdoorsman in horse country should learn how to pack. You never can tell when it may be necessary to lend a hand or to proceed on your own.

One mounts and dismounts from the left side of the horse as it faces forward. This is known, therefore, as the "on" or "near" side. Some horses become so accustomed to having this side the master side that they become skittish at any change.

When packing it saves time to work in pairs, but the offside person goes about the task as an assistant only, taking care of the tasks that can't be handled from the near side.

The first thing to make sure of is that the animal's back is clean. A curry comb and a brush will keep it well groomed and fit, especially if you are gentle with the animal at tender spots as where bones lie close to the surface. Care must be taken, too, that the saddle blanket is likewise as clean as possible. Never approach an animal, of course, before making it calmly aware of your presence.

Saddle Blanket

A good woolen saddle blanket, or other adequate pad, goes on initially. It must be smooth and soft. Throw it on close to the neck and then slide in toward the tail so that the hair will lie right. It should extend at least some three inches from where the saddle is to rest. When it has been smoothed into place, put a finger under its center front and back and lift it slightly from the backbone so as to provide ventilation, as well as to prevent the load from pressing unduly on the spine. The saddle goes on next.

Saddling Pack Horses

Some latigos (the long strap used to secure the cinch) have buckles. The trick with these is to make certain that all reasonable slack is taken up between the ring and the cinch, or the tongue of the buckle may slide loose and cause the load to slip.

More commonly, the off-side packer will hand you the cinch under the belly. Shove the latigo through the cinch and then continue it up through the ring on the saddle from the outside in. Depending on the length of the latigo and the size of the horse, repeat this until you have made at least two complete loops, one over the other. Although the saddle should be forward, the cinch must not be too close to the front legs, or friction will cause a sore. If the saddle has a rear cinch, do the same with that, only more loosely.

Now let the animal stand awhile, going on to saddle the others. A lot of horses, mules, and burros tense up at this stage and often take enormous breaths that will make for slack when they let the air exhale.

When you come back, shove your left hand between the animal and the cinch ring to keep the hide from wrinkling. Draw up on the latigo until it is so tight that you can barely get two fingers between the leather and the animal. Secure with two half hitches to the saddle ring—in from the top on the left-hand side, out from the back, around to the front and across to the right, and down inside the loop made by the crossover. Tuck any remainder out of the way.

The rear cinch, which is fastened the same way, should go just behind the middle of the animal, but should not be as tight as the front cinch, lest it interfere with breathing.

Slinging on the Load

Some panniers are made with leather loops or sling straps. When the panniers are smooth, a sling rope must be used to attach them to the pack saddle. This is an easy matter, however.

Take the light sling rope and, still standing on the near side, toss one end of it over the animal's back just ahead of the saddle. At about the middle of the rope, tie two half hitches or a clove hitch (see Chapter 1 for illustration of clove hitch) on the forward fork of the saddle.

Take the free end of the rope on your side and make a half hitch on the rear fork, leaving a large enough loop to go over the pannier. Bring the free end of the rope back and shove it under the loop. The same thing is done on the opposite side.

The off-side packer gets his pannier into place first because, with this routine, it is easier to remove this last when unpacking alone. Lift it well up into

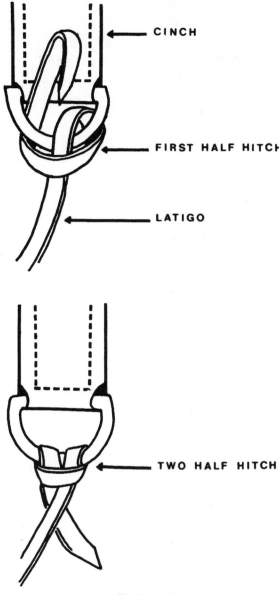

Cinching
Top: First step. *Bottom:* Second step.

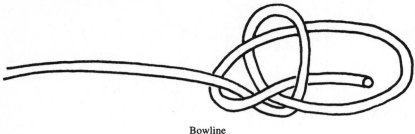

Bowline

the forks. Hold it in position with the palm of the right hand. With the left hand adjust the loop around the lower side of the pannier. Pull up the slack with the free end of the rope where it passes across the middle of the pannier. Now tie a bowline in the end of the rope so this will reach the top center of the load. Flip the loop over the animal so it can be reached from the near side.

Now sling on the near pannier in exactly the same fashion, except that no bowline is tied. Instead, slip the end of the near rope through the bowline on the far side, draw everything tight, and tie off.

After the panniers have thus been slung and secured, lay what you choose across or between them and spread your pack cover into place. Then, with a strong half-inch rope braided to the ring of a canvas pack cinch which, at its other extremity has something such as a large wooden hook, bind down the entire load.

One of the hitches shown in the illustrations can be used for this purpose. This should be made as tight as possible, particularly as the tension will be on the pack and not on the animal. Get purchase when you have to by bracing a foot against the animal's side.

SADDLING TO RIDE

The natural tendency when saddling, especially with the heavier western rigs, is to heave the girth rings and stirrups too high. This causes them to bang noisily against such tender spots as leg points and ribs. A lot of resultant shying and sidestepping can be avoided by swinging these just high enough to land easily on your mount's back, where they'll slide down smoothly.

Or place the right stirrup and the cinch of the breeching across the seat of the saddle. Then, gripping the horn with the left hand and the back center of the saddle with the right hand, swing the saddle just high enough so you can settle it easily on the blanket. Incidentally, you'll probably get so that you'll be able to do this with just one hand on the horn. Go around and straighten up, at the same time taking down the stirrup, cinch, or breeching.

The same fundamentals that apply to readying the animal for the pack saddle apply when it comes to saddling for riding. The knees are not used in western riding as they are in the east. With the western saddle, therefore, the

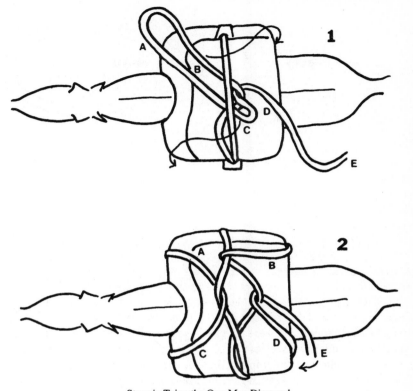

Steps in Tying the One-Man Diamond

Working from the on side of the animal, facing the tail, toss the cinch over the animal's back, reach under and pick up the cinch, and bind the running rope to the cinch hook from in to out. Pull up slack, run the loose rope up the side of the load, double, and then shove loop under the standing rope from back forward at the top of the pack to hold slack. Heave the running rope to the off side, go around there, and pull the free end of the running rope forward from the standing rope at the top of the load.

Put the end of the running rope over and under the forward end of the off load, then backward under the standing rope and pack, all as shown. Then pass the rope forward over the side of the load, double, and press the doubled part over and under the forward rope in a loop. Using the left hand, grab the double rope at loop just to the back of the standing rope. With the right hand pass the running rope down and close to the rear of the standing rope. Now pull up all slack.

Heave loose end across animal to the on side, across the center of the load. Move back to the on side and repeat what you've just done on the off side. Tighten everything. Finish off the hitch by passing the loose end of the line over and under the forward standing and running ropes, take up any slack with your foot braced against the load, and tie off.

stirrups should be long enough so that you'll clear the seat by about two inches when standing in them. You'll then be able to rely on balance and on the grip of your thighs, employing your partly tensed knees and ankles as

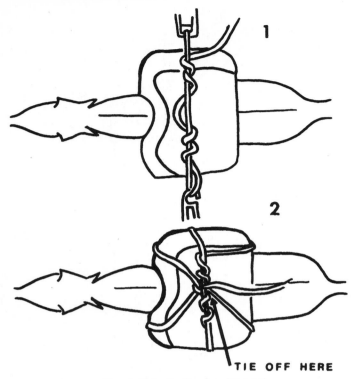

TIE OFF HERE

Steps in Tying the Crosstree Diamond

Stand at the on side of the hose, facing tail. Ease cinch over top of pack so that enough hangs loose under the horse's belly to be grasped and engaged in hook from in to out. Pull tight and hold by grasping the standing and running ropes in left hand.

Double loose part of running rope and thrust under standing rope from rear forward at top and middle of load. Then bring center of loop over and under standing rope again as shown, thus giving rope at either end of loop another complete turn around standing rope. Toss loose rope to off side of animal.

Go around back of the horse, with a reassuring hand on his rump, and bring line down along front, bottom, and back end of load, shoving rope end up through loop at top of pack. Take up slack and come back to on side of animal.

Pass running rope around front, bottom, and back end of what it is you're packing, then under the standing rope at the opposite middle of the loop. Take up slack, tighten all the way around, proceeding in sequence. Finish by pressing foot on load, pulling as tightly as you can, and finally tying off.

springs to absorb any roughness that would be jarring or jolting. There is a tremendous difference in horses in this respect. Without exaggeration, a very few actually trot more smoothly than others can walk.

MOUNTING AND RIDING

A smooth and sure way of getting into the western saddle is to take the lines in the left hand, stand to the left of the head of the animal and, facing the tail,

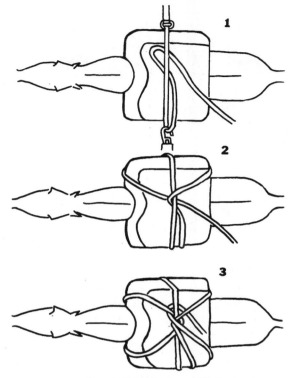

Steps in Tying the Squaw Hitch

Stand at on side of horse, facing tail. Toss the cinch over the top and middle of the pack so that you can readily reach it under the horse. Pass from in to out on the hook and draw up slack, being sure as always that the cinch passes smoothly under the middle of the horse's belly. Grab standing and running rope with left hand to keep tight.

With the right hand double the running rope, shoving this doubled part under the standing rope from rear forward in a bight as shown. Pull through sufficient slack line to make a loop big enough to pass over and around the off side of load. Move, carefully so as not to spook the animal, to the other side, turn loop over, and pass the loop around the ends and bottom of load from rear to front.

Come back to on side. There pass the running rope around the forward end, the bottom, and then the rear part of the load. Pull the end of the rope from above down, over, and beneath the standing, running, and back ropes at the top center of whatever it is you're packing. Starting at the beginning, tighten all the way around, bit by bit, pull taut, usually with the help of a foot braced against the load, and tie off.

Two packers can do a much faster job than one. The load must be smoothly installed and centered on all these hitches, then tightened evenly, or you're in for shifting packs and sore backs.

secure a firm grip on the bridle cheek with the left hand, put the left foot lightly in the stirrup, grab the horn securely with the right hand, and then swing aboard in one fluid motion while using the horn as a pivot. This natural arc is spoiled, as we can readily understand, by the awkward, if common, habit of grasping the back of the saddle with the right hand.

In any event, when you're ready to get on, particularly if you and the animal are strangers, the main thing is to be in control. Horses differ. With a very few, you'll have to rein the head around, forcing the animal into a turn while it insists on moving ahead before you're ready. Others begin to fret and to pitch if you're heavy on the bit. Mostly, a firm but light hold on the lines will be sufficient.

Keep the lines low ordinarily, although if a knothead is inclined to pitch, you may want to curb that impulse by holding its head high. Don't fall into the practice, very common among dudes, of knotting the ends of the reins together as soon as you climb on a strange horse. Then, if anything goes wrong or even if you get off for some reason, you're apt to find yourself plumb afoot.

The times when you want to ride reinless, twist them a couple of times around the horn and perhaps top with a single half hitch. Then, if anything goes amuck, the lines will soon be dangling, to halt the animal if it's been broken to ground-rein or to impede it long enough for you to have a chance to ease around and catch it.

HITTING THE TRAIL

When the outfit is ready to hit the trail, the lead rope of all but the front pack animal is tied to the tail, pack, or to a rope loop fastened for that purpose around the rear fork of the pack saddle on the horse ahead. The knot used is one that can be instantly jerked free if something goes wrong. The wrangler holds the head of the foremost animal and rides off.

Or, with the pack horses turned loose, occasionally with a wire mask on each so that it won't stop to graze, the wrangler starts ahead, and the other partner closes in behind. Occasionally, a horse bolts or strays out of line, and the rear man urges him back. This he does slowly and quietly, so as not to excite the string.

Some days may be full of all kinds of trouble; spooked horses, turning packs, and snagged or bogged-down animals. Little distance then will be covered. On other days, you may traverse as much as a rousing thirty miles. The thing is to try to keep the pack train moving, all the time watching for slipping loads that will necessitate repacking on the spot.

The wrangler is the man to say where the next camp shall be made. He is responsible for the horses, and he must stop where the feed is good, where there's water, and where he can hold the animals reasonably close. Of course, with two individuals it's often an equal partnership.

MAKING CAMP

Everyone generally turns to when camp is reached, catching the animals and tying them well apart. Preferably the lead ropes should be secured at least waist high and short enough so that the animals can't step over them or become entangled in nearby brush.

Knots are loosened and panniers eased to the ground in pairs, in such a way that their marks can be easily identified. Ropes are coiled and laid together in one place. Pack covers are folded and stacked or, if the weather is foul, spread protectively over the gear.

Saddles, which have probably been selected to fit certain animals and identified by names or numbers, are lined over a convenient log or upside down on the ground. Blankets are spread out, down side up, over their respective saddles to dry. If precipitation is falling or threatening, all these may be stacked in piles beneath the waterproof pack covers.

Finally, after perhaps some grooming, hobbles and bells should be strapped on and halters removed so that the animals will not accidentally get hung up by them. These halters, with their attached lead ropes, should be suspended in one place, away from little forest folk who would gnaw them for their salt.

PACK HORSE TRIPS FOR TWO

There is no reason why two individuals reasonably accustomed to handling horses, to camping in the wilderness, and to traveling safely in strange country should not take an extended pack horse trip by themselves. It means a lot of work for, if we fish for instance in virgin waters during the day, we will have cooking, tackle repairs, and odd jobs to take care of sometimes late into the night. Horse wrangling, too, will frequently interfere.

Two outdoorsmen can rent—or often more cheaply buy—four to six horses and live the life for months at a time. As for taking care of your own animals, lone trappers and prospectors often travel with six and seven.

Or, to a lesser extent, we can do the same thing with mules. In many ways most easily of all, one or both of us can pack gear on one or two burros and hike wherever we want to go.

THE TONIC OF WILDNESS

As Thoreau said, "We need the tonic of wildness—to wade sometimes in marshes where the bittern and the meadow hen lurk, and hear the booming of the snipe; to smell the whispering sedge where only some wilder and more solitary fowl builds her nest, and the mink crawls with its belly close to the ground.

"We can never have enough of nature. We must be refreshed by the sight of inexhaustible vigor, vast and titanic features, the wilderness with its living and its decaying trees, the thundercloud, the rain.

"If you have built castles in the air, your work need not be lost; that is where they should be. Now put the foundations under them."

PART SIX
SURVIVAL SKILLS: FINDING FOOD
AND BEING YOUR OWN DOCTOR

CHAPTER THIRTEEN

DOWN TO NOTHING: FINDING FOOD WHEN YOU'RE DESPERATE

Starvation is not a great deal more pleasant than most would expect. The body becomes auto-cannibalistic after a few foodless hours. The carbohydrates in the system are devoured first. The fats follow.

This might not be too disagreeable, inasmuch as reducing diets seek to accomplish much the same result. But then proteins from muscles and tendons are consumed to maintain the dwindling strength their loss more gravely weakens.

No reasonable nourishment should, therefore, be overlooked if one needs food. Furthermore, if you are ever stranded and hungry in the wilderness, be sure, while your strength is near its maximum, not to pass up any promising sources of sustenance.

Practices ordinarily contrary to both game regulations and good sportsmanship are justified in extreme emergencies by the more ancient law of survival.

Under ordinary circumstances many of the methods of securing food here considered are illegal practically everywhere and reasonably so. Repugnance accompanies even the thought of some, while at best their successful commission during emergencies will not be joined by any satisfaction except that resulting from the thus answered instinct to stay alive.

OVERCOMING FOOD PREJUDICES

Few will disagree, at least not when the moment of decision is at hand, that there is a point when luxuries as such become relatively unimportant.

One of the luxuries which is valued most highly is the freedom to indulge taste prejudices. These taste prejudices are commonly based on two factors.

First, there is a human tendency to look down upon certain foods as being beneath one's social station. When grouse are particularly thick in the Northeast, for example, they are often scorned among backwoodsmen as a "poor

247

man's dish." The same season, in the Northwest where there happens to be a scarcity of grouse but numerous varying hare, the former are esteemed while you hear natives apologizing for having rabbits in their pots. As it is everywhere in such matters, the lower the often self-designated station in life is, the more pronounced such evaluations become.

Second, it is natural to like the food to which you have become accustomed. Individuals in the United States and Canada have their wheat. The Mexican has his corn, the Asian his rice. These grains Americans and Canadians like also, but it would seem a hardship to have to eat them every day as one does wheat bread.

One's fastidiousness, too, is sometimes repelled by the idea of a Scandinavian's eating raw fish, although at the moment you may be twirling a raw oyster in grated horseradish. The Eskimo enjoys fish mellowed by age. Many farther south regard as choice some particularly moldy, odoriferous cheeses.

INSECTS AND REPTILES

Grasshoppers are edible when hard portions such as wings and legs have been removed. So are cicadas. Termites, locusts, and crickets are similarly eaten.

Some natives have capitalized on ants' acidity by mashing them in water sweetened with berries or sap to make a sort of lemonade. The eggs and the young of the ant are eaten also.

Both snakes and lizards are not only digestible, but often are considered delicacies for which some willingly pay many times the amount they expend for a similar weight of prime beef. The only time snake meat may be poisonous is when it has suffered a venomous bite, perhaps from its own fangs. This also holds true with lizards, the only poisonous ones in North America being the Southwest's Gila monster and Mexico's beaded lizard. To prepare the reptiles, behead, skin, remove the entrails, and cook like chicken to whose white meat the somewhat fibrous flesh often is compared.

An ancient method for securing already cooked insects, reptiles, and small animals is to fire large tracts of grassland and then to comb them for whatever may have been roasted.

Turtles

Turtle fat, from which no more heat than that from the sun renders a clear, savory oil, is so nutritious that the reptile is an unusually valuable food source. Blood and juices often are used to relieve thirst.

Occasionally it is possible to backtrack a female to a fresh nest of eggs, generally buried in sand or mud not far from water. Although not greatly esteemed for taste by those more accustomed to hen's eggs, these are nourishing at all stages.

A turtle can be killed by concussion or by beheading, care being taken even after it is dead to avoid both jaws and claws. If it is convenient, the turtle then can be scalded for several minutes by being dropped into boiling water. The under shell then may be quartered and the entrails removed, whereupon the meat can readily be simmered free of the upper shell.

FISH

Nutritional Value

Freshly caught fish also provide a completely balanced diet when sufficiently fat and not overcooked. The main difficulty with subsisting exclusively on fish arises from the fact that in calories they often are far less nourishing than one might expect. This fact can be vital.

Suppose there comes a time when you have nothing to eat but, say, trout. You're stranded in the wilderness, for example, about two days east of the Alaska Highway. No one knows you're missing, and therefore no one is searching for you. You know the general lay of the country well enough, by map, to be confident of cutting the Alaska Highway if you keep heading west by compass.

The area seems barren of game, but by really working at it, you may reasonably expect to average catching a half-dozen one-pound trout daily. Should you remain where you are for a few days and live on fish, with the idea of building up your dwindling strength for the journey that still lies ahead?

An office worker undergoing very little physical exertion requires some 2,000 to 2,500 calories daily. It is reasonable to generalize that an individual living a rugged outdoor life needs at least twice as many of these energy units. Any not supplied directly by food will be taken from the body's own carbohydrates, fats, and proteins.

A one-pound rainbow trout when caught, Canada's Department of National Health and Welfare has ascertained, contains only slightly more than 200 calories. So to eat 4,500 calories daily, you'd have to catch twenty such trout each day. Instead of gaining vigor on six pounds or so of fresh trout daily, you'd be very gravely losing strength. You'd do better to finish the journey as soon as possible.

Other considerations, of course, could alter the situation. You might have unlimited fish. You might be able to supplement the fish with sufficient other wild nutriments. The fish might be some more nourishing species, such as, in many localities, fat salmon averaging closer to 900 calories per fresh raw pound.

Too, the wild food available might be yours so easily that you could conserve a decisive amount of energy by relaxing most of the time beside a warm blaze. For although the basal energy requirements of the human system decline but little even when one is starving, a man lounging comfortably beside a campfire may consume only about 100 calories an hour, whereas struggling through the bush he can burn six times as much.

Emergency Fishing Methods

Just because you do not happen to have a hook and line doesn't mean you can't catch fish. Unravel a bit of sweater, for example. Tie on a small strip of bright cloth, such as the corner of a handkerchief. When the fish closes its mouth over the cloth, give the line a tug. There is a reasonable chance, especially where fishing is virgin, that you'll flip the quarry out on the bank. This doesn't always work, of course. Fish won't always take regular bait, either.

Homemade Hooks

You can devise almost any number of different types of hooks. A bent pin really works, as many a youngster has learned, the only trick being to maintain pressure so the fish won't slip off. An open safety pin is a somewhat larger hook of the same variety. Bent nails have been used with considerable success.

It follows, therefore, that hooks can be made out of practically any workable metal of sufficient rigidity. To make a really rugged one, lash the blade of a pocket knife partly open against a wooden wedge. A second blade, so opened at an opposite angle, can form a barb of sorts. The knife, so prepared, then can be hidden in a gob of bait.

You also can cut hooks from wood, preferably wood that is hard and tough. Whittle the shank first. Lash one or more sharp slivers so they slant upward from the lower end. You can even add a barb by lashing another sliver even

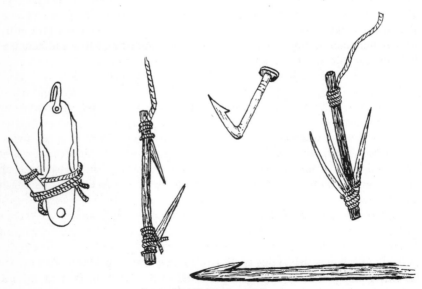

Improvised Fishhooks and Spear

more acutely downward from the top. Thorns, if available, can be utilized. Fish bones, too, will furnish both serviceable points and barbs.

Primitive Fishing Device

One of the most primitive fishing devices, still used successfully if not sportingly, is made by tying the line to the middle of a sharp piece of wood or bone that has been sharpened at both ends. Hidden in bait, this is swallowed by the fish, whereupon a jerk of the cord pulls it crossways.

Making Fishing Lines

Fish lines can be improvised in numerous ways. One method is to unravel a piece of fabric and to knot lengths of four or so threads together at frequent intervals. Another is to cut around and around a section of leather, forming a continuous lace, as described in chapter 3.

Line can be more scientifically made, after cutting or raveling any fabric or fiber that may be available so as to procure a number of long strands. Take four of these threads and fasten them at one end. Hold two threads in each hand. Roll and twist each strand clockwise between the thumb and forefinger of each hand, while turning those in the right hand counterclockwise around those held in the left. This twisting and winding must be done tautly, so the completed line will not unravel.

Depending on the lengths of thread, conclude each of the four strands about two inches apart so as to make the splicing on of new strands easier. About an inch before any thread stops, twist on a new strand to replace the one just ending.

This procedure can be continued, as long as material holds out, to make a line of any length. The same operation that will provide a small cord for ordinary fishing can be employed with a dozen or more strands to manufacture a fish line capable of landing a tuna or big lake trout.

Gigging

Gigging, which is illegal in many localities and not without reason, is the practice of catching fish by hooking them in the body. An Eskimo method is to dangle a long, smooth hook above which are suspended bits of bone that flutter and shine in the water. When a fish approaches to investigate, the line is suddenly jerked up the intervening two or three inches, with a good chance of being driven into the prey, which is at once hauled up before it has a chance to work loose. Gigging is often resorted to in waters where fish can be seen but not readily induced to bite.

Buttons and Spoons

A button often is successful as a lure. So is any bright small bit of metal. In its emergency kit the Hudson's Bay Company includes a tablespoon with a hole drilled in it so a hook can be wired in place for trolling or gigging.

Finding the Best Bait

Various insects, and even fuzzy seeds resembling them, will catch fish. Widely effective are grasshoppers, which, when available, can themselves be harvested with particular ease at night with the aid of a light.

"Experiment with bait," the Hudson's Bay Company advises any of its employees who may be in distress. "Look for bait in water, for this is the source of most fish food. Insects, crayfish, worms, wood grubs, minnows, and fish eggs are all good. After catching your first fish, examine the stomach and intestines. See what it is feeding on and try to duplicate it. If it is crayfish (a form of fresh-water crab), turn over the rocks in the stream until you get one."

If you succeed in finding many crayfish, incidentally, there's your meal, for once they are cooked by being dropped into boiling water, the lower portions are easily sucked free of the shells. One way to catch these is by driving a school into a restricted pool and dipping them out with a net made either by tightly interlacing foliage to a frame consisting of a bent green sapling, or by attaching some porous article of clothing to such a loop.

Fishing with Bare Hands

Fish such as salmon and herring throng up streams in such numbers at certain times of the year that one can catch and throw ashore large numbers of them with the bare hands. It also is possible, on occasion, to secure by hand alone quantities of such fish as smelt, when schools come up on beaches to spawn in the surf.

You also can find such fish as perch and trout wedged among rocks of fast little rivers. Still another way to capture fish with the bare hands is by feeling carefully among the nooks and cavities in stream banks. You can even catch fish, strange to say, by forming a sort of cave with your cupped hands held motionless against a bank. Trout in particular will investigate, whereupon, by the acquired art of closing the hands quickly enough but not too hurriedly, you'll have them.

When rations are short one sometimes can splash up shallow brooks, driving any fish ahead of him. When these are cornered in a pool, he can, if he must, block their retreat with piled stones and go in and kill them with a club. Small streams, too, often can be diverted so as to strand fish in pools.

If one is really up against it in beaver country, occasionally it is possible to strand a life-sustaining catch by prying an opening in a beaver dam. Another technique is to wade in, riling with the feet the muck that amasses behind such a dam and catching with bare hands the temporarily mud-blinded fish.

Building a Fish Trap

Fish often can be trapped with considerable success in cases of dire need. One such basic trap, recommended by the Hudson's Bay Company for use under life-or-death conditions, can be built by driving sticks and branches into the bottom so their tops protrude above the water. The trap consists of a narrow-mouth enclosure into which the fish are led by a wide funnel-like V.

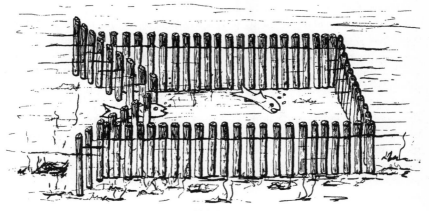

Fish Trap

Attracted by some such bait as spoiled fish or decomposed meat, the prey guided into the pen through the slit at the apex are, in enough cases, unable to find their way out.

Materials used in making such a trap vary. Stretching a net around stakes will, if the former is available, save considerable energy. Stones can be utilized, perhaps leading into a natural fresh-water or tidal pool.

Spearing

You may have already experimented with making spears, perhaps sharpening a long dry stick for the purpose and hardening this point over the embers of a campfire. It's also possible to fashion a barbed spear by whittling the point in this instance at the joint of an inverted crotch, an inch or two of whose angle you have slivered into a sharply restraining projection. You also may test the efficacy of barbs and tips of bone, stone, or metal that you have lashed into place.

One procedure is to thrust the spear very slowly through the water toward the target, often to within inches of the fish before making the final jab. With the help of a light, perhaps a torch of flaming birch bark or a burning pine knot, you can, many times, spot a fish at night lying practically motionless in shallow water. By advancing the spear cautiously, aiming low to counteract deceptive refraction, it becomes increasingly easy to pin a majority of such fish against the bottom.

Drugging

Certain Indian methods of fishing may prove life savers to the hunger wayfarer. One procedure is to crush the leaves and stalks of the mullein, or fishweed, *Croton setigerus*. These are dropped into a still pool or temporarily dammed brook. The fish therein, momentarily narcotized, will float to the surface where they should be immediately secured.

The bulbous root of the so-called soap plant, *Chlorogalum pomeridianum,* can be similarly used. Fish caught by these emergency means are as wholesome as if merely dazed by concussion.

OTHER MARINE FOODS

Seaweeds

All seaweeds are good to eat. You can munch them raw, simmer them in fresh water to make soup, boil them with meat or vegetables, and even dry them for a number of other future uses. Algae, of which seaweeds are one type, are, in fact, regarded by research scientists as potentially valuable sources of the gigantic amounts of protein-rich food that may be needed if the increasing world population becomes so burdensome that present supplies are inadequate.

Sea Cucumbers

Sea cucumbers are eatable boiled, fried, stewed, and raw. Actually an animal, the sea cucumber also is dried and smoked by some natives. The easily recognizable organism, so common along seashores, has a rough and flexible body about six to eight inches long when contracted and about twice that length when expanded. The five long white muscles, left after the insides have been discarded and the slimy outer skin scraped away, are what is used. Their taste is not unlike that of clams.

Sea Urchin Eggs

The sea urchin, a marine animal related to the starfish, is a principal source of nourishment in many localities. Safe when found in the temperate and arctic waters of this continent where they often can be gathered in quantity at low tide, sea urchins are shaped like slightly flattened balls. They have thin, fragile shells that often bristle with movable spines. The lengths of eggs inside the top shell are edible both raw and cooked.

Abalone

The abalone, a large, rock-clinging mollusk, is particularly well known along the Pacific coast of North America. There hundreds at a time, attached

Sea Cucumber

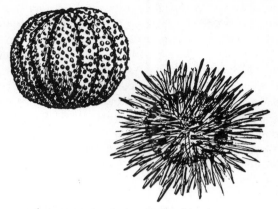

Sea Urchin. *Left:* spineless. *Right:* with spines.

to boulders and ledges, are revealed by low tides. Also they are occasionally seen floating free in seaweed. Their flattened shells, which vary from black and green to red, are fantastically lined with mother-of-pearl.

By abruptly inserting a long, thin instrument such as a sheath knife or stick between the abalone and the rock and prying quickly, the shellfish can be detached, usually with little trouble, before it has a chance to adhere more tightly. The operation otherwise requires a heavier tool and considerable pressure.

The abalone then can be levered from the shell, which not infrequently has a diameter of ten inches or so and therefore considerable utility as a bowl. Or the shell can be cracked with a rock and picked off. The hard white meat is what is retained. This may be sliced into thin steaks and tenderized by pounding with the flat edge of a stone, then very briefly fried, broiled over open coals, or diced and simmered into chowder.

Shellfish

Any time we may be up against it for food, there will be, in general, no more promising areas in which to seek nourishment than those near water. Piles of shells beside a creek may be the clue to clams that often can be seen in clear water or felt beneath the bare feet.

Saltwater clams, although not so easily dug, may be secured at low tide. Evidence of these bivalves' presence is furnished by elongated siphons or the marks left by the withdrawals thereof. Along Pacific shores below the Aleutians, all dark portions should be discarded for the six months beginning with May and ending with October because of possibly dangerous concentrations of toxic alkaloids therein, the white meat alone then being eaten.

Snails are edible and, by some peoples, particularly relished. So are scallops, oysters, and shrimps. Eels also are very much edible, in many localities being regarded as superior to any other fish.

Mussels, with one important exception, may be safely eaten if care is taken to avoid any that do not close tightly when touched. The small, bluish-black mussels found attached, usually in clusters, to seashore rocks become poisonous at certain times of the year along the Pacific Coast below the Aleutians. The poison, which, being alkaloid, cannot be destroyed by heat, is the result of a diet which includes venomous organisms that drift shoreward from about the end of April through October. If there is any doubt whatsoever about when, in any particular area, these mussels are fit for food, they should be avoided entirely.

Crabs are all good. Usually they can be immobilized in shallow water for a long enough time either to crush them or reach behind and pick them up. They will attach themselves readily to flesh lowered on a line. Although saltwater varieties may be eaten raw, land crabs are sometimes infected with parasites and should be dropped live into boiling water for at least twenty minutes.

BIRDS

All birds are good to eat. When they are moulting and unable to fly, it is not difficult to corner them on foot. Large flocks may occasionally be captured by driving them into nets or traps. Roosting or nesting birds can be secured by a noose fastened to the end of a pole. Birds also can be caught in fine snares placed where they nest, feed, or congregate. Deadfalls get them, too.

Even the riper eggs, or any eggs it may be possible to secure, are nourishing. If one has continued access to a large colony at nesting time, one way to be assured of fresh eggs is to mark whatever is already in the nests, perhaps removing all but a few, if conditions seem to justify it.

Bagging Birds without Guns

Game birds such as ptarmigan and grouse promise feasts for anybody lost in the wilderness, especially as a few stones or sticks are often the only weapons needed. If one misses the first time, such fowl usually will afford a second and even a third try. When they do fly, they generally go only short distances and may be successfully followed, particularly if this is done casually and at such an angle that it would seem that you were going to stroll on past.

Bird Traps

Traps also work well with birds. A stick fence, put up in a narrowing spiral and baited, will sometimes catch in its center fowl such as quail. Geese can be bagged in a ditch some four feet deep into which they are led by bait such as wild grain. When one rushes suddenly at the geese, they try to fly but are unable to spread their wings.

Turkey also are taken by the use of bait, one ruse consisting of attracting them head down under a low fence. Once turkeys so pen themselves and, upon finishing their pecking, raise their long necks, it often takes them too long a time to figure how to retreat.

Bola

One can improvise a bola, a primitive missile consisting of stones attached to the ends of thongs. Although the Spanish peoples generally are thought of in connection with the bola, Eskimos use a device of this type consisting of several cords about a yard long with a small weight at the extremity of each.

The bola is grasped at the center from which all cords radiate, and the weights are twirled above the head. Hurled at flying birds, the spinning strings often twist around one or more and bring them to the ground.

Easily Caught Scavengers

Gulls and other scavenger birds can be easily although unsportingly caught by a man who is desperate enough for food. A short bone or stick sharpened at both ends is secured in the middle by a line, preferably tied to something limber, such as a sapling, and then concealed in some bait such as decomposed fish.

GAME

Utilizing the Whole Animal

Some natives roast the bland young antlers of the deer family when these are in velvet. Others esteem the stomach contents of herbivorous mammals such as caribou, for such greens, mixed as they are with digestive acids, are not too unlike salad prepared with vinegar.

Some aborigines, as desirous of wasting nothing as those gourmets who cook and eat whole plucked woodcock, do not bother to open the smaller birds and animals they secure, but pound them to a pulp which is tossed in its entirety into the pot. Other peoples gather moose and rabbit excrement for thickening boiled dishes. Even such an unlikely ingredient as gall has, among other uses, utility as a seasoning.

Animals should not be bled any more than can be helped if food is scarce. Blood, which is not far removed from milk, is unusually rich in easily absorbed minerals and vitamins. Our bodies, for illustration, need iron. It would require ten ordinary eggs to supply one man's normal daily requirements. Four tablespoons of blood are capable of doing the same job. Fresh blood can be secured and carried, in the absence of handier means, in a bag improvised from the entrails. One way to use it is in broths and soups, enlivened perhaps with a wild vegetable or two.

The skin of the animal is as nourishing as a similar quantity of lean meat. Baking a catch in its hide, although ordinarily both a handy and tasty method of preparing camp meat occasionally, is therefore a practice to be avoided when rations are scarce.

Rawhide, incidentally, also is high in protein. Boiled, it has even less flavor than roasted antlers, and the not overly appealing look and feel of the boiled skin of a large fish. When it is raw, a usual procedure, naturally enough adopted in emergencies, is to chew on a small bit until that becomes tiresome, and then to swallow the slippery shred.

The mineral-rich marrow found in the bones of animals that were in good physical condition at demise is not surpassed by any other natural food in caloric strength. What is, at the same time, the most delectable of tidbits is wasted by the common outdoor practice of roasting such bones until they are on the point of crumbling. A more nutriment-conserving procedure is to crack them at the onset, with two stones if nothing handier is available. The less the marrow is cooked the better it will remain as far as nutrition is concerned. All this is something to consider if anyone desperate for food happens upon temporary salvation in the form of a skeleton of a large animal.

When food supplies are limited, nothing should be cooked longer than is considered necessary for palatability. The only exception is when there may be germs or parasites to be destroyed. The more food is subjected to heat, the greater are the losses of nutritive values.

Nearly every part of North American animals is edible. An occasional exception is the polar bear and ringed- and bearded-seal liver, which become so excessively rich in vitamin A that they are poisonous to some degree at certain times and are usually as well avoided. All fresh-water fish are likewise good to eat.

You will probably want to eat most of any animals you can secure if short of food. Some parts, as, for example, the liver, whose abundance of vitamin A has caused it to be recognized even among primitive tribes as a specific for night blindness, contain in more concentrated form certain of the necessary food elements. But any section of plump fresh meat is a complete diet in itself, affording all the necessary good ingredients even if you dine on nothing but fat, rare steaks for week after month after year.

Capturing Small Game

How to Use Deadfalls

For the capture of food animals, the Hudson's Bay Company recommends the use of deadfalls by any of its employees who may be stranded without

Figure-Four Trigger

adequate sustenance in the northern wilderness. The Company of Adventurers' pattern of the deadly figure-four trigger is effective.

Essentially, you might prepare a deadfall by lifting one end of a heavy object such as a log. Prop up this end with a stick, doing so with such studied insecurity that any animal or bird who moved the support would knock it loose. You can encourage this by affixing some bait to the prop. It's possible to go even further, arranging a few branches so that, to reach the bait, the victim would place himself so as to receive the full weight of the dislodged deadfall back of the shoulders.

Snares

Even if you have a gun, you may want to set a few snares, the principles of which are as simple as they are primitive. With a strong enough thong or rope, you can snare deer and larger animals. With nothing huskier than light fishline or horsehair, squirrels and rabbits can be caught.

A snare is, in effect, a slip noose placed with the object of tightening about and holding a quarry if the latter inadvertently moves into it.

The size of the snare depends on the size of the animal to be trapped. For example, on a rabbit trail the loop should be about four inches in diameter and hang 1½–3 inches above the ground.

Snare

Suppose you want to snare a rabbit for the pot. It's evident that they, like other animals, follow regular paths. Try, therefore, to hang the slip noose so the rabbit will run headfirst into it and quickly choke itself.

It helps to go one step further and narrow the trail at that particular spot. This can be accomplished in one of several ways. You can drop a branch or small tree as naturally as possible across the track, making a narrow slit in it in which to suspend the noose and shove a few sticks into the ground to serve as a funnel. You can block the top, bottom, and sides of the runway with brush except for a small opening where the loop awaits.

All possible guile should be bent to make everything seem as natural as possible. The necessity for this increases in direct proportion with the intelligence of the prey sought. Trappers customarily prepare snares months ahead of time and leave them, with the nooses harmlessly closed until fur season, to blend them with the surroundings. Small pot animals, however, usually can be snared by beginners with a minimum of artifice.

A quick way to collect squirrels, for instance, is to lean a pole against a conifer under which there is considerable squirrel sign, and at six or so points on the pole attach small, closely lying nooses. A squirrel scampering up the incline runs his head into the waiting loop and falls free. Its dangling there does not seriously deter other squirrels from using the same route and being so caught themselves.

You can tie one end of any snare to a stationary object such as a pole or tree. You can tie it, particularly if snow makes tracking easy, to a drag such as a chunk of deadwood. Preferably, you can bend a sapling and arrange a

Bent-Branch Snare

trigger so the animal will be lifted off its feet and, if not choked as humanely as possible under the conditions, at least rendered unable to exert direct pressure.

Other Weapons

Both slingshots and bows and arrows are so familiar that, inasmuch as you will be limited in any event by the materials at hand, there is probably no need to do more than suggest them as survival weapons. As for their successful use, this will depend largely on practice. Do the best you can. If you have the ingenuity and resourcefulness necessary for survival under extreme conditions, you are likely to do extremely well.

Smoking Out Game

Distasteful as it may be to him, a starving man is occasionally forced to smoke small animals from places of concealment. Sometimes an animal also can be driven to within reach of a club by quantities of water poured into a burrow.

The opening may be such that it will be possible to impale the creature on a barbed pole or to secure it by twisting a forked stick into its hair and skin. One frequently is able to dig with success. One also may have some luck by spreading a noose in front of the hole, hiding a short distance away, and jerking the loop tight when the quarry ventures out.

LEMMINGS

Lemmings have been found valuable as an emergency food by members of the Royal Canadian Mounted Police on extended patrols. Lemmings are the little stub-tailed mice that, when reaching the ocean on their migrations, occasionally start swimming in the possible belief that it is just another pond or lake.

"In winter they rest on or near the ground, deep in snow drifts," say Mounted Police sources, "and you will have to dig for them. In summer you can find them by overturning flat rocks. You can get them by setting snares of very fine wire along the runways. Lemming are constantly preyed upon by shrews, weasels, foxes, and owls."

PORCUPINES

Porcupines, like nettles and thistles, are better eating than it might seem reasonable to expect. The sluggish rodent is the one animal even the greenest tenderfoot, although weak with hunger, can kill with something no more formidable than a stick.

Porcupines cannot, of course, shoot their quills, but any of these that are stuck in the flesh by contact should be pulled out immediately, for their barbed tips cause them to be gradually worked out of sight. This danger from quills is one reason why it is poor practice to cook a porcupine, as is sometimes done, by tossing it into a small fire. Very often all the quills are not burned off. Even if they are, a considerable amount of the valuable fat will be consumed as well.

The best procedure is to skin out the porcupine, first turning it over so as to make the initial incision along the smooth underneath portion. Many who've dined on this meat consider the surprisingly large liver especially flavorful.

FROGS

Frog meat is one example of the often disdained foods, sometimes so expensive in the more fashionable dining salons of the world, that nature furnishes free for the taking. The amphibians can be hooked with fishing tackle and small fly. They can be caught with string and bit of cloth, the former being given a swift yank when the latter is taken experimentally into the mouth.

Frogs can be secured with spears of various types. A sharpened stick will do. They can be so occupied at night by a light that you'll be able to net them and even, if you go about it slowly, to reach cautiously around and clamp a hand over one.

Most of the delicately flavored meat is on the hind legs which can be cut off in pairs, skinned, and in the absence of cooking utensils, extended over hot coals on a green stick for broiling. If rations were scant, you'd use the entire skinned, cleaned frog, perhaps boiling the meat briefly with some wild greens (see chapter 18).

Letting Predators Hunt for You

If you are ever stranded and hungry, it may be worthwhile to watch for owls, for spying one roosting in a quiet, shadowy place is not unusual, and it may be possible to steal close enough to knock it down. Although not so large and plump as might seem from outward appearances, an owl nevertheless is excellent eating.

What is more likely, however, is that you may scare an owl from a kill and thus secure yourself a fresh supper. You may also have such good fortune, perhaps earlier in the day, with other predatory birds such as hawks and eagles. It is not uncommon to come upon one of these which has just captured a partridge, hare, or other prey that is proving awkward to lift from the ground, and, by running, to drive the hunter away with its talons empty.

Wolves, coyotes, and foxes also may be surprised at fresh kills that are still fit for human consumption. Such carnivora will seek new whereabouts at the sight or scent of an approaching human being.

Coming up to a bear's kill may be something else again. A wild bear probably won't dispute your presence. Then again it may. Although the chances are very much against this latter probability, that is all the more reason not to take disproportionate risks.

If you are unarmed and really need the bear's meal, you must plan and execute your campaign with all reasonable caution. This probably will mean, first of all, spotting in the minutest detail preferably at least two paths of escape in case a fast exit should be advisable. This should not be too difficult where there are small trees to climb.

You'll then watch for your opportunity, and if, for instance, the kill is a still warm moose calf, perhaps build a large fire beside it, discreetly gathering enough fuel to last for several hours—until morning if night is close at hand. Take care, in any event, to be constantly alert until well away from the locality, realizing that bears, especially when they have gorged themselves, have a habit of dropping down near their food.

If you have a gun, you will be able to judge for yourself if the best procedure may not be to bag the bear itself. Fat becomes the most important single item in almost every survival diet, and the bear is particularly well fortified with this throughout most of the year. Usually, except for a short period in the spring, bear flesh is particularly nourishing.

Many people, most of whom have never tasted bear meat nor smelled it cooking, are prejudiced against the carnivore as a table delicacy for one reason or another. One excuse often heard concerns the animal's eating habits. Yet the most ravenous bear is a finicky diner when compared to such offerings as lobster and chicken.

It is only natural that preferences should vary, and if only for this reason, it may be interesting to note that many who live on wild meat most of the time relish plump bear more than any other North American game meat with the single exception of mountain sheep. Furthermore, these individuals include a sizable number who, after long professing an inability to stomach bear meat in any form, found themselves coming back for thirds and even fourths of bear roast or bear stew, under the impression that anything so savory must be, at the very least, choice beef.

CHAPTER FOURTEEN

THE WILDERNESS DOCTOR: YOU!

What would be a very minor accident in a city, with assistance as near as the telephone, could be an extremely serious and even fatal misstep in the wilderness. So, both consciously and subconsciously, most individuals are wholesomely careful to sidestep trouble when in remote areas. Away from the masses, too, one is not so apt to become involved in the lapses and shortcomings of others.

All this is a major reason why among able-bodied men and women the probability of an accident or serious physical trouble in the deep wilderness is extremely small. In the comparative cleanness of the silent places, furthermore, there is correspondingly little likelihood of infection.

The exception to this latter circumstance has to do with the progressive lessening of built-up immunities when you are not in continual contact with the ills of civilization. An example is the common cold. This is a gradual matter and, being important only on recontact, is at most a minor consideration unless you are going to remain in remote country for months or years.

FIRST AID KITS

Anyone who goes more than a half a day from civilization and a doctor should, whenever possible, be armed with an adequate first aid kit and the working knowledge of how to use it. This precaution he owes, at the very least, both to himself and to any who accompany him. No more than a reasonable measure, it sometimes can mean the difference between an easily repaired disability and one that lasts a lifetime.

The ready-packed commercial kits, fine as they are for many purposes, seldom are satisfactory for the individual who wanders far from beaten trails. One reason is that their assembly is based more or less on the assumption that the patient can be placed under a doctor's care within a comparatively brief period. Furthermore, these kits do not always include provisions for those

264

accidents most likely to occur in wild country. As for the Army first aid kit, this is designed for the emergency treatment of battle wounds.

It is not necessary that such an emergency aid kit be carried on the person, although it should be readily available at the camp, canoe, cabin, or other base of operations. Even a small and compact affair attached to the belt soon becomes an unwarranted nuisance, however, particularly as, at best, one would be useful in no more than a disproportionate few emergencies. Something can always be extemporized on the spot to do for a short time. Even a functional splint, for example, can be improvised from a thick live roll of birch bark peeled from a tree whose circumference is similar to that of the injured limb.

Basic Wilderness Medicine Kit

Medical Supplies	Treatment Uses
1 triangular 40" sterile bandage, with 2 safety pins	Direct application while sterile over wounds, covering sterile dressings, padding, splint and traction ties, tourniquet.
6 gauze roller bandages of assorted widths in individual sterile packages; 6 gauze compresses, 3 inches square, each in sterile packing	Direct application over wounds, direct pressure to stop bleeding, holding compresses in place.
1 package small adhesive compresses with plastic tape and plain sterile pads	Cover minor wounds, tape abrasions to guard against irritation and infection, protect blisters, draw cuts together, etc.
1 small bar soap	Cleanse hands before applying first aid, scrub wounds.
50 or less aspirin tablets, 5-grain	Counteract pain, relieve shock, lower temperature.
2 rolls adhesive tape, 2" wide	General taping, holding compress in place, emergency repairs.
2 elastic bandages, 4" wide	Applied fully stretched over compress, one or more of these as needed to control severe bleeding while, unlike the dangerous and temporary tourniquet, permitting circulation. Furthermore, these can be used anywhere, while tourniquets will serve only for the extremities. Even here, application will many times permit the gradual and fairly immediate removal of an already applied tourniquet. Good for strapping chest to exclude air in puncture wounds, for bandaging of fractures and dislocations, and for pressure bandages when applied at half stretch for strains and sprains.
1 snake bite kit	In bad snake country, each individual should have a personal kit on his person at all times.

¼-oz. tube of antiseptic-anesthetic eye ointment	Soothing and treating eye injuries and minor infections, deadening eye prior to removing imbedded particles, treatment of pain and irritation of snow blindness.
1 good fever thermometer	Average normal temperature is 98.6, fluctuations of one degree not usually being regarded as significant.
1 small high-quality scissors, pointed	Spreading in preference to slashing the incisions indicated in snake bite treatment. Such disruption of the tissues, although painful, will more safely avoid injury to blood vessels and tendon.
1 sharply pointed tweezers or splinter forceps	Removing thorns and splinters. Forceps also valuable for spreading open, rather than cutting, certain incisions.
2 curved surgeon's needles, with ligature and needle holder	For emergency sewing, when sterilized, of wounds not easily closed by other means. Cleanse wound first, as by flushing liberally with sterile water. Pick out any debris and scrub with soap if that seems necessary.
Oil of cloves	To treat toothache. Dip bit of cotton in oil and insert in freshly cleaned cavity that is causing toothache. More modern treatment may well be favored by your doctor.
Vitamin B complex and vitamin C in high-potency, stress doses	To replenish body supplies being drained by severe accident or illness. It is then important to maintain adequate nutrition, emphasizing B complex, C, and protein.

In addition to the items in the list above, be sure to take along on wilderness treks a first-aid guide, supplemented, preferably by marginal notes made with your doctor's help, with information about the additional steps that may become necessary in remote areas. The terse, compact booklet put out by the U.S. Forest Service is excellent.

Versatile Household Pharmaceuticals

There are other odds and ends that you may want to put in the emergency aid kit, as for example something such as salve for lips chapped by wind and sun. Items available elsewhere in your outfit can frequently be made to perform double duty, however.

Baking Soda

Baking soda, according to the medical and dental professions, is as good a dentrifice as most and far less expensive than any of the manufactured products.

A paste of baking soda and water applied to insect stings and bites often will help to reduce the swelling and irritation. Soaking in water when possible is even simpler. Daubing on mud will do, too, in a pinch. The itching from hives, skin irritation caused by chafing, allergies, and so on, can often be relieved by patting on a paste of baking soda and water or by applying bandages or compresses soaked in a saturated solution of sodium bicarbonate.

For indigestion, ¼ teaspoon of baking soda in ½ glass of water, not to be repeated more than two or three times any day and definitely not to be used habitually, often helps ease the discomfort of acid indigestion and heartburn. If the necessity for an antacid is prolonged, one of the inert alkalies should be used, instead.

Half a teaspoon of baking soda in a glass of water will serve as a gargle or mouthwash.

Salt

Half a level teaspoon of salt in a glass of water is regarded by many doctors as equal to commercial mouthwashes. No larger a proportion of salt should be used, for when a solution is employed that is stronger in salt than the body fluid, its tendency is to draw natural moisture out of the system, dehydrating tissue and causing irritation.

Plain ordinary table salt, a rounded teaspoon in a quart of warm water taken preferably before breakfast or at any rate on an empty stomach, will serve as a purge if you ever need one, passing through the digestive system in about half an hour. A quart of cold spring water, enjoyed while one is washing up the first thing in the morning, is also often effective as a laxative.

WHAT TO DO WHEN THINGS GO WRONG

Keeping healthy and fit is especially important when you're on your own. Protection against cold and heat, as well as knowledge of how to find water and food, will be vital to your health. But there are more rules you should heed.

Drink enough water to avoid dehydration, an important consideration, too, in winter. If water is scarce or difficult to obtain, avoid excessive dehydration from sweating.

Save your strength, avoid fatigue, and get enough sleep. If you can't sleep at first, get a fire going if you possibly can and lie down beside it relaxing and loosening up. If you are walking out or doing other hard work, try resting for a few minutes each hour, not long enough to stiffen up. Resting this way, you rid your body of some 30 percent of the lactic acid buildup in the first five to seven minutes. But during an additional quarter hour you'd lose only some 5 percent more.

Take care of your feet. These will be most important, particularly if you plan to walk out. If your feet hurt, take care of them right away. Examine your feet when you first stop to see if there are any red spots or blisters. Apply adhesive tape smoothly on your skin where shoes rub.

Guard against skin infection. Your skin is the first line of defense against this trouble. Try to wash even the smallest cut or scratch, preferably with soap and water. Keep your fingernails short, especially in fly season, to prevent infection from scratching. Cuts and scratches are more apt to become seriously infected particularly in hot country, and a bad infection could hurt your chances of coming out safely. Wherever you are, make a habit of personal cleanliness. Keep your body, clothing, and camp clean.

Guard against intestinal sickness. Purify all water used for drinking, brushing the teeth, dish washing, and the like, either with water purification tablets or by boiling it for five minutes. At altitudes above sea level, boil it an additional minute for each thousand feet of elevation.

Don't worry about a slowdown of the digestive functions. This will take care of itself harmlessly in a few days if you exercise and drink plenty of water.

This section is intended as a reference for those who may venture into the wilderness—places in which ready access to professional medical help would be impossible. This is not a home reference for the health problems of everyday life or a treatment substitute for those traveling where physicians and medical facilities are readily available.

There are occasions when it's tough and even terrifying to be the one who has to decide what to do and to assume all of the responsibility. That's when not knowing what ought to be done hurts. And bad decisions—made in ignorance—are truly sometimes the hardest kinds to outlive.

If you love visiting the backlands, follow good general rules. The outdoorsman having a special health problem such as diabetes or epilepsy should always get complete counsel from his doctor before heading for the remote reaches.

It is strongly recommended that before traveling in the wilderness you enroll in an advanced first-aid training course, and follow up with periodic refresher classes. Emergency care treatment is constantly being improved, and the serious outdoorsman should stay on top of the most current procedures.

Always seek medical help when it's available.

TREATMENT OF CUTS

The object of treatment of lacerations is the stopping of bleeding, apposition of the skin edges to promote healing with a minimum of scarring, and prevention of infection.

If the bleeding is heavy, this will have to be stopped first. It is surprising how bleeding usually will stop spontaneously, even in the nastiest cuts. The bleeding, even in a completely severed finger, usually will stop with only pressure over the bleeding area.

Using a Compress

The first thing to do, then, is to make *steady,* firm pressure over the cut with a folded gauze, handkerchief, or whatever is available. Do not keep dabbing, as many do, and do not keep looking to see what is going on beneath the compress. Hold the compress for a minimum of five minutes before looking. The chances are that this will have stopped, or at least controlled, all or most of the bleeding.

Cleaning the Wound

The wound should be cleaned next. If it is a clean knife or ax cut, irrigation with drinking water may be adequate. If the wound is dirty and contaminated with foreign material, all bits of dirt, twigs, and the like should be meticulously picked out. Then the wound should be gently but thoroughly irrigated with soapy water until clean. Do the job well. There is no hurry.

There is no place for the use of alcohol, Merthiolate, or similar antiseptics in these injuries, although year after year first-aid books tell you to douse wounds liberally with them. It is true that these substances kill germs, but they also kill tissue, and using them in open wounds will devitalize (kill) tissue. Because germs grow best in devitalized tissue, and some germs are always present, you can see that these preparations set the stage for a future wound infection. At the very least, they delay rather than hasten healing.

Bits of frayed and devitalized tissue are best trimmed off with manicure scissors. This usually is painless because the tissue already is torn loose and is without feeling. Frequently some small amount of bleeding restarts during the cleansing, and again this will respond to pressure. In dirty wounds, it is best to use water which has been boiled for five minutes at sea level, and an additional minute for each extra 1,000 feet of altitude, then cooled.

The best way to handle a cut or scrape is to wash it well with plenty of soap and water, dry it well, and apply a dressing.

Butterfly Tape for Gaping Cuts

If the wound is gaping, it will have to be brought together. This is done most easily with a Butterfly. A Butterfly is a plastic tape which, as illustrated, is applied across the laceration to pull and hold the edges together. This will suffice in most cases.

Severe Bleeding

There are two types of bleeding, venous and arterial. You should always examine the injury carefully, as some bleeding wounds that appear serious can in reality be minor. Venous bleeding is usually dark and flows smoothly.

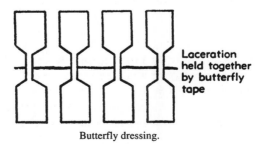

Laceration held together by butterfly tape

Butterfly dressing.

Arterial bleeding, on the other hand, is usually bright red and pulses or spurts from the wound. Massive arterial bleeding can be fatal within a few minutes, and quick action is mandatory.

The direct pressure method already described stops bleeding in the majority of cases. If this method fails, three other techniques are recommended: elevation, pressure on the supplying artery, and applying a tourniquet. A tourniquet should be used only in a critical emergency, if all other methods fail.

If there is no evidence of a fracture, the affected part should be raised to a level higher than the victim's heart. This method helps to slow blood loss by reducing blood pressure in the injured area. Direct pressure on a thick pad over the wound should be continued during elevation.

If direct pressure and elevation fail to stop bleeding, you can use pressure points in addition to these techniques. It's best if you can get some help to apply these three methods simultaneously. Do not use a pressure point any longer than is necessary, as it stops blood circulation to and within the limb.

There is one pressure point on each arm and leg. For an arm wound, apply pressure on the brachial artery, which will hold the artery shut by pressing it against the arm bone. This pressure point is located on the inside of the arm in the groove between the biceps and triceps, about midway between the armpit and elbow. Grasp the middle of the victim's upper arm with your thumb on the outside of the arm and your fingers on the inside. Press your fingers towards your thumb, using the flat surface of your fingers, not your fingertips.

For a leg wound, apply pressure on the femoral artery, pushing it against the pelvic bone. This pressure point is on the front of the thigh just below the middle of the crease of the groin where the artery crosses over the pelvic bone on its way to the leg. Place the victim on his back and put the heel of your hand directly over the pressure point. With your arm straightened, lean forward to apply pressure.

A tourniquet should be applied only when the pressure point technique fails, and the bleeding is severe and uncontrollable. Essentially, it's a decision to risk sacrificing a limb in order to save a life. Applied too loosely, a tourniquet can increase, instead of control, bleeding. If left in place for an extended period, uninjured tissues may die from lack of blood. Once a tourniquet is in place, medical attention is imperative.

A tourniquet should be made from a wide band of cloth or similar material, not a narrow band or rope. Place it just above, not touching, the wound. If the wound is in a joint area or just below, place the tourniquet immediately above the joint. Wrap the band of cloth tightly twice around the limb and tie a knot. Place a short, strong stick (or something similar that won't break) on the knot, and tie two additional knots on top of the stick. Twist the stick until bleeding stops, and secure it in place with the ends of the tourniquet or other improvised material.

Tag or mark the victim with a note indicating the location of the tourniquet and the time it was applied. Do not cover a tourniquet. Treat the victim for shock, and seek medical help immediately. Once the tourniquet is in place, don't loosen it, as this increases the danger of shock, and bleeding may resume.

BLISTERS

These should never happen in the first place. Gear should be well broken in before the big trip beyond, socks changed frequently, feet kept clean and dry, and any sensitive spots protected, if they develop, with little adhesive bandages.

If a blister still should form, leave it alone. The best sterile dressing is the covering that nature put over it; therefore it should not be opened. If it should break spontaneously, trim off the dead skin with manicure scissors, apply a little antibiotic ointment, and keep dressed until new skin grows over.

Keep Merthiolate and alcohol off open blisters. Clean them instead with soap and water. Alcohol and Merthiolate are skin disinfectants, not *wound* disinfectants. They kill delicate tissue, and while reducing the germ count initially, they harm the tissue. Germs multiply best on injured tissues, so you see you actually foster infection rather than reduce it with the use of these so-called disinfectants. Soap and water are best for cleansing a wound.

FISHHOOKS

If the hook is imbedded in the skin beyond the barb, it is best to push it all the way through rather than attempt to pull it out. The shank is cut off and the hook is pushed through, or the barb is clipped off, and the hook is pulled back whence it came.

BURNS

If a blister should form from a burn, it should be left alone, as with ordinary blisters. A first-degree burn requires little treatment. Only the skin will become red. As pointed out, aspirin relieves the sting of a burn. Ointments are messy and do little good.

A second-degree burn involves blistering or the loss of some of the top skin. Vaseline makes a soothing dressing. Sterilize this by melting and bringing it to the boiling point, then allowing it to cool. Apply to gauze flats or some other dressing material by buttering, as on a piece of bread. This is preferable to attempting to spread it on the burn and then covering with gauze.

Third-degree burns are nasty at best. The skin is burned all the way through and the area either will have to be grafted on or granulated in from the sides.

HYPOTHERMIA—A DEADLY HAZARD

If body heat loss exceeds heat gain for a prolonged period of time, hypothermia results. Deaths have been attributed to a loss of body heat at air temperatures between 30°F. and 50°F. Combined with strong wind, internal temperature slides downward even more rapidly.

The peculiar danger of this condition is that the victim doesn't realize what's happening. Without immediate treatment, stupor, collapse, and death can follow in as short a time as 2 hours. Watch yourself and others carefully for the following symptoms of hypothermia: uncontrollable fits of shivering, slurred speech, inability to use the hands, incoherence, stumbling, drowsiness, and apparent exhaustion.

Prevention is your best defense. Stay dry and warm at all times. Use rain gear before you get wet. If this is impossible, change into dry clothes at the first opportunity. Make camp and build a fire rather than prolonging exposure.

If you must treat a victim of hypothermia, relieve the symptoms, not the victim—he may deny he is in trouble. Get the victim out of the cold. Strip off all his wet clothes and get him into a sleeping bag which has been warmed by another member of the party. Body contact is the most effective treatment. It's even better to put the victim into a sleeping bag with another person, also stripped. Build a fire next to the victim.

Try to keep him awake and give him warm drinks if he can swallow. Never treat a hypothermia victim with alcoholic beverages, which can seriously worsen the condition.

Seek medical attention for the victim as soon as possible.

If You Ever Fall In

If you ever fall in water in cold weather, roll in dry snow to blot the moisture. Brush off the excess snow, then roll again until as much as possible of the water is absorbed. Don't take off your boots until you are in some warm shelter or until you have a fire crackling outdoors.

FROSTBITE

Frostbite is the freezing of some part of the body. It is a constant hazard in subzero temperatures, especially when the wind is strong. As a rule, the first sensation of frostbite is numbness rather than pain. You can see the effect of frostbite, a greyish or yellow-whitish spot on the skin, before you feel it. Therefore, if you have someone with you, get in the habit of watching each other for visible frostbite. If you are alone, keep feeling your face and ears for stiffness.

If the freezing is only minor and local, a cupped warm hand will thaw it. Otherwise, try to get the frostbite casualty into a heated shelter if possible.

When only the surface skin is frozen and it becomes spongy to the touch, it can be rewarmed by body heat. If toes and feet are superficially frozen and you have a cooperative companion along, thaw them against his warm abdomen.

If deeper tissues are involved, the thawing process must take place quickly. Because the refreezing of a thawed part means the certain loss of tissue, it is often best on the trail to continue with a frozen part for a reasonable length of time rather than to thaw it when there is a strong chance of refreezing. Thawing, in any event, must be accomplished as soon as possible.

Warm the frozen part rapidly. Frozen members ideally should be thawed in warm water until soft, even though this treatment is painful. The procedure is most effective when the water is between 99°F. and 104°F., that is, when it is comfortably warm to a normally protected part such as an elbow. If warm water is not available, wrap the frozen part in blankets or clothing and apply improvised heat packs, perhaps stones warmed in the fire. Thawed extremities should be immobilized.

Use body heat whenever possible to aid in thawing. Hold a bare, warm palm against frozen ears or parts of the face. Grasp a frostbitten wrist with the other warm, bare hand. Hold frostbitten fingers against the chest, under the armpits, or between the legs at the groin.

Never forcibly remove frozen shoes and mittens. Place in lukewarm water, or thaw in front of the campfire, and then take them off gently.

Never rub frostbite. You may tear frozen tissues and cause additional damage. Never follow the old-fashioned custom of applying snow or ice, as this just increases the cold injury. Rubbing a frozen cheek with snow in very cold weather, in fact, is comparable to scrubbing a warm cheek with sand and gravel. Never make the terrible mistake of trying to thaw the frozen part in cold gasoline, oil, or alcohol at subzero temperatures, just because they are still liquid.

SHOCK

Shock may be immediate, or it may be delayed for several hours after its incitement. Usually it follows a severe injury, blow, or fracture. It may be induced by such circumstances as rough handling, cold, severe pain, or hemorrhage, particularly when the loss of blood is excessive. The skin is cold and clammy, and the patient feels light-headed and faint. The pulse is rapid, over ninety mostly, and not strong.

Often the shock can be more serious than the original injury, and must be treated in every instance.

Keep the victim flat on his back. If he has no head, neck, back or leg injuries, raise the legs by bending the knees. Keep the victim warm with extra clothing, blankets, or sleeping bag. Avoid further movement or manipulation and get medical help as soon as possible.

CARBON MONOXIDE POISONING

Carbon monoxide is a danger in any closed space where there is combustion of any kind. The common product of incomplete burning, carbon monoxide is both odorless and cumulative. This latter characteristic is particularly dangerous.

Carbon monoxide usually gives no recognizable warning. For example, there is no difficulty with breathing, although in a shelter you may be tipped off by the fact that a light starts to burn poorly. What ordinarily occurs is that the individual is so entirely overcome that when he first realizes something is wrong, he already is nearly if not completely helpless.

The peril heightens as cold deepens because of the natural inclination to curb ventilation in favor of warmth. Restricted circulation of air allows the invisible and odor-free vapor to build up in an enclosed space. There is very real danger, even in a tent, if the spaces in the weave of the fabric are closed by waterproofing, or by rain, snow, or even frost; a small heater can be very dangerous. By far the best preventative is to make sure of good ventilation.

Especial danger confronts the motorist stalled by ice or snow. The inclination in such an emergency is to keep the windows snugly shut and the motor going so that the occupants can keep warm. The peril when any closed vehicle is so parked, especially if a white smother of snow is heaping around it, is that carbon monoxide can build up inside the unventilated car.

Symptoms of carbon monoxide poisoning, if you notice any, begin with tightness over the forehead, headache, and a slight flush. The headache becomes progressively worse with continued exposure. Then weakness, dizziness, decreased vision, nausea and vomiting make their appearance followed by collapse.

With collapse, the pulse and respiration are increased. Breathing may be labored, then alternately slower and then labored again. Eventually there is coma, convulsions, decreased respiration and pulse, and finally death.

The prescribed treatment is immediate removal to fresh air. To decrease the oxygen requirements of the tissues, the victim should be kept warm. Steady observation is necessary because improvement may be followed by reverses. Keep quiet to decrease the oxygen requirements.

If the victim is unconscious, mouth-to-mouth resuscitation should be commenced immediately.

The carbon monoxide in the system will dissipate faster if 5 or 10 percent carbon dioxide is supplied with the air that is being breathed. This can be done by taking a deep breath, exhaling in a paper or plastic bag, and then having the patient take a deep breath of the air expired into the bag by a person not afflicted. If several people can supply such bags of air, the effects will pass more quickly, perhaps taking only thirty to forty minutes instead of several hours.

The effects are not necessarily gone when all the carbon monoxide is out of the system. Small hemorrhages in the heart muscle, brain, and other organs may persist. Depending on their location, there may be serious after-effects if these hemorrhages are in vital areas.

Again, carbon monoxide poisoning can be chronic. That is, continued exposure for four to five hours at a time, for example, can cause chronic headaches, a general feeling of sickness, digestive ailments, and so on, but never proceed to the full poisoning effect.

The diagnosis of the acute case is easy. There is the history or evidence of exposure, plus a cherry-red color to the nails, the mucous membranes of the mouth, and the tissues.

No matter what the circumstances, always maintain adequate ventilation, wherever you are, at all times.

Mouth-to-Mouth Resuscitation

Immediate action is necessary whenever breathing stops as a result of drowning, smoke inhalation, or electric shock as from lightning.

Lay the victim on his back. Check the mouth and make sure the air passage from the mouth and nose to the lungs is not blocked. Remove mucus, water, etc. If the tongue has been swallowed or is stopping the throat, hook it free with a forefinger. Pull the chin upward until the head is fully tipped back.

Now place your mouth solidly over the victim's mouth. Pinch his nostrils shut. Exhale sharply. With a small child, place your mouth over both his nose and mouth while blowing. The chest of the victim should expand during this procedure.

Good skin color and adequate chest motion will show whether the procedure is effective. A blue cast to the skin and failure of the chest to move point to an immediate need to re-check the victim's head and jaw position. His tongue may be blocking the air passage. If you still get no chest action, turn him on his side and slap him sharply several times between the shoulder blades in an effort to dislodge any foreign matter in the throat. If the victim is a child, hold him momentarily head downward while you do this. Wipe the mouth clean and resume the mouth-to-mouth breathing.

With adults, blow one vigorous breath twelve times a minute. For small children, blow shallow breaths twenty times a minute. *Don't give up* until the victim begins to breathe. Success sometimes requires hours of artificial respiration.

WHAT ABOUT SNOWBLINDNESS?

Symptoms of so-called snowblindness, when you're not actually blind, are redness, burning, watery or sandy feeling eyes, the halo one ordinarily sees when looking at lights, headaches, and poor vision. Remember, snowblindness may not appear until four to six hours after exposure. It is often not suspected, for this reason, particularly because the symptoms may not manifest themselves until well after sunset.

Treat snowblindness by protecting the eyes from light and by relieving the pain. You can accomplish the first by staying in a dark shelter and by wearing a lightproof bandage. For the second, keep cold compresses on the eyes if there is no danger of freezing and take aspirin. Most cases recover within eighteen hours without medical treatment. However, one attack of snowblindness will make you more susceptible to future attacks.

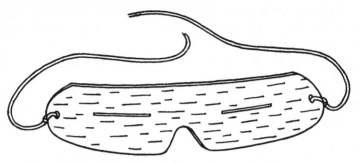

A leather mask will protect the eyes from snowblindness.

Snowblindness is caused by the exposure of the unprotected eyes to glare from the snow. It can occur even on cloudy days and in tents. You can prevent snowblindness by wearing dark glasses whenever you are exposed to glare. Prevention is the best answer. Don't wait until your eyes hurt to wear your glasses.

A handy substitute for sun glasses is a piece of wood, bone, leather, or other material with narrow eye slits cut in it. These and similar eyeshades are fine in snow country because the slits can be kept clean by brushing them off, whereas regular glasses may give trouble by frosting. Too, it is a good idea to blacken the area around your eyes with soot from the fire. Even though the glare may not seem to bother you, it will affect your ability to see objects at a distance and will retard your eyes' adaption to night vision. If your eyes hurt and you have boric acid ointment, apply some to the eyelids and the corners of the eyes.

PRIMITIVE SUNBURN AID

When sunburned, besides protecting yourself from additional exposure, you can cover the affected area with ointment or with a tannin-rich substitute made by boiling the bark of a hemlock, oak, or chestnut tree. Keep the burned area covered and at rest if possible. Drink large amounts of water, partly to rid the body of wastes formerly lost through the now-blocked sweat glands.

GUARDING AGAINST HEAT INJURY

In hot climates develop a tan slowly by gradual exposure to the sun. Sunburn in the desert can be dangerous, so if you must be in the sun, try not to expose your head. Avoid strenuous exertion in the hot sun, as there is the danger of fatal heat stroke.

The lesser illnesses caused by heat can be prevented by consuming enough water and salt to replace the sweat. Salt tablets or table salt ideally should be taken in the proportion of two tablets or one-fourth teaspoonful to a quart of water. Treatment of heat casualties consists of cooling the body and restoring water and salt. Exposure to the desert sun can cause several types of heat collapse.

Heat Cramps

The first warning of heat collapse generally is cramps in the leg or abdominal muscles. Rest. If possible, drink water in which salt has been dissolved in the proportions suggested above.

Heat Exhaustion

You're first flushed, then pale. You sweat profusely, and your skin is moist and cool. You may even become light-headed or unconscious. Treat by lying in any shade, flat on your back. Take salt dissolved in water, the same two tablets or one-fourth teaspoonful to a quart.

Heat Stroke

This may come on suddenly. Your face is red, your skin hot and dry. All perspiring ceases. You have a severe headache, and your pulse is fast and strong. Unconsciousness may result. Treat by somehow cooling yourself off. Loosen your clothing. Lie flat in the shade, preferably about a foot off the ground. If at all possible, cool by saturating your clothing with water and by fanning. Never take stimulants.

TROUBLE IN BUG COUNTRY?

The real danger in hot, swampy country especially, is the insects, many of which pass on diseases and parasites. If you are in an area where it's prevalent, malaria may be your worst enemy. It is still transmitted by mosquitoes, the Anopheles variety normally encountered from late afternoon until early morning. Too, they may bite in the shade during the day. All in all, guard against bites. Camp away from swamps, preferably on high land. If you have no mosquito netting to snooze under, smear mud on your face as protection

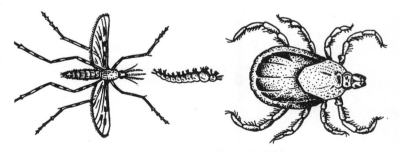

Anopheles mosquito and larva; hard tick.

against insects while you are asleep or sleep within the smoke area of a camp-fire turned into a smudge by green or damp fuel, unless you can find a bare windy ridge or shore.

Wear full clothing, especially at night, and tuck your trouser legs into the tops of your socks or boots. Today's more effective insect repellents afford comfort with the least time and trouble. The best yet to reach the sporting goods stores is a product with 95 percent DEET, the key ingredient in the better insect repellents ever since it was made available commercially as N. N.-Diethyl Toluamide.

Ticks may be numerous, particularly in grassy places, and you may get dozens of them on your body. Strip to the skin at least once a day and inspect your hide for ticks, leeches, bed bugs, and other pests. If you have a companion, examine each other. Brush ticks off your clothing. Flick them off the skin. If ticks get attached, covering them with an irritant such as a drop of iodine will sometimes make them let go. So may heating them with a stick from the fire, but don't burn your skin. Wash the bite if possible with soap and water. Be careful when removing a tick, as the heads have a tendency to stay in and start infection.

Some ticks, especially in certain areas in and around Montana, are bearers of Rocky Mountain spotted fever which may be fatal, away from antibiotics. Immunization with spotted fever vaccine is often recommended if you're likely to be spending much time in infected areas.

Where fleas are common, it is a good idea to keep your trousers tucked into your shoe tops or socks. Female fleas will burrow under your toenails and into your skin to lay eggs. Use a sterilized knife point to remove them, keeping the cut clean.

Mites and chiggers will burrow into the skin, often around the waist. Touch the spots with iodine, or with a drop of resin, oil, or pitch, which will kill them. Do your best to avoid scratching all bites.

If you are in an area inhabited by biting ants, never walk barefoot. Try never to camp near an anthill or ant trail. Treat ant stings, as well as those of wasps and bees, with cold compresses or mud.

Your shoes guard against crawling mites, ticks, ants, cuts, and subsequent bacterial infections. When you are accidentally dunked or forced to wade in fresh waters suspected of being infected with fluke parasites, wring out your clothes, drain and dry your shoes, and rub your body dry. Apply insect repellent over exposed areas.

SNAKEBITE

Poisonous snakes are far less abundant than most people think. There is little danger of a bite if you wear adequate boots, sleep off the ground, and are careful where you put your hands.

In country where there are poisonous snakes, however, it will be well to carry a small and compact snakebite remedy.

PLANTS POISONOUS TO TOUCH

Most of the plants that are poisonous to touch belong to either the sumac or the spurge family. The three most important poisonous plants in the United States are poison ivy, poison oak, and poison sumac. All these plants have compound leaves and small, round, white or greyish green fruits.

Poisonous plant juices are especially dangerous in the vicinity of your eyes. Danger of becoming contaminated increases with overheating and perspiring. Using the wood of any contact-poisoning plant as firewood is dangerous. The worst case of poison oak I ever incurred was a result of the inclusion of a few sticks of dead poison oak into my cooking fire.

Symptoms of plant poisoning are reddening, itching, swelling, and blistering. The best treatment after contact with these plants is an immediate and thorough wash with the strongest soap available.

WILL A WOLF GET YOU?

North American animals, except those that are so accustomed to man that they have lost most of their native timidity, are not dangerous. The polar bear is an exception. So to a lesser degree is the grizzly, which is easily provoked. A walrus can be dangerous at close quarters. Wolves are perilous only in fiction.

When in the course of ordinary events you come face to face with a large animal that, startled, shows no inclination to disappear, the best thing you can do is freeze. Then start to talk in as calm, quiet, and friendly a way as you can manage. Such a monotone has a soothing effect on any animal, large or small. Any I have so encountered in the open have, unless they fled at once, regarded me for a short time and then sifted into the shadows, usually slowly and in any event without sign of undue excitement.

Poison ivy; poison oak; poison sumac.

If you have a rifle, you'll of course get that to your shoulder as coolly and smoothly as you can, especially if the animal is so near that any sudden motion may provoke a similar reaction. Unless absolutely necessary, it will seldom be wise to shoot under such conditions. If you must, aim an instantly anchoring shot at the brain.

If the animal shows no sign of giving ground, perhaps because it feels it is cornered or because of regard for young ones, back away as casually as you can manage, still continuing to avoid any abrupt actions and still talking quietly.

CHAPTER FIFTEEN

LET NATURE SET THE TABLE

Few of the American and Canadian Indians had gardens when Columbus re-discovered the New World, instead regularly supplementing their meat and fish with wild fruits, nuts, roots, tubers, greens, seeds, beverages, and the like which they gathered free from the land. We can have the satisfaction of doing the same thing today, for these edible wild plants still grow everywhere.

You needn't be any kind of an expert to begin eating what remains un-spoiled and free. If you will positively identify everything before you gather it, you will never have any trouble. I strongly suggest, however, that you avoid mushrooms entirely. They have very little food value, and the risk in eating them is way out of proportion to the possible gain. It cannot be over-emphasized that no single test, short of eating, can distinguish between a poi-sonous mushroom and a safe variety.

If you've ever sat down to a well-prepared meal that included wild vegeta-bles, maybe you've noticed that many of them seem to taste better than domes-ticated varieties from the store. I'll let you in on a trade secret. They *are* better.

Green leafy vegetables, to give just one example, deteriorate very rapidly. Even when purchased as fresh as obtainable from the finest nearby market, they'll already have lost a sizable proportion of vitamins. Some of the food values of greens diminish as much as one-third during the first hour after

picking. But gather them fresh from nature's own garden and eat them while they're at their tastiest, and you'll enjoy the best they have to offer.

Wild greens can be successfully frozen, but they must be blanched first. This is necessary to halt the enzymic action which, if not stopped, would change the flavor, color, texture, and even the nutritive values of these delicacies.

To blanch, have a large kettle of water boiling. Place the cleaned greens, not more than two cups for each gallon of fluid, in either a basket or a section of cheesecloth. Lower into the water. Starting counting as soon as boiling is commenced, scald for two minutes at sea level. Add roughly 10 percent to this total time for each 1,000 feet of higher elevation.

Then cool immediately by plunging the greens into preferably ice water. Drain as well as you can. Get the greens in the form in which you are going to use them, perhaps tearing them into bite sizes. Then dry pack in plastic or laminated containers or bags, leaving one-half inch expansion space at the top. Label, freeze immediately, and store like any other food.

Cooked without defrosting, such wild vegetables can do much to capture for midwinter enjoyment all the rousing satisfaction and nostalgia of a sunny spring day.

Freshly picked and carefully handled berries retain their refreshing flavor and rich color for a long time when frozen by the dry pack method. Just pick them over and stem them. Spread on trays until frozen. Then pour like marbles into rigid containers or plastic bags and store. When these are served, a few remaining ice crystals will enhance both their savor and shape.

Rum cherries, which may be pitted if storage space is a problem, may well be covered with a cooled syrup made by dissolving three cups of sugar in every quart of water, along with one-half teaspoon of ascorbic acid to prevent further darkening.

Today gourmets, campers, and stay-at-home cooks alike will find pleasure in harvesting their meats from the wild lands where nature is the farmer and where nothing is ever due at any checkout counter.

BLUEBERRY (*Vaccinium*) (*Gaylussacia*)

Family Heath (*Ericaceae*)

Other Names Whortleberry, Bilberry, Huckleberry, Oval-Leaf Whortleberry, Dwarf Bilberry, Sierra Bilberry, Great Bilberry, Bog Bilberry, Mountain Bilberry, Twin-Leaved Huckleberry, Blue Huckleberry, Mountain Huckleberry, Evergreen Huckleberry, Lowbush Blueberry, Swamp Blueberry, Farkleberry, Blueridge Blueberry, Box Blueberry, Big Whortleberry, Sour-Top Blueberry, Velvet-Leaf Blueberry, High Blueberry, Early Blueberry, Low Sweet Blueberry, Deerberry, Squaw Huckleberry, California Black Buckleberry, Tangleberry, Blue Tangle, Dangleberry, Late Low Blueberry, Early Sweet Blueberry, Sugar Blueberry, Dwarf Blueberry, Western Blueberry, Thin-Leaf Blueberry, Alaska Blueberry, Bog Blueberry, Dwarf Huckleberry, Whorts, Hurts.

Description   None of the blueberry-huckleberry tribe is inedible. As for the differences between these two very similar berries, the former, *Vassinium,* is filled with numerous soft seeds, while the latter, *Gaylussacia,* contains precisely ten stony, seedlike nutlets. Too, if you bother to notice, huckleberries have waxy little spots on their foliage and fresh shoots. Blueberries and huckleberries are so much alike, however, that they are often picked and eaten together.

The berries, sometimes bright red when mature, are more often blue to black. A few ripen to a greenish or yellowish hue. They frequently have a bloom to them that can be rubbed off. Making the fruit unmistakable is a puckery-edged indentation at each summit.

These members of the heath family many times grow by the acre on bushes so heavily laden that you can spread a sheet on the ground and gather mostly the ripe fruit by the bushel merely by shaking the limbs. A pioneer method of later cleaning them is to let them fall, a few at a time, from a tipped pail onto a slanted, preferably new and fuzzy woolen blanket, stretched tightly a few feet below. The ripe blueberries will roll into a large, wide container placed just below the lower edge of the blanket. Most of the harder green berries will bounce free. The leaves and other debris will remain on the blanket which can be brushed clean from time to time. Finally, stirred about in water to float away the remaining clutter, the booty will be ready to eat.

As may be judged from the difference in names, blueberries as a whole grow on a variety of shrubs from small low plants to thickets of tall bushes, all free of brambles. They like acid soil and sunlight, frequently springing up

Blueberry. *Left:* in flower. *Right:* with fruit.

on freshly cleared land and on vast fire-blackened wilderness expanses. In fact, the woodlands and forests of this continent are frequently set afire to encourage blueberry crops which, aside from direct human use, bring in abundant game.

Distribution   About 35 different members of this genus grow throughout Canada and the United States, some in swamps but most in open woodlands and clearings. They are among the most important berries of the Arctic and sub-Arctic.

Edibility   Because the digestive system of the bear is better adapted to handling meat than fruit, anyone who has followed many bear trails in blueberry country can attest to the fact that this fruit forms a major part of the grizzly's and black bear's diet in late summer and fall.

The berries are also a prime portion of the diet of a number of the grouses, who also feast on the leaves and the pretty, bell-shaped, little blossoms. Gulls, cranes, pigeons, turkeys, and dozens of songbirds seek the fruit, especially as some of it clings, dry but still nourishing, to the shrubs well into winter. Living, too, in part on the fruit, twigs, and foliage is a large host of wildlife from foxes, opossums, raccoons, and squirrels to deer, moose, caribou, and elk.

Indians preceded the settlers and their present-day descendants in enjoying the fruit both raw and cooked in all sorts of ways, even to thickening stews and soups. In addition to its wide use as preserves, the plain fruit also keeps well frozen, as well as dried at room temperatures, both without additives of any sort.

Wild Blueberry Pie

For one 9-inch pie, pick over and wash a quart of blueberries. Put a cup of these into a saucepan along with 1¼ cups of sugar, 2 tablespoons butter, ⅛ teaspoon salt, and 2 tablespoons cornstarch mixed with ¼ cup of cold water. Cook over low heat until thick, stirring occasionally and crushing the fruit. Then remove from the stove, mix in a tablespoon lemon juice, pour over the remaining berries, and let stand until cold.

In the meantime, make your pastry. If you don't have a favorite recipe of your own, this may be started by sifting together 1¼ cups flour and ⅛ teaspoon salt. Cut in ¼ cup apiece of butter and of bear grease or commercial shortening, add 4 tablespoons cold water, and mix gently. Roll out thin. Line the pie dish or pan. Use the remaining pastry for strips to lay across the top of the pie.

Pour the filling into the uncooked pie shell, spread evenly, and lay on the latticework of upper crust. Bake in a moderate 375°F. oven about 50 minutes, or until the crust is golden brown.

Wild Blueberry Flapjacks

Wild blueberry flapjacks are something special the year around, bringing back as they do the familiar vision of the unspoiled earth, the murmur of insects, the distant cowbells, and the soft stirring of a light breeze. Make your regular batter and drop it, ⅓ cup at a time, on a hot griddle lightly greased with bacon rind. Do not let your griddle get so hot that it smokes.

If you're cooking for two and don't have a favorite flapjack recipe, sift together a cup of flour, a tablespoon of baking powder, a tablespoon of sugar, and ⅛ teaspoon of salt. Beat an egg with ⅔ cup of milk and 2 tablespoons melted butter. Add to the dry ingredients, mix quickly, and have everything ready to move without any waiting.

Sprinkle 2 tablespoons of blueberries over each saucer-sized flipper. When the hotcake begins showing small bubbles and its underside is golden, turn it and brown the other side. Have the butter dish loaded and enough syrup waiting to match the appetites.

CATTAIL (*Typha*)

Family   Cattail (*Typhaceae*)

Other Names   Flags, Rushes, Bulrushes, Cossack Asparagus, Cattail Flag, Broadleaf Cattail, Narrow-Leaved Cattail, Cat-o'-Nine Tails, Reed Mace.

Description   Everyone knows these tall sharp-leaved plants with their sausagelike heads which, growing in groups from about two to ten feet tall, enliven wet places throughout North America except in the Arctic.

The slender, flat, 3- to 6-feet long, ½-1 inch wide, tapering, pointed basal leaves, dried and then soaked to make them pliable, afford rush seats and backs for chairs, as well as rugged material for mats and rugs. The longest of them are nearly always at least a couple of feet shorter than the round, smooth stems and spring up in the very early spring among the dried leaves of the year before.

Atop each unbranched stalk is a thickly flowered spike of tiny brown blossoms, each on its separate stem and maturing from the base upward. The lower several inches of these massed flowers, at first green, are a crowded, sausagelike compactness of female blossoms. Just above these, enabling them later to produce their cottony seeds, are the male flowers which, without benefit of the usual insects, drop their golden pollen as the summer proceeds, eventually leaving the naked upper part of the stem spiking and withering above the feminine inflorescence.

Red-winged blackbirds and many other kinds of birds find cattails fine protective nesting and roosting cover.

Distribution   Cattails grow throughout the United States and Canada except in the far northern regions.

Edibility   Although cattail seeds are too minute and hairy to attract most birds, some like the teal feed on them. The starchy underground roots and the bright green shoots are relished by geese and muskrats. The shoots, too, are sought by moose and elk when they first appear each new spring.

Cattail.

The roots, as well as the lower portions of the stems, are sweetish with more than half weight-sustaining carbohydrates. These are fairly easy to pull up or to dig out, even in deep snow, with no more help than a pointed stick. They are delicious and nutritious raw, baked, roasted ash-sheathed in the glowing embers of a campfire, or briefly boiled. First scrub, then peel while still wet.

The cores can also be dried and ground into a substantial white flour, which you may want to sift to get out any fibers.

The tender young shoots, which somewhat resemble cucumbers in taste, are very much edible. If they are starting to get tough, drop them into boiling salted water to simmer to tenderness. These young shoots also make tasty pickles.

Peeled of their outer rind, the tender white insides of the first 1 or 1½ feet of the young stems give this worldwide delicacy its provocative name of Cossack asparagus. Again, these are edible both raw and cooked.

The greenish-yellow flower spikes, before they become tawny with pollen, can be gathered, husked as you would corn, and dropped into rapidly boiling salted water to simmer until tender. Or steam them to retain even more of the goodness. Eat like corn, dripping with butter or oleomargarine. Or scrape these boiled flower buds from the wiry cobs and use them like cooked corn kernels.

These flower spikes later are gilded with thick pollen which, easily and quickly rubbed or shaken into a container, is a flour substitute for breadstuffs. It can be cleaned if necessary by passing through a sieve. For delectable golden hotcakes in camp, mix half and half with the regular flour in any pancake recipe.

Finally, there is a pithy little tidbit where the new green stem sprouts out of the rootstocks which can be roasted or boiled like young potatoes.

CURRANTS AND GOOSEBERRIES (*Ribes*)

Family   Gooseberry (*Grossulariaceae*)

Other Names   Buffalo Currant, Wax Currant, Whitestem Gooseberry, Sticky Currant, Western Black Currant, Golden Currant, Red Garden Currant, Swamp Red Currant, American Red Currant, Fetid Currant, Skunk Currant, Wild Black Currant, Missouri Currant, Clove Bush, Black Currant, Wild Gooseberry, Prickly Gooseberry, Smooth-Fruited Gooseberry, Slender Gooseberry, Missouri Gooseberry, Northern Gooseberry, Bristly Gooseberry, European Gooseberry, Eastern Wild Gooseberry, Garden Gooseberry, Swamp Gooseberry, Trailing Black Currant, Northern Black Currant, Blue Currant, Feverberry, Groser, California Black Currant, Dog Bramble, Hudson Bay Currant, Round-Leaved Gooseberry, Smooth Wild Gooseberry, Rock Gooseberry, Sierra Gooseberry.

Description   Some 75 species of currants and gooseberries, both of the *Ribes* genus, grow in this country where they are easily reachable, being sim-

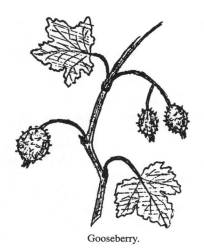

Gooseberry.

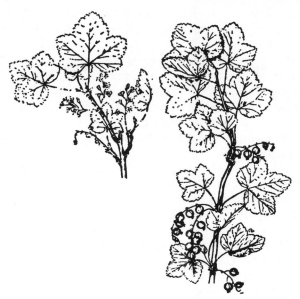

Currant. *Left:* with flowers. *Right:* with fruit.

ilar to domesticated species. In fact, some of the more popular wild varieties are refugees from gardens. Generally speaking, the members of the *Ribes* family without spines are known as currants, while the better protected, thorny varieties are called gooseberries. The fruit of these latter shrubs may be either smooth or bristling. A maplelike leaf is common to both.

For example, there is the golden currant (*Ribes aureum*) also known as the buffalo currant and as the Missouri currant, which was first made known to civilization by Captain Meriwether Lewis who found it on the headwaters of the Missouri and Columbia Rivers during the Lewis and Clark Expedition in 1805. Here, feasting on the berries themselves, they found the Indians using them in the making of pemmican, concocted by a mixture of dried buffalo meat and rendered fat, flavored by dried berries of one kind or another.

Found now from coast to coast because of the way it has repeatedly escaped from Eastern gardens, the golden currant is a native shrub whose slenderly curving branches reach sometimes ten feet high. The maplelike leaves, each with three to five sawtoothed lobes, taper to a broadish base that is sometimes wider than the leaf is long.

Spicily fragrant golden blossoms, up to about an inch long and growing in short elongated clusters along single stalks with small modified leaves near their bottoms, give the edible its additional and descriptive name of clove bush. The lower parts of these yellowish flowers are shaped like little tubes.

The berries, about ¼ inch across on the wild shrubs but larger and frequently more agreeable on the varieties cultivated from this native, are yellow, reddish, or dark black.

Distribution   The currants and gooseberries, partly because they are so prone to escape from gardens, grow from the Gulf of Alaska to the Gulf of Mexico and from the Pacific to the Atlantic.

Found in cool woods, swamps, ravines, near streams, foothills, and along many a thus more interesting fence, they generally prefer moist soil, and their presence at the base of an elevation in the desert often indicates the presence of water close underground.

Edibility   The use of gooseberries and currants by the wildlife of North America was greater before so many of the shrubs were destroyed when it became known that the fungus known as blister rust, which kills the white and other five-needle pines, lives in one of its stages first on *Ribes* before spreading to the evergreens. Thus by eradicating the currants and gooseberries in or near our conifer forests has the life cycle of the blister rust been interrupted and its spread restrained.

Blue and sharp-tailed grouse vie for the fruit and foliage, while a number of songbirds including the robin and the cedar waxwing peck away at the berries. Coyotes, foxes, racoons, and squirrels eat both fruit and foliage, while such small mammals as the chipmunk confine their appetites to the former. Deer, elk, and mountain sheep browse on the twigs and leaves. Black bear feast on the fruit.

Currants and gooseberries differ wonderfully in taste, especially raw, but even the seemingly less appetizing fruit can be appealing and refreshing when one is hungry and thirsty. Most, however, are generally more palatable cooked. All supply good fruit, and since colonial days, when they were introduced to the first settlers and frontiersmen by the Indians, they have been famous in the United States and Canada for pies, tarts, sauces, jams, jellies, and wine.

Green Currant Pie

This is best when the currants are just starting to ripen. You'll need a quart. Mix them with 2 cups of sugar, a teaspoon cinnamon, ¼ teaspoon nutmeg, and either 3 tablespoons cornstarch or ⅓ cup flour.

The pastry suggested for blackberry pie is a good one for this double-crust pie, too. Bake in a hot 450°F. oven for 10 minutes. Then reduce the heat to a moderate 350°F. and bake 35 minutes more or until the crust is browned the way you like it. By then the room will be filled with the smell of spices and hot fruit.

Gooseberry Catsup

Important as Indian food, gooseberries were among the native American fruits quickly adopted by settlers and frontiersmen. A gourmet catsup made of them, excellent with game, was famous even back in Colonial days. Just simmer 5 pounds of stemmed and cleaned gooseberries, 4 pounds brown sugar, 2 cups cider vinegar, 1 tablespoon cinnamon, 2 teaspoons each of cloves and allspice, and ¼ teaspoon cayenne pepper for 2 hours. Then fill sterilized bottles, seal, and label.

DANDELION (*Taraxacum*)

Family   Composite (*Compositae*)

Other Names   Common Dandelion, Red-Seeded Dandelion, Arctic Dandelion, Blowball, Alpine Dandelion.

Description   There's hardly a month in the year except when snow's on the ground, and sometimes even then, when you can't see the golden smile of the dandelion, probably the best known flower in the world if often the least appreciated.

The big yellow blossoms, often the first wild flowers that foretell the spring and one of the last in the fall, are composed of numerous, individual, tiny flower tubes, each broadening into a slim long strap. The golden tubes are arranged on a round disk with the straps extending in a circle, those at the edges unfurling first.

Because these yellow petals are like the golden teeth of the lion of heraldry, there is some dispute as to whether they or the toothed leaves are responsible for the French cognomen, *dent de lion,* from which the English name has

Dandelion.

been slurred. In any event, it is interesting that in almost every European country the local name is of similar significance.

Each of the flowers nods by itself at the end of a long hollow stalk which, when broken, emits a bitter milky juice similar to that which oozes from the cut or abraded roots. Directly beneath the golden head is a verdant cup composed of slender, pointed, green leaves, a few of which twist backward toward the cylindrical stem. Nights and on rainy days, the leaves of the cup lift and cover the gilded petals with their greenery.

Once the blossoms wither, the round disks that bear them become white with the unbranched, short, white hairs that radiate in tiny tufts from the tips of each of the multitudinous seeds. When winds blow on them, these whiten the landscape, spreading all the further this wild edible that still follows man throughout the civilized world. In the meantime, children blow the more fragilely mature of them and count everything from the time of day to the numbers of their future offspring by the seeds remaining.

The leaves of the dandelion are smooth and appetizingly green, unless you are looking at them from the eye of a gardener who is seeking to expel them from his lawn. They grow in rosettes directly from the roots, either upright or close to the ground, depending to some extent on both the environment and to which of the same twenty-five species in the world, three or more in the United States, they belong. Their edges are indented into large teeth which, many say, resemble those of the king of beasts.

Distribution   The humble and beautiful dandelion has followed man abundantly to almost every inhabited corner of Canada and the United States.

Edibility   The dandelion's flowers and seed heads are a favorite spring and summer food of Canada geese, grouse, partridge, pheasant, prairie chicken, and quail. Blackbirds, siskins, and sparrows are among the songbirds relishing the seeds. Deer, moose, elk, both the black bears and the grizzlies, the little prairie dogs, and the even sprier and smaller chipmunks eat the plants.

The dandelion, which has saved peoples from starvation, is a three-tiered food; the succulent roots, the tender and tasty crowns, and the tops from young leaves to flower buds all being exceptionally tasty and sustaining. Even the older leaves are good, although ordinarily you can find enough young ones for a meal, always starting them in boiling water and when someone objects too strenuously to the clean tang of the bitterness, changing the water at least once. Interestingly, the first few frosts in the fall revive the sweetness of the leaves.

Scraped and sliced, then boiled in salted water, the roots are of pleasant taste and texture and when you haven't tried them before surprisingly sweet. Incidentally, these roots can be roasted in an oven until nut-brown all the way through, grated, and used as a coffee stretcher or substitute, dandelions being close cousins of the similarly used chicory.

The white crowns, the parts of the perennial between the roots and the surface of the ground, are even finer flavored than the young leaves in many's estimations.

Raw dandelion greens, 85 percent water, have an abundant 14,000 international units of vitamin A per 100 grams, plus .19 milligrams of thiamine, .26 mg. riboflavin, and 35 mg. of the vital ascorbic acid, all of which helps to explain why the lowly dandelion was so highly regarded as a tonic and general remedy by frontiersmen and early settlers long before the days of vitamin pills.

This same portion of edible greens is further enriched with 198 milligrams of calcium, 76 mg. of sodium, and 397 mg. of potassium. To get all this goodness undiluted, let the tender young greens enhance your fresh salads.

Creamed Dandelion Greens

The familiar dandelion, all too well known because of the way it dots many a lawn, is among the best of the wild greens. Four cups of the washed and very thoroughly dried young leaves, with a few buds included for flavor and appearance, will make a salad for as many feasters. Put these into a bowl and sprinkle them with 1½ teaspoons salt. Pour a cup of sour cream over the top and color this with ¼ teaspoon of freshly ground black pepper and ⅛ teaspoon of paprika.

Add a tablespoon of chopped chives if the greens are very young. If they are older, just short of being tough, their own singular flavor will be sufficient. Toss at the table.

GREEN AMARANTH (*Amaranthus*)

Family   Amaranth (*Amaranthaceae*)
Other Names   Wild Beet, Pigweed, Redroot, Amaranth.
Description   Every wild edible manufactures its own vitamins, and the nutritious and delicious green amaranth is rich in minerals as well. An edible 100-gram portion, as picked, contains a healthful 6,100 international units of vitamin A. It also has 80 milligrams of vitamin C and a multitude of B vitamins, including .08 milligrams of thiamine, .16 mg. of riboflavin, and 1.4 niacin.

Added to all these, the tender tops, stalks, and leaves of this wild spinach, which have none of the strong taste of market varieties and which are delightfully esculent from early spring to frost-blighting fall, boast 267 mg. of calcium, 67 mg. of phosphorus, 3.9 of blood-reddening iron, and a big 411 mg. of potassium. And they're all free for the eating.

It is easy to mistake green amaranth for lamb's quarter, discussed elsewhere, although this does not make too much difference as both are almost equally delectable. But for the record, the stems and leaves of the amaranths are usually softly hairy, whereas those of the lamb's quarter or *Chenopodium* are smooth and whitely powdered. Too, the amaranths have strong, noticeable veins.

Green amaranth.

Growing as a weed over much of the continent including the tropics, the green amaranth, as well as the other edible amaranths, is familiar to most individuals although not usually as a food. The stout, rough stalks, generally unbranched, sometimes reach the height of a man, but small, tender plants can usually be found growing in the same patch. As has been suggested, even these are slightly fuzzy.

The alternately growing, dull green leaves are long-pointed ovals with wavy edges. Their stems, also edible, are nearly as long as are they themselves. The roots, the reason for the occasional name of redroot and wild beet, are attractively red. Another name is pigweed, applied because the green amaranth prefers rich, manured soil such as that found around pigpens, barns, and farm yards.

The flowers are small and greenish and, being such, are generally not recognized as blossoms. They grow, in the top angles between leafstems and stalks, in long, sometimes loosely branched, densely filled clusters. Exuding the faint, evocative scent of spring, they have a pleasant taste raw.

The resulting shiny black seeds were threshed by some of the Indians, roasted, and then used for cakes and porridge. In fact, Arizona tribes cultivated the amaranth for its seeds, over one hundred thousand of which are sometimes to be found on a single plant. Some outdoorsmen, including myself, still like to scatter a handful atop a bannock before consigning this frypan bread to the heat.

Distribution   The amaranths grow all over the North American continent except where it is too cold.

Edibility   Some of the thousands of seeds persist on their thickly clustered spikes into the winter and spring, when other foods are scarce, and are a boon to birds. The teal, dove, pheasant, and quail are among the game birds eating them. These are joined by a wide group of songbirds which include the bunting, finch, goldfinch, junco, lark, longspur, pipit, towhee, and well over a dozen different species of sparrows. Cottontails enjoy the plants.

The extremely delicate flavor of green amaranth is something many prefer to that of almost any other green. This fragility of taste lends itself to a wide range of cooking procedures. You can also influence the final results by including some less bland vegetable such as dandelions or mustard. Young green amaranth is also notable raw.

The plants do toughen and become overly bitter to many palates after they blossom.

The seeds can easily be rubbed free of their husks, then cleaned by being poured back and forth between two receptacles in a wind. The dark flour resulting from the grinding of these seeds is good for mush or for breads, waffles, hotcakes, and the like, especially if the somewhat mustily unfamiliar flavor is brought into line with the addition of store flour or cornmeal. The seeds, like the rest of the plant, are also nourishing raw.

Green Amaranth Soufflé

Green amaranth, whose seeds can later be ground into meal for use in cereals and breadstuffs, makes a delicate, wonderful vegetable when young. Melt 3 tablespoons of butter in a frypan over low heat. Gradually stir in 2 tablespoons of flour and then, bit by bit, ½ cup of warm milk. Season with ½ teaspoon salt and ⅛ teaspoon freshly ground black pepper. Cook until smooth and thick.

Beat the yolks of 4 eggs in a bowl. Gradually stir in the hot sauce, then 2 cups of tender, young, shredded green amaranth leaves. Allow everything to cool. Then fold in the stiffly beaten whites of the 4 eggs, turn into a buttered soufflé dish, and bake in a moderate 375°F. oven for half an hour or until firm. This is as uniquely enjoyable as it is nourishing.

GROUNDNUT (*Apios*)

Family   Pea (*Leguminosae*)

Other Names   Indian Potato, Wild Bean, Bog Potato, Potato Bean, Hopniss.

Description   Asa Gray, the noted botanist, once opined that if civilization had started in the New World rather than the Old, the little groundnut would have been the first tuber to have been cultivated as a food. Many trying it for the first time do like it better than the modern potato. Although it is edible raw, the secret is that when it is cooked to eat, it should be eaten hot, as it loses both tenderness and taste when cold. It can be successfully rewarmed, however, as when buttered and roasted.

Known in some regions as the wild bean, this edible is a climbing and twin-ing perennial with alternate compound leaves, made up of three to seven or nine broadly oval, sharply pointed, roundly based leaflets, each one to three inches long, arranged on either side of a common leafstalk.

If the wind is right, you can smell the lush, heady fragrance of the maroon to chocolate blossoms long before you discover the vine, where it is perhaps climbing a bush. The numerous velvety, pealike, often brownish-purple flow-ers are grouped in short, thick clusters in the angles between the leaves and soft stems which have a milky sap. Each individual bloom is some ½ inch in diameter and formed like that of a pea or bean. One of the ten stamens stands apart prominently.

As with other members of the pea family, the fruit is a beanlike pod, in this instance slim, almost straight, pointed, and some two or three inches along. When you can gather sufficient of them, the seeds inside can be cooked in salted water like peas.

Groundnut.

The rootstocks have tuberous enlargements, some as big as eggs and others no more than an inch long, connected by fibrous strands a great deal like beads strung on a necklace. These take more than one season to develop fully, one of the characteristics that balked Europeans trying to make the groundnut a garden vegetable.

Lying in strings just beneath the surface, these can be easily uncovered, perhaps with the help of a sharp stick, unless the ground under the then dryly white vines is frozen.

Distribution   Requiring damp but not wet soil, the groundnuts are selective in the moist woods and bottomlands where they grow from the Maritime Provinces to North Dakota, south to Florida, and west to Colorado and New Mexico, often as smooth slender vines, four to eleven feet long, along the rims of ponds, swamps, and marshes.

Edibility   The Pilgrims, introduced to the groundnut by friendly Massachusetts Indians, depended on them to a large extent their first rugged winter in Plymouth. Other Indians along the Eastern Seaboard in particular regularly ate those potatolike vegetables. They thus became familiar to early European settlers, many of whom found the tubers very acceptable substitutes for bread. The beanlike seeds when you can find enough of them, are also edible.

Groundnut Omelet

Groundnuts, which helped Swedish settlers through breadless days on the Delaware during Colonial times, still cook up into mighty special food. If you are serving two, for instance, thinly slice 2 cups of them, leaving them unpeeled. Sauté them in 3 tablespoons olive oil until well colored. Add ½ cup of diced onion and cook this until it is limp. Add ½ cup chopped watercress and mix thoroughly. Salt and pepper to taste.

Then break 4 eggs into a bowl. Add a tablespoon of water, ¼ teaspoon salt, and just a dash of freshly ground black pepper. Beat vigorously with a fork until the yolks and whites are blended. Pour this over the other ingredients. Cook until the eggs no longer run freely when the pan is slanted, but the moistly inviting top still looks creamy.

HORSERADISH (*Armoracia*)

Family   Mustard (*Cruciferae*)
Other Names   Red Cole, Wild Horseradish, Sting Nose.
Description   The tiny white blossoms of the horseradish, like those of the other members of the tasty mustard family, have just four petals in the form of a cross. They also boast four long and two short stamens. Although seeds are not very often produced, there are the occasional roundly egg-shaped pods, each of which is divided into two cells with perhaps four to six seeds in each.

Numerous very large leaves grow from the white roots on strong, long stalks. These green leaves, often six inches wide and nearly twice as long,

Horseradish.

have wavy, scalloped edges. The much smaller, stemless leaves that grow directly from a smooth, round, erect, central spike, often several feet long, are oblong and serrated.

The fleshy roots, sometimes as long as a foot and as thick as one or two inches, are tapering, conical at the top, and many times abruptly branched near the end. They are white, both within and without. When scraped or bruised, they give off a strongly pungent odor. When a particle is transferred to the tongue, it is immediately hot and biting.

Distribution   The perennial horseradish, regrowing in the same places for dozens of years and spreading where there is sufficient moisture, came to the New World from England. Originally planted about the cabins of the northeastern United States and southern Canada, it has thrived and dispersed until it now grows wild throughout much of the same general area.

Edibility   The leaves when tender in the spring make greens that are tastier than most when dropped into a small amount of boiling salted water, cooked uncovered only until tender, and then served immediately with a crowning pat of butter or margarine. Caught young enough, they are also good raw.

But it is for its heartily peppery, raw roots that horseradish has been famous for thousands of years. There is little comparison between the freshly grated horseradish you can prepare yourself, using the wild roots and lemon juice instead of the commonly employed wine vinegar, and that from a store. Mouth-tickling horseradish, popular the world over, has been used for food seasoning for centuries.

There are innumerable refinements to the preparation of this masterful condiment, the easiest of which is to add by taste a small amount of sugar to the original mixture. In any event, for the most pleasing results make only small amounts of the sauce at one time, an easy thing to do as horseradish roots can be freshly gathered much of the year, except when the ground is frozen too hard.

Keep the sauce covered when not in use, preferably in a tightly closed jar or bottle. You may well want to keep this in the refrigerator. For best results, however, it should be allowed to return to room temperature before being used. Otherwise, some of its taste-tingling piquancy will be trapped by cold, and more will have to be used to achieve the same results.

Grated horseradish and sour cream make a combination that really brings out the flavor of meats. Freshly grated horseradish will also do much for sandwiches and for crisp small crackers—tidbits that will arouse the appetite even more if decorated with slices of pimento-stuffed olives.

Horseradish is also nutritious, there being 87 calories to 100 grams of the raw roots, plus 140 milligrams of calcium, 64 mg. of phosphorous, 1.4 mg. of iron, and a big 564 mg. of potassium. There are also 81 milligrams of the necessary ascorbic acid that the body can't store.

Besides enjoying horseradish roots and leaves, pioneers used to apply the freshly scraped roots externally as they would mustard plasters. Horseradish was also used as an internal medicine, a teaspoon of the grated root to a cup of boiling water. This was allowed to cool. One or two cupfuls were then drunk throughout the day, several sips at a time, as a stimulant to the stomach.

JERUSALEM ARTICHOKE (*Helianthus*)

Family Composite (*Compositae*)

Other Names Sunflower Artichoke, Earth Apple, Sunflower Root, Canada Potato, Wild Sunflower.

Description This native of North America is a large perennial sunflower, often growing in congested clusters. Slender and branched 6 to 10 feet tall, it has narrower and more sharply tipped leaves than most of the other wild sunflowers. The lower of these often grow opposite one another, but the upper leaves are more frequently alternate, occasionally in whorls of three. Shaped like jagged lanceheads, they are thick, broadly based, rough, and hard. Their stems are apt to be coarsely hairy.

Characteristic are numerous flower heads, two to three inches in diameter, which are lighter yellow than most other wild sunflower blossoms and which lack the brownish and purplish centers of these latter where develop the

Jerusalem artichoke. *Left:* stalk with leaves and flowers. *Right:* tubers.

edible, oil-rich seeds. The yellowish Jerusalem artichoke disks are very much smaller. What this wild edible looks like above ground is more than compensated for, however, by slender flattish, medium-size tubers that are potatolike in appearance and that bulge from a thickly creeping root system.

They lack any connection with the Holy City. Sent back to Europe by the early settlers who found the Indians using the tubers and soon followed suit, the edibles became popular along the Mediterranean where they were known as *girasol* in Spain and *girasole* in Italy. These names, referring to the sun, became changed in English to Jerusalem. The artichoke part of the title arose from the circumstances that even centuries ago the flower buds of some of the edible sunflowers were boiled and eaten with butter like that vegetable.

Distribution   Liking damp but not wet ground, Jerusalem artichokes grow along roads, ditches, streams, paths, and fences and in abandoned fields and other wastelands from Saskatchewan to Ontario, south to Kansas and Georgia. Formerly cultivated in the East by Indians and later the settlers, it has widely escaped and grows wild throughout much of this area, as well as in widely scattered parts of the United States for the same reason.

Edibility   Root-eating animals such as the prairie dog and the groundhog seek these tubers.

They should not be dug until after the first frosts of fall. Sought here then by the Indians and later the colonists, they took the place for years in the New World of the later popularized potato. They are still regarded as a favored, sweetly flavored food for invalids to whom other vegetables are denied.

A simple method of preparation is scrubbed, simmered in their skins in enough water to cover until just tender, then peeled, and served either with salt and butter or with a cream sauce. Or peel, oil, and roast. They are also turned into pickles and pies and are edible raw.

LAMB'S QUARTER (*Chenopodium*)

Family   Goosefoot (*Chenopodium*)

Other Names   Wild Spinach, Goosefoot, Pigweed, White Goosefoot, Smooth Pigweed.

Description   This wild spinach, a branching annual growing from one to about six feet high, was widely used as a green, both raw and cooked, by the North American Indians, many of whom also gathered its abundant seeds, nearly seventy-five thousand of which have been counted on a single plant.

A characteristic is that the greyish-green or bluish-green leaves have a floury white, water-repellent mealiness, particularly on their underneath portions. Adding to the color, there is frequently a red-streaked appearance to the stalks of the older plants. The more or less diamond-shaped leaves are like egg-shaped parallelograms with oblique angles, those on top being formed more like lanceheads with broadly toothed edges. From one to four

Lamb's quarter.

inches long, their general overall shape has given the wild edible its name
Chenopodium which is Greek for goosefoot.

The flowers, all the more inconspicuous for being green, although this may
turn reddish, grow in spiked clusters at the tips of the plants or in angles between the stalk and leaves, as well as in additional clusters on the topmost
parts of the stems. They later evolve into tiny, black, often dullish, flattish but
convex seeds.

Distribution   A native of Asia and Europe, this relative of beets and
spinach is now distributed throughout the United States and Canada from
Alaska to Labrador southward. It is found mainly where the soil has been disturbed, as in old gardens and yards, once-ploughed meadows, ditches, and
along fences and roadsides.

Edibility   The lambs quarters' seeds are devoured in quantity by mourn-
ing doves, grouse, partridge, pheasants, quail, buntings, finches, juncos, larks,
and by more than a dozen different species of sparrows. Chipmunks, gophers,
ground squirrels, and kangaroo rats also relish them. Deer and moose are
among the animals browsing on the entire plants.

Because lamb's quarter has no harsh flavors, many deem it the best of the
wild greens. The entire young plant is edible, whereas from the older ones
quantities of tender small leaves can generally be stripped. The seeds, ground
into a dark meal, were utilized by the Southwest Indians in particular for
everything from cakes to gruel. Today they make a hearty flour when mixed
half-and-half with the regular wheat product. Or for a nourishing breakfast
cereal, just boil the whole seeds until they are soft.

Lamb's quarter has been found to contain 309 milligrams of calcium per
100 grams of the raw edible portions and 258 mgs. after this same amount has
been boiled and drained, a percentage that is all the more remarkable when you
consider that the green is roughly from 80 percent to 90 percent water. The
same portion boasts 11,600 international units of vitamin A when raw, 9,700
when cooked, plus significant amounts of thiamine, riboflavin, and niacin.

Lamb's Quarter Salad

Even when the majority of lamb's quarters' pale green leaves with their
mealy-appearing underneaths become too tough to eat raw, you can still enjoy
a salad with this tastiest of the wild spinach family. Pick enough of the greens
to simmer in salted water into 2 cupfuls.

For the dressing, combine 4 tablespoons olive oil, a tablespoon fresh lemon
juice, 2 teaspoons grated onion, 1 teaspoon salt, ¼ teaspoon dry mustard, and
⅛ teaspoon freshly ground black pepper. Mix this thoroughly with the cooked
greens and chill.

Even late in the summer, you can strip a quantity of small tender leaves
from this wild vegetable, also widely known as pigweed and goosefoot. Do
this just before your meal, providing 4 verdant layers on which to heap the in-

dividual servings of the salad. And, particularly if it's hot weather, see what the family's idea is for vegetables the rest of the week.

MINT (*Mentha*)

Family   Mint (*Labiatae*)

Other Names   Spearmint, Oswego Tea, Beebalm, Lemon Mint, Wild Bergamot, Horsemint, Peppermint, Pennyroyal, American Pennyroyal, Mountain Pennyroyal, Western Pennyroyal, Lamb Mint, Fieldmint, Brandy Mint, Watermint, Wild Mint, Horehound, American Mint, Giant Hyssop.

Description   The various wild mints—important to us from ancient times to the present as foods, scents, flavorings, medicines, and the like—are numerous and widespread but, fortunately, easy as a whole to recognize because of their square stems, opposite leaves, and pleasantly familiar fragrance. This characteristic aroma may not be perceptible in the air where just a few mints grow together, but you've only to rub a leaf between thumb and forefinger to smell it.

For instance, there is spearmint with its square stems, oblong or lancehead-shaped leaves growing opposite one another, and its odor that is so familiar to anyone who's chewed gum. Growing from about one to two feet tall, this is a smooth green perennial whose creeping roots spread it rapidly through wet areas. Blanched, it has odoriferous green leaves that are stemless or nearly so, a bright inch or two long, pointed, narrow-based, and unevenly sawtoothed. Small, pinkly purple to white blossoms encircle a thronged spike at the top, which is usually set off at each lower side by a smaller flower cluster.

Peppermint grows similarly in the same sort of habitats but has leaves that are somewhat shaggy beneath rather than smooth like the spearmint's and which are different, too, in that their edges are uniformly indented. There is also the marked variance in scent.

Mint.

Oswego tea, or beebalm as it is frequently called, blooms from June through August with distinctively large, showily beautiful lavender to scarlet flowers, usually bunched on unbranched stems, atop a one to three-foot, square, branching stalk. The opposite, bright green, sawtooth-edged leaves are oval or shaped like lanceheads. The plant as a whole is rather coarse, sharply pointed, and hairy.

Distribution   The wild mints, many of which have escaped from cultivation, are widely distributed throughout the United States and the southern half of Canada, preferring damp ground.

Spearmint, to be more specific, is abundant in spots from British Columbia and the State of Washington to the Maritime Provinces, south to Florida and California.

Peppermint is common from the Maritimes to Manitoba, south to Florida and Louisiana, being scattered elsewhere. Oswego tea brightens the landscape particularly from British Columbia to Quebec, south to Tennessee and Arizona.

Edibility   The mint family as a whole has glands filled with aromatic oil. This is so volatile, incidentally, that much of it will be wasted if you try to extract it by boiling unless your purpose is to perfume the surroundings. Instead, immerse a handful or so of fresh mint leaves in hot water, cover, and leave to steep overnight. Then strain and use. This not only conserves a large part of the aroma, but it is also saving of the abundant vitamins A and C.

Another thrifty way to use fresh young mint leaves is finely chopped in green salads. You'll want to do a bit of experimenting first, though, as there are considerable taste differences among various species.

For off-season use, young mint leaves freshly picked during a dry morning can be dried at room temperatures, then put away in tightly capped jars to conserve the volatile aroma. Tea can be made from these is similar proportions to regular orange pekoe and formosa oolong.

Wild Mint Sauce

Wild mints, quickly identified by their square stems, opposite leaves, and familiar aroma, grow everywhere. Mint sauce, with an agreeableness all its own, brings out the flavor of venison and other wild meats, especially the king of them all, mountain sheep.

I like mine made by mashing a cup of chopped fresh mint into 2 tablespoons sugar and ¼ teaspoon salt. Mix this with ¾ cup of white vinegar and ¼ cup of freshly squeezed lemon juice. If you concoct this about lunch time and then set it resolutely aside to assume its own mellowness, it will be ready for dinner.

MULBERRY (*Morus*)

Family   Nettle (*Urticacaea*)
Other Names   Red Mulberry, White Mulberry, Black Mulberry, Texas Mulberry.

Mulberry. *Left:* winter twig. *Center:* branch with leaves and fruit. *Right:* bud and leaf scar.

Description   Although up to some dozen different species of mulberries are distributed over our north temperate regions, the best of the fruit comes from our native red mulberry. This becomes so abundant that I have gathered it by the gallon merely by shaking a heavily laden branch over an outspread tarpaulin.

The red mulberry is a small tree, generally twenty to thirty feet high but sometimes reaching eighty feet into the sky, with a trunk diameter of from one to three or four feet, which prefers the moist richness of bottomlands and foothill forests. It is the only mulberry native to the eastern United States, although its range has been extended by its introduction to many yards and streets.

Summers, the big, roundish, dark green, sharply tipped, saw-toothed leaves, with their upper-surface deeply sunken veins, are characteristic. Three to ten inches long and almost as wide, these are often irregular from their generally heart-shaped bases to their pointed ends, some of them being lobed and a few resembling a mitten in silhouette. The underneaths are paler than the rough tops and many times slightly downy. Perhaps the most positive characteristic of these leaves is the fact that the stems, when cut, emit a milky sap. This is also true of the twigs, which have a sweetish taste.

Winters, the silhouette of the entire tree is characteristic, the often crooked branches of the red mulberry commonly spreading into dense, broad, round domes. The twigs are clean, usually smooth, and a pale greenish-brown. They have hollow and oval leaf scars, in which there are many bundle scars that form closed ellipses, where fibers formerly ran to the leaves. The buds have some half-dozen scales, the end buds being false. The thinnish bark is red-dish-brown to greyish-brown, flaky, and ridged.

In May and June the flowers appear in dense, dangling spikes, growing like catkins from the angles between leaves and branches, male and female blossoms thriving separately but generally on the same tree. The June and July berries are composed of many one-seeded drupes, growing rather like the blackberry in shape as well as color, becoming dark purple when mature. They average about a juicy inch long.

Although the wood of the red mulberry is soft, it is surprisingly tough and proves durable when in contact with the ground, making excellent fence posts for many a farmer. It is also used in making furniture.

The white mulberry, introduced here by the British prior to the American Revolution in an unsuccessful try to set up a silkworm industry, is a similar tree. However, the leaves are hairless, the buds reddish-brown without darker scale borders, and the bark a yellowish-brown. The fruit, which is whitish with sometimes a pinkish or purplish tinge, does not have the same keen flavor, being rather tasteless though very sweet.

Distribution   A standby of Indians and of early European explorers and settlers, the red mulberry (*Morus rubra*) grows as a native from New England to the Dakotas and south to Texas and Florida, being especially prolific in the Mississippi and Ohio Valleys.

The white mulberry (*M. alba*) although seen most frequently east of the Appalachians from New England to Florida, has extended its range as far west as Texas and Minnesota.

The so-called Texas mulberry (*M. microphylla*) grows from Texas and Arizona to Old Mexico, being a shrub or small tree seldom much more than a dozen feet high. The fruit is pleasant but not as sweet as the previous two species.

Edibility   When mulberries ripen in early summer, they become one of the fruits sought most avidly by songbirds. In fact, a lot of the birds eat them green, apparently partly influenced by the seeds which some experts hold to be about as nutritious as the fleshy portions. Birds not deterred by the disfigurement known as witch broom, caused mostly by the action of various fungi on some of the trees, include the band-tailed pigeon, cardinal, catbird, crested flycatcher, purple grackle, rosebreasted grosbeak, northern blue jay, scarlet and summer and western tanager, russet-backed wood thrush, tufted titmouse, cedar waxwing, and red-headed woodpecker. The armadillo, fox, opossum, skunk, raccoon, and several of the squirrels also relish the fruit.

Mulberries, popular raw, are also widely favored for pies, jellies, and such, especially when their sweetness is modified by a dash of lemon. Hot mulberries and steaming dumplings are a happy combination. The juice makes an excellent and often easily obtained warm-weather drink.

Incidentally, the twigs are sweetish and, particularly when tender in the spring, are edible either raw or boiled.

Mulberry Pie

The ripe fruit of the red mulberry resembling that of the blackberry in color as well as shape when it ripens to a dark purple, makes a long-remembered pie with a minimum of bother. The pastry recipe suggested for blueberry pie is an ideal one.

Just fill an uncooked pie shell with the fruit. Sprinkle with a cup of sugar mixed with ¼ cup flour, and the juice of a lemon. Add the second crust and bake in a moderate 375°F. oven about 50 minutes, or until the crust is your idea of a tempting brown. Served when a heady breeze is moving through the dining room, making the candles drip, this is really delicious.

PLANTAIN (*Plantago*)

Family Plantain (*Plantaginaceae*)
Other Names Seaside Plantain, Goosetongue, Cart-Track Plant, Pale Plantain, English Plantain, Seashore Plantain, Common Plantain, Plain Plantain, Indian Wheat, Snake Weed, Rippleseed Plantain, Cuckoo's Bread, Ribwort, Soldiers Herb.

Plantain.

Description   Although nearly everyone knows plantain, few realize it is edible. It is a sturdy, persistent, little plant, and I've seen it poking up through sidewalks in such busy cities as Boston, New York, and San Francisco.

It is the short, stemless perennial, instantly recognizable from its picture, where strongly ribbed, spadelike, green leaves lift directly from the root about one or more straight central spikes. What there is of a stem is troughlike.

Seaside plantain grows along the shores, cliffs, and a bit inland from both the Pacific and Atlantic Coasts, and the leaves of this are fleshier, longer, and less tough. Many are up to 10 inches in length and about an inch wide. The flowers are crowded into a spike at the end of a leafless stalk. It is the shape of these leaves, as well as those of the alien English plantain which has become common on this continent, that give the potherb its name of goosetongue.

The spikes of the plantain, although likely you've never noticed it, flower with tiny greenish or drab bronze blossoms that mature into equally inconspicuous seeds.

Plain plantain, another of the same 19 varieties of the wild edible that thrive in the Eastern Hemisphere, has thinner and brighter green leaves than the first-described common plantain. The stalks are reddish at their bottoms. The flower heads are not as dense and are even thinner and less crowded at their tips.

Distribution   Plantain grows from Alaska to Labrador, southward throughout Canada and the United States.

Edibility   Grouse eat the plants, while cardinals, sparrows, and a host of other songbirds feast on the seeds. Rabbits, squirrels, and deer are among the animals eating the plants.

Rich in vitamins A and C and in many of the minerals, plantain is used raw when caught young enough and is later cooked like spinach. The narrow-leaved varieties are the tenderest. When older, it has a woodsy flavor and is best appreciated with a cream sauce, after the plant has been pureed and pressed through a fine sieve to exclude its fibers.

The leaves also make one of the backwoods teas, each ½ handful being covered by a cup of boiling water and steeped for ½ hour.

RASPBERRY AND BLACKBERRY (*Rubus*)

Family   Rose (*Rosaceae*)

Other Names   Cloudberry, Baked-Apple Berry, White-Flowering Raspberry, Purple-Flowering Raspberry, American Red Raspberry, Wild Red Raspberry, Dewberry, Thimbleberry, Western Thimbleberry, Swamp Blackberry, Salmonberry, Western Raspberry, Virginia Raspberry, California Blackberry, Running Blackberry, Highbush Blackberry, Blackcap, Purple Raspberry, Black Raspberry, Creeping Blackberry, Mountain Blackberry, Tall Blackberry, Bake-Apple, Arctic Raspberry, Flymboy, Sand Blackberry, Rocky Mountain Raspberry, Flowering Raspberry, Wineberry, Nagoonberry.

Black raspberry.

Description The most valuable wild fruit on this continent both in terms of money and of importance as a summer wildlife food, the raspberry-blackberry genus combines from some fifty to four hundred species in the United States alone, depending on whether the equally competent botanist doing the counting is a lumper or a splitter. The fact that some plants are thornless makes no difference in the general classifications, nor does the color, the so-called black raspberry being one of the more delicious of the tribe. Although there are differences in taste, all are good to eat, so as far as the amateur gourmet is concerned the precise identification can be a matter of no more than casual curiosity.

All plebes in good standing in the rose company, they provide closely and for the most part delectably related fruits in commonly differing reddish, tawny, black, and even bluish hues. Size and consistency vary also, but all are berries that are composed of numerous, small, usually juicy, pulp-filled ovals in the center of each of which is a hard seed, frequently not too noticeable when the fruit is devoured raw but becoming more predominant with cooking. The easiest way to separate them is through their similarity to domestic species.

The fruit, in particular, has a readily identified sameness to market products even when, as in the instance of the Far North's red nagoonberry or so-called wineberry, the erect stems are less than 6 inches long, lifting directly, first with dark rose to red flowers, from a spreading rootstock to ground level. More have greater familiarity with the white-flowered salmonberry or thimbleberry which, growing juicy red fruit on spineless stems, is seen on bushes from several to six feet tall.

Quickly picked in encouraging quantity, the mature blackberries and raspberries separate easily from their white-coned, five-tailed hulls, leaving a hollow entity in which each section has developed from its own ovary, forming a loosely adhering whole.

Distribution   The genus is common along the northern rim of the continent and, in fact, throughout the world although the heaviest distribution is in the north temperate zone. Species, growing from the deepest valleys to mountainsides 1½ miles higher, reach all the way to the Mexican border.

The majority of the common species prefer moist, relatively open areas. Others, with a preference for shade, are typical woodland natives. Wild raspberries, dewberries, and blackberries frequently enliven roadsides, fence rows, field borders, abandoned meadows, and deserted farmyards.

Edibility   Wildlife from the smallest towhee to the largest wild turkey, and from the chipmunk to the grizzly, make the fruit and sometimes the stems of the raspberry-blackberry family their foremost summer food. Despite the thorns or fuzz on many of the species, moose, deer, elk, caribou, and mountain sheep and goat browse on the stems and foliage wherever they can reach them.

The fresh fruit is an extremely rich source of the antiascorbutic vitamin C. When frozen immediately after gathering and kept hard until ready to eat, it retains much of this vitamin. One sample of *Rubus chamaemorus* kept iced from harvesting in the autumn to April of the succeeding year was found to contain 356 milligrams of the ascorbic acid per 200 grams, approximately a cup. This is from 2½ to 3 times that contained in an orange. On the other hand, when these berries are kept in a warm place and allowed to mold and ferment as is sometimes done, the vitamin C is totally obliterated.

The tender, young, peeled sprouts and twigs are also pleasant and nutritious to eat when you're outdoors and hungry.

Beside the usual kitchen uses, blackberries and raspberries lend themselves to superior cordials and wines. A refreshing non-alcoholic beverage can be made from them, too, by letting the ripe fruit stand in vinegar for a month, then straining, sweetening to taste, and diluting with iced water.

Blackberry Pie

Like many of the other members of the vast rose family, blackberries make superb pies. Mix 2 tablespoons cornstarch, a cup sugar, and ⅛ teaspoon salt. Blend gradually with ½ cup cold water. Bring this slowly to a simmer and, stirring, cook a minute. Combine with 3 cups wild blackberries, turn into an uncooked pie shell, cover liberally with chips of butter, and top with a second layer of pastry.

Bake in a preheated hot 450°F. oven for 10 minutes. Then reduce the heat to a moderate 350°F. and bake 30 minutes longer or until done.

A good crust for this and for other 9-inch, double-crust wild berry pies can be made by carefully combining ⅓ cup of good shortening with 2 cups all-purpose flour sifted with 1 teaspoon salt until what you reach is about the same consistency as cornmeal.

Then add another ⅓ cup shortening and blend until the flour is completely absorbed and you have a consistency like that of large peas. Incidentally, by far the best shortening both for flavor and for texture that we have ever found for pies is rendered bear fat.

Add by teaspoons 5 to 6 tablespoons cold water, tossing lightly with a fork until the mixture is barely dampened. Gather into a ball in waxed paper, then chill. Cut this in half. Roll each half out, on a plastic or other surface well dusted with the same type of flour, until it is about ⅛ inch thick.

Invert the pie dish or preferably, the well-browned pie tin on the dough. Allow ½-inch margin when you trim. In those cases when you want a pre-cooked shell, prick the shell with tines of a fork, then bake in a hot 450°F. oven until tan, about 15 minutes.

Devoured hot during a snowstorm, with the vague moving whiteness becoming grey as darkness approaches, such blackberry pie really brings back the languid days of summer.

Raspberry Pie

You'll need a baked pie shell to start with, a quart of chilled ripe raspberries, a cup of confectioner's sugar, and ½ pint of heavy cream.

To make this pie shell, sift together a cup of sifted flour and ½ teaspoon salt. Cut in ¼ cup of shortening. Handling this lightly and quickly, add only enough water—about 3 tablespoons—to make a dough that will stay together when rolled. Roll out and place in a pie pan. Prick to prevent puffing. Bake in a hot 450°F. oven for 12 to 15 minutes or until done.

Line the baked and cooled shell with the soft raspberries. Sprinkle with confectioner's sugar. Add layer after layer until the fruit and the sugar are all used. Just before serving this pie, whip the cream and pour it in a fluffy white mound atop the crimson fruit.

RUM CHERRY (*Prunus*)

Family Rose (*Rosaceae*)

Other Names Wild Black Cherry, Capuli, Black Cherry, Cabinet Cherry, Sweet Black Cherry, Wild Cherry.

Description The rum cherry is the only native species of this estimable edible wild growth which reaches the size of a large tree, sometimes attaining heights in excess of one hundred feet with trunks four and five feet through.

Too, it is possible to distinguish it at any time of the year by its irregularly cracking bark. This is nearly black on older trees and rough with irregular, thick scales that have a tendency to curl upwards along their edges. The bark

Rum cherry. *Top left:* blossom. *Top right:* branch with leaves and fruit. *Bottom:* branch with leaves and blossoms.

on young trunks is shiny, reddish-to-olive brown, and predominantly marked with horizontally elongated, breathing pores that appear at a casual glance to be white lines

The inner bark has an almondish odor and characteristically bitter taste due to the presence of poisonous hydrocyanic acid.

Furthermore, when in bloom the edible can be picked out from the other wild cherries in that its white flowers droop in cone-shaped spikes, appearing in May and June while the tree, which may be little larger than a shrub, is still leaving.

The fruit is a drupe in that, like the plum and peach, it consists of skin-enclosed pulp, surrounding a single seed. Ripening to a bright black or dark purple in August and September, it varies in size and quality from tree to tree. Usually about the size of garden peas, it grows even larger in Mexico where, the only native wild cherry to be had there, it finds its way to markets as *capulinos*.

The leaves vary from narrow ovals to oblong lancehead shapes, with widely rounded or wedge-formed bases and long-pointed tips. Measuring from about two to five inches in length by about one-third that width, they have edges that are minutely toothed with incurving and somewhat blunt teeth. Thick and firm, they are a shiny dark-green above, lighter and smooth underneath. The stems, seldom more than an inch long, have twin reddish glands at their tops.

Commonly some 45 to 55 feet high, with trunks 1½ to 3 inches through, the rum cherry has irregularly oblong tops when it grows in the open, although in forests it shoots up tall and straight with lofty, comparatively small crowns. The hardy strong, moderately heavy, beautifully close-grained wood is valuable for panels and furniture, both solid and as a much less expensive veneer, both all the more desirable because of the way it accepts a high polish, while neither splitting nor warping.

Distribution   The rum cherry, whose range alone among the native wild cherries reaches through Mexico into South America, grows from the Maritime Provinces to Florida, west to North Dakota, Texas, and Arizona. Thriving best in moist and fertile deep soil, it also springs up in the dry gravelly and sandy uplands.

Edibility   Game birds and songsters feast on rum cherries summers and autumns when they ripen, and even before, and animals feed on the fruit that falls to the ground. Bear gorge themselves on all they can reach. Moose, deer, elk, and mountain sheep are among the big game adding the foliage, twigs, and the aromatic if bitter bark to their meals. Deer mice and chipmunks deem the pits a favorite repast, the latter storing them in quantity for the periods during which they rouse and eat in the wintertime.

Their richly bittersweet, winy juiciness makes rum cherries popular raw wherever they grow, particularly among small boys. They get their name, incidentally, from the way the simmered and sweetened juice was added to raw liquors to smooth and thriftily stretch them. They are still used in various combinations with ardent spirits.

Rum cherries make rich dark jelly when combined with apples, or they will jell alone with added pectin. Sauces, pies, sherbets, and flavoring juices are also successfully concocted from them in the kitchen.

SHEPHERD'S PURSE (*Capsella*)

Family   Mustard (*Cruciferae*)

Other Names   Pickpocket, Mother's Heart, Pepper and Salt, Lady's Purse.

Description   This is one of the commonest of our wayside edibles, having accompanied Europeans in all their navigations, establishing itself with wayfaring persistency wherever they have settled long enough to till the soil. It flourishes most of the growing year in all parts of the world except the tropics, even in the Arctic, and being so pleasant an addition to the table is a good and easy plant to know.

The flowers, which are not particularly attractive, grow near together on stalks close to the tip of the stem. Very small, each has two pairs of opposite petals, characteristic of the mustard family. Because the blossoms lowest on the stalk open first, flowers are blooming while there is still a cluster of green buds at the top.

Tiny yellow stamens are in the center of these four petals, below which are a quartet of small green sepals. Once the blossom has withered, the seed vessel clinging to the center of the stalk increases in size until it resembles a

Shepherd's purse.

jewel-like emerald heart with a hard little mass in its middle. These flattish, triangular, heartlike seed pods are more noticeable than the preceding blossoms. When mature, the seed pouches burst open readily.

The leaves at the base of each shepherd's purse, growing in a rosette, are dandelionlike, being long and narrow with edges that are deeply indented, almost to the center vein. The leaves higher on the flower stem are formed like arrowheads, their bottoms clasping the stalk tightly.

Distribution Following civilization through most of the world, this alien now grows throughout most of Canada and the United States, beginning its activity especially where the ground has been disturbed.

Edibility Grouse, larks, and the cheery little goldfinches are among the birds making a practice of eating the seeds of the shepherd's purse.

The young leaves are enjoyed in salads and later as a potherb. The seeds can be gathered and ground into a nutritious meal.

Wilted Shepherd's Purse

Thriving so close to the ground and in such accessible places, shepherd's purse is apt to pick up a lot of grit and dust, so it is best to gather the leaves young and then to wash them well.

To steam enough for four people, melt 4 tablespoons of butter in a heavy frypan over high heat. Stir in 6 loosely filled cups of greens, along with 6 tablespoons of water. Cover, except when stirring periodically, and cook for several minutes until the leaves are wilted. Salt, pepper, and serve.

STRAWBERRY (*Fragaria*)

Family   Rose (*Rosaceae*)

Other Names   Wild Strawberry, Scarlet Strawberry, Virginia Strawberry, Wood Strawberry, European Wood Strawberry, California Strawberry, Earth Mulberry, Beach Strawberry, Yukon Strawberry, White Strawberry.

Description   This most delectable of all berries, wild or tame, is known to everyone because of its similarity to the far larger but always infinitely less sweet domesticated varieties. The fruit is usually the familiar red, an exception being a strain of wild white strawberries, also delicately sugary and delicious, that grows in New York, Pennsylvania, and West Virginia.

Ripe from June to August depending on the elevation and latitude, wild strawberries are mostly tiny and grow in loose clusters close to the sheltering ground. I've enjoyed them all over the continent, except in the deserts, and the largest I have picked have been some inches long, growing in Southeastern Alaska. This same juicy fruit, *Fragaria chiloensis,* is also found in the Aleutians, on the Seward Peninsula, and along the Gulf of Alaska. Yet even as nearby as the dry hillsides of the upper and central Yukon River in the interior of this 49th state, the plants are more slender and the berries of more usual minuteness, with tighter clinging hulls.

In fact, the difficulty of disengaging the hulls of wild strawberries is the most time-consuming part of the joy of gathering these wilderness delicacies everywhere, particularly when they are not fully ripe.

Strawberry.

It all starts with the five-petaled flower, the members of this frequently having notched outer edges. Underneath the five parts of these sweet-smelling blossoms are five leaflike sepals, each pointed, and five bracts—the modified leaves, actually the reproductive spore cases, at the base of the flower cluster. To save a lot of picking over, it is best to take the time initially to separate the berries from the hulls. When you're feasting as you harvest, the easiest way to rid an individual berry from a tenacious calyx is just to bite the fruit from it.

Twenty or more stamens lift in a dense ring around the seed vessels of each blossom, being united so fast to the sepals that they do not fall off when the white petals wither. Once the flower shrinks and shrivels, the receptacle under the central seeds starts to swell, expanding finally into a luscious berry. The minute yellowish or brownish seeds still cling to the outside of this, in such a variety as the *Fragaria virginiana* being sunk in pits that indent the fruitlike berries. Actually, strawberry fruits are the tiny surface seeds. What we enjoy are actually the enlarged flower containers.

The dark green leaves of the typical wild strawberry grow separately from the roots. Each is made up of three roughly toothed leaflets, further armed with soft hairs.

Distribution   Wild strawberries perfume the air from Alaska, the Yukon, and the Northwest Territories to Mexico, thriving nearly everywhere except in arid areas.

Edibility   Grouse, prairie chickens, pheasants, and quail, along with a host of songbirds among which the robin is especially ravenous, seek the luscious strawberry. Hare, rabbits, possums, chipmunks, and squirrels dine on both fruit and the tenderer leaves. White-tailed and mule deer are among the hoofed browsers nuzzling the plants.

Wild strawberries make shortcakes, tarts, sauces, jellies, jams, and preserves whose flavor and sweetness is difficult to approach with any other fruit, wild or tame. Not only are they delectable raw, but in home desserts it is unnecessary to cut them up first as a sprinkling of sugar soon draws out their unexcelled juices.

They are unusually nutritious in that they are rich in such necessary food ingredients as quickly assimilated iron, potassium, sulphur, calcium, sodium, silicon, and the related malic and citric acids. A part of a cup, the proportion depending on the environment and the season, equals the vitamin C content of an orange.

The leaves not only make a tasty tea, but they can provide one that is unusually rich in the scurvy-preventing-and-curing C vitamin. For refreshing enjoyment, cover two full handfuls of the sawtoothed, fresh, green leaves with a quart of boiling water, allow to steep five minutes, and then serve either plain or with a bit of fresh lemon juice and a trifle of sweetening. For free medicinal quantities of vitamin C, immerse newly picked, green, young strawberry leaves with boiling water, cover, and drink cold the next day.

If you are ever outdoors and hungry and if the strawberry crop about you is limited, remember that the stems and stalks of this ever-popular-perennial are also tasty.

WATER CRESS (*Nasturtium*)

Family   Mustard (*Cruciferae*)

Other Names   Pepperleaf, Water Nasturtium, Scurvy Grass.

Description   The usually prostrate and often floating plant thrives in cold water and wet places, growing in mats or clumps, characterized by innumerable, little, white, threadlike roots. The roots are tough and should in the main be left, in any event, so that the cress can continue to spread.

The minute white flowers, arranged in their mustardlike crosses, many of them extending from the stem joints and all blossoming on a succession of tiny stocks attached to a longish stalk, are usually inconspicuous. They develop needlelike pods from about ½ to 1 inch long which, if still tender to the bite, are tasty, too.

Dense green leaves, dark and shiny, with smooth but wavy edges, grow with three to eleven smooth and roundish segments, the biggest of which is at the end.

Depending on the location, water cress flowers from May to August.

Distribution   Water cress is common throughout Canada and the United States, growing in every state and throughout the world, especially in this

Water cress.

Northern Hemisphere. A native of Europe, it is cultivated there and in this country, often escaping to the wilds. You can even buy the seeds and, following the directions on the packet, start your own patch.

Edibility Pungently tasty both cooked and in its native state, it is generally preferred raw. However, briefly simmered leaves, stems, flowers, and young pods are not only hard to beat among the boiled greens, but a handful of them adds zest to most other edible greens.

Boiling, too, does away with the danger of contamination. The familiar plant prefers clean, clear, cold water, but you can't always be sure that those pools, trout streams, expanses of mud, and even springs are pure. In case of doubt, it is a sensible precaution to soak the well-washed leaves and tender shoots in water in which purification tablets have been dissolved.

A tangy and interesting supplement to any salad, water cress, stimulating the appetite, is also a prime appetizer and will enliven hors d'oeuvres. Enjoy its characteristic peppery flower in sandwiches, too, where it has been relished as long as these food snacks have been known.

A memorable, nutritious, vitamin-and-mineral-swarming tea can be made by covering a teaspoon of the leaves or roots with a cup of boiling water and steeping for five minutes.

Fried Water Cress

To complete that epicurean enjoyment of freshly caught fish or shellfish, garnish them with fried water cress. Just toss the individual sprigs into hot oil for scarcely a minute. Drain briefly on absorbent paper. This really touches up those mouthfuls of hot steaming trout, especially when served with a delicate white wine.

CHAPTER SIXTEEN

TIPS AND TRICKS FOR GREAT WILDERNESS COOKING

Nothing is more important on a camping trip than the grub.
—Colonel Townsend Whelen

When your appetite is sharpened by the healthy sort of outdoor living for which mankind was made, the mealtimes can include some of the best moments of any vacation—if you outfit yourself with foods that keep well, cook readily, and are easy to handle.

Now is not too soon to get started on your provisioning for that next trip back of beyond, for done right it's going to take some time. You'll do best to take foods you personally like and know how to prepare. Experimenting at home and on weekend journeys is the soundest way to find out how much of each item you'll need to round out the sort of satisfying meals you're going to need to keep going under full power.

And they should be satisfying as well as sustaining. As the Hudson's Bay Company says, "There is usually little object in traveling tough just for the sake of being tough."

Rough it, sure, if you want to prove to yourself the actually very important fact that you can rough it. One day, it's true, anyone at all may be thrown entirely upon his own resources and forced to get along the best he can with a minimum of comforts.

But as far as the preference goes, roughing it is a development stage. Once we've successfully tested our ability to take it, a whole lot of doubts and inhibitions disappear. We find ourselves realizing that the real challenge lies in smoothing it. We come to appreciate that making it easy on ourselves takes a lot more experience and ingenuity than bulling it through the tough way.

319

As Colonel Townsend Whelen has pointed out, "Most of us go camping to have a good time. If the food is poor, unwholesome, or not what we crave, we have a continual grouch. If it is excellent and there is plenty of it, everything is rosy. Good food even makes up for rain and hard beds. Good fellowship is at its best around good meals."

Far from the humdrum concerns of manmade civilization, it is possible as nowhere else to appreciate the simple pleasures of life—browning frypan bread, steaming coffee, and bacon sputtering over apple-red coals. The crackle of your campfire takes on unexpected coziness, and even the smallest tent all at once seems as snug and satisfying as a mansion.

HEATING AND EATING EQUIPMENT

That unforgettable first fire at dawn. Because of the air currents set into motion by the blending of day and night, it's colder now than it was during total darkness. The cook maybe deposits an old pine stump, saved for the purpose, in the center of the fading overnight embers. This gives him a blaze like the light of a pressure lantern, and it also helps him to get some warmth into his extended fingers. Pretty soon he's thawed out enough to shove the coffee pot grumpily into the heat. He then begins banging pans around, a little more expressively than necessary. Further sleep soon becomes impossible. The coffee smells too good, anyway, particularly when joined by the aromas of flapjacks and bacon.

Much of the success of a camping trip, as well as a considerable deal of the pleasure, is going to depend on your having the right kinds of cooking fires. This does not mean that campfires, if those are what you use, should be built in just one way. It all depends upon where you are and what you have.

Various Cooking Fires

The round fire is generally not too convenient for cooking purposes. One answer is to arrange a number of such small fires of varying intensities, just as you use different burners on a city range.

But the problem becomes one of most easily supporting the various cooking utensils. As usual, solutions are numerous. One handy method that will do away with a lot of teetering and tipping is to scoop, scrape, or stamp a trench. This may be about six inches wide and deep and perhaps two feet long. Running this trench in the same direction as the wind will assure a better draft. Get a good fire going in this trench, perhaps by raking it there after it gets blazing well. Then kettle, frypan, and pots can be steadied across it. Such a fire, however, probably won't be successful if either the day is quiet or the fuel is none too ardent.

The answer then may be the more usual above-ground fire but one that's some eight inches wide and four or five feet long. This fire may be contained by two fairly dry logs some four to six inches in diameter, laid either parallel

Cooking a Full Meal

Indian fireplace.

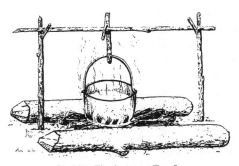

Cooking Fire between Two Logs

Two types of hunter's fire.

or at a slight angle with the open end toward the wind. If these logs are raised an inch or two by stones or billets, air will be able to circulate advantageously beneath them. Fuel this fire with preferably long split hardwood, and if possible let it burn down either to a hot bed of coals or to a steady blaze which does not flame up more than a foot.

Meanwhile, cut two substantial forked green poles. Drive these upright into the ground at each end of the fire, so that a green crosspiece laid between the crotches will extend the length of the center of the fire. Make pothooks for each kettle by cutting handle-holding notches in forked sticks that can be inverted over this crosspiece. Or carry several pothooks made by bending short lengths of coat-hanger wire into "S" shapes.

A convenient variation of this technique is to use two green poles on either side of the fire instead of the somewhat seasoned logs. Take pains to raise these evenly above the ground, perhaps notching the supporting billets if that's what you're using. Such green poles will take a long time to burn through. Just set your cooking utensils across them.

Grates and Irons

A substantial wire grid, available from dealers in camp equipment, will provide a convenient base on which to set pots and pans above a wood fire and over which to broil meat. Some of these have folding legs which, stuck into the forest floor, will hold kettles and frying pan above the heat.

My own experience, however, has been that these sharp extremities can be somewhat of a menace when one is on the move. I have removed them, also partly to save weight. The grids can as handily be laid across rocks or billets. In a stony and often in a treacherously soft spot, this has to be done anyway.

Camp Stoves

In spite of all that can be said for an open fire, there are times when a stove either is necessary or is at least indicated by common sense.

Tiny fire for a quick lunch.

The most popular camp stove today is a one-burner, white gas stove. In many cases the gasoline stove solves the cooking problem admirably, especially when it comes to boiling and frying. A separate oven can be used for baking.

This type of stove is ideal and often a must for many public camping grounds. It is good for the places where firewood is no longer to be had and where space may be limited. Available with two or three burners, it is excellent for those automobile tourists who like to cook their own meals beside the road.

Such a cooking fire can be lighted immediately. The even and easily regulated heat will allow the refugee from the city range to put out good meals with a minimum of effort and guesswork. Such a stove is fine, too, for travelers in those areas where nonresidents are prohibited from lighting an open fire except when accompanied by a resident or a licensed guide.

Trench fire.

Gasoline stoves are inexpensive, easily and compactly packed, and durable. They can be used if desired atop a handy metal stand that supports them at normal stove height and, when not in use, folds into a small bundle that is easily stowed in the car or boat.

Dutch Oven

Here is the one and only. It's not that this old-fashioned oven of cast iron doesn't have its disadvantages. It's awkward and heavy to carry unless you're traveling by pack train, boat, or car. Furthermore, although it holds the heat, it will rust if not kept well greased. Other varieties, such as those made of aluminum, are both lighter and easier to keep clean. But they're for city stoves if anywhere. They wouldn't even come close to getting the job done over outdoor fires.

What you want for food in the farther places is a heavy, thick, cast-iron pot with a similarly rugged top, lipped to hold a ruddy bed of coals. The model I find most satisfactory for my own use with small parties is 12 inches in diameter, 4 inches deep, and 17 pounds in weight. Models are also available 8, 10, 14, and 16 inches in diameter.

The dutch oven you get should have squat legs both to keep the bottom safely above the otherwise scorching ardor of hot embers and to anchor the contraption levelly. It will also need a convenient handle by which the hot top can be lifted and a likewise easily manipulated bail by which the entire contrivance can be moved. Both of these jobs can be performed with the help of a forked stick cut on the spot. When I'm shifting the coal-heaped lid, though, I help balance it with a second stick held in the other hand. You'll also need a shovel. One of the husky, folding models available at surplus stores is convenient to carry. Dutch ovens are used both above and below ground.

Dutch oven.

Old-timers season their dutch ovens, when they first buy them, by boiling grease in them. Otherwise, they'll tell you, the cast iron which is porous will give trouble in making food stick. This is a sound precaution when you buy those heavy iron frypans, too.

Reflector Baker

The way to add a really luxurious touch to meals cooked over open fires is to bring along a reflector baker. One of these holdovers from pioneer years can also be effectively utilized with ovenless stoves and with the most modern charcoal grills. Dealers sell reflector bakers in sizes to fit your needs.

Some hints? Because these contrivances roast and bake with reflected as well as direct heat, you'll get better campfire results if the warmth from your open blaze is directed toward the opening by some reflecting surface such as a rock or a high back log. Two ways to keep this oven from cooking too fast on the bottom are to place the oven several inches lower than the fire or to base the blaze on a slow-burning green wood so that its concentration of heat will be a bit higher than the lower part of the oven. You need flames for this sort of cooking; not coals. The reflector baker may be as close as 8 inches to the leaping blaze.

Griddle

A griddle will clear the way for the quick serving of bacon, eggs, and flapjacks in quantity. One of these plates can be laid across a couple of logs between which a cooking fire has largely burned to coals. Matter of fact, such a griddle can also be used as a substitute stovetop to keep cooking utensils steady and free of soot. Magnesium griddles are the lightest available. Unless you plan to wrap them in papers, it's a good idea to make or buy a protective traveling cover so as to keep the rest of the outfit clean.

Foil

Aluminum foil cookery is the modern version of enclosing food for cooking by bundling it in moist leaves, clay, or dripping green seaweed. This modern method also encourages food to retain its juices and to warm evenly. Therein, as a matter of fact, lie the shortcomings. Meat wrapped in foil, for example, is steamed rather than roasted or broiled. The deliciously crisp brownness is missing. There are ways around, of course. But these largely erase the virtues of simplicity.

A fish can be roasted directly on the coals if it is first wrapped in oiled foil, and in the case of small catches you can impart a certain charred touch by toasting it unwrapped beforehand on a forked stick. With large fish, you can help along the taste by cooking sliced tomatoes, diced onions, bacon, chopped peppers, and the like in the foil along with the fish.

Then there are the vegetables and such whose taste this variety of cooking does not seriously impair. The major drawback to any large amount of foil cookery, from the vacationist's viewpoint, is that its nature is more that of an occasional novelty. It does not really lend itself to serious cookery. Once in a while it's fun. But in the long run you save no time or energy. Most importantly for go-light campers on extended trips, you also save no weight.

Nested Cooking Utensils

You'll need cooking and eating paraphernalia. Pots, pans, dishes, and tableware from home will often do.

For the lone camper, the practical minimum is two small kettles with covers and with bails by which they can be hung over a fire, a frypan with preferably a folding handle, a tablespoon and usually a light fork, and a cool cup. The frypan will serve as a plate; the cup as a bowl. One's pocket or sheath knife can be used whenever necessary.

Two nesting aluminum kettles, the larger holding about 1½ quarts, together with an 8-inch frypan with conveniently folding handle, are available from dealers in camping goods. Weighing less than two pounds, they add no appreciable bulk to a pack, inasmuch as food and other essentials can be packed within them. Even when there are two or three people in the party, this same outfit can suffice; along with a plate, cup, spoon, and fork for each individual.

Best of all for camping is a small nested cooking and eating kit made of a light, tough aluminum compound. Anyone who has ever burned himself on aluminum, however, will agree that the nested cups, and preferably the plates as well, may be of stainless steel. The frypan, too, should be stainless steel. I bought an outfit of this sort when I first started going into the real wilderness, and I've used it without replacement or changes ever since. Matter of fact, many of the components are so handy that even when I'm in the city one or another of them is still used almost daily. However, some flimsy and highly impractical sets are on the market. Buy your nested outfit, if you get one, from the best established and most reliable sporting goods dealer you can get in touch with.

Light fabric holders available for the pots and frypan permit their being cleanly packed, when camp is moved frequently, without a whole lot of work scouring off the black every time. Actually, a certain amount of this exterior blackness makes for faster and more even cooking. You can also secure fabric knife, fork, and spoon rolls that, when you set up camp, can be handily hung to a tree or tent.

When you get home, spots and discolorations on aluminum ware can be removed by using a solution made by dissolving a tablespoon of cream of tartar in a pint of water.

A durable set of nested aluminum measuring spoons takes up very little space and can be handy in both the kitchen and eating areas. If you do not take a regular measuring cup, mark accurate proportions plainly on one of your drinking cups.

Mixing Surface

Simplest and handiest thing to take along for mixing and working purposes is a thin sheet of plastic. This can be easily washed, quickly refolded, and conveniently carried from one vacation spot to another with a minimum of bother.

OTHER VALUABLE TOOLS

Meat Saw

A lot of hunters carry only hatchets or, if they're traveling by canoe, axes. I also like a meat saw, small enough to stow in my packsack. Besides other uses, such a saw is the only conservative way to cut up frozen portions.

Cook's Knife

You need a knife constantly afield, and for many purposes. For example, the camp cook will require one for slicing bread and meat, paring vegetables, and for a dozen other chores. Any fair-sized knife will do for such duties. Unless you're traveling particularly light, however, it is better to have a special one for kitchen work. This blade is almost sure to get such rough treatment that it would take a lot of work to keep it sharp enough for other jobs. Aside from that, a kitchen knife both performs better and holds up more satisfactorily if not given the fine edge desirable for pocket and sporting knives.

One reason for this is that meat is carved and bread sliced more easily with what is actually a sawing action. A coarse edge made by sweeping the blade forward a few times against a carborundum diagonally from heel to tip, first on one side and then on the other, actually resembles saw teeth. This most functional edge can be quickly renewed by the same process.

A small butcher knife, particularly one of those stocked by specialists in outdoor equipment, goes well with most outfits. Have a sheath for it, and keep it in the bundle with the knives, forks, and spoons. Do not oil and thus soften this leather. Not only does the knife then become difficult to encase, but the point has a tendency to catch and puncture the flexible and often curling leather. Saddle soap the sheath instead, or use ordinary shoe polish on it.

Cleaning Carborundum

Carborundums are used so often in camp that it's little wonder that these abrasive stones become more and more clotted with grime, thus progressively losing their effectiveness. To restore the cutting ability of your dirt-clogged carborundum, just put the stone in a good bed of coals until it is red hot. Then it will be all right again.

Pails

Plenty of water is wanted at most campsites, and sources of supply are often some distance away. Collapsible and folding canvas or rubberized buckets are procurable and are handy for certain kinds of camping. For other types of vacationing, such as automobile camping, two galvanized pails will be cleaner and more convenient. Breakables can be packed in them during traveling.

BASIC GRUBSTAKES

The standard foods taken by experienced outdoorsmen on trips into the farther places of this continent, and which in general form the basis of most grubstakes, include: all-purpose flour, triple-action baking powder, baking soda and a packet of dry yeast if sourdough breadstuffs are to be used, sugar, compact cereals such as quickly cooking rice and oatmeal, corn meal, side bacon which has nearly triple the calories of back bacon, salt pork, oleomargarine, salt, spaghetti and such, powdered milk and eggs, and dehydrated fruits and vegetables. All these are practically free of water.

Some of the more nutritious spreads such as honey, jam, and peanut butter work in well. So does cheese. Practical beverages are concentrated tea powder or tea itself, one of the instant coffees, malted milk, and chocolate. Bouillon solids and dry soup mixes, although short on nourishment, are often welcome because of the easy variety they afford, especially with small game that hasn't had time to age. Seasonings such as powdered celery and onion, pepper, a favorite spice or two, as well as an unseasoned meat tenderizer, may be desirable.

The old Three B days are gone; not that steady diets of beans, bacon, and bannock ever had much glamor in real life after the first couple of days.

HOW MUCH OF EACH

No one can give you more than an idea of the quantities to take of various items. It all depends on the number of meals you expect to make of each food, how many are to be in the party, and how much of each particular nutriment it will take to make a satisfying portion for each individual concerned.

To determine quantities, you can experiment at home. If you want oatmeal every morning, for example, find out just how much rolled oats are needed to make the breakfast you will likely eat in the woods. Just as a suggestion, take at least double the amount of sugar and sweets you would use at home, for your desire for them in camp will be out of all proportion to what you want in the city.

HOW TO PACK

Dry foods such as flour, cereal, beans, salt, and sugar may be packed in small waterproof sacks which are available in a variety of types and sizes from most camp outfitters. You can make them, too. Each should be plainly labeled. Repackage prepared dry foods whenever this can be done advantageously, cutting out and enclosing any special directions. Unless you've plenty of room, foods such as corn flakes should be compressed into as small a space as possible.

Dried meats may be wrapped in wax paper or aluminum foil. Lard, butter, and the like travel well in tightly closed tins such as half-pound and pound tobacco cans. Plastic flasks and bottles made for carrying most liquids are safer and lighter than glass for syrup, oil, and such; but not for most extracts. Powdered eggs and milk will keep better in snugly closed receptacles. Beverages in powder form should also be kept tightly covered.

Wilderness Refrigeration

Foods can be kept cool by placing them in a pail that is partly submerged in a shady portion of a brook, lake, or spring. Small amounts of fresh meat will keep for several days this way in hot weather if air is allowed to reach it. Cooked meat, broth, mulligan, greens, and the like will keep better if covered individually. Several yards of inexpensive cheesecloth tucked in the outfit will protect such food when flies become pestiferous.

ABOUT FREEZING

Some of the foods will spoil if allowed to freeze. Days these can be wrapped in bedding. Nights they can be stowed near enough to the reflected warmth of a fire. When traveling with a small outfit and sleeping out in temperatures 60°F. and more below freezing, I've kept a few canned goods, that otherwise would be burst by the cold, stowed safely out of the way at the foot of my sleeping bag.

When food does freeze, it preferably should not be thawed until it is to be used. Fresh meat and fish keep well frozen. So do cheese and eggs, although their flavors are impaired. The taste and texture of such fruits as oranges are best preserved by letting them defrost in cold water. Frozen potatoes, which take on the aspect of marble, should be dipped in boiling water and their skins scraped off. Then drop them singly into boiling water that is kept bubbling. Cold weather increases a potato's sugar content, so you may find the resulting flavor especially appealing.

CANNED FOODS

Canned goods are usually ruled out except on trips when transportation is of little worry. Otherwise, their weight and bulk can quickly add up to prohibitive proportions. If you cannot expect to procure fresh game or fish, however, you may care to pack along a few of the canned meats. Canned tomatoes always go particularly well in the woods if you can manage them.

The most economical way to heat canned vegetables is to puncture the top of the can slightly, as with a small nail, and then to place the container in a deep pan of water. This should not cover the tin, which should be left in the hot water only the brief time necessary to heat the contents thoroughly. It will then give no trouble in opening. Incidentally, if a tenderfoot ever tries to heat that unopened can of soup or beans by dropping it in the campfire, either rake it out in a hurry or stand a long way back.

Nutriment that you may as well capitalize on to the fullest, especially after packing it for miles, is wasted by emptying commercially canned vegetables into a pan for heating. But if you do this, simply warm them before using. Boiling destroys much of their food value.

Don't throw away any of the juice in the can. Containing both vitamins and minerals, it can be profitably used in sauces, gravies, and soups. Seasoned if you want, it also makes a tasty beverage, especially in the bush.

If there are any cans without distinguishing markings except for paper labels and if there is a reasonable chance that your outfit may become wet, scratch the identity of the contents on an end of each tin. I neglected to take this precaution on a month-long river trip in Eastern Canada. We had ample room, no portages, and plenty of hunting and fishing to do in preference to cooking. Therefore, we had an abundance of canned goods, packed loosely in burlap bags so we could trim the canoe more easily. After paddling mostly in rain the first day, and shipping some water in rapids besides, we had to try from then on to pick what we wanted from a perfectly blank array of tins.

The cleanest and safest place to keep the contents of an open can, incidentally, is in that can. Cover this, perhaps with one of several elastic-trimmed little plastic fabrics brought for the purpose, and store away from squirrels and their like in as cool a place as possible. With acid foods such as tomatoes, however, a metallic though harmless taste may insinuate itself because of the acids' eating into the iron of the opened can, so these may as well be shifted to a non-metallic container. Unopened canned goods should preferably be kept at moderate temperatures.

Inspect all cans before buying them for a camping trip. Do this again before opening them. Such commonplaces of wilderness travel as denting, rusting, and freezing all can cause trouble. One test is to press each end of the can. Neither should bulge, nor should it snap back unless the can has been sprung or unless the contents have been frozen sufficiently to exert pressure against the ends although not enough to break the seal. Ordinarily, both ends should either be flat or should curve slightly inward. Seams should be tight and clean with no evidence of any leakage.

When you open a can, watch out for spurting liquid and for any off colors or odors. All are danger signals. Cans should be clean and smooth inside with very little corrosion. If the metal of a meat product can has merely turned dark inside, though, this is only a harmless reaction with the sulphur in the meat. Whenever there are any signs of spoilage, the wise thing to do is to discard all contents without tasting.

Instead of puncturing the evaporated milk can on top and plugging, taping, or sealing the holes with congealed milk, try making these small openings on opposites sides just below the rim. Then you can close them with a wide elastic band.

THE BASICS

The Least with the Most

Fat is, in calories, the most concentrated food. It is also the hardest to come by when living off the wilderness. Butter, oleomargarine, lard, and cooking oils have double and triple the amount of calories that even such a quick energy food as honey contains. If you plan to augment your meals with fish and game, the staples you carry should include a large proportion of edible fats.

Other concentrated foods that have figured conspicuously in rations where space and weight have been stringently restricted include dried shelled nuts, peanut butter, chocolate, dried whole eggs, dried whole milk, and malted milk tablets. If you want a bulky starch, rice is one that cooks up appetizingly with nearly everything.

Even when you're sleeping relaxed in the most comfortable of eiderdowns, your system is consuming heat units (or calories) at the rate of approximately ten calories a day per pound of body weight. In other words, if you weigh 160 pounds, the least number of calories you will use each day is 1,600.

The more you move around and the more energy you expend in keeping warm, the more calories you use. Even lying in your sleeping bag and reading will increase your basic caloric needs about 25 percent. The city man who gets very little exercise consumes on the average 50 percent above his minimum requirements. To maintain his weight, therefore, such a 160-pound individual requires about 2,400 calories daily.

It is reasonable, both from these scientific facts and from personal experience, to generalize that a healthy and fit man enjoying a robust outdoor life can require 20 calories of food a day per pound of body weight—and perhaps more, depending on his activity and on the climate. Cold weather, for example, compels the system to put out more and more heat to keep itself warm. The same 160-pound city man hunting in the north woods can very easily take in 3,200 or 4,000 calories a day, and more, and still trim down lean and hard.

Fats

Oleomargarine, largely because it keeps so well, is recommended for general camp use. To cut hard margarine or butter cleanly, use a knife that has been heated in hot water.

To protect yourself from popping hot fat, stop the spattering by sprinkling a bit of flour in the frypan. If the grease catches fire, throw a handful of flour on it; either that, or extinguish the flames by covering the burning fat and shutting out the air.

The camp shortening pail can be replenished by pouring in your surplus bacon grease. Excellent lard can also be secured from game fat not eaten along with the lean. Cut this into small bits and melt them down in a pan over low heat. Pour the liquid grease into some handy container, such as a friction-top can, where ordinarily it will harden and become easy to pack. Save the cracklings to eat with lean meat or to munch for lunch some cold noon.

Jams

An outdoor trip is where you really appreciate jams and marmalades. Some campers are bothered by the white crystals that often form in these foods. Looking like mold, such crystals tend to spread through the mixture once the first of them have appeared. Actually, they're the result of sugar combining with the water in the preparation. Although they do nothing for texture and appearance, they are not at all harmful.

Yeast

It is a good idea when using sourdough breadstuffs to carry a recently dated package of dry yeast in case something happens to the sourdough starter. It's true enough that a fresh starter can be made on the spot by mixing a cup apiece of flour and water in a scalded jar, covering it loosely, and stowing it in a warm place to sour. If the first results are not satisfactory, you can always try again with a new mixture. But the addition of yeast to these sourings will eliminate the guesswork.

Vinegar

Here's a pioneer stratagem to stretch supplies of sometimes hard-to-pack vinegar. When half of the vinegar is used, dilute the remainder with an equal amount of water. Then restore its authority by adding a cup of sugar, brown sugar if you have it. The sugar will ferment and supplant the missing acid.

Cheese

Cheese is one of the most versatile and delectable of camp foods. It may be relished in its natural state or added to everything from soups and salads to sauces to make all sorts of delicious combinations. More than one day I've enjoyed it at breakfast with scrambled eggs, at lunch in a sandwich melted over the noonday tea fire, and at night in a baked macaroni and tomato casserole. Preferences vary. A sharp, aged Cheddar keeps well, as do Edam and Gouda. Provolone is probably the best choice in high temperatures.

If heat makes the cheese rubbery, a solution is to wrap it well and to revive it in a cool stream. If you're going to spend a month or more away from civilization, sew one-week portions snugly in cheesecloth and immerse them in melted wax. You can harmlessly keep mold off cheese to a large extent by wiping the cheese with a clean cloth soaked either in baking soda solution or in vinegar.

Milk

Whether or not you use powdered milk and eggs will depend to a large extent on your preferences and upon where you are. As far as nutrition goes, both compare favorably with the fresh products.

Powdered milk is especially handy in cold weather if only because the quality of evaporated milk is impaired by freezing, which, as far as that goes, may cause it to spoil entirely by bursting the can. Besides, evaporated milk is still ¾ water. Condensed milk is ¼ water and nearly ½ sugar. Depending on the product, one pound of whole milk powder makes one gallon of liquid whole milk.

Whole milk powder is sometimes a little difficult to mix with water, but there are several ways to get around this. When you open the container, stir the powder and lightly take up the amount you want without packing it down in any way. Even measures are best obtained by leveling off the top of the cup or spoon with the straight edge of a knife. Place the powder on top of the water with which it is to mix. Then stir with a spoon until smooth. The mixing can be speeded somewhat by having the water slightly warm. You can also shake the water and powder together in a tightly closed jar which will subsequently serve as a pitcher.

Dried skim milk has all the nourishment of fresh skim milk. It has the calcium, phosphorous, iron, and other minerals, the B vitamins, natural sugar, and the protein that make liquid skim milk such an important food. Powdered whole milk has all these, plus the fat and vitamin A found in the cream of whole milk. Adding two teaspoons of butter or margarine to a cup of reconstituted skim milk will make this equal in food value to a cup of whole milk. And it's often a lot easier to mix.

You can even use dried skim milk to make a whipped topping for desserts. Mix ½ cup of the milk powder with ½ cup of preferably ice water. Beat for 3 or 4 minutes until soft peaks form. Then add 2 tablespoons lemon juice, fresh or reconstituted, and beat about the same length of time until it is stiff. Fold in ¼ cup sugar. About 3 cups of topping will result. Serve while you're still ahead.

Containers holding any of the dry milk products should be kept tightly closed, as the powder attracts moisture and becomes lumpy if long exposed to the air. It also picks up odors unless care is taken.

Powdered milk, mixed dry with the flour, makes a valuable addition to biscuits and other breadstuffs. Mornings when you're in a hurry to get away hunting or fishing, milk powder can be mixed directly with cereals such as oatmeal and the breakfast food then cooked as indicated on the package.

Evaporated milk, which is what you may settle for, is homogenized whole milk concentrated to double strength by evaporating part of the water. If you use equal parts of evaporated milk and water, you can utilize evaporated milk as you would any other fluid whole milk. The lumps in evaporated milk are formed by solids settling during storage and are harmless. Cans of evaporated milk can be turned or shaken at frequent intervals during a vacation trip to prevent such lumping.

Powdered Eggs

An egg is 11 percent waste unless you are going to bake the shells and then pulverize them, as many do to increase the calcium content of their dogs' feed. Seventy-four percent of the remaining yolk and white is water.

Yet dried whole egg has virtually the same food value, includes no waste whatsoever, and is only five percent water. More efficient processing equipment and methods have improved the quality of dried eggs. Varying somewhat with brands, a pound of desiccated eggs is the equivalent of some five dozen fresh eggs. One level tablespoon of the yellow powder, beaten until smoothly blended with two tablespoons of water, again depending on the individual product, equals one hen's egg. And you don't have to bother cushioning those perishable ovals with crumpled newspaper in the more stable types of their own cartons, nor arranging them with the large ends up while camping so as to keep the yolks centered.

In any event, scrambled eggs prepared from the powder come to taste mighty good in the farther places. If you haven't prepared these before, dissolve powdered eggs and milk in lukewarm water to make the proportions of these fresh products you might ordinarily use. Add salt, pepper, and any other seasoning, together with a chunk of butter or oleomargarine. A little flour may be stirred in for thickening. Scrambling all this with ham or bacon gives the dish added flavor.

Desserts

The dehydrated fruits such as raisins, apricots, apples, prunes, peaches, pears, dates, and figs give everyone plenty of choice. Numerous prepared dessert mixes of one sort or another also afford a wide selection, but find out by experimentation which ones you like before you take to the woods. Especially delicious and nutritious in the wilderness? That dense, heavy fruitcake that ordinarily seems a little too rich for city consumption.

Spices and Flavorings

Everybody has his own ideas on these, which is as it should be. Nearly everyone wants a little pepper. Small containers of powdered (not salt) celery, onions, and garlic pack a lot of possibilities. Paprika and powdered parsley combine taste and eye appeal. Then there are nutmeg, cinnamon, and their ilk. Small containers of thyme and rosemary afford occasional taste variations with fowl and red meats respectively. Like the rest, they only cost a few cents and occupy little room. Among the flavorings that seem to taste particularly good in the woods are vanilla, banana, and the peppermint which really touches up chocolate. Then there are lemon and other pure fruit juice powders, crystals, etc. Suit yourself.

Camp Coffee

The way I like to make camp coffee is to put a rather coarse grind into fresh cold water, using 2 level tablespoons for every cup of water. Amounts can be varied, of course, for a stronger or weaker brew. Hang or set this over the fire. Watch it carefully. As soon as it boils up once, lift it to a warm sanctuary to take on body for five minutes. Then settle the grounds if you want with a couple of tablespoons of cold water and start pouring.

Unless you have decided preferences to the contrary, though, powdered instant coffee is far preferable to the ground article for general camp use except, perhaps, for those first cups in the morning. It is more economical in weight and bulk, cheaper, better lasting, and both quicker and easier to prepare. It can be made to individual order and without waste.

If you'd like to pocket several pleasant pickups before going on a hike or for a day's fishing, you can ready a number of these in a jiffy beforehand. For each, mix one teaspoon of your favorite instant coffee with an equal amount of sugar. Roll securely in foil. Dissolved pleasantly in the mouth, each will provide the same amount of stimulation and energy as would a similarly based cup of black coffee.

Other Beverages

Fruit juices are particular treats in the bush. Lemon, for example, is also sometimes welcome with fresh rainbow trout. A number of consolidated fruit juices are available, both dried and in concentrated liquid.

Bouillon cubes and powders make hot drinks that taste good around a campfire. A lot of times you'll appreciate them a lot more than you would either tea or coffee. They are also useful for flavoring broths, soups, gravies, and stews. Other worthwhile beverage concentrates include cocoa, malted milk, and chocolate.

Chocolate

Hot chocolate and cocoa in particular have a way of easing those last few steps between fire and bed. As for chocolate bars, these are one of the best known and liked energy foods. It's a common thing on extended camping trips to find a whitish appearance in such chocolate. This does not indicate spoilage, however, but is due to cocoa butter that has separated out. At a temperature no more than 85°F., the cocoa butter in ordinary chocolate melts and comes to the surface. It whitens upon hardening. Only the appearance of the chocolate is affected.

Instant Everything

Try the individual dehydrated product first. Do this before you leave home. Then suit yourself. Tastes differ. So do needs. A major error is to load up with dehydrated meals for the entire trip without everyone's doing considerable sampling beforehand.

Ordinarily, you'll be heading out for fun and relaxation, and the enjoyment of the meals is going to be a determining factor. Unless weight, space, and perhaps temperatures are basic considerations—as in mountain climbing, on extended backpacking hikes away from supply points, and during forced trips into remote regions—dehydrated foods despite their continuing improvements are still most satisfactorily used to supplement, rather than replace, regular victuals.

Trip Tip

Keep a record for future reference. Note what is left over at the end of the journey. Such intelligence can guide your efforts when you provision for that next sojourn in the silent spaces.

POTPOURRI

Baking Temperatures

If space and weight are no problems, one thing to do while accumulating experience is to bring along a small oven thermometer unless such is already attached to your cooking contraption. One costs only a few cents, occupies very little room, and takes much of the initial guesswork out of baking with outdoor fires. The following table will then apply; all temperatures mentioned being the commonly used Fahrenheit, whereby at sea level fresh water freezes at 32° and boils at 212°.

Slow oven	250° to 325°
Moderate oven	325° to 400°
Hot oven	400° to 450°
Very hot oven	450° to 550°

If you're starting out with no such thermometer, you will be able to get a fairly accurate idea of the temperature by using the following test. With experience, of course, you'll be able to make the same approximations by holding the bare hand in the heat. In the meantime, sprinkle some white flour in a pan and place this in the heated oven or baker. If you're short on flour, a piece of white tissue paper can be used instead.

Wilderness Cookery

Turns light tan in 5 minutes	Slow oven
Turns medium golden tan in 5 minutes	Moderate oven
Turns deep dark brown in 5 minutes	Hot oven
Turns deep dark brown in 3 minutes	Very hot oven

High Altitudes

Water, being under less pressure the loftier the altitude, boils at lower and lower temperatures the higher we go. This means that foods boiled or simmered at higher altitudes require a correspondingly longer cooking time. There are so many variations in foods themselves that it is difficult to give any definite rules. In general, such cooking times must be increased from 4 to 11 percent per 1,000 feet above sea level. Until you've had experience with a particular food, a safe rule is to add roughly 10 percent per 1,000 feet. A few minutes before that time is reached, start testing or tasting.

At high altitudes, sourdough and other yeast bread should be allowed to rise for a shorter time, only until about doubted in bulk. Either that, or less leavening should be used. The first technique assures better results.

Because flour dries out faster at high altitudes, it may be necessary to use more liquid to compensate for this loss and to give the dough the desirable consistency.

Dish Washing

Washing dishes is not really much of a chore if you have some system about it and if you always clean up immediately after a meal. With your cook kit, you'll find it helpful to include such items as detergent, two small tough cellulose sponges or dish cloths, a little dish mop for that hot campfire water, and scouring pads that combine steel wool or such with soap.

While you are eating, have your largest kettle over the fire heating dishwater. Or at the jumping-off spot, perhaps, buy a cheap tin dishpan if you've the room and ditch it when the trip is over. This will not take up much space if you select a model into which other items in your outfit can nest.

If you prefer, you may take along a small canvas wash basin. Such a 7-ounce affair that I've carried on go-light trips for years is 4 inches high and 12 inches in diameter. It squashes down flat to pack.

Every camper, as he finishes his meal, scrapes his probably nearly clean plate into the fire. When you are through with the frypans, pour off all grease and wipe them clean. Then fill them with water and put them on the fire to boil. Do the same with any kettle containing the sticky residue of mush.

Pans in which cereals like rolled oats have been cooked are particularly bothersome. If you will put a little square of butter or oleomargarine in the water when you are preparing the cereal, it will make the pot ten times easier to clean.

If you have a pet aluminum pot whose exterior you want to keep bright, coat the outside with a film of soap before you place it on the fire. All trace of black will then quickly wash off. Eventually, most kettles get thoroughly darkened on the outside with soot which sticks most tenaciously and which can scarcely be removed by anything short of abrasives. But this soot does no harm whatever and even makes food in such a kettle cook faster and more evenly. If you scour with sand, very little will rub off on other things when you pack. It is customary to have a canvas bag in which to stow the nest of pans and kettles. This helps to keep them from blackening other articles in the outfit. Individual fabric containers may also be convenient.

It has been the experience of a great many of the old sourdoughs in Alaska and the Northwest that when a utensil used for cooking meat is washed with soap, they get bad digestive disturbances akin to poisoning and that this ceases when such washing is stopped. One way to clean a steel frypan is to heat it very hot, then quickly plunge it into cold water. If this does not remove all the dirt, then scrub with sand and rinse in clear boiling water. Another way of loosening grease is to fill the pan with water into which some wood ashes have been dropped and allow the whole thing to come to a boil beside the blaze.

PART SEVEN
WILDERNESS COOKING:
SKILLS, TOOLS, RECIPES

CHAPTER SEVENTEEN

BASIC WILDERNESS COOKING RECIPES

BANNOCK, SOURDOUGH, AND OTHER BREADS

About the only cooking odors that even approach the aroma of bread baking outdoors are the sizzling smell of good grilled bacon, coffee bubbling in the heat of a campfire, and fat venison sputtering over hardwood coals.

Unless you can replenish it frequently, bakery bread soon becomes moldy, stale, and thoroughly unappetizing in the out-of-doors. Furthermore, its airy softness is unreasonably bulky and unsubstantial when it comes to packing.

Frying Pan Bread

This is the famous bannock of the open places. The basic recipe for one hungry outdoorsman follows. If you want more, increase the ingredients proportionately.

1 cup flour
1 teaspoon baking powder
¼ teaspoon salt

Mix these dry, taking all the time you need to do this thoroughly. Have the hands floured and everything ready to go before you add liquid. If you are going to use the traditional frypan, make sure it is warm and greased.

Working quickly from now on, stir in enough cold water to make a firm dough. Shape this, with as little handling as possible, into a cake about an inch thick. If you like crust, leave a doughnutlike hole in the middle. Dust the loaf lightly with flour, so it will handle more easily.

Lay the bannock in the warm frypan. Hold it over the heat until a bottom crust forms, rotating the pan a little so the loaf will shift and not become stuck.

Once the dough has hardened enough to hold together, you can turn the bannock over. This, if you've practiced a bit and have the confidence to flip strongly enough, can be easily accomplished with a slight swing of the arm and snap of the wrist. Or you can use a spatula, supporting the loaf long enough to invert the frypan over it and then turning everything together.

With a campfire, however, it is often easier at this stage just to prop the frypan at a steep angle so that the bannock will get direct heat on top. When crust has formed all around, you may if you wish turn the bannock over and around a few times while it is baking to an appetizing brown.

When is the bannock done? After you've been cooking them awhile, you will be able to tap one and gauge this by the hollowness of the sound. Meanwhile, test by shoving in a straw or sliver. If any dough adheres, the loaf needs more heat. Cooking can be accomplished in about 15 minutes. If you have other duties around camp, twice that time a bit farther from the heat will allow the bannock to cook more evenly.

Makeshift Ovens

Instead of slanting the pan in front of the fire to cook the top side only, you can often bake it throughout at this second stage. This may be accomplished by the use of an existing boulder or some such reflecting surface, perhaps several large stones laid up beside the campfire for the purpose. When the reflecting area is hot, lean the pan with its back to this and its face to the direct heat.

A reflector can also be made by thrusting several stakes in a line a foot behind the fire to support an expanse of aluminum foil. Or, with a small bannock, you can just bend a small sheet of foil in an arc over the frypan so that the heat rising about the pan will be reflected back down onto the top of the food.

You can also scoop a small pit in front of the campfire, rake a few red coals into it, and set the frypan on these so the bannock will be cooked both by the embers below and the blazing forelog of the fire above. For best results, this forelog should be a well burning one that's lying several inches off the ground at this point and blazing upwards with a generally vertical flame.

Suppose you're short on utensils and long on appetites? As soon as each loaf is crusty enough to hold its shape, slide it out of the pan and lean it on the ground near enough to the campfire to finish cooking. Immediately start another.

Bannock, in any event, never tastes better than when devoured piping hot around a campfire. It should then be broken apart, never cut. A cold bannock sliced in half, however, and made into a man-size sandwich with plenty of meat or other filler in between is the best lunch ever.

Biscuits

Start with the basic bannock recipe. Work 3 tablespoons of solid shortening per cup of flour into these dry ingredients. Mix thoroughly, perhaps by cutting through the flour and shortening again and again with two dull knives, until the mixture has the consistency of coarse meal.

Then, working quickly, add enough water or milk to make a dough just soft enough to be easily handled. From ¼ to ⅓ cup of fluid per cup of flour will generally suffice. If the dough becomes too sticky, rapidly scatter on a little more flour. For best results, knead no more than half a minute.

Flatten the dough speedily into a sheet about ¾ inch thick. A cold bottle or can makes an effective rolling pin. Cut square biscuits with a sharp cold knife or press out round ones with perhaps the top of the baking powder tin. Dust each with flour.

Place on a lightly greased pan or sheet. Bake in a very hot oven or reflector baker until a rich brown, by which time the biscuits should have risen to about 2 inches high. These biscuits can also be cooked in a frypan like bannock, in which case you may have to turn each one several times to assure even cooking. If you do not care for crust, keep them close together.

Want something special? Dip each biscuit into melted shortening before baking.

Baking Powders

When liquid is added to baking powder, gas is released. This is the same harmless carbon dioxide that gives such beverages as ginger ale their bubbliness. Its function in breadstuffs is to raise the dough. Without some such effervescence you'd end up with a chunk of hardtack; the way to make this, incidentally.

It follows that you want to prevent as much as possible of this gas from wastefully escaping. Aside from speed, you can conserve it several ways. Cold fluid, as might be expected, releases the carbon dioxide more slowly than hot. It is also better to do as much of the necessary mixing as possible with a cold spoon or peeled stick rather than with the warm hands.

Why not just put in more baking powder? The answer is that food tastes better and digests more easily with a minimum of this acid-alkali combination. Some outdoor cooks do tend to take out insurance by using more than the teaspoon of baking powder that's generally sufficient for each cup of flour. It's true that strengths of this leavening agent vary. Furthermore, all baking powder tends to become weaker with age, particularly if the container has not been kept tightly closed and in a dry and preferably cool place. It's sound practice to stir baking powder a bit before measuring, partly to break up any lumps but mainly to assure a more uniform mixture of ingredients. The outer layer is apt to lose some of its leavening power because of contact with air.

Directions on the particular can if the contents are fresh, experimentation if they are not, will provide a functional yardstick if you've any doubts. Double action baking powder, the so-called combination type which releases part of its gas when heated, packs more power than either the tartrate or the calcium phosphate varieties. The recipes in this book are geared to it.

The ideal, insofar as flavor and digestion are concerned, is to use the smallest amount of baking powder that will raise the breadstuff enough for your liking.

How to find out if the baking powder in your camping outfit it still active? Stir a teaspoonful into ½ cup of hot water. If the mixture does not bubble diligently, better use sourdough instead.

Bannock Changes

Variations on the basic bannock recipe are innumerable. Inclusion of a tablespoon of sugar with every cup of flour will make for a more pronounced taste and a crisper crust. Fresh or powdered eggs, ½ to 1 egg for every cup of flour, will add thickness and richness. Substitution of milk for water, or the addition of powdered milk, will improve both flavor and characteristic golden brownness.

Addition of a shortening, usually from 1 to 3 tablespoons per cup of flour, will increase tenderness. This is especially desirable in winter sports weather when even larger proportions of fat are sometimes necessary to keep the breadstuff from freezing hard on frosty trails. Solids like butter, margarine, bacon drippings, and lard are most effective when either creamed with the sugar or thoroughly mixed with the flour. Liquids such as cooking and salad oils, which make for a more crumbly but not so tender product, may be added mixed with water, milk, and any fresh eggs.

Such fruits as raisins, currants, and blueberries make bannock tastier, although their inclusion calls for the use of a bit more baking powder. Combine these fruits with the dry ingredients to avoid any overmixing. Spices, particularly nutmeg and cinnamon, are unusually zestful when their odors mingle with the keenness of pine trees and wood smoke.

Maple Muffins

You don't need maple trees for these. If you want, just make up some of the substitute maple syrup described elsewhere in this book. Then take:

2 eggs
⅓ cup milk
½ cup syrup
4 tablespoons liquid shortening
2 cups flour
2 teaspoons baking powder
¼ teaspoon salt

Add the eggs, either whole or dried, to the milk and beat together. Mix the syrup and shortening. Stir this into the eggs and milk.

Combine the flour, baking powder, and salt. Add the rest, mixing just enough to moisten the dry ingredients. Pour into a greased muffin pan and bake in a moderate oven or reflector baker. About ½ hour should do it. If these muffins are not devoured on the spot, loosen them in the pan, tip them so that air can get around them, and put them in a warm place.

Snow for Eggs

In the North when we have lacked eggs for this and other breadstuffs, we have successfully used snow instead. Fresh dry snow is best for this purpose.

It is rapidly stirred in just before the breadstuff is put over the heat. It must not be allowed to melt until the cooking is underway, for its function is entirely mechanical.

The air-loaded flakes of snow hold the ingredients apart. Cooked while these are so separated, such breadstuffs come out airy and light. Egg is able to accomplish the same end result, as you can appreciate by watching the way an egg readily beats into air-holding froth whose elasticity heightens its raising and spacing prowess. Two heaping tablespoons of fresh dry snow will take the place of every egg in the batter.

Homemade Dry Mix

Fresh bannock is a simple thing to cook on the trail, even when the nearest utensil is a dozen miles away. Then the handiest method is to mix the dry in-gredients before leaving the base of supplies. In fact, you can make up a num-ber of such batches at home, sealing each in a small plastic bag. This mix has multiple short-notice uses.

The following basic mix, given here in one-man proportions, will stay fresh for six weeks or more in camp if kept sealed, dry, and reasonably cool.

1 cup all-purpose flour
1 teaspoon double action baking powder
¼ teaspoon salt
3 tablespoons oleomargarine

If this mix is being readied at home, sift the flour before measuring it. Then sift together the flour, baking powder, and salt. Cut in the margarine with two knives, with an electric mixer at low speed, or with a pastry blender, until the mixture resembles coarse meal. For increased food value, add 2 tablespoons of powdered skim milk for every cup of flour.

Place in plastic bags. Seal with a hot iron or with one of the plastic tapes. A large quantity can be made at once, of course, and divided into smaller por-tions. Before using, it is a good idea to stir the mixture lightly.

If compounding this mix in camp, do it with the ingredients at hand and in the simplest way possible. Any solid shortening may be utilized if the mix is to be used within a short time. Such mix may be carried in a glass jar or just folded in wax paper.

For Hot Trail Bread   When the fire is going and everything else is ready, quickly add enough water to basic mix to make a firm dough. Shape into a long, thin roll, no more than an inch thick. Wind this ribbon on a preheated green hardwood stick, the diameter of a rake handle, so trimmed that several projecting stubs of branches will keep the dough in place. A particularly sweet wood for the job is birch. Hold the bannock in the heat, occasionally turning it, for a couple of minutes. Once a crust has been formed, the stick may be leaned between the fringes of the fire and some reflecting surface such as a log or rock for the 15 minutes or so required to form a tasty brown spiral. Or you can just shove a sharpened end of the stick into the ground beside the fire and turn this holder now and then while readying the remainder of the meal.

For Frying Pan Bread   When ready to go, add to mix about ⅓ cup of cold water for an easily handled dough. Cook like regular bannock.

For Drop Biscuits   Mix with a little less than ½ cup cold water to make a soft dough. Drop by the spoonful atop a hot greased metal surface and bake in a very hot oven or reflector baker for 10 to 15 minutes.

For Fruit Cobblers   Proceed as with the above biscuits, but drop each daub of dough atop a frying section of apple, apricot, or other cooked dry fruit.

For Muffins   Add 1 tablespoon sugar, 1 well-beaten whole or reconstituted egg, and ½ cup milk. Stir just enough to dampen all the dry ingredients. Fill greased muffin rings, improvised if necessary from aluminum foil, about ⅔ full. Bake in a hot oven about 20 minutes. Eat at once. For a dessert, cook with a teaspoon of marmalade or jam atop each muffin.

For Shortcake   Add 1 tablespoon of sugar to make half a dozen medium-size shortcakes, which will assure a pleasant change of diet in berry season. Mix with ⅓ cup cold water to form an easily handled dough. Flatten this to ¼ inch and either cut squares with a knife or punch out ovals with something like a can top. Brush half of these with melted margarine. Cover each with one of the remaining pieces. Bake in reflector baker. Serve hot with fruit.

For Corn Bread   Add a previously mixed 1 cup corn meal, 1 tablespoon sugar, 1 beaten egg, and 1 cup milk, stirring only until blended. Bake in hot oven or reflector baker about half an hour. Corn bread, like biscuits and baked potatoes, should be served as promptly as possible.

For Flapjacks   Add ½ cup milk, with which a whole or dried egg has been mixed, to the homemade dry mix. Stir only enough to moisten the flour. Cook like regular flapjacks.

For Dumplings   Stir in ¼ cup of cold milk or water. Proceed as with regular dumplings. These can also be dropped by the tablespoon atop a meat or vegetable casserole and baked in a hot oven approximately 20 minutes.

For Coffee Cake   Stir 3 tablespoons sugar into the mix. Combine a scant ¼ cup milk with 1 egg, fresh or dried, and stir well into the mix. Pour into

Wrap bread dough around a stick, then bake it over your campfire.

shallow greased pan. Sprinkle something such as nutmeg, cinnamon, powdered instant coffee, and sugar over the top if you want. Bake in a hot oven or reflector baker about 25 minutes. Delicious!

Sourdough

Sourdough was the first raising agent ever used in bread making. The primitive leaven contained wild yeasts as well as numerous kinds and types of bacteria, some of which produce gas and acids. If desirable organisms were to gain supremacy, the leaven was a success. If the fermentation was dominated by undesirable organisms, the product was inferior. Knowing all this, we can now control our sourdough to a large extent.

You can still make a primitive sourdough starter by mixing a cup apiece of plain flour and water in a scalded jar, covering it loosely, and placing it in a warm place to sour. If the first results are not satisfactory, you may try again with a new mixture. Trouble is, you run into all sorts of different flavors and consistencies. If you will enlist the help of store yeast, however, you can almost always come up with a satisfactory starter of your own on the first try.

Sourdough Starter   The starter can be readied at home. Once you have it, you have commenced growing your own yeast. That's what you are actually using when you bake with sourdough. Here's the sure, simple way to begin:

2 cups flour
2 cups lukewarm water
1 yeast cake or package of dry yeast

Mix the flour, lukewarm water, and yeast thoroughly. Then set overnight away from drafts in a warm place. By the next morning, the mixture should be putting forth bubbles and a pleasant yeasty odor. This overall process need not stop for as long as you're going to be in the wilderness.

For best results, keep the starter in a well-washed and scalded glass or pottery container. Never leave any metal in contact with it. Keep the starter as much as possible in a cool spot. As a matter of fact, if you want to store the starter or part of it for a period of months, just freeze it.

The sourdough starter can also be kept fresh and clean by drying. If you want to carry it easily and safely, work in enough flour to solidify the sponge into a dry wad. A good place to pack this is in the flour itself. Water and warmth will later reactivate the yeast plants for you.

Starters occasionally lose their vigor, particularly in cold weather. Oldtimers then sometimes revive them with a tablespoon of unpasteurized cider vinegar. This puts new acetic acid bacteria on the job. A tablespoon or two of raw sour milk or cream, of unpasteurized buttermilk, or of cultured buttermilk or cultured sour cream will get the lactic acids functioning again.

Sourdough starters should never be stored in a warm place for very long. Heat encourages organisms hurtful to yeast to grow at an extremely rapid rate. These may soon gain sufficient control to produce putrefactive changes; the reason for some of the unpleasant smells one occasionally runs across in old starters. Another result is that the starter becomes progressively weaker in dough-fermenting ability.

The sometimes necessary solution? Begin a new starter. This is a practical reason for including some spare yeast in the camping outfit. Best to take is recently dated, packaged dry yeast. Stored where reasonably cool, this will keep several months or more.

A sourdough starter is best kept going by the addition of flour and water only. The starter, unless temporarily frozen or dried, should be so fed about once a week at least. If you are regularly cooking with the starter, this process will take care of itself.

Sourdough Bread   If commencing from the beginning, set your starting sponge as already directed. The commercial yeast is used only to get the starter going. From then on, the mixture will grow its own yeast. When doubling a recipe, by the way, you needn't double the starter.

Take your starter. Add enough flour and lukewarm water in equal volumes to make about 3 cups of sponge. Let this stand in a warm location overnight or from 6 to 8 hours, whereupon it should be bubbling and giving off an agreeable yeasty odor.

From here on, the general procedure remains the same. Take out, in this instance, 2 cups of sponge. Place the remainder aside. That's your next starter. No matter what the recipe, at this stage always keep out about a cup of the basic sourdough.

To these 2 cups of sponge add the following:

4 cups flour
2 tablespoons sugar
1 teaspoon salt
2 tablespoons shortening

Mix the flour, sugar, and salt. Make a depression in the center of these dry ingredients. Melt the shortening if it is not already liquid. Blend it and the sponge in the hollow. Then mix everything together. A soft dough should result. If necessary, add either flour or fluid. The latter may be water or milk. Knead for 3 or 4 minutes on any clean, floured surface.

"Keep attacking," I can still hear an old trapper cautioning, eyes blinking amiably behind thick-lensed spectacles. "Don't gentle it. That is where most cheechakos make their mistake. Too much pushing and pressing lets the gas escape that's needed to raise the stuff. Just bang the dough together in a hurry, cut off loaves to fit your greased pans, and put them in a warm place to raise."

The dough, once it has plumped out to double size, should be baked some 50 to 60 minutes in a moderately hot oven or reflector baker that, preferably, is hottest the first 15 minutes. Baking should redouble the size of the loaves.

One tests "in the usual way," the old trapper added. He explained, probably because it seemed necessary, that the "usual way" is to wait until the loaves seem crisply brown, then to jab in a straw. If the bread is done, the straw will come out dry and at least as clean as it was when inserted.

Sourdough bread is substantial in comparison with the usual air-filled bakery loaf. It keeps moist for a satisfactorily long time. When the bread is made according to the preceding suggestions, the flavor is unusually excellent, being especially nutty when slices are toasted. If your crew likes real tasty crust, bake the bread in long slim loaves to capitalize on this outstanding characteristic.

Baking in the Ground   During the Gold Rush days at the turn of the century, when gravel punchers stampeded past my present Hudson Hope, British Columbia, homesite toward where dust lay yellower and more beckoning beneath the northern lights, prospectors used to bake sourdough bread in the shallow steel vessels used for panning gold. A few still do, for that matter.

A shallow hole was scooped in the ground, often in the heat-retaining sand of a stream bank. A fire was allowed to turn to coals in this cavity. Dough, in the meantime, was rising between two gold pans. Some of the ruddy embers were raked out of the hole. The pans were inserted and covered with the hot residue, plus maybe a few coals from the regular campfire. One hour's cooking in this makeshift oven was generally the minimum. The bread would not ordinarily burn if allowed to remain longer. The crust would just thicken and become more golden, that's all.

You do not need gold pans to do this today. Other utensils, as for example two preferably large heavy frypans, will accomplish the same thing. If the metal is light, insulate it all around with a thin covering of ashes.

Beaten Sourdough Bread   This bread is especially popular with outdoorsmen cooking for themselves. One reason is that its unnecessary to touch the dough with the hands, sometimes a particular boon as when you've been blazing a trail and your fingers are sticky with pine pitch.

Proceed as with regular sourdough bread. Instead of kneading the dough, however, beat it for two minutes. Then leave it standing in the mixing bowl until it has bubbled itself to lightness.

Add 1 teaspoon baking soda. Mix another minute. Then turn into a well-greased container and let stand 10 minutes in a warm place. Bake in a moderately hot oven or reflector baker 50 to 60 minutes or until done.

Sourdough Flippers   A lot of fishermen, campers, and other frequenters of the farther places don't figure they've started the day right until they have stoked up with a stack of hot, tender, moist sourdough flapjacks. These flippers, as sourdoughs often call them, are so easy to prepare that there's no need for even the greenest tenderfoot to be dependent on store mixes. They're so tasty and wholesome, furthermore, that many a vacationist looks ardently for more when he's shut in again by city streets.

For a couple of breakfasters, add 2 cups flour and 2 cups lukewarm water to your sourdough starter. Set overnight away from drafts in a warm location. The next morning return the original amount of starter to its scalded glass or earthenware container. To the remaining batter add:

2 eggs, fresh or dried
½ teaspoon salt
1 tablespoon sugar
1 teaspoon soda
1 teaspoon warm water
2 tablespoons liquid shortening

Mix the eggs, salt, and sugar with a fork. Melt the baking soda in the teaspoon of warm water. Stir all these into the batter, along with either cooking or salad oil, or melted lard, margarine, etc.

For variations from time to time, if you ever want them, add a little whole wheat flour, corn meal, bran flakes, or such to batters after the starter has been saved out.

If the flapjack batter becomes a bit too thick to pour easily, thin it with just enough milk. Flour, on the other hand, will provide stiffening. But if the batter is on the thin side, the flippers will be more tender.

Once the preferably heavy frypan or griddle is hot, grease it sparingly with bacon rind. Do not let the metal reach smoking temperatures. Turn each flipper once only, when the hotcake starts showing small bubbles. The second side takes about half as long to cook. Serve steaming hot with margarine and sugar, with syrup, or with what you will.

Corn

Hush Puppies   Colonel Townsend Whelen makes these by mixing 2 cups yellow corn meal, ¾ cup flour, 2½ teaspoons baking powder, and 1 teaspoon salt with 1 cup water to make a medium thick dough. Drop big gobs into deep hot fat. Cook until a rich brown. Hush puppies are particularly good with fresh fish. In fact, the Colonel and a lot of us prefer cooking them in fat where fish and onions are also being fried.

Frypan Corn Bread   Get this cooking a half hour before come-and-get-it time. For two hungry men you'll want:

1 cup corn meal
1 cup flour
2 tablespoons sugar
1 teaspoon salt
2 teaspoons baking powder
2 eggs
4 tablespoons liquid shortening
1 cup milk

Combine the dry ingredients. If using fresh eggs, beat them separately. Blend the eggs, shortening, and milk. Then quickly mix everything.

Pour the batter into a warm, well-greased frypan. Cover and place immediately over low heat.

Spoon Bread   This is the recipe that Colonel Whelen's daughter, Mrs. William G. Bowling, uses for spoon bread; good when eaten with butter or margarine along with the main dish instead of potato, and also when served with syrup to provide a special treat for dessert.

2 cups milk
½ cup corn meal
1 teaspoon salt
1 tablespoon melted butter
½ teaspoon baking powder
3 eggs

Scald the milk in a pan by heating it nearly to the boiling point. Stir in the corn meal bit by bit. Continue cooking for several minutes, stirring to avoid scorching. Then remove from the heat and add the salt, melted butter, baking powder, and the egg yolks beaten until light. Beat the egg whites stiff and fold them in.

Pour the batter into a buttered baking dish in which it will lie about 2 inches deep. Bake for 30 minutes or until the spoon bread is roofed with a thick brown crust.

Canoe Bread   This went well on the most recent deer hunting trip I took by canoe down the famous Half Moon of the Southwest Miramichi River, shortly before the New Brunswick freeze-up. Matter of fact, the hunting and the eating were so good that the ice caught us. I had to cache my canoe above Big Louie rapids and walk out to the railroad, and I've never had a chance to go back after it.

For enough hot bread for two of us, it took:

4 tablespoons shortening
1 teaspoon salt
¼ cup corn meal
2 teaspoons baking powder
1½ cups flour
½ cup water

The amount of flour was always approximate because we were spending as many hours as possible in the bush and shying away from any unnecessary culinary chores. We dropped the shortening in one gob in the top of the rolled-down flour sack. The salt, baking powder, and corn meal went atop it. Then the cook for that particular meal worked the ingredients into the lard, picking up whatever flour clung to them. He next dented the flour with his fist, poured in the ½ cup of water, and without any delay mixed a soft wad of dough.

Flattened, this went into a warm, greased frypan for cooking over birch coals. The salty, thick, brown crust always tasted particularly good after a hard, dehydrating day among the alders.

MAIN AND SIDE DISHES

Bacon

"Bacon," a sourdough friend translated when asked what he meant by saying he'd gorged himself with vast quantities of *tiger*. "That's because it's striped. Sounds nobler when called tiger."

The main troubles that camp cooks experience with bacon arise from their submitting it too soon to too much heat. Not only is the bacon thus burned and toughened, but very often the frypan becomes a mass of leaping flames. Aside from resulting offenses to taste and digestion, this is wasteful if nothing worse. The nearly 3,000 calories per pound that fat side bacon contains lie largely in its grease, any excess of which should be saved, particularly in the bush.

We'll do better to start the bacon in a *cold* frypan and to fry it slowly over a very few coals raked to one side of the blaze. Move and turn the bacon from time to time. If you like it crisp, keep pouring off the grease. Do not waste any of this, though. It has numerous camp uses.

More satisfactory still is the practice of laying the strips well apart in a pan and baking them evenly to a golden brown in a moderately warm reflector baker.

Slabs of bacon have a tendency to mold. This mold can be harmlessly wiped off with a clean cloth moistened either in vinegar or in a solution of baking soda and water.

Cereal

Prepare according to the instructions on the package. A favorite camp cereal of a lot of us is oatmeal. The quickly cooking variety saves time. What I do is ready it the night before by adding ½ cup oatmeal and ½ teaspoon salt to 2 cups cold water. A ¼ cup of raisins, more or less, plumps out overnight to add flavor. The next morning I hunch far enough out of the sleeping bag to get the fire going, put on the covered pan, and let the contents come to a boil before setting it to one side for a few minutes. Then I either pour in evaporated milk straight out of the can, or in colder weather add a liberal spoonful of margarine, and begin satisfying the inner man.

This is really luxury when deepening cold has condensed, close above the throbbing earth, a twinkling ceiling of ice crystals to which the smoke of your solitary campfire ascends in an unwavering pillar.

Poached Eggs

There's a gimmick to this one. Fill a frypan 2 inches deep with water, with roughly a teaspoon of salt for every 4 cups of water. Bring the water to the bubbling point. Then take a spoon and start the water revolving in one direction.

Now slide each egg gently into the water from a saucer. The movement of the liquid will keep the whites from spreading. Dip some of the water over the top. Three minutes of simmering suits most people. Or once the eggs are in, you may set the water off the heat for 5 minutes. Try these eggs sometime on a small mound of buttered rice, noodles, spaghetti, macaroni, or potatoes.

Scrambled Eggs

The addition of milk has a tendency to toughen scrambled eggs. Instead, add 1 tablespoon of cold water for each egg. Mix the eggs and water well with salt and pepper to taste. Heat a tablespoon of fat in a frypan just hot enough to sizzle a drop of water. Pour in the egg mixture and reduce the heat. When the eggs have started to harden, begin stirring them constantly with a fork. Remove while they're still soft and creamy.

Fried Eggs

Have about ½ inch of fat warm, not hot. Break in your eggs. Keeping the heat low so that the whites won't become tough and leathery, baste the yolks until they are well filmed. Salt, pepper, and serve on a hot plate.

Or get a tablespoon of fat just hot enough to sizzle a test drop of water. Break in the eggs. Take the frypan off the heat at once. Baste the eggs with hot fat 3 or 4 minutes.

Omelet

Break the eggs into a bowl or mixing dish. Add 1 teaspoon water for each egg. For a 3-egg omelet, season with ¼ teaspoon salt and just a dash of pepper. Beat vigorously with a fork until yolks and whites are blended.

Melt 1 tablespoon butter (1 teaspoon for each egg) in a frypan until it just begins to brown. Pour in the eggs. Keep shaking and slanting the pan slightly while cooking so as to keep the omelet from sticking. As soon as the bottom of the omelet starts to harden, slip a thin spatula or knife well under the edges and lift the middle of the omelet so that uncooked egg can flow beneath it. This liquid egg, incidentally, will repair any resulting breaks and tears.

An omelet takes only about 5 minutes from shells to heated plates. It is done as soon as the eggs no longer run freely but the top still looks moist and creamy. Omelets will toughen if they are allowed to brown at all. Fold the omelet by tilting the pan sideways with one hand and then lifting the uppermost section about ⅓ over the middle. Now tilt, shake, and slide the folded omelet onto the hot plate. It's actually easier to make one such easily handled 3-egg omelet for each camper than to try to manipulate any more than, at most, a 6-egg omelet.

French Toast

For half a dozen slices of hard bread, beat 3 eggs well. Add 1 cup of milk, 3 tablespoons sugar, and 1 teaspoon vanilla. Melt 3 tablespoons of margarine or other fat in a frypan. Dip each slice of bread in the egg mixture and brown lightly on both sides in the skillet. Sprinkle with cinnamon while hot and serve at once with sugar and margarine, tart jelly, or syrup.

Tomatoes, Onions, & Eggs

This nourishing and easily digestible dish, with the mild and provocatively elusive flavor, is unusually good when someone hauls into camp late, especially as its preparation is both simple and swift. Proportions, which are flexible, may be varied in ratio to appetite.

For two late arrivals, brown a couple of diced onions with a little grease in a frypan. When these have cooked to a dark blandness, add a small can of tomatoes. Let these begin to bubble. Then break in 6 eggs. Season with salt and pepper. Keep scrambling over low heat until fairly dry.

Whelen Sandwich

You'll need bacon, onion, eggs, cheese, seasoning, and patience enough to make seconds and maybe thirds. For each sandwich start 2 slices of bread toasting over the heat. Cut a slice of bacon into small bits. Fry these until they are crisp, pouring the excess grease into the camp shortening can. Fork the bacon together into a small rectangle and place a slice of onion atop it. Cook the onion until it begins to soften and tan.

Then break an egg over it. Puncture the yolk with the fork. Salt and pepper. Cover with a square of cheese. Cook slowly until the egg is done and the cheese has melted. Place each such serving between two slices of toast. If any water cress is handy, add several sprigs of that. With the average camp frypan you can usually have four such sandwiches going at once.

Welsh Rabbit

Melt 1 tablespoon margarine or butter in a pan. Add 1 tablespoon flour, ⅛ teaspoon pepper, and ¼ teaspoon salt. Mix thoroughly. Gradually stir in 2 cups of grated, shredded, or diced cheddar cheese, as aged and tangy as is available. Keep stirring over low heat until the cheese has melted. Heat ½ cup of milk and stir that in gradually and thoroughly. Add a slightly beaten fresh or reconstituted egg. Cook an additional 2 minutes. Serve at once on toast or hot crisp crackers.

Baked Macaroni and Cheese

Boil ½ pound macaroni in 4 quarts of water with 4 teaspoons of salt, according to the preceding directions. Cut ½ pound of cheese into cubes. Open a small can of tomatoes.

Alternate layers of cooked macaroni with cheese in a greased pan or baking dish, seasoning each layer with salt and pepper. Add 1 tablespoon of solid tomato to each layer. Then pour enough tomato over everything to come within ½ inch of the top. Roof with sliced onion if you want. Bake in a hot oven or reflector baker until well browned.

Camp Baked Beans

"Take 3 cups of dried navy beans. Pick out any small pebbles you may find. Soak the beans overnight in cold water, and the next morning put to boil in a large kettle with a tablespoon of salt. Boil for about 2½ hours, adding boiling water as the fluid level goes down.

"Then drop in about a dozen 1-inch cubes of salt pork or bacon with the rind on it. Keep bubbling for about an hour and a half more or until the individual beans are soft, but not mushy. You have been keeping about 2 inches of water on top of the beans in the kettle. This water is now the finest of bean soup. Pour most of it into another container and serve while hot, but leave enough so that the beans are still quite damp.

"Then, usually the next day, place these beans about 2 inches deep in a pan, shift the cubes of pork or bacon to the top, sprinkle a little sugar over the entire surface, and bake in a reflector baker or oven for an hour or more, until they become a little brown on top." (Colonel Townsend Whelen)

Pea Soup

Now and then there are few things more delicious when the bunch gets home, cold and agreeably tired from a long day's hunt, than a bowl of thick, hot pea soup. This sort of thaws everyone out and loosens the stomach kinks in preparation for more thorough enjoyment of that roast or steak.

Fast cooking split peas, both green and yellow, are now available that save the bother of overnight soaking and over-tedious cooking. Let a pound of these simmer until tender in 4 cups of meat stock, or in bouillon made by dissolving 4 chicken bouillon cubes in 4 cups of water. Then crush the peas with a spoon or fork and continue simmering, covered, along with salt and pepper to taste and a finely chopped onion.

The finishing touch, as far as I'm concerned, is furnished by those small chunks of bacon or salt pork scattered through the savory hotness. Put these in now. Here's the place, too, for that flavor-filled bacon rind you've been wondering what to do with. When everything is cooked, keep the soup hot and ready on the back of the fire.

Corn Meal Mush

Mix 1 cup of corn meal with 1 cup of cold water. Get 3 cups of water, seasoned with 1 teaspoon salt, bubbling diligently. Pour in the corn meal mixture slowly and stir for 5 minutes or until the combination has thickened. Move to low heat for 30 minutes and occasionally stir. If it becomes necessary to thin this, use boiling water. A double boiler is a handy gadget when you're making corn meal mush or polenta. It's often easy to contrive one, as by arranging several pieces of silverware in the bottom of a pan of boiling water and setting the mush pot atop those.

If you prefer a thicker mush to begin with, use a total of 2 cups of water for every 1 cup of meal. Such mush may also be used with margarine as a vegetable, sliced cold for frying, or topped with molasses and milk for dessert.

Fried Rice

The nutty flavor of this is so good with such repasts as steaks, chops, and fried grouse that sometimes you don't know in which direction to reach first for seconds. Stir and cook 2 cups boiled rice in 2 tablespoons fat in a frypan over low heat for about 5 minutes. Add 2 tablespoons chopped, preferably green onions and if you want a similar volume of cooked meat chopped and shredded into tiny bits. Cook this several minutes longer. Then break in 1 egg. Season with 2 teaspoons soy sauce or with salt to taste. Stir vigorously until the egg is set.

Green Rice

Melt 2 tablespoons margarine or butter in a pan. Stir a chopped small onion in this until it is lightly browned. Add 2 cups cooked rice, 1 cup warm milk, and 1 tablespoon powdered parsley.

Beat 2 eggs with a fork. Mix with 1 teaspoon salt and 1 cup grated, shredded, or cubed cheese. Add these to the above. Mix thoroughly. Bake in a moderate oven or reflector baker for about 45 minutes or until firm.

Or try this version. Mix 2 cups of hot cooked rice with 2 tablespoons melted margarine and 1 tablespoon powdered parsley. If you can come by them, add small amounts of shredded water cress, young mustard, or dandelion leaves, etc. Season the savory result with salt to taste and serve.

Pilaf

Stir 1 cup raw rice in 3 tablespoons shortening in a frypan over low heat until the rice begins to tan. A small, chopped onion may also be included. Season with salt and pepper. Then pour on 2 cups broth or bouillon. Canned soup may be used instead, mushroom being a tasty choice. Cover the frypan and simmer over very low heat for about 30 minutes until the rice is tender and almost dry. If the rice is nearly dry, however, and is still hard in the center, add a bit more hot liquid and cook as long as necessary. Top with butter or margarine.

Cheese Balls

Grate or chop preferably dry, stale cheese. Mix it with an equal volume of flour. Add salt and pepper to taste, ½ teaspoon mustard, and bind with a well beaten egg. Drop by the spoonful into hot fat and fry until a light brown. In the Far North they serve these over boiled macaroni, topped with tomato sauce hot from the fire.

Vegetable Casserole

You can get this started in a hurry by opening small cans of peas, corn, and tomatoes. You'll also need a cup of bread, bannock, or cracker crumbs, seasoned with 1 teaspoon salt and ⅛ teaspoon pepper. Arrange the vegetables in layers. Sprinkle each layer with the seasoned crumbs. Dot the top with margarine or crisscross it with strips of bacon. For a one-dish meal, cut any of the canned meats into small pieces and include layers of this. Bake 25 minutes in a moderate oven or reflector baker.

Baked Potatoes

A good way to cook this native American vegetable is to bake the large ones in their skins in hot ashes, not glowing coals, until they become pretty well blackened on the outside. They're done when a thin, sharpened stick will run through their middles easily. Rake out, break in half, and serve at once with margarine and salt.

A more complicated way to go about this on occasion, in camps near civilization, is to cut well scrubbed potatoes lengthwise into 3 slabs. Lay thin slices of onion, salted and peppered, between these sections. Then reassemble each potato, wrap in a sheet of heavy foil or several thicknesses of lightweight foil, and bake in a nest of ashes among hot coals for about a half hour or until done, turning once during this period.

Potatoes may be scrubbed, rubbed with melted fat or salad oil, pricked with a fork, (or prepared as above and held together with skewers) and baked in a hot oven or reflector baker. This method is handiest when combined with some other cooking, as about an hour of baking is required.

Potato Cakes

An easy way to make potato cakes is to shape cold mashed potatoes as desired, then to cook them slowly in margarine or drippings, turning once, until they are tan and crusty.

Hashed Brown Potatoes

Heat 4 tablespoons margarine, cooking oil, or other shortening in the frypan. Add enough potatoes, peeled and cut very fine. Salt and pepper. Then press down and cook over low heat until brown and crisp on the bottom. Loosen this crust with a knife. Then cover the frypan with a plate and invert it quickly, so that the potatoes will come out with the brown underside on top.

Potato and Onion Puff

Cook equal quantities of potato and onion together. Mash. Add milk, margarine, and 1 or 2 well-beaten eggs. Beat until fluffy. Season with salt and pepper. Spoon into a greased pan. Top with grated or sliced cheese if you want. Bake until browned.

Potato Salad

Here's my favorite year-around recipe for potato salad, unless you already have one of your own. For use as a main dish for 2 people, scrub and boil 6 medium potatoes, removing them from the salted water while they're still hard. Peel as sparingly as possible so as to preserve the utmost flavor and nourishment. Hard boil 6 eggs at the same time; then plunge them under cold water and peel them.

Slice some of the hot potato into an earthenware bowl, if one is at hand, or into whatever else is handy. Slice some egg atop it. Now pour on a liberal amount of preferably olive oil or of salad oil. Douse on about ¼ as much vinegar. Salt and pepper. Sprinkle on a very small amount of powdered garlic if you have any and if you don't object to it. Paprika and dried parsley will add eye and taste appeal. Repeat, keeping on doing this until you've used all the potatoes and eggs. Cover so that the flavor will permeate everything.

Preparing this salad half a day or more ahead of time will give the best results. Take off the lid once or twice and carefully, so as not to break up the eggs and potatoes, spoon the mixture around a bit to redistribute the oil and vinegar.

Onion Soup Au Gratin

Saute 2 large, sliced onions very slowly in 2 tablespoons of margarine or butter. When they have become lightly browned, add 4 cups of broth, canned bouillon, or water in which 4 beef or chicken bouillon cubes have been dissolved. Salt to taste. Then simmer 15 minutes.

In the meantime, cut a substantial slice of preferably sourdough bread for everyone. Spread lightly with prepared mustard if you want. Cover with grated or sliced cheese and toast until crisp in the reflector baker or oven. If no reflector baker or oven is available, the bread can be toasted on anything from a campfire grate to a forked green stick, then turned, covered on the hot side with cheese, and very slowly toasted on the other side until crisp throughout. Put each slice in a bowl, breaking the toast into bits if necessary, and cover with the hot soup.

Roast Corn

You'll want sweet, young corn for this. Carefully strip the husks down to the end of the ear, leaving them attached. Pull off the silk. Soak the corn in cold salted water for ½ hour. Drain. Then brush the kernels with margarine or butter and sprinkle them with salt and a little pepper. Pull the husks back up around the corn and twist tightly together. Make a hollow of coals at the edge of the campfire, cover it with an inch of ashes, lay in the corn, cover with more ashes and then hot coals, and roast about ½ hour. Peel the husks back again and use as a handle.

If you're where there is green corn, probably aluminum foil is available, too. If you want, then, wrap and twist each ear tightly in foil before consigning it to the ash-insulated coals. This way you can poke the corn around occasionally to assure more even cooking, and even take a look, while it is roasting to taste.

TOPPING IT OFF

Ice Cream

Ice cream is one of the quickest and easiest of all desserts to make outdoors, especially after a fresh snow. Best for the purpose are dry flakes. You can also use the granular interior of the perpetual snowbanks found in the higher mountains, although the result will be more a coarse sherbet.

Just empty a can of evaporated milk into a large pot or bowl. A similar amount of dry milk, reconstituted with water, will do as well. Add 2 tablespoons of sugar, ⅛ teaspoon of salt, and some flavoring. Vanilla or one of the other extracts will serve. So will cocoa, powdered coffee, and the like. Mocha? Balance 2 teaspoons of powdered instant coffee with 1 teaspoon chocolate; enough, incidentally, for a quart of ice cream. If the flavoring, as for instance chocolate syrup, is already sweet, just omit the sugar.

Then quickly stir in fresh snow to taste. More sweetening and flavoring may be added at the end if you want. For this reason it is safest to go light on these initially. Otherwise, you'll have to repair any mistake with more milk and snow—not that this isn't a good excuse.

Three varieties that come out especially well, if you happen to like them to begin with, are the universally favored vanilla, rich dark chocolate with overtones of peppermint extract, and banana ice cream made with that particular extract.

Treeless Maple Syrup

The sugar maple grows only in North America. Like all green trees, it mysteriously changes water and carbon dioxide into sugar. So exceptional is the sugar maple's capacity for storing the sweet that this talent is a double boon. In autumn it produces some of the loveliest hues of the American forest; in spring, the amber succulence of maple syrup.

The only trouble many wilderness cooks have is that these latter activities are largely confined to such Eastern regions as the St. Lawrence Valley, New Brunswick and Nova Scotia, and such New England states as New Hampshire and Vermont. But there's a slightly incredible way around. You'll need:

6 medium potatoes
2 cups water
1 cup white sugar
1 cup brown sugar

Peel the medium-sized potatoes. Boil uncovered with 2 cups water until but 1 cup of fluid remains. Remove the potatoes, for use any way you want. Stirring the liquid until the boiling point has again been reached, slowly add the sugar. Once this has entirely dissolved, set the pan off the heat to cool slowly.

"Ghastly concoction," the old mountain man who gave me the formula nodded agreeably when, the initial time around, I first sampled the elixir at this primary stage. "Like home brew, it has to be aged in a dark place. After a couple of days in a bottle it'll be noble."

See if that first spoonful you doubtfully try doesn't seem to justify your worst suspicions, too. But bottle the syrup and tuck it away for several days to age. Taste it again at the end of that time and see if you, also, aren't pleasantly amazed.

Hard Sauce

For hard sauce, cream ½ cup butter or margarine and gradually add 1½ cups of preferably powdered sugar. Beat until creamy. Toward the end add ½ teaspoon vanilla or some other flavoring.

Baked Dried Apples

Put 2 cups dried apples in an equal volume of boiling water. Set immediately off the heat and allow to stand 1 hour. Grease a shallow baking dish. Place the apples and liquid into this. Sprinkle with ½ teaspoon nutmeg, ½ teaspoon cinnamon, and 1 cup sugar. Slice ½ cup of margarine over the top.

Bake in a moderately hot oven or reflector baker ½ hour. Serve hot with milk. Or if you're where you can do it, mix up a quick batch of vanilla ice cream with the help of preferably light snow, and put a few spoonfuls of that atop the hot apples.

Peach Shortbread

3 cups quick-cooking oats
½ cup sugar
¼ cup flour
¼ teaspoon salt
¾ cup margarine
1 teaspoon vanilla extract
stewed dried peaches (to taste)

Mix the dry ingredients. Cut in the margarine. Finally, stir in the vanilla extract. Press across the bottom of a greased oven pan. Put in a preheated moderately warm reflector baker or oven and bake 1½ hours or until lightly browned. Cut or break into chunks. Drench with stewed dried peaches.

Strawberry Shortcake

All you need for this tip-top treat is wild strawberries and hot bannock. To match about 2 quarts of berries, freshly picked and left standing drenched with a cup of sugar, here's one way to go about the latter:

2 cups sifted flour
2 tablespoons sugar
2 teaspoons baking powder
1 teaspoon salt
4 tablespoons shortening
½ cup (or more) cold milk

The first time I ever ate this one was on Ottertail Creek, in the middle of the Canadian Rockies, with trapper and riverman Billy Kruger doing the cooking. We'd run out of lard a week earlier. Instead, Billy used some oil he'd previously rendered from a couple of young grizzlies.

Billy Kruger commenced the rites by sifting all the dry ingredients together into a bowl. He worked in the shortening, then stirred in enough cold milk to make a soft dough.

This dough Billy kneaded very briefly on a floured board. Using a clean cold bottle, he rolled it out about ½ inch thick. Half of the dough he laid in a greased pan and dotted with chunks of canned butter. The other half he spread on top. If you prefer individual biscuits, just cut the dough into ovals with a floured can top or glass. Baking in a very hot oven or reflector baker takes 12 to 15 minutes.

Afterwards we carefully separated the steaming layers, ladled the sweetened berries between and above, and fell to it. Raspberries, blueberries, saskatoons, blackberries, and similar wild fruits are also good with this hot bannock.

Whipped Cream

That particular summer evening we crowned the shortcake with whipped cream made from evaporated milk. There's a simple gimmick to this. Milk and utensils have to be icy cold. This we arranged easily enough by submerging bowl, beater, and can of milk in the mountain stream that sparkled past Billy Kruger's cabin on its way to mingle with the Peace River.

So chilled, most evaporated milk quickly whips to about triple volume. A couple of tablespoons of lemon juice can be used to increase the stiffness after the milk is partially whipped. Some bush cooks also use an envelope (1 tablespoon) of unflavored gelatin, dissolved in a minimum of water, for this purpose.

Blueberry Slump

Bring 4 cups blueberries, 1½ cups sugar, 4 tablespoons cornstarch, and 1 teaspoon nutmeg slowly to a boil in a heavy saucepan. While the mixture is simmering, make a batter of:

4 tablespoons sugar
3 tablespoons shortening
½ cup milk
1½ cups sifted flour
1½ teaspoons baking powder
¼ teaspoon salt

Cream the sugar and shortening. Add the milk and blend thoroughly. Mix the flour, baking powder, and salt. Stir rapidly into the other ingredients.

Then begin dropping the batter, spoonful by spoonful, over the bubbling berries. Cover and cook at the same speed for 10 minutes. Serve hot with cream, if you have it, or with vanilla ice cream if there's snow for quickly stirring together a bowlful.

Tomato Soup Cake

Cream 2 tablespoons of shortening with 1 cup sugar. Add 1 well beaten egg. Sift together 2 cups flour, 1 teaspoon cloves, ½ teaspoon mace, ½ teaspoon nutmeg, ½ teaspoon baking soda, and 3 teaspoons baking powder. Stir these into the above, along with 1 can of condensed tomato soup. Add 1 cup seeded raisins, lightly floured.

Pour the batter into a small greased pan. Bake in a moderate oven 1 hour or until done. And unless you're an old hand with this sort of thing, be ready to be rather pleasantly surprised.

CHAPTER EIGHTEEN

PREPARING AND COOKING FISH AND GAME

PREPARING GAME ANIMALS

How good would the choicest corn-fed beef taste if the steer were shot four times through the paunch and chased several miles? Suppose the rancher hacked into the entrails while butchering it, letting additional juices and waste matter mingle with hair in the meat. He might then leave the unskinned carcass lying a couple of days, with the sun working on one side, the damp ground on the other, and flies all over. Eventually, suppose he hauled the beef over the sweltering hood of his car and jolted it through dust, heat, and fumes for a few hundred miles before flopping it down for the locker man to skin, section, and refrigerate. That's the way more than one deer is mishandled, and if the prime steers got the same treatment there'd be as much conversation about "gamy" beef as there is about "gamy" venison. When people honestly and open-mindedly react this way to wild meat, the odds are that the animal was not dressed out properly and that, in addition, the meat wasn't cared for afterwards as it should have been. There is no good reason for any of this.

Butchering

When you come to your kill, don't try to hang up the animal unless this can be quickly and easily accomplished. Ordinarily, the job is apt to be difficult and unreasonably time consuming. If this is the case, it will be sufficient to have the carcass with the head uphill and the rest of the body slanting downwards. If even that is not possible, try to get the animal's chest up on a rock or log.

Turn the animal belly up, propping it in that position with rocks, logs, stakes, or whatever else may be handy. Or a line between a hind leg and a tree will hold it. Then make a very short center cut at the lower end of the breastbone just below the lowest ribs. As soon as the knife slits through skin, fat, and meat into the body cavity, insert the first two fingers of whichever is your master hand into the opening.

363

Hold the entrails down and away so that the knife will not penetrate them. Then extend the incision down to the rectum, circumventing the active external milk glands if any and then returning to lift and cut away these easily disengaged tissues. Cut around each side of the major sexual organ and around the rectum, taking care not to puncture either. The contents can quickly taint the best meat unless any areas of contact are trimmed away. Carefully free the ducts leading to each. Preferably, tie them off with a piece of string or lace so that nothing will escape from them.

Then with your sleeves rolled up and wrist watch removed, reach up into the upper end of the abdominal cavity and cut the diaphragm loose all around. This is the membrane that separates the organs of the chest from those in the abdomen. Now reach with your secondary hand into the top part of the chest. Find and pull down on the windpipe, gullet, and large arteries. Cut them off as close to the neck as you can. This is one operation where, because of the close and obscure quarters, you have to take particular care not to slash yourself.

Now the entire contents of the chest and abdomen are free except for occasional adhesions along the backbone. These can be quickly torn loose by hand. You can now turn the animal on its side and dump out the viscera. As you work down towards the stern, take care to poke the two tied ends free so they will fall out with the remainder. It is then that you wipe the inside of the animal as dry as possible, after dragging it away from the discards.

Delicacies

Save the heart, cutting this free from the little pouch of membrane in which it is lodged. Be sure to lay the liver beside it on some clean area such as a piece of bark, a rock, or a patch of snow. Secure the two kidneys as well. All are delicious. You may also care to save the white sheets of abdominal fat which will render into excellent lard for cooking. Unless you are going to have the head mounted, slit the underneath of the jaw deeply enough so that you can pull the tongue down through this opening and sever it near the base. A blood-proof bag is handy for carrying these back to camp.

Cooling

What you do next will depend to a large extent on circumstances such as weather, weight, and terrain. You may be able to hang the game by the head. You will at least be able to turn it so that the body opening can be propped down with sticks in order that the meat will cool as soon as possible.

Covering the carcass with a mass of well-leaved boughs will protect the flesh to a large extent from the shifting sun, as well as from birds which may be already waiting for a chance to whittle away at the fat.

If blowflies are bad, you should either have enough cheesecloth to cover the cavity or a cheesecloth bag in which the entire animal can be placed.

Bluebottles and other winged pests will still probably get at it to some extent. When these have been particularly thick, I've found it effective to douse the underneath few of a mass of evergreen boughs with one of the effective and unobjectionable personal fly dopes, taking care of course to keep this off the meat. You can examine all openings and exposed spots when you pack the animal out, in any event, and wipe or cut away any eggs and larvae.

If rain is threatening, a better procedure is to turn the animal so that it is draped, back uppermost, over a rock or log. The body cavity must be freely ventilated in any event. Turning a freshly butchered deer on its belly in the snow, for example, will cause the meat to start to putrify noticeably even overnight in temperatures well below zero.

Skinning

If you are an old-time hunter, you'll very possibly prefer to complete the skinning on the spot. You may pretty well have to do this if your trophy is big. There are exceptions, of course, depending generally on the available methods of transportation and to some degree on the weather.

You'll want to get the hide off as soon as reasonably practical. The meat should be allowed to cool thoroughly with the least possible delay. Unless the animal is a small one and is opened wide, it won't cool quickly in temperate weather with the skin on. And if you're in a cold climate, you'll want to be sure to complete the skinning before the hide freezes on, or what would have been a few minutes' work may very easily develop into a cold and disagreeable all-day chore. Besides, bacterial growth is prevented on the surface of the meat when the air can get to it.

To skin a deer, first remove the lower legs or shanks. The novice is likely to begin too high at what most of us think of as the knees. Cut deeply through skin, flesh, and muscle about an inch below these joints. Then brace your knee against what are actually the ankles. Pull forward briskly in the case of a front leg, backward with the hind leg, and the shank will snap off.

Now we come to the actual skinning. Slit the hide along the inside of each leg to meet the belly cut. Extend this latter incision on up to the neck just short of the jaw. Then cut completely around the neck, close behind the jaws, ears, and antlers.

Slit the underside of the tail, also. Then start at each of these cuts in turn to peel the skin from the flesh. If you are working on the ground, use the hide throughout as a clean rug on which to keep the meat unsullied. Generally, the skin will come away neatly, particularly if the animal has just been shot. In places where it adheres rather firmly, such as along the neck, use your knife carefully to cut it loose.

Avoid as much as possible making any nicks in the hide. You will notice between skin and flesh a thin, white film resembling parchment which, as a matter of fact, it is in a sense. Touch this film with a sharp blade, and the skin will continue to peel off. If anyone is helping you, have that individual keep the hide pulled taut while you free it with the long easy sweeps of a keen knife.

Despite all your care, there will be a few places where thin layers of meat and fat will adhere to the skin. When you have the latter off and can find some time to work on it, perhaps leisurely beside the campfire at night, neatly flesh it. One way to make this task easier is to stretch the section on which you are working tightly and comfortably across a knee. Fleshing consists of cutting, scraping, or peeling off all pieces of meat and fat that adhere to the hide.

If a rug is what you want, lace the skin to a frame. Or stretch it, with the hair against a building or a big tree, with nails around the edge. Or, leaving the fleshed side up, stake it out on clean and dry ground by pegs driven around the perimeter through little slits made six inches apart. Let it dry away from moisture and sunshine. If there are blowflies and bugs around, rub the inside of it with salt to discourage them. A day or so later, wipe the wet salt off and let the skin dry as before.

You may be on the go, however, and unable to stretch the skin. It can still be kept in fine shape for a rug by salting it thoroughly all over the fleshed side, turning the ends and edges in, and rolling the whole thing into a limp bundle that may be stowed in a loose burlap bag if one is handy and hung in a cool dry place. The hide does not have to be fleshed too closely when handled this way.

Quartering

Once the carcass is free of the skin, which you have been shifting about so as to keep the meat as clean as possible, quartering will be in order. Ease the point of your blade deeply into the cartilages between the skull and the first vertebra, severing them as well as you can. Then twist the head abruptly in one direction and then in the other, and it will snap free.

With a hatchet, ax, or meat saw, split the bone from the belly cut to the neck. Open the neck on the same line and remove the windpipe and gullet. Then split the backbone from neck to tail. The animal will now be in two halves. Quarter it by dividing each of these halves along the line of the lowest ribs.

You may now wrap these quarters, perhaps rubbed with flour, separately in cheesecloth to discourage pests. Sprinkling black pepper on the flesh will, if necessary, also help to keep bluebottles and such annoyers off while the meat gets a protective casing over its outside. You will also probably want to examine the meat every day or so to make sure it remains unbothered, giving particular attention to bullet wounds and to folds and nicks in the flesh. Any eggs or larvae so detected can be quickly and harmlessly scraped, wiped, or cut away.

In any event, the quarters can now cool quickly, especially if you hang them high in a tree to hasten the chilling the first night. Some of the pack trains in the mountains, hunting early so as to be back down in the lowlands before snow drifts in too deeply, keep fresh game sweet by trimming the branches out of a tree and pulling the meat high up into the clear 20 feet or more from the ground where blowflies do not operate. Days, the quarters can be wrapped in canvas or bedding to keep them cool.

A meat tent is a handy thing to pack along in hot weather if you have a large enough outfit to warrant its inclusion. A handy model, often seen in work camps in the wilderness, consists of canopied netting with a zipper opening. This shelter is customarily tied in a dark, well ventilated spot by a single rope that runs from its top center.

Refrigeration

Keep these quarters as cool and as dry as possible. If you are heading outside, get them into refrigeration as soon as you can. If a long and warm auto trip lies ahead, try at the earliest opportunity both to pack each quarter in a carton of dry ice and to protect those containers in larger ones with crumpled newspapers between for insulation. Circumstances may be such, too, that you'll prefer to travel in the comparative coolness of the night.

If the weather is hot and the distance far, you will probably do well to lay over a day in some locality where you can have the meat frozen solid. This may be a desirable time to cut and wrap it in plainly labeled packages that can be retrieved from the freezer and used one by one. Odd portions can be ground into hamburger, along with a desirable proportion of beef fat unless you object.

It should then be an easy job, with the help of dry ice which is obtainable along most routes, to bring these packages frozen to your cold storage cabinet, drawer, locker, or butcher's cold room. You'll have some really fine meat.

PREPARING FISH

Cleaning a Fish

Slit the abdomen from the vent to the neck as soon as possible after catching. Take out the entrails. Scrape the kidney tissue from along the backbone with the knife tip or thumbnail. Some of the sweetest meat is in the head and tail, but if you'd prefer to have them off, sever them with a sharp knife. If you're by a stream, you'll probably rinse the cavity in cold running water. Otherwise, it is preferable to wipe it out well with a clean damp cloth. Keep the fish dry and cool.

Removing the Fins

Cut into the flesh on either side of the fin. Then grasp the fin and yank it abruptly toward the head so as to pull out the bones. If you ever trim fins with shears or knife, leave these bones in sight so that they can be dislodged easily after being loosened by cooking.

Scaling

Hold the fish firmly on a flat surface. Scrape off the scales with a blunt knife, working swiftly from tail to head. Scales are most easily removed if you can give a few moments to the job while the fish is still wet from the water.

Skinning

Slice off a thin ribbon of skin along the entire length of the backbone once the back fins have been removed. Then loosen the skin around the gills. Grasp the skin, finally, and peel it from head to tail. With tough hides like that of the ling, pliers are handy. Turn the fish over and do the same thing on the other side.

Filleting

Cut down from the head to the tail, along the backbone, with a sharp pointed knife. Turn the knife flat and cut the flesh along the spine to the tail, letting the knife slide over the ribs. Lift off the side of the fish in one piece. Turn the fish over and remove the other fillet the same way. Fillets are those slices, boneless or nearly so, cut lengthwise along the ribs parallel to the backbone. Steaks, on the other hand, are slabs cut at right angles to the backbone.

Boning

Lay the fish on its side and with a sharp pointed knife cut from the head to the tail close to the spine. Turn the fish on its other side and make a similar cut. Sever the head if this hasn't already been done. Then carefully lift out the entire backbone. Pick out as many remaining small bones as possible.

Keeping Fish in Camp

Clean immediately after catching, wipe dry, and then put in a dry nest of grass or other green vegetation within a creel or similar container. Completely surround each fish with the grass or such, so that no fish touches another. The top layer of vegetation may be moistened slightly, inasmuch as evaporation will make for added coolness. But no more dampness should touch the fish. Keep them cool, dry, and clean.

One way to keep such fish several days without refrigeration is to swathe the fish and vegetation in a lot of newspapers, early in the morning after they have been chilled by the night air. Then pick a spot that will remain shaded all day and bury the package underground. Or the package can be rolled during the day in dampened burlap or such, then laid out each night to air and cool.

Another method is to wrap each fish, sprinkled with salt or corn meal if you want, in wax paper after it has been cleaned and dried. Then roll in dry fabric or newspaper and wrap a second time. Sacking or other material may then be soaked, wrung out, and then lashed over the dry bundle with each end roped tight. Keep in as cool a place as possible, preferably away from open air. Do not open until the fish are to be used.

PREPARING GAME BIRDS

For best results, unless you have preferences to the contrary, remove the crop and entrails as soon as possible. This may often be successfully delayed for a few hours, but if the bird is badly shot up, the flavor of the meat is apt to be affected. Also, such dressing, in the opinion of many of us, desirably hastens the cooling process.

The crop is situated loosely beneath the skin at the base of the throat. Slit open the skin, take it out, and pull out the windpipe.

Then make a crosswise slit below the breastbone. With small birds that are not going to be stuffed, you can often just hold the legs in one hand, the breast in the other, and pull the bird open. Reach into the abdominal cavity and carefully draw out the insides. Cut out the vent. Then wipe the bird dry. Do not leave any blood clots on the interior.

Save the liver, gizzard, and heart. Very gently cut out the little gall bladder intact and discard it. Its contents are so bitter that any dark portions where they may have spilled on the liver may well be cut from this delicacy as well. Clean the gizzard by easing the knife through to the hard center, then pulling the flesh away from this central sac.

Before using you may remove the oil sac at the base of the tail, disjoint the legs below the thighs, and cut off the head.

Birds should be cooled as quickly as possible. Separating them rather than piling them into a hot game pocket will speed this. If allowed to hang in a cool place soon after they have been shot and drawn, a protective glaze will be formed from contact with the air. They should be kept cool until used. Flavor will be better if they are hung for at least several days before being used.

To save yourself work and to avoid tearing the skin, dry pluck the fowl while it is still warm. Remaining pinfeathers may be removed with the fingernails or with tweezers. Singe the down off quickly, being careful not to burn the skin. Do not pass the bird through the flames of a lighted newspaper, however, as the ink has a blackening effect.

Birds may be plucked later, of course. Scalding is then recommended for grouse, pheasant, quail, and similar fowl. Hold the bird by the feet and quickly plunge it several times into hot, not boiling water, until the feathers loosen readily. Scalding waterfowl, however, usually makes the plucking even more difficult and results in loss of flavor.

Small duck, coot, and such may as well be skinned. Just slit open the back. Pulling in opposite directions with both hands if you want, peel off the skin like a glove. Cut off head, wings, and feet.

Despite a loss in flavor, many hunters skin other birds rather than bother plucking them. As a matter of fact, how you handle your game birds is decided by your own palate. Each of us is a gourmet in his own right.

PREPARING SMALL GAME

Clean, skin, and cool as soon as possible. Remove any scent or musk glands if they do not come off with the hide. These small, waxy or reddish kernels or glands, located under the forelegs and along the spine or under the lower part of the abdomen, often pull away with the skin. Cut out all imbedded glands, removing them intact if possible so as not to give a musky flavor to the meat.

If you can handle big game, you'll have no trouble with small meat animals. Matter of fact, if you're not going to save the skin, just ring it with your knife around the middle part of the body. Pull half toward the head and the other half toward the tail. Cut off the head, feet, and tail, and that's that.

Rabbit and certain other small game are susceptible to infections that can be passed on to man. These are less likely to exist after the first heavy frost and during cold weather. One precaution is to pass up all but lively game. The prudent hunter will also take particular pains to avoid cutting himself while handling any small game and will don rubber or plastic gloves whenever he has any cuts or wounds on his hands. Thorough washing of the hands with a strong soap, followed by the use of a disinfectant after dressing the game, will vastly reduce the danger of any infection.

The liver of each animal, the rabbit especially, should be examined for possible infection. The liver of a healthy animal is clear, dark red in color, firm, and unspotted. Small white cystlike spots, the size of peas or smaller, may indicate the presence of tularemia. Germs of this, incidentally, are destroyed by thorough cooking. But the thing to do when you are aware of its presence, of course, is to burn or deeply bury the infected carcass. Painstaking cleansing of the hands is essential after an infected carcass has been handled.

Thoroughly cooked meat, it may be repeated, is completely safe. By observing the above few simple rules for handling freshly killed small game animals, and by cooking the meat until well done, danger of contracting tularemia from infected animals is removed; one reason why more wild rabbits continue to be happily taken by hunters each year on this continent than any other game, large or small.

BIG GAME FOR THE GOURMET

What too many well-meaning cooks do to big game meat shouldn't happen in a nightmare. The result? The hunter is crestfallen. The cook feels unappreciated. A lot of top-notch grub is wasted.

More game meat is ruined by overcooking than by any other misadventure. The major reasons for this are two. The cook has the mistaken opinion that an abundance of heat is the way to assure tenderness. There is also the erroneous notion that high temperatures will burn away the wild flavor.

If your deer or moose tastes best to you rare, that's fine. If not, there's still a way around. Overcooking is ordinarily fatal to most big game, with the exception of bear, because of its general lack of the layers of fat common to comparable domestic meats. Such wild meat dries out under heat, and the fibers quickly tend to harden and toughen. An antidote? A non-seasoned meat tenderizer. For best results with game, use more than the instructions suggest and let it stand a shorter time.

Whether or not some people like a particular game meat largely depends on their taste prejudices. In other words, individuals sit down for the first time to deer that's kept sassy on willow shoots, and they expect it to taste like corn-fattened beef. It does not. The instinctive reaction, no matter how delicious the venison may be in its own right? Unfavorable.

Such taste prejudices can work themselves out in a while, when repeated servings begin to assume a familiar taste. There are better ways around, however. One of these shortcuts is to present the meat in as favorable an aspect as possible, surrounded with familiar and favorite side dishes, especially the impressionable first time.

Most of the other methods have to do with actually reducing any objectionable wild game flavors. These latter efforts start in the field with immediate cleaning and rapid cooling, as already considered. They continue with proper handling and storage. When the meat reaches the cooking area, there is an even wider range of choices. Among them are the following general methods, often used both with modifications and in combination.

Cut and pull off all loose fat, inasmuch as this carries most of the game's flavor. Replace this, if at all possible, with beef fat. Your meat man, or any cattle raiser who's been butchering, will sell you a bag of beef fat, and it can make all the difference. While you're in the woods, other fat will do, of course. The whiteness or yellowness of fat, incidentally, is no indication of quality or age. Yellow fat merely indicates that the carotin, the yellow substance found in all vegetation, has not yet been converted to vitamin A.

Trim the meat well before using it, removing all discolored and dehydrated portions and especially any hard or dry outer husk.

You can use spices, herbs, sauces, and the like if you want to alter or modify flavor. The trouble is that you are apt to get too far from the natural deliciousness of game meat. A more natural method? Plain, ordinary bouillon cubes, beef extracts, and similar preparations.

There's this, too. Roasts and stews will have far fewer unfamiliar flavors than steaks. As for such delicacies as heart and liver, these can seldom be distinguished from those bought at the butcher shop.

Finally, if you want, you may soak the meat overnight in a solution of vinegar, water, and spices. Some cooks employ wines, combinations of oil and weak acids such as lemon and tomato juice, barbecue sauces, and the like.

Most of us who love the woods prefer fine game meat quickly cooked, on the rare side, with only salt, pepper, and melting butter or margarine to bring out the delectable natural flavors. However, for one reason or another usually having to do either with age or mating, some meat is below average in savor. Also, everyone is a gourmet in his own right. If an individual prefers to marinate either a prime slab of beef or an equally choice moose sirloin, who is to say that he is wrong?

For those who may be interested, here is a better than usual marinade that will flavor and tenderize some 7 or 8 pounds of steak cut no less than 1½ inches thick. This marinade can be prepared at home by blending the following: 2 tablespoons olive oil, ½ cup wine vinegar, 1 rounded teaspoon oregano, and a sparsely measured ⅛ teaspoon apiece of salt, black pepper, Italian red pepper, and cayenne pepper. When ready to use, pour this into a flat dish where it will lie about ½ inch deep. Immerse the meat about suppertime, topping it with a thinly sliced medium-size onion and covering the dish. Turn the meat once the last thing at night. The steaks will be ready the next day.

This will give a general idea. Actually, if you taste occasionally, use a certain degree of restraint, and have the inclination, you can usually concoct an adequate marinade from the materials at hand. A virtually foolproof wild game marinade can be made, for example, by diluting a cheap red wine such as a claret with half its volume of water, then returning its authority by adding small amounts of pepper, bay leaf, rosemary, tarragon, thyme, mustard seed—anything that gives a pleasing taste.

WHAT TO EAT FIRST

The first parts of the big game animal to eat, while the body of the meat is taking on flavor and tenderness with age, include the liver, heart, kidneys, brains, and tongue. If you don't utilize at least most of these, you're passing up some mighty fine feasting.

Liver

Slice about ½ inch thick. Brown in a heavy frypan in bacon drippings or other fat until done to taste. Include onions and bacon by all means if you want. Liver is best when it is kept on the rare side. Overcooking gives you a tough, dry, tasteless, and far less nutritious product.

Grilled liver beats the frypan product four ways from go. This is one reason why, if you're hungry by the time you've collected that deer, bear, or sheep, you may choose to emulate the Indian hunter. If so, build a small fire and drape the liver, or slices of it, over a rack made of green wood. Or just shove a pointed stick into the ground and impale the liver on it, turning it occasionally in any event. It will not take long to cook. Fresh liver is delicious without seasoning, although if you want you can do like many sportsmen and always carry a small container of salt.

Liver sliced an inch or so thick and grilled briefly over an open fire until crisp outside and pinkly juicy within is delectable. Cutting into the meat will show you when it is ready. Butter liberally just before serving.

Heart

Brown the heart in natural fat or shortening in a Dutch oven. Season with salt and pepper. Then set the heart on a rack. Pour in a cup of boiling water. Cover and pot roast slowly in an oven or atop the heat for about 20 minutes per pound, only until the meat cuts easily. It should be rare to be tender. If you prefer yours well done, it is well to help it along with one of the tenderizers. Too much heat will give you a dry chunk of leather. Add more boiling water if necessary. Peeled onions, carrots, potatoes, and such may be put in toward the end. Basting the heart every half hour seems to improve the flavor. It certainly stimulates the appetite.

Big game hearts are also excellent broiled over cooking coals. Cut into thin slices, season, baste with butter or margarine, and cook about 3 minutes to a side. Eat while still sizzling. A tart jam or marmalade served on the side makes these taste even better. So does a kettle of hot black tea steeping within arm's reach.

Kidneys

"If I could eat just once more, I'd sure pick bear kidneys," King Gething told me up on the headwaters of the Peace River. "I'd want them simmered awhile with butter, salt, cloves, celery if I had any, and a mite of onion. Matter of fact, let's get 'em on the fire before somebody else shows up."

Cut or divide the kidneys into segments about the size of chicken hearts. All you have to do with bear kidneys to achieve this is strip away the connective membrane. Let the kidneys and other ingredients simmer in low heat until tender. Best way to establish proportions is by taste. These kidneys are especially tasty atop either steaming mountains of mashed potato or hot crusty bannock, streaming with butter or margarine.

Brains

This one is worth the trouble. It's also a practical way of reminding yourself how small and precisely positioned a target the brain of a big game animal actually is. Best way in is with a meat saw, although a battered woodpile bludgeon will get the job done. If you have a dog along, wire the head loosely to a tree, so he won't burry and forget it, and he'll worry away happily at it for as long as you're in camp.

Remove the other membrane of the brains. Dip them in beaten egg, roll in cracker or bannock crumbs seasoned with salt and pepper, and sauté uncovered in butter or margarine. These have a delicate flavor and go well with scrambled eggs.

If you haven't any fresh eggs in camp, however, immerse the brains in melted butter or margarine and then crumbs. Pan-broil slowly until crisp outside and hot throughout. Serve with buttered toast, hot biscuits, or boiled potatoes.

Marrow Bones

"They can keep them filly-minions and sech," an old prospector told me once over coffee in Seattle. "Me, I'm heading back to where I can knock over a caribou. I'd roast me the tongue first, except the liver is durned near as good and won't keep as long. I ain't forgetting the leg bones, either. Ever heat them in your campfire, then bust them open with rocks to get at the marrow? Then you savvy what I'm palavering about."

Marrow bones from any of the large game animals are an epicurean's delight.

Tongue

Tongue is another delicacy you shouldn't let get by you. Those from the larger animals are special tidbits, that from a moose being as big as a beef tongue. Caribou tongue is also excellent. So is elk tongue. The only drawback to that from the usual deer is its small size.

In case you've heretofore passed up this choice bit, there's a trick to securing it. Feel for the bones under the lower jaw. Make a deep slit between them up into the mouth. Press the tongue down through this opening. Grasp and cut off as close to the base as possible.

Cover with cold, salted water. Bring to a boil. Spoon off any scum that has come to the surface. Then simmer until the tongue is tender. When it has cooled sufficiently in the stock to permit its being handled easily, skin it. A sharp knife will help, although much of the skin can be peeled off with the fingers alone. Remove any small bones at the base.

This meat is especially good thinly sliced, either hot or cold. If you want something special, smoke the cooked and peeled tongue over a smudge of ground birch, alder, willow, or similar hardwood for several hours.

ASSORTED GAME RECIPES

Sweet and Sour Spareribs

Saw some 2 pounds of ribs into serving portions. Brown in a frypan over moderate heat about 5 minutes on each side. Add ½ cup water, ¼ cup raisins, and ½ teaspoon salt. Cover pan tightly and cook over very low heat 20 minutes. Add two sliced green peppers if you have them; a similar bulk of some other green such as celery, wild mustard leaves, watercress, peas, etc. if you don't.

Blend 1½ tablespoons of cornstarch with 1¼ cup sugar, 1¼ cup vinegar, and 1 cup of water. Mix this with the other ingredients in the pan. Re-cover and continue cooking over low heat for another 1½ hours. Stir occasionally and if necessary add more water to prevent drying. Before serving, perhaps with rice, sprinkle on soy sauce if possible. I most always keep some of this latter

in my outfit. If you've never tried it, you'll better appreciate why when you discover the elusively different flavor a few drops give such wilderness dishes as cold venison and boiled wild greens.

Baked Venison Chops

Arrange four thick chops in an open baking pan. Measure out a cup of canned tomato, using the solid portions. Spoon this over the chops. Then distribute a sliced onion atop the meat. Salt and pepper.

Pour in a cup of water and bake in a moderately hot oven for 45 minutes. Turn the chops once. Another 30 minutes should see them tender and ready to serve, perhaps along with mashed potatoes into each serving of which a spoonful of the juice is depressed. If they've had this before, you'll only have to call them once for dinner.

Venison Steaks with Pepper

Here's one that will amaze you with its deliciousness if you've never tried it before; that is, if you do not make the mistake of using ordinary ground black pepper which will be much too pungent. Instead, coarsely grind your own peppercorns in the electric blender or in a pepper mill, or crush them with a rolling pin. Even then, sift out the powdery particles for use elsewhere. You can also buy small bottles of suitable cracked or crushed peppercorns.

Cut the steaks an inch thick. Rub them with soft butter. Working one side at a time, sprinkle each slab liberally with the coarse black pepper, then press this into the meat. Let stand at room temperature for an hour.

Sprinkle a teaspoon of salt over the bottom of a very hot frypan. As soon as this begins to tan, put in the steaks. Turn once, as soon as they are well bronzed on one side. For the tenderest, tastiest meat, cook not more than 2 minutes in all.

Then knife a large chunk of butter atop each steak, sprinkle with chopped parsley and chives, set ¼ cup of warmed brandy alight with a match, pour flaming over the meat, and serve on hot plates with all the savory juices. Such steaks, robust and hearty, will make the world seem more real.

Venison Cutlets

Cut thin layers of otherwise tough venison across the grain from the long round leg muscle and pound them even thinner. For about a pound of these, enough for two people, beat an egg with 2 teaspoons water. Dip each cutlet in flour, then in the egg. Finally, roll in a mixture of 1½ cups fine bread crumbs, a teaspoon salt, and ¼ teaspoon freshly ground black pepper.

Allow to dry for 15 minutes. Then sauté the cutlets over low heat in a stick of butter until they are tanned short of browning. Serve with water cress and lemon wedges. This is the kind of delicately hearty meal to be particularly enjoyed when autumn is bustling out, red-faced and angry, slamming the doors of the hills behind her.

Steaks

These are always best over an open fire. I mostly pan broil all top grade steaks, cutting them 2½ inches thick, quickly searing both sides in a hot and preferably heavy frypan, and then cooking with slightly less heat until done to taste. Salt the metal well before putting the meat in and have it really hot. No grease at all is used, and that sputtering from the meat is tipped out. Salt and pepper if you want, and daub with butter or margarine after cooking. Serve on preheated plates.

Cooking over open embers is still unbeatable, however. A good trick at the start is to get a glowing bed of coals, then to sprinkle on a few chips and shavings. These will flare up enough both to help seal in the juices and to give that flavorsome char relished by so many. As you're already aware, the grill should be greased beforehand to prevent sticking.

Individual steaks can also be very pleasingly grilled merely by holding them over the heat by means of sturdy, forked green sticks.

Lean meat cooks more quickly than fat meat. Aging also progressively shortens the cooking time. Then there are such factors as size, shape, and the amount of bone. Outdoor fires add another variable. A practical way to test is to prick the steak with a sharpened stick. If red juice wells out, the meat is rare; pink, medium rare; colorless, overdone unless that is the way you want it.

Swiss Game Steak

This is good both for a change and for those days when you're confronted with the tougher cuts. Flank handled this way will work into a tasty steak of sorts. Slitting such game meat every few inches along the trimmed edges will keep it from curling unduly.

For about a 3-pound slab, mix 2 teaspoons salt with ½ teaspoon black pepper. Season one side of the steak with half of this. Then with the back of your camping knife pound all the flour you can into the meat. Turn the steak and repeat both processes.

Melt 5 tablespoons of bacon drippings, bear grease, lard, margarine, or the like in a Dutch oven or in a large skillet which has a cover. Quickly brown the meat all over.

Then spread a large onion and an equal bulk of carrot, diced together, over the steak. Add a can of tomatoes. Cover and simmer over low heat 1½ hours. Then bank the meat with enough small, peeled potatoes for the ensuing meal. Cook for an additional half hour or until the potatoes are tender.

Gameburgers

Ground venison, properly prepared, has fewer wild flavors than steaks or roasts. The main essential is to include as much beef fat as you like to lighten your ground beef.

Also, if this should be necessary, trim the meat well, removing any deer fat or any dried or discolored portions before consigning it to the grinder. Otherwise, gameburgers can include venison that is below par in tenderness and plumpness.

Seasonings go better if mixed directly with the venison when the meat is to be used at once, *not* however if it is scheduled for freezing. For each pound of gameburger, ½ teaspoon of salt and ⅛ teaspoon of freshly ground black pepper is ordinarily sufficient. You may also like to include ¼ teaspoon of mustard. Shredded Cheddar cheese, about ½ cup to each pound of meat, also blends well.

Gameburgers are best when they accumulate the charred, smoky taste associated with grilling. They are next best pan broiled with just enough butter to prevent sticking. If you like them rare, that's all to the good. They toughen rapidly when cooked too long. Serve the way you like, perhaps with salted slices of tomato and wisps of lettuce, and have plenty for replacements.

"Boiled" Meat

Cut the meat into about 2-inch cubes. Drop these individually into just enough bubbling water to cover. Do not boil. Don't salt until almost ready to serve. Meat so cooked can best be relished after it has been simmering covered only 5 minutes or so. However, many get the habit of letting it cook an hour or more.

Often rice and other vegetables, particularly onions, are cooked along with the meat to make what is often called mulligan. The addition of any such components, except when included for flavor only, should be so staggered that everything will be done at the same time. Any extra fluid should be heated before it is added.

If you are going to use the meat cold, let it cool in the broth. For a tasty treat with moose and caribou eaten this way, try sprinkling a little soy sauce over it and serving wild berry jam on the side.

The dutch oven will conveniently so "boil" a big solid chunk of game meat. Place the meat in the bottom of the oven along with onions if you have any, perhaps a sliced carrot or two, and 1½ teaspoons of salt per pound. Half cover the meat with simmering water. Cook about an hour for every pound, at the end of which time the meat should be tender but not stringy or mushy. If you want to use it in cold sandwiches, let it cool in the broth. Then move to a flat utensil that will also hold a little of the broth. Press it into shape with a weighted cover or plate so that it can later be more handily sliced.

Pack Train Mulligan

This trail mulligan is a favorite of some of the cooks on big game hunting parties when their pack trains make camp late after a long ride. Cut 3 pounds of caribou or other game meat into inch squares. Brown with 2 tablespoons of margarine or lard in the bottom of a stew pail. Then put in 2 quarts of water and 1 tablespoon of salt. Cover and boil until the meat is done.

Add hot water as necessary to bring the water back to its original level. Add 1½ cups macaroni, spaghetti, noodles, or the like. When this is nearly soft enough to eat, put in two large (15 oz.) cans of chili con carne or anything of the sort that may be handy in an accessible pannier. Salt and pepper to taste. Cook only a few minutes, just long enough for the mulligan to thicken. Serve with piping hot bannock. And if you want seconds yourself, you'd better get your refill in a hurry.

Stewing

Stew meat, which can be the toughest in the critter, is best browned at the onset with fat, chopped onion, and seasonings in the bottom of the kettle. You can then if you want stir in enough flour to make a thick smooth gravy.

For liquid, use any fluid in which vegetables have been cooked or canned, broth from boiled meat, or water. Season to taste, bring to a bubble, and then place tightly covered where it will simmer all morning or all afternoon.

A dutch oven is a handy receptacle for stew inasmuch as you can dig a hole, always in a safe place where fire can not spread, and leave it buried there among hot coals while you spend the day hiking, fishing, or hunting.

Broth

When trophy hunting in pack-horse country, you sometimes find yourself back of beyond with more good game meat than you can ever hope to bring out. Maybe you'll delay in camp a few days longer. Still, you can scarcely begin to eat it.

On occasions like this, why not really splurge on broth and enjoy all you possibly can? What I've done such times is get the kettle simmering, hang a ladle nearby, and let everyone help himself until the pot is exhausted. Then begin another. Thing to remember is that the liquid will boil down, so don't get it too salty at the start.

Just cut the meat into small pieces so that you'll get the most good out of it. Shot portions are fine. So are all lesser cuts that you haven't time or room to handle otherwise. Marrow bones, split or sawed, are unequalled. Those necks and backs of game birds can be used this way, too. Add about 1 cup of cold water for every ½ pound of meat and bone. Cover and simmer (not boil) upwards of 4 hours.

Incidentally, if you get hungry between meals, the meat itself is wonderful hot and swimming in melting butter or margarine.

Soup

Start like the above. In fact, you can ladle out what broth you need for the liquid part of the soup. If the broth you want to use for the soup has somehow become too salty, let is simmer along with some raw potatoes. Then remove the potatoes. Gently sauté in the bottom of the kettle whatever vegetables you're going to use. Figure out your times so that these will not be overcooked. Then add the broth and cover. Do not boil or you'll spoil the flavor. Do not season until 5 minutes before you're ready to serve.

Camp Hash

When you have cold vegetables left over and maybe not enough cooked meat to go around, here is a solution. Cut the venison or other meat up fine. If you're a bit short on meat, help the flavor along with a bouillon cube. Add enough chopped vegetables, usually potatoes mostly, to go around. Season to taste.

Be melting several tablespoons of fat in a frypan. If rawish onions bother anyone in the party, cook these first until thoroughly soft. Otherwise, chop up whatever amount you want and mix them with the other ingredients.

Press the hash down into the pan. Cook over slow heat until a crust has formed on the bottom. Fold over and serve while hot.

Upland Fowl

The trouble many cooks have in cooking some of the upland game birds stems from the fact that woodcock, quail, pheasant, and the like tend to run on the lean side. For half a dozen woodcock or quail, or an equivalent bulk of quartered pheasant, try:

¼ cup margarine
¼ teaspoon thyme (optional)
¼ cup chopped onion
1 teaspoon dried parsley
1 cup apple juice
1 teaspoon salt
⅛ teaspoon paprika (optional)
flour

Spread open the small birds, cutting along the backbone and removing the nearly meatless bony parts. Quarter the pheasant. Roll sparingly in flour.

Melt the margarine or other fat in a heavy frypan. When it is hot, brown the fowl. Sprinkle on the thyme. Cover and cook over low heat for 10 minutes.

Mix the chopped onion, dried parsley, and cup of juice which may be from cooked dried apples. Cover and keep simmering an hour or until done. About 10 minutes before the cooking is finished, sprinkle on the salt and paprika. A good accompaniment is rice—wild rice, by all means, if you can gather this expensive seed in your neck of the woods.

Creamed Game Bird

Cut into strips or cubes the cooked meat of any leftover partridge or similar game bird. For every cup of meat, you'll want 2 tablespoons margarine, 2 tablespoons flour, ⅛ teaspoon salt, and 1 cup milk. A little powdered or plain dried celery will further enhance the flavor, as will a small amount of dried parsley.

Melt the fat in a heavy frypan. Stir in the seasoned flour until it is smoothly blended. Continuing to stir, gradually pour in the milk. Cook over low heat until creamy. Season to taste. Then put in the fowl and slowly cook until warm. Sprinkle lightly with dried parsley and serve.

Two Game Bird Sauces

In some regions, even when your major objective is big game, you can dine on ptarmigan, partridge, and other game birds about as often as you want. Here's a sauce that will afford a change of taste.

2 tablespoons margarine
1 medium-size chopped onion
1 tablespoon flour
1 can evaporated milk
1 tablespoon vinegar
salt and pepper to taste

Melt the fat and fry the onions at low heat, turning them constantly and not allowing them to brown. When the onions are tender, gradually stir in the flour. Then add milk and vinegar. Bring to a boil and allow to simmer 15 minutes, stirring frequently. Season. This sauce goes well with all upland fowl.

When gunning is so good that you have a quantity of breasts to cook separately, mix:

½ cup cooking oil
1 cup vinegar
2½ tablespoons salt
1½ teaspoons poultry seasoning
¼ teaspoon pepper
1 minced clove of garlic

Bring these to a simmer. Then set off the stove and permit to cool. Soak the breasts in this sauce for an hour. Then broil or roast them until tender, basting with the remaining sauce. See if this one doesn't prove to all doubters that grub can be a pleasure as well as a necessity.

Roasted Wild Duck

Early-season duck that are still in the pinfeather stage, duck that are to be stored frozen, badly shot birds, and those with fishy and other strong odors in the fatty tissue just beneath the skin will be considerably choicer eating if skinned.

Wild duck ordinarily are not stuffed. However, chopped or sliced onions, stalks or leaves of celery, soaked prunes or dried apples, or a few juniper berries are frequently placed in the cavity.

Set the well-wiped duck in an open roasting pan with the breasts uppermost. Roast up to 25 minutes or so, depending on the size, in a very hot oven. Baste about every 5 minutes by spooning the hot juices over the birds. Duck will be tastier, juicier, and tenderer if kept very definitely to the rare side. Season to taste with salt and pepper after cooking.

This recipe is good, too, for sand hill crane.

Wild Geese Sputtering

Roast wild geese in a slow oven until well done, allowing 18 to 20 minutes per pound. If you'd care to try a dried apricot stuffing, I can recommend this one:

¼ cup chopped onion
½ cup margarine

3 cups cooked rice
1 tablespoon celery seed or powder
1 teaspoon dried parsley
2 cups chopped dried apricots
1 diced carrot
1 teaspoon allspice
½ teaspoon salt
⅛ teaspoon pepper

Sauté the onion lightly and politely in the margarine, only until tender. Remove from the heat. Add the other ingredients. Mix them together with just a few stirs. Stuff the goose. Truss. Roast in a moderate oven.

Wild geese, unlike their less active domestic brethren, tend to be dry and need frequent basting. The bird will be ready for the table when legs are loose and skin is appetizingly bronzed. Gravy may be concocted with drippings and giblets.

Wild Goose Pâté

Sauté the livers, preferably in goose fat, until soft, which takes only a few minutes. Add an equal volume of eggs that have been hardcooked by being simmered, completely covered by water, for 15 minutes.

Mash to a paste. Then season to taste with salt, paprika, a few flakes of freshly ground black pepper, and a bit of grated onion. If the resulting paste seems too thick, thin it with a spoonful of fat drippings. It is especially tasty on thin, hot toast.

Mallard

"My method of preparing this supreme wild fare is fairly simple," says Duncan Hines. "After washing and drying the duck, put a whole onion, a tablespoon vinegar, and a stalk of celery cut into long pieces inside it. Then set in a covered pan in a cold place overnight. This is for the purpose of eliminating all fishy flavor. These contents should be removed and discarded the next day.

"A sliced apple and a cut stalk of celery go inside the mallard next, but these, too, are discarded after the roasting. Lay 2 slices of salt pork diagonally across the breast of the duck. Put ½ cup olive oil and 3 tablespoons butter into a small roaster, and be certain it is very hot before putting in the duck. Roast in a hot oven for 15 to 20 minutes, basting every 4 to 5 minutes. My favorite accompaniment is wild rice and cranberry sauce."

Quail

Here is another savory and mouthwatering delicacy passed along to me by Duncan Hines. Dredge 6 quail lightly in 1 tablespoon of flour, salted and peppered to taste. Now heat ½ cup butter and a tablespoon lard as much as possible without scorching. Add the birds and, turning them, brown fast to seal in the juices.

Then lower the temperature, add a cup of boiling water to the birds, cover the pan, and cook until tender. Add water as needed until you are ready to brown the breasts. After the water is gone, place the quail breasts down in the butter and brown over low heat.

For the gravy, remove the birds and stir a tablespoon of flour into the butter and juices. Add 1 to 1¼ cups of water to the flour mixture and scrape all the brown coating off the roaster into the gravy. Stir and cook until quite thick.

Quail in Sour Cream

This recipe both successfully overcomes quail's dryness and complements the fragile flavor of these birds. With 4 quail, melt 2 tablespoons of butter in a large frypan. Sauté the foursome that have been well wrapped with toothpick-pinned salt pork, turning them as they brown.

Crush ½ dozen juniper berries, put them in the pan with the quail, pour a cup of boiling water over everything, and simmer until the tiny fowl are tender, adding more hot water whenever this should become necessary. Salt and pepper to taste. Then add a cup of sour cream, ¼ cup of sherry, and bring to a simmer.

In the meantime, start the cleaned and diced heart and gizzard simmering for ½ hour in a cup of white wine, ⅛ teaspoon celery seed, and salt and freshly ground black pepper to taste.

When the meat is browned, move it to a well-buttered casserole. Remove the cooked heart and gizzard to the hot frypan, reserving the liquid in which they were cooked. Stir them around in the butter until the bits are bronzed. Pour in the cooking liquid and stir vigorously over a moderate flame to loosen all the brown particles in the frypan. Then pour everything into the waiting casserole.

Add a dozen tiny onions and a cup of shredded carrots. Stir in sour cream to cover and set in a slow 325°F. oven until the vegetables are tender, about ½ hour. Sprinkle with paprika, and open an alley to the table.

Giblets

These are just about the best part of any fowl, for my money. Clean the gizzards by carefully cutting to the hard center, then pulling this sac away from the meat with the fingers. Gently separate the bitter gall bladder from the liver, cutting out any part of the liver that is left with a greenish tinge.

Here's a good dish for sometime when you have a lot of these giblets; enough, say, for a couple of heavy eaters. Place the hearts and sliced gizzards into enough cold water, with ½ teaspoon of salt, so that you'll end up with 2 cups of broth. Adding feet and necks will give you a richer broth. Simmer for about 2 hours or until the hearts and gizzards are tender. Put in the livers the last 5 minutes of cooking.

Now get 2 tablespoons margarine or other fat melting in a frypan. Gradually add 2 tablespoons flour, stirring until it is smooth and thick. Sauté ½ cup onion and ½ cup celery over low heat until tender. Then add the 2 cups of broth and get everything hot.

The hearts, gizzards, and liver go in next. Stir everything together over the low heat. If you want the gravy a little thinner or a little whiter, add evaporated milk. Salt and pepper to taste. Top with paprika and powdered parsley if you happen to have any.

All giblets taste pretty much the same. So, during off seasons back in town, you may like to buy frozen chicken hearts so that you can repeat this repast often.

Pigeon and Dove

The meat is dark of color and fine of flavor, that of pigeon having a tendency to be tough. Both are best cooked, tightly covered, in a small amount of water or tomato juice at low temperatures, either atop the heat or in the oven or reflector baker. Brown the birds first in a bit of cooking oil. Season with salt, pepper, celery or parsley flakes, and a small amount of chopped onion. Simmer usually from 30 to 45 minutes or until just tender.

Potted Dove or Pigeon

Sometime when you are having another couple over for dinner, cut 4 large pigeons or 6 doves into pieces, rub well with butter, salt liberally, speck with a few flakes of freshly ground black pepper, and sauté briefly in 6 tablespoons butter. When the fowl has taken on a tempting tan, move to a casserole.

Add to the hot butter remaining in the pan ½ cup of chopped onion and ¼ cup of chopped celery. Cook, stirring, until the onion is soft but not brown. Then pour in a cup of boiling water in which a chicken bouillon cube has been dissolved, or use chicken or similar stock. Add a small can of pieces and stems of mushrooms, the juice included. Mix thoroughly, then turn everything over the birds. Cover and cook in a moderate 350°F. oven for about an hour or until the meat is tender.

Unless you have wild rice for this, try stirring and cooking 2 cups boiled rice in 2 tablespoons butter in a frypan over low heat for 5 minutes. Add 2 tablespoons chopped, preferably green, onions. Cook several minutes longer. Then add a beaten egg and stir vigorously until the egg is set. Season with parsley flakes and salt. Serve everything hot. This will really set off the arriving night when the pale saffron glow overhead begins to fade into velvet darkness.

H.B.C. Pasties

Some of the best eating you'll find in northern Canada is at the Hudson's Bay Company trading posts. The following flexible recipe, geared in this instance to 4 partridge, is one of the reasons.

You'll also need 1 cup of raw potato and 2 tablespoons onion. Chop and mix these and the meat thoroughly. Salt and pepper to taste.

Now roll and cut some pastry dough into rectangles, about ¼ inch thick. Moisten the edges. Put generous portions of the meat mixture on one half. Then fold over the other half and seal the edges of the pastry well. Prick with a fork to make an escape vent for steam. Place on a pan and bake in moderate oven or reflector baker ¾ hour or until done. If any last that long, these are also memorable cold.

Blue Grouse

The subtly flavored white meat of one of these big, plump fellows is just about the best you're going to sit down to in the game bird realm. Way I like them is cut into serving pieces, well rubbed with cooking oil, liberally salted, dusted with a few flakes of pepper, and slowly broiled over hot coals. Start with the bony side toward the heat. Turn after about 10 minutes, again basting and seasoning. When a fork slips in easily and there's no gushing or red juices, the grouse is done.

You sometimes get a coat full of blue grouse, though, in high windy country where there's no satisfactory hardwood for coals. One way around is to use just the legs and breasts, saving the giblets and the rest for soup. Dredge the legs and breasts in salted and peppered flour. Now bring 6 slices of bacon slowly to a sputter in a heavy frypan. Remove the bacon to a hot dish when it is crisp. Quickly brown the grouse on both sides in the hot fat. Salt and pepper it, then remove to more moderate heat. Cover and cook 15 minutes, turning at about the halfway point.

Put the grouse on the hot dish with the bacon. Stir 2 tablespoons of flour into the fat and juice. Still stirring, slowly add 1½ cups of rich milk. When this has thickened the way you like it, season it to taste. Let each banqueter spoon his share over grouse, bacon, and any vegetables. With one ridge after another lifting in front of the late northern sun as you eat, and a breeze starting to trumpet a cool blue note, this is grub you're never going to forget.

Northern Partridge

The most memorable roast partridge I ever ate goes back to a day when I was alone in a small log cabin in the Far North, with the temperature hovering a frigid $-50°F$. The two birds were big and old, but I had all day with nothing to do but keep a wood fire stoked up and to sit close beside it with a Dumas book, while outside trees and river ice snapped and banged as they froze even more deeply.

I wanted a moist stuffing, from ingredients at hand, so I mixed well-soaked dried apples in equal amounts with cream cheese, and stirred in a minced clove of garlic and 4 tablespoons of rendered bear fat. Butter, I proved later, would have served almost as well.

The brace of partridge, well rubbed with the fat and crisscrossed with bacon, went into a bread pan apiece and into the hot oven. There I basted them with their own juices about every half-hour until the meat was falling away from the bones, by which time it was deliciously permeated with the savor of the dressing.

Partridge in Mustard Leaves

Partridge are frequently so plentiful that, on occasion, you may like to try something different with them. Allowing one fowl per diner, rub well with fresh lemon juice. Then, depending on how many birds you're cooking, make a mixture proportionately of a tablespoon of salt, ½ teaspoon of freshly ground black pepper, 1 teaspoon cloves, and ½ teaspoon powdered ginger. Dust the birds liberally with this. Then strip with thin slices of salt pork.

Set breast side up in a roasting pan. Arrange a layer of wild mustard (*Brassica*) leaves over the birds. If these are not available where you live, substitute some other peppery wild edible, such as water cress. Roast in a hot 425°F. oven for 15 minutes or until tender. Then remove both the leaves and the slices of salt pork, brush with melted butter into which a little lemon juice has been squeezed, and brown.

Cold Partridge Sandwiches

These are superior for an informal lunch when you have several cold roast partridge. For the utmost in flavor, do not slice the birds until ready to eat. The other ingredients you'll need are a liberal supply of garlic toast, especially some made from crusty sourdough bread. Let everyone serve himself.

For the odds and ends of meat that will be left, mix with enough gravy to moisten, add a few chopped nuts such as freshly gathered hazelnuts or walnuts, season to taste with celery salt, and spread between thin slices of well-buttered bread.

Young Pheasant with Cream

Disjoint two young pheasants, putting the backs and wings aside for soup. Season with freshly ground black pepper and salt. Sauté in ½ stick of butter in a frypan until lightly browned. Then cover with a pint of heavy cream, add ¼ cup of dry sherry, and simmer until the pheasant is tender and the sauce has thickened. This repast really deserves wild rice.

Pheasant Hash

When you're served roast pheasant and some is left over, here's a way to resurrect it that retains all the delicate flavor of this nobleman among game birds. Cut the meat into about ¼-inch cubes. For every cup of fowl, stir in ½ cup of light cream. Cook, along with a tablespoon of butter for every cup of poultry, until the cream warms and thickens. Season to taste with salt and with freshly ground black pepper. This is the sort of fine food that evokes so many praises.

Roast Wild Turkey

This prince of the game birds, one of the most prized of all trophies, has a delicious wild flavor that sets it far above the domestic Thanksgiving fowl. Incidentally, because of feeding practices, you do not find this flavor in the so-called wild turkey from game farms.

Wild turkey, though, because of these same eating and living habits, are leaner and tougher than the domesticated varieties. So as to offset this, and at the same time to enhance rather than diminish the natural savor, you won't go wrong in first steaming your bird for ½ hour over moderate heat with a quart of water in a closely covered roaster. Then, shifting the fluid to a handy pot, dry the bird with clean toweling.

Rub with salt and with at least 2 sticks of butter. Place in the now dry and uncovered roaster in a hot 400°F. oven and brown. Then lower the heat to a moderate 325°F. and roast until tender, which won't take as long as otherwise because of the initial steaming. Baste frequently with the water from the steaming process and with the melted butter.

For the gravy, stir enough flour, previously mixed to a smooth thin paste with double its volume of cold water, with the juices and the remaining stock over low heat until it bubbles to a rich deliciousness. Such wild turkey is something long to be eulogized, especially when the wind suddenly has teeth in it and there's enough snow in the night to make sequins in the starlight.

Ovenless Turkey

If you have to cook your wild turkey without the benefit of an oven, which may be the case in camp, there's still a way to conserve that wonderful flavor, also ideal for the home patio. Cut and disjoint the bird into serving portions. Rub the pieces with salt and with a very generous amount of butter.

Lay on a large, doubled rectangle of heavy aluminum foil and wrap, crimping all edges securely. Place on a grill over glowing coals or in the edge of a small campfire.

Cook 1½ hours, carefully, turning the packet every 20 minutes to insure that every part will be evenly cooked and basted. When the supreme moment for unwrapping arrives, take care to save the juice. This should be distributed in cups, so each feaster can punctuate an occasional forkful of steaming meat by immersing it in the engaging savoriness.

SMALL GAME: FOOD FOR A KING

'Possum

The opossum's light colored and fine grained meat, all the tenderer because of mild flavored fat that's well distributed among the bands of lean, make it one of the most prized game animals in the southern states particularly. I prefer to skin them, at the same time removing the glands in the small of the back and inside the forelegs. The meat is better after it has aged a few days. If the

'possum is particularly plump, the answer as with bear is to cut off most of the outside fat and to keep grease from accumulating in the cooking pan. Salt and pepper. Roast in an oven or reflector baker.

'Possum is also exceptionally good when broiled over the open coals of the campfire. Cut it in half for this purpose. Or divide it into serving pieces. A small 'possum can then be individually cooked on forked sticks. If you want, baste it with your favorite barbecue sauce, although a lot of us would rather keep this latter for some less delicately flavored meat.

You can also brown 'possum in its own fat in the bottom of a dutch oven. Season it with salt and pepper and perhaps ⅛ teaspoon of sage, add enough vegetables including sweet potatoes to go around, pour in 2 cups of hot water, and cook slowly until the meat is tender.

Squirrel

Squirrel, too, has little if any gaminess. The firm, lean meat needs added fat, but it can be advantageously cooked about every way. Lard it with bacon, season, and roast 1½ hours in a moderate oven. Or broil about a half hour or until tender, basting frequently. Or fry uncovered in a small amount of fat for from ½ to 1 hour, turning occasionally.

Or, particularly if the squirrel are the elders of their tribe, cut them up and roll each piece in flour. Brown slowly in a small amount of bacon drippings in a heavy frypan or dutch oven. Season with salt and pepper. Then add enough tomato juice or water to cover the bottom of the receptacle. Cover tightly and simmer in low heat from 1 to 1½ hours or until the meat is tender, turning it occasionally and if necessary adding enough liquid to maintain steam. Remove the cover the last 15 minutes for a crisper crust. Serve hot with gravy made by adding a small amount of water to the pan drippings, stirring it diligently over the heat, and seasoning to taste.

Squirrel Stew

If you only have a couple or so squirrel and some robust appetites to satisfy, the following stew may be the solution. Cut up the squirrel. Brown the pieces in the bottom of a pan in 3 tablespoons of margarine. Then cover with 3 cups water. Season only with 1 teaspoon salt and ½ teaspoon pepper so as to maintain the distinctive natural flavor. Simmer 1 hour.

Add ¼ cup chopped onion, ½ cup diced celery, and ½ cup sliced carrot. Thicken with a smooth paste made by blending 3 tablespoons flour with ¼ cup water. Cook an additional 15 minutes. If you want to really top this one off, roof it with dumplings.

Wild Game Soup

This recipe is another from the Hudson's Bay Company. It calls for cutting up a rabbit or ptarmigan, although any similar game is also satisfactory. Put in a pot and simmer slowly for 2 hours with some left over vegetables, either 1 onion or 1½ tablespoons onion flakes, ¼ cup rice, 4 cups cold water, and salt and pepper to taste.

Brunswick Stew

This huntsman's stew has been famous for centuries, so the recipes vary. The following is a good one, particularly when a day outdoors has whetted everyone's appetite. For four servings, disjoint a large rabbit or several squirrel or partridge so as to come by about 2 pounds of meat. Brown this in

2 tablespoons of fat in a heavy pot or frypan, along with ¼ cup of diced onions.

Add 1 cup tomatoes, 1 cup boiling water, and ⅛ teaspoon pepper. Cover and simmer until the meat is tender. Then put in 1½ cups lima or other green beans and 1½ cups of corn. Simmer 10 minutes or, if the vegetables were raw, until everything is ready. Season to taste with salt.

Rabbit

The mildly flavored, finely grained meat of the rabbit and hare can be cooked like chicken, which it resembles. First, remove the glands from under the forelegs. Rabbit is so lean that even if you had all of it you could eat, you'd still starve to death on it alone. Add fat, though, and it's both nutritious and delicious. Cook like fowl and like other small game.

Smothered rabbit is a way out when you run into some of the older animals. With 2 rabbit, you'll need:

1 teaspoon salt
⅛ teaspoon pepper
½ cup flour
¼ cup fat
½ cup diced onion
1 cup milk

Mix the flour, pepper, and salt. Roll the serving pieces in this and brown them with the fat in a frypan or dutch oven. Add the onion and milk. Cover and simmer slowly for about an hour or until tender. Then remove the meat. Stir enough flour into the remaining juices to make gravy. Pour this over the meat. Sprinkle on paprika if you have it. Garnish if possible with parsley, either fresh or powdered, or with watercress. Serve over potatoes, rice, or hot bannock.

Rabbit Fricassee

One hungry wet night up by Sherwood Lake in New Brunswick, when our tent was leaking so much that we pitched it under an old brush lean-to, Old Bill MacDonald took a couple of small rabbit I'd managed to bag, clattered around some in the grub box of our canoe, and came up with a fricassee that pushed back the rain and the shadows. By the next morning the rain had turned to tracking snow, and we were soon paddling back toward his Seven Mile Lake camp with a heavy buck.

Old Bill cut those rabbit into serving pieces and rolled them awhile in flour, salt, and pepper. Then he got ½ cup of butter sizzling in the bottom of a big iron frypan and slowly browned the chunks, forking them around all the time. He then poured in 2 cups of hot water from the boiling kettle, covered the frypan, and shoved it to one end of the grate where enough birch coals were falling apart to keep it simmering merrily.

After about an hour, he tested a meaty slab with a fork, nodded, and then stirred in a large chopped onion and a small can of peas. It couldn't have taken any more than 15 minutes to whip together a steaming batch of baking powder biscuits. Our stainless steel plates were so hot by then that I remember we had to put on a glove apiece to handle them. Old Bill eased a couple of biscuits on each plate, saturated them with butter, and then spooned rabbit over them until I begged quits. There was still enough for the seconds, at that.

Fried Rabbit

This is my favorite way of cooking America's most hunted game. Divide the rabbit or hare into serving pieces, disjointing whenever possible. Dip each portion in milk. Salt and pepper, and then roll lightly in flour.

Put ½ stick butter and 4 tablespoons cooking oil in a frypan over high heat and set in the pieces, any bony sides uppermost. Lower the temperature at once and cook, uncovered, until the portions are brown on one side. Then turn, just once, and brown the other side. The meat will be crisp and done in a total of slightly more than ½ hour. Spread it out on absorbent paper and keep warm while concocting the gravy.

For this, pour off all the fat except just enough to cover the bottom of the frypan. Stir in 2 tablespoons flour, ½ teaspoon salt, and ⅛ teaspoon freshly ground black pepper, smoothing it into a paste. Using the milk into which you dipped the meat, add enough additional milk to make a cupful. Pour this, then a cup of water slowly into the pan, all the time stirring. Simmer over low heat for 12 minutes, adding more milk and water if the gravy becomes too thick. Finally, sprinkle with paprika and parsley flakes. With everything served hot, the gravy has enough distinctiveness to transmute fried rabbit into an art form.

Marinated Rabbit or Squirrel

Soy sauce gives a different and highly agreeable flavor to wild meat, as we discovered one winter in the Far North while living on moose meat and not much else except for the occasional varying hare and red squirrel bagged for the sake of variety. It can really impart that special something to serving pieces of either of these latter, marinated all afternoon in, if you are preparing enough for four: a cup of soy sauce, ¼ cup sherry, 1½ teaspoons sugar, and a minced clove of garlic.

Place the portions on a rack in a shallow pan and roast them uncovered in a preheated moderate 350°F. oven until tender, brushing them every 10 minutes with the marinade. They'll then be sheer gastronomical delights.

Small-Game Kabobs

These are always good. On the patio or in the fireplace, you can really dress them up. For about 2 pounds of any tender small game—rabbit, squirrel, raccoon, opossum, or such—you'll need ½ stick butter, 2 tablespoons lemon juice, ¼ pound sliced bacon, and enough sliced onions, firm chunks of tomatoes, to be impaled through the skin, and mushroom caps to go around.

Cut the boned game into cubes about 1½ inches square. Brush these well with melted butter and lemon juice, and let them stand ½ hour.

Using green sticks, metal rods, or whatever you have, thread loosely in succession a piece of game, sliced onion, 2-inch strip of bacon, chunk of tomato, mushroom, game, and so on, ending up with a chunk of game. Brush with the mixed lemon juice and melted butter. Then sprinkle with salt and freshly ground black pepper.

Broil in the rotisserie or 2 inches above glowing coals until the meat is tender, turning occasionally and basting frequently. These kabobs are best when charred outside and still juicily red inside. Serve with potato chips, pickles, and hot garlic bread. Such a blending will convert these refreshing tidbits into a delicacy that will rate high on almost anyone's list of favorite foods.

FISH AND ITS PREPARATION

The way you cook your fish may be determined to some extent by their fatness. Plumper varieties such as lake trout, salmon, and whitefish are best for baking, as in a reflector baker or dutch oven, and for broiling over the cherry-red coals of a campfire. Their fat content helps keep them from becoming too dry.

Leaner catches such as pike, bass, perch, and Arctic grayling are preferable for poaching and for steaming because they remain firmer. They can also be satisfactorily baked and grilled if frequently basted or if topped with a sauce.

All fish are eminently suitable for frying. As far as that goes, any fish may be satisfyingly cooked by any of the basic methods if allowances are made for the fat content.

The main thing is not to overcook the catch. To keep fish moist and tender, and to bring out its delicate flavor, cook only until the flesh is no longer translucent. Once the fish is easily flaked, it is done. The taste will be further enhanced if the fish is salted, inside and out, as much as an hour in advance of cooking.

Second thing to avoid? Never soak any fish before or after it is cleaned.

Spitted Fish

Some time when you have a mess of small brook trout or such, let everyone roughly trim and peel his own green hardwood wand. Thread a slice of bacon on the wand and broil it over ruddy coals until translucent. Then place the opened and cleaned fish lengthwise over the bacon, fastening the fish by skewering it with sharpened twigs. Cook slowly over glowing embers. Repeat as long as fish and appetites hold out.

Large fish may also be spitted and roasted over hot coals. They have a tendency to roll on the stick, however, and usually must be lashed to it with twine or old fishline. Unless the fish is fat, it will be the better for basting.

Sautéed Fish

This is hard to beat when it comes to fillets and small fish. Open and clean these latter as soon as possible after catching, saving the livers, hearts, and any roe. Unless you object to them too strenuously, leave on the head and certainly the tail where, in that order, lies the sweetest meat. Keep dry, cool, and well ventilated.

Get the frypan just hot enough that the butter or margarine in it barely begins to brown. You can roll the fish in flour, crumbs, or corn meal if you want, although I much prefer the rich crispy skin when it is unadorned. Brown on both sides only until the flesh flakes easily. The heart, liver, and any roe will then also be well done and tender. Transfer to a hot plate, unless you're eating alone maybe, and add any desired salt. If near civilization where such supplements are available, you may also like to squeeze on a few drops of lemon juice.

Fried Fish

Dip the fillets, steaks, or the cleaned but otherwise whole pan fish into evaporated milk. For a richer crust, immerse next in beaten eggs. Roll finally in cracker, bannock, or bread crumbs. This will seal the flavor in and the cooking fat out.

Get this latter ½ inch deep and thoroughly hot, just short of smoking, in a heavy frypan, so that a protective coating will be quickly formed on the fish. Do not let the fat get any warmer, as this will cause both dryness and loss of flavor. Turn each piece of fish once. Although the cooking time will depend on the thickness of the catch, keep it on the underside if anything. When the fish flakes easily with a fork, it's ready for eating.

Fish so prepared can also be cooked in a hot reflector baker. Once they have been rolled in crumbs, place them in a warm greased pan and either dot with butter or margarine or pour a small amount of oil over them. This cooking method will give you more time for other chores. In about a dozen minutes, depending on the fish and the fire, the flesh will flake easily and be ready for the table.

Baked Fish

A reflector baker and a large fish make a winning combination. Cover the fish well with butter, margarine, or cooking oil. Place in the greased pan with the skin down. Bake in front of a rousing fire as you would bannock. Baste occasionally. Turn the pan end-for-end about halfway through. About the only thing to beware of is overcooking. Test for flakiness as usual with a fork or twig. Too, baked fish must be fresh, or it will fall to pieces.

The larger fish can also be stuffed and baked if you want. A bread filling is a favorite. For a 5-pound fish, come as close as you can to:

¼ cup chopped onion
¼ cup margarine
5 cups bread crumbs
1 teaspoon salt
⅛ teaspoon pepper
1½ teaspoons thyme or poultry seasoning
¼ cup water

Cook the onion in the margarine until tender. Mix with crumbs, salt, pepper, and seasoning. Then add the water. Fill the fish loosely so that it won't burst and close it with whittled skewers. Bake in a hot oven or reflector baker, basting frequently. This will take about 10 minutes a pound. The usual flaking test will indicate when done.

With leaner fish in particular, this bread stuffing may seem somewhat dry. If you want and have the raw materials, substitute sliced tomatoes for the crumbs and omit the thyme and poultry seasoning.

Grilled Fish

The smaller the fish, the hotter the grill should be. If the fish sticks or breaks when you attempt to turn it or to take it up, then odds are you did not let the grill get hot enough to start with. Too, grease it well at the onset.

Either salt the inside and outside of the fish up to an hour before broiling, or sprinkle the inside with pepper and lemon juice just before it goes on the heat. Whole fish may be split or not, depending on your preferences and on the size. Even when the fish has a thick skin well cushioned with fat, basting will add to the flavor. Once the translucency of the fish has clouded to opaqueness, the fish will be ready for serving.

Planked Fish

These days if you can't easily come by a clean, sweet hardwood plank several inches thick, you can use almost any handy slab, shake, or other piece of wood of suitable size by first sheathing the working side with aluminum foil. The wood should be slightly longer and wider than the split fish.

Nail or peg the opened and flattened fish to the plank with the skin toward the back. Salt and pepper. Either spread it with butter or margarine or brush it with cooking oil. Lean near the fire, turning the plank now and then and occasionally basting. As soon as the fish is flaky, it is ready. The saltiness of melting butter touches up the taste. If you've enough to go around, serve each fish with its individual hot plate attached.

Poached Fish

Use serving size portions. Place in a frypan. Barely cover with hot salted water, tomato juice, or milk. Add diced onions if you want. Cover and simmer for about 10 minutes or until the fish is flaky. Then remove the fish and thicken the remaining gravy by stirring in flour and margarine. Pour the hot sauce over the fish and serve.

When fish is so poached in salted water, an egg sauce is a particularly fitting accompaniment. Melt 2 tablespoons of margarine in a separate pan. Blend in 2 tablespoons flour. Gradually stir in 1 cup of milk and cook about 5 minutes or until the sauce is thick and smooth. Remove from the heat. Season with ½ teaspoon salt and a sprinkle of black pepper. A ¼ teaspoon of paprika and 1 teaspoon of dried parsley will add eye and taste appeal. Finish by stirring in 2 finely chopped, hard boiled eggs. This sauce can be richly made with dried milk and eggs.

Fish may also be cradled in cloth or cheesecloth, lowered into salted bubbling water, and simmered gently until done. This is an easy way to prepare for recipes demanding flaked cooked fish. It is also a satisfactory way to cook a large salmon, part of which is to be eaten cold.

Fish Cakes

Colonel Townsend Whelen taught me this way of making fish cakes. You'll need:

    1 small onion, chopped fine
    2 tablespoons shortening
    1½ cups cooked fish
    3 cups diced, boiled potatoes
    ½ teaspoon salt
    ¼ teaspoon black pepper
    1 tablespoon dried egg
    ½ cup water

Fry the onion in a small mount of the shortening until soft. Then mix with fish, potatoes, and seasoning. Stir the egg in the water. Add this and the remainder of the shortening to the other ingredients. Form into small cakes ¾ inch thick and fry in a greased pan until brown.

Another way both the Colonel and I like fish cakes on occasion is in the proportions of:

    1 cup cooked fish
    2 cups mashed potatoes
    2 eggs, fresh or reconstituted
    3 tablespoons shortening
    ½ teaspoon salt
    ¼ teaspoon pepper

Mix the potatoes and fish. Then stir the other ingredients into the mixture. Form cakes as before and fry them slowly until you can't wait any longer.

Fish Chowder

You can prepare for this before leaving on your vacation by packing and sealing dehydrated equivalents of the following or similar ingredients, except for the bacon and fish, in a plastic bag. Or you can make a quart of it on the spot with:

    1 cup diced potatoes
    ½ cup diced carrots
    2 tablespoons diced bacon
    1 tablespoon chopped onion

½ cup dry milk
1½ tablespoons flour
2 cups liquid (that from cooked vegetables plus water or fluid milk)
2 cups flaked cooked fish

Cook the potatoes and carrots until tender in just enough boiling water to cover. Drain and save liquid. Fry bacon until crisp, adding onion long enough to make it tender.

Add milk powder and flour to the liquid and beat until smooth. Cook over low heat, stirring constantly until slightly thickened. Then combine all ingredients and heat thoroughly.

Oven-Fried Trout

For enough small, whole fish or fillets for four, melt a stick of butter. Pour half of this into a baking dish and warm for 5 minutes in an oven preheated to a very hot 500°F.

In the meantime, beat an egg yolk with ¼ cup of light cream. Salt and pepper to taste. Then stir in ½ teaspoon of chopped watercress and ¼ teaspoon paprika. Dip the fish in this before rolling in fine, dry cracker or bread crumbs.

Remove the baking dish from the oven long enough to arrange the coated fish in it. Distribute the remainder of the melted butter over them. Return to the heat for 8 minutes or until the fish flakes readily. Serve immediately, perhaps with lemon wedges to lend a special flavor.

Baked Brook Trout

Another engaging way with brook trout is to bake it to a flaky goodness, each cleaned but otherwise whole small fish wrapped in 2 strips of bacon. For 6 of these trout, prepare the scene by lightly sautéing a tablespoon of chopped green onion with 3 tablespoons butter in a shallow baking pan. Then put in the catch, slide into a hot 400°F. oven, and bake until opaque.

Shift the trout to a hot platter. Stir a teaspoon of lemon juice, ½ teaspoon parsley flakes, and salt and freshly ground black pepper to taste into the juices in the pan. Bring quickly to a simmer and pour over the trout. Serve with watercress and lemon wedges. There is a gusto and a sensuous, open-eyed delight to be experienced from food like this.

Baked Lake Trout

For a smooth golden taste with about a 4-pound lake trout, mix a teaspoon of salt with the juice of a large lemon. Rub the trout inside and out with this.

For the stuffing, blend 2 cups of soft bread crumbs, the drained contents of a small can of mushroom stems and pieces, ½ stick melted butter, and a small diced onion. Stir in a teaspoon of very finely chopped celery, ⅛ teaspoon thyme, and a coloring of freshly ground black pepper. Add a tablespoon of brandy and a tablespoon of heavy cream.

Stuff the trout about ¾ full and fasten with toothpicks. Place in a buttered, shallow baking dish and bake uncovered in a preheated moderate 350°F. oven for about 45 minutes, or until the trout is flaky, basting with melted butter. Any extra stuffing may be baked for ½ hour in a shallow pan. Serve on a hot platter, tastefully surrounded with parsley sprigs and lemon wedges.

Lake Trout With Mint

You'll often find wild mint (*Mentha*) in dark green stands beside the waters in which you catch lake trout. This can be gathered and taken home, as it will keep indefinitely. For about a 4-pound fish, mix ¼ cup olive oil, 4 tablespoons fresh lemon juice, 3 tablespoons of the chopped mint leaves, ½ teaspoon thyme, and salt and freshly ground black pepper to taste. Brush the trout with this.

Lay the fish on a well-buttered grill and set 4 inches below the heat. Broil until golden and flaky, brushing several times with the spiced oil. Bring the unusual and intriguing results to the table on a preheated platter, garnished with sprigs of mint and surrounded by lemon wedges.

Trout with Almonds

Let's face it. The fishing can be too good! Some weeks, both by the shore and later at home, we gorge ourselves so nobly with brook trout and such that the day arrives when we guiltily realize we'd almost rather reach for a plebeian hamburger. When this happens, the following recipe can be a passport to further piscatorial pleasure.

In a small skillet, heat 2 tablespoons butter and toss in 3 tablespoons slivered almonds, bought that way if you prefer. When the nuts are lightly browned, stir in a teaspoon paprika, 2 tablespoons lemon juice, and 2 tablespoons chopped parsley.

Then, in a frypan large enough not to crowd 6 trout, melt 3 tablespoons butter and, when this is hot, sauté the salted and peppered catch over medium heat until their undersides flake readily. Now turn the fish, tip the little skillet of sizzling almond butter over them, and finish cooking.

Poached Atlantic Salmon Steaks

This is one of the ways I've enjoyed these fighting beauties on the *Half Moon* of the Southwest Miramichi River in New Brunswick and later at home in Boston. For enough steaks for four, bring 6 cups of water, 1 tablespoon of vinegar, and 1 teaspoon of salt to a bubble in a large frypan. Add the salmon and simmer for 10 minutes or until the fish is flaky. Serve drenched with melted butter.

Salmon Loaf

It's a common thing in both the Northeast and the Northwest to cook more salmon than you can readily eat. Baked salmon loaf is then often the solution.

With every 2 cups of skinned, flaked, and boned salmon, mix a cup of finely crumbed bread or crackers, a cup of rich milk, a beaten egg, a tablespoon of minced onion, a tablespoon chopped watercress, ¼ teaspoon salt, and a sprinkling of freshly ground black pepper.

Level in a buttered baking pan and bake in a moderate 350°F. oven for ½ hour or until set. Then cool 3 or 4 minutes in the pan before turning onto a hot platter.

This is good with a rich onion sauce. To make this latter in proportions for the above, melt a tablespoon of butter in a pan, remove from the fire long enough to stir a tablespoon of flour smoothly into the butter, and then return to low heat to bubble—but not brown—for a minute.

Add a tablespoon of grated onion and cook this until yellow and soft. Pouring slowly and stirring constantly, add a cup of heated half-and-half milk and cream and simmer for 10 minutes. Stir in a teaspoon of lemon juice. Then salt to taste. Pour over the hot salmon loaf and start serving. The plates must be very hot.

Smallmouth Bass Salad

The friend who used to serve this salad to us made it with smallmouth bass, caught just outside his island cottage, but like the other recipes in this section, it will work with other fish as well, either frozen or fresh. With every cup of flaked cooked fish, mix ½ cup of finely chopped raw carrot, ½ cup of chopped raw apple, and 2 tablespoons of chopped raw tomato. Salt to taste.

For the dressing, blend 2 tablespoons mayonnaise, ½ cup heavy cream, 1 teaspoon prepared brown mustard, ⅛ teaspoon paprika, and a tablespoon of fresh lemon juice.

Shape the portions on beds of crisp lettuce, flavor liberally with the dressing, and lightly with parsley flakes. This is a distinctive and unusual salad, mingling as it does so many different flavors in concentrated form.

Baked Bass

This recipe is one to reach for when everyone's mouth is watering for something a little different. For a 4-pound bass, mix a teaspoon of salt, ¼ teaspoon freshly ground black pepper, and ⅛ teaspoon apiece of parsley flakes and paprika. Rub the prepared bass inside and out with this.

Distribute the slices from a medium-size onion inside the fish. Lay in a well-buttered baking dish and cover with 6 slices of bacon. Bake, uncovered, in a moderate 325°F. oven for 45 minutes or until the fish flakes readily.

When the bass is nearly done, make a cheese sauce for it, starting by blending ½ stick of butter with 3 tablespoons of flour. Slowly, add this to 1½ cups of milk over low heat, stirring constantly. Then remove from the stove.

When the sauce has cooled a bit, begin stirring in ⅔ cup of good grated Cheddar cheese, putting in only small amounts at a time and mixing vigorously before adding any more. If you want a more decided taste, include ½ teaspoon of prepared mustard. Then return to very low heat, continuing to stir. If the sauce still is not as velvety as you would like, try rapidly mixing in a tablespoon of cognac. Serve everything hot, blended into one delectable savory whole.

Pan-Fried Blue Gills

Dust the blue gills with flour, salt and pepper them liberally, and lay them carefully in a yellow pool of fresh butter in a sizzling frypan. Brown lightly but crisply on both sides over moderate heat until the white flesh flakes easily. Serve with all the butter cascaded over them and with perhaps a little more added.

Fisherman's Respite

Fisherman's Respite is for that moment when you feel that tomorrow you may be sprouting fins. Melt ½ stick of butter in the frypan. Add 2 cups cooked, cold, diced potatoes and ½ cup diced onion. Cook slowly, turning everything gently and often until it is lightly browned.

Pour on 3 tablespoons good dry sherry and bring to a boil. Then add 2 cups of flaked cooked fish. Cook a minute or two to warm through; then lower the heat.

Mix ¼ cup whipping cream, 2 slightly beaten eggs, ¼ cup shredded sharp Cheddar cheese, ½ teaspoon salt, ⅛ teaspoon freshly ground black pepper, and ¼ teaspoon tarragon. Stir into the fish mixture. Cook, turning with a spatula until the egg mixture is slightly set, and serve your hungry quartet with this welcome change of pace.

SHELLFISH YOU WILL ENJOY

If you'd like to enjoy a wonderfully lazy day in the sun, with the nearly certain promise of catching a delicious meal, shellfishing is hard to beat. Everyone is sure to get something. And what's better eating? Matter of fact, some of the best fun of all can be gathering driftwood, putting on a big kettle of salt water, and doing your feasting right on the shore.

Crabs

It's perhaps the crabs that provide more good sport and fine dining than any other North American saltwater delicacy. There are so many ways to catch these pugnacious individualists that no one should have much trouble in getting his share. Just a chunk of meat tied to a string will turn the trick. Crabs attracted to it will hold on so persistently that you can easily yank them, dripping, from the water. By moving quickly enough at low tide, you can also scoop crabs of all dimensions out of the shallows where they sometimes lurk by the hundreds in swaying sea grass. A night light will bring them, swimming like luminous ghosts, to within easy reach of a long-handled net.

Any rake, its sharp tines blunted by tape, will excite some of these crustaceans to combat if advanced slowly through grasses and seaweed. When they've clamped tight, just lift them out. Similarly blunted garden forks will also serve. Or you can just poke around with a stick, pinning the crab if necessary until you can flip it into the damp burlap bag or pail of brine you're carrying.

Crabs are plunged live into boiling water. After 20 minutes of seething, they're ready for breaking open and eating with melted butter. Or the cracked legs may be dipped into a mixture of egg and crumbs, then fried in butter until brown and delicious. How about when crabs are in the soft-shell stage? Leaving the delicate new shell undisturbed, just sauté them in a little butter. Once you've finished devouring the first batch, odds are you'll be out looking for more.

Crab Newburg

Melt a stick of butter in a double boiler. Stir in 3 cups of freshly cooked crabmeat and cook directly over low heat for 5 minutes. Add 2 tablespoons of sherry, ½ teaspoon paprika, ½ teaspoon salt, and ⅛ teaspoon nutmeg, and place over hot water.

Beat 5 egg yolks with 1½ cups of light cream. Add this gradually to the crabmeat mixture, stirring for about 4 minutes or until everything is thick and smooth. Serve immediately on hot wedges of toast to the delighted gourmets.

Crabmeat Salad

Even the widely used mayonnaise is really too strong a dressing for crab-meat salad, overpowering too much of the delicate flavor. A small amount of fresh lemon juice and a sprinkling of salt is all you need. Other ingredients? I like crisp fresh lettuce, several chopped, hard-cooked eggs, and perhaps a lit-tle diced celery.

Clams

Then there are the clams. Almost all our coastal waters are enriched with these, and at least half the fun is getting out to harvest them. Sandy beaches, salty mud flats, gravel-loaded reefs, bright headlands, and foggy bays all yield their savory treasures. These vary from tiny bean clams, which after storms can sometimes be picked up by the hundreds along Southern California beaches, to huge geoducks weighing a dozen pounds and more.

Some of these clams are dug with shovels, rakes, forks, hoes, and trowels. Others are felt by barefooted waders who then casually reach down and trans-fer them to a convenient bag or basket. There are even clams, such as the suc-culent rough piddock, that hollow out homes in rocks and are hunted with such unlikely tools as sledgehammers and chisels.

On many a beach, the technique is to stroll along and tap the hard-packed sand ahead, all the time watching for tiny holes to appear. At this sign that a clam is on the move somewhere beneath, the idea is to begin instantly digging on the seaward side. Some experts scoop away only the hard top surface, then grope for the fleeting clam with their hands. With a lot of species, you have to move surprisingly fast.

If there's any way clams can be cooked more delectably than they have been for centuries at New England clambakes, then a lot of us haven't discovered it yet. All you have to do is dig a pit on the beach, line it with rocks, and kindle a roaring fire within. When the burning driftwood has crumbled to hot coals, spread on fresh wet seaweed. The clams go in next. They are immediately covered with more soggy live kelp. Then come such old standbys as unhusked corn and potatoes in their jackets, and a final topping of more wet seaweed. A thick layer of sand seals in both the heat and the wonderfully fragrant steam.

After about an hour, if you can wait that long, the now dry seaweed is raked out. The food is gingerly extracted. And everyone begins making with hot melted butter. But if your appetite precludes even these relatively simple preparations, just lay your live clams on a piece of sheet metal under which driftwood is flaming in all its different colors. When the shells have opened, cut out the clams, dip them in butter, and wash them down with sips of their own shellcupped juices.

Steamed Clams

This one brings memories of some particularly congenial hours spent with good companions beside rousing fires. A good way to get ready for such sessions is by washing your clams well in several changes of water, then spreading them out in a big shallow pan. Barely cover them with cold water, with 1 cup of salt to every 3 gallons of water, and let them stand 3 or 4 hours to cleanse themselves. This process you can help along by sprinkling on a cup of corn meal. Then, before you use the clams, make sure each is still alive. Any with yawning shells that don't close when handled should be discarded.

Place the clams in a dutch oven or large kettle. Add ½ cup boiling water for every 4 quarts of clams. Put on a tight lid and allow to steam over the fire until the shells partially open. This usually takes about 15 minutes.

Set the pot in the middle of the table. Have dishes of melted butter ready. Ladle some of the steaming hot broth into individual cups. Then let everyone use his hands, opening the shells one by one, stripping off the membrane and the outside of the neck, swishing the clam a bit in the broth, then dipping it in the butter, and plopping it into the mouth. By being careful not to disturb the sediment in the bottom of the cups, you can intersperse the eating with frequent sips of the rich salty liquid.

Clam Chowder

Nothing's better on a cool, foggy day. Separate the hard necks from the soft, plump bodies of a quart of shucked and cleaned clams. Let these necks simmer ½ hour, or until tender, in a cup of water.

Add a bay leaf, a teaspoon salt, ⅛ teaspoon thyme, and ⅛ teaspoon freshly ground black pepper to a quart of milk. Simmer a cup of diced potatoes and ½ cup of diced onion in this until they are barely tender.

Then stir in all the clams and liquid, a cup of heavy cream, and a cup of fine sherry. Simmer for 5 minutes. Dust with paprika and ladle out piping hot for four hungry clam diggers.

Clam Pie

Growing up on the New England seacoast, I began to enjoy clam pie early. Recipes for this substantial dish vary considerably, but the one I prefer is heavier on the bivalves than on the accompanying vegetables.

Shuck and clean a quart of clams, always saving the liquor. Dice a large onion and 2 medium-size potatoes. Add enough rich milk to all but 3 tablespoons of the clam juice to give you a quart of liquids. Bring everything to a simmer in this.

In the meantime, cube ¼ pound of salt pork. Keeping most of the fat poured off, fry this over low heat until it is brown and crisp. Then add to the other ingredients. Season with salt and freshly ground black pepper to taste. Keep simmering until the potatoes are just short of being done.

Turn into a large, fairly shallow casserole and top liberally with paprika and parsley flakes. Cover with a rich crust made by sifting together 1½ cups of flour and 1 teaspoon salt, cutting in ½ cup of well-chilled butter, and then gradually adding the 3 tablespoons of remaining clam juice to make a ball of dough.

Roll this out, fit over the dish, press the edges to the rim, prick to make steam vents. Any leftover pastry may be cut into decorative shapes, brushed with beaten egg, and placed atop the crust. Bake in a preheated hot 450°F. oven for 15 minutes or until the top is golden brown. Serve immediately on hot plates. All the work of preparation will be more than overbalanced by the excellent taste.

Fried Clams

I have boyhood memories of smelling these for miles along the traffic-clogged Massachusetts shores of Essex, Ipswich, and Gloucester, and I still don't know of any odor more conducive to hearty eating. Dry your shucked and cleaned clams. Dip each in beaten egg. Then roll in fine dry crumbs. Fry in deep, hot fat only until golden brown.

Tenderness depends on not cooking these too fast or too long. Drain, if you can wait that long, on paper toweling. To my way of thinking, these are the best after being swirled a bit in tartar sauce.

Oysters

There are the savory bay scallops, the cockles, prawns, shrimp, the rock lobsters, and the picturesque and exciting conches. There are also the tasty mussels that in the United States and Canada are found inland as well as along the coast. And there are the oysters; some of them even attached to the roots of trees. No other waters anywhere in the world will give the family or individual more fun or finer eating.

It is the oysters that guarantee some of the best meals our open places can provide. Eat them live. Roast them like clams. Roll in eggs, milk, and seasoned crumbs, and then fry in hot fat about 2 minutes or until brown. Steam and serve in the shells with melted butter. Shuck, drain, sprinkle with seasoned and buttered bread crumbs, and broil on the half shell for 5 minutes. Simmer them into stew with salt and pepper, butter, and a quart of milk per pint of shellfish. Alternate them on a green wand with slices of bacon and cook over the coals of the campfire.

Or conjure up what's known as Angels on Horseback with:

1 pint oysters
12 slices bacon
½ teaspoon salt
⅛ teaspoon pepper
2 teaspoons dried parsley

Drain the oysters. Lay each oyster on half a slice of bacon. Sprinkle with salt, pepper, and dried parsley. Loop the bacon around the oyster and fasten with a toothpick or whittled skewer. Arrange the oysters on a rack in a shallow pan and bake them in a hot oven or in the reflector baker before a leaping fire. Pick up by the toothpick or skewer and eat hot.

Broiled Scallops

Swirl the rinsed and dried scallops in melted butter which has been flavored with lemon juice. Sprinkle with powdered parsley. Place on a preheated broiler pan about 3 inches from the heat and heat until they are a subtle and voluptuous gold, turning them so they will cook evenly.

Sautéed Scallops

Rinse and dry the scallops, quartering them if they are too large. Then dip in lightly beaten egg. Roll in bread crumbs that have been seasoned with 4 parts salt and 1 part freshly ground black pepper. Turning them occasionally, sauté in butter for 2 minutes or until they begin to brown. Sprinkle with chopped parsley and cook until colored a bit more. Eaten hot, these will be gastronomic delights, not merely just another seafood.

PART EIGHT
YOUR WILDERNESS HOME

CHAPTER NINETEEN

BUILDING A CABIN

Everyone talks about building a log cabin. Very few, however, ever get around to it, as Henry David Thoreau did. This is too bad in a lot of ways, for log cabin living is a delightful experience that is absolutely unique.

"Near the end of March, 1845, I cut down some tall pines by Walden Pond and hewed timbers, studs and rafters with my axe," wrote Thoreau. "By the middle of April, for I made no haste in my work but rather the most of it, my house was ready for raising.

"I dug my cellar in the side of a hill where a woodchuck had formerly dug his burrow, down through sumach and blackberry roots. In May, with the help of acquaintances—rather to improve as good an occasion for neighborliness than from any necessity—I set up the frame of my house and as soon as it was boarded and roofed, I began to occupy it."

Thoreau's home in the woods cost him $28.12.

"I intend to build me a home that will surpass any on the main street in grandeur and luxury, as soon as it pleases me as much," he wrote, "and it will cost me no more than my present one."

Cabin building itself is very simple. The job takes work but no particular skill. Best of all, it proceeds with satisfying speed.

Any reasonably able-bodied boy or man can put up a comfortable cabin by himself. If he has help, the construction will go all the faster. You don't even have to swing an ax if you don't want. All the necessary cutting and trimming can be done with a saw, with occasional assistance from mallet and chisel.

BUILDING MATERIALS

Choosing and Seasoning Logs

Straight, smooth cedar, lodgepole pine, fir, and similar evergreens make the best logs. About 50 of these, averaging 8 to 10 inches in diameter, will make a cabin.

Ideally, these should be cut in the late fall or early winter and allowed to season on skids, up off the ground, for at least six months. For all practical purposes, however, generally you can do well enough right away with whatever may be at hand. It will pay, though, to scout around and find some sound standing dead dry wood for at least the foundations and the ridgepole.

Logs should be peeled. Even when one goes to a tremendous amount of care, unpeeled cabin logs almost always turn out to be dirty or otherwise unsatisfactory. Ideally again, the best procedure is to hew or shave off two narrow strips of bark the length of each log, top and bottom, when you fell it. These strips should follow the straightest length of the log. This is so the cracks, that will largely concentrate here as the logs dry and shrink, can be hidden in the walls. When the bark eventually loosens in the spring, while the logs are still on skids, just pry it off.

If you're going to build right away, get the bark off in the easiest way possible when you drop the trees. If you're building in the springtime, the bark will strip off in great rolls.

Manufactured Materials

Although it is possible to build a cabin entirely with such wilderness materials that may be at hand, you'll do better to buy planed lumber for floor, window and door frames, shelves, bunks, tables, and the like. Rough lumber and roll roofing will save time and trouble when you come to topping off the structure. Some two-by-fours, especially for use as floor joists where they'll be hidden, are quicker to fit than poles. You'll also need an assortment of spikes and nails, a thimble for the stovepipe outlet, windows, hinges, etc.

In the semiarid interior of the country, cabins are often put up with their lower logs actually resting on the ground. Many such cabins stay sound for twenty years or more. In wet country, though, unless the bottom legs are kept dry, they'll begin to rot the first year.

Where decay is a problem, as in coastal regions, it may be feasible to use a preservative on the logs. Local inhabitants can give you a line on these, as homemade mixtures are compounded for the purpose. An excellent commercial product is pentachlorophenol. Directions accompany this preparation, commonly known as "penta."

PICKING THE SITE

A good way to visualize your future wilderness cabin is to mark its proposed outline with stakes and strings. When these are in place, look over the location from every angle, both inside and out. Consider every point that may be important to you: sunlight at different seasons, view, wind, drainage, access, etc. If the answers aren't satisfactory, keep moving your markers until the best possible site is located.

Before you do any actual building, get your plans and measurements down on paper. It is possible to get along quite happily in a very small, easily heated area. But every inch of space must be utilized to the fullest.

The dimensions of your log cabin will be determined to a large degree by your personal needs and by the materials at hand. For one or two people, a cabin about 20 feet long and 12 feet wide is an agreeable size. Room can be saved effectively by massing all the windows in one of the long walls. No matter what else you do when building in the woods, make sure that the cabin interior will get plenty of cheerful light. You'll appreciate this, especially in the north woods, during rainy weather and the long, darkish days of winter.

FOUNDATIONS

Four large stones, solidly embedded with the flat surfaces up, will serve for cornerstones. If the locality is at all wet, however, you'll get a far better foundation by laying another slab loosely without cement atop each base stone. Moisture which will climb the first stone by capillary attraction will then be checked by the second. Similar supports should be placed about every six feet beneath the foundation logs.

Then get the four bottom logs into position. These should be the sturdiest of the lot. Lift the two long logs into place first, if you want. Then roll up the two short logs. These should set half a log higher than the side logs. This can be accomplished by notching them, as will be considered in a moment. These four bottom logs should be solid, square, and of nearly equal height at the corners. When you get them ready, spike them together.

KEEPING THE LOGS PLUMB AND LEVEL

The inside measurements are what you use when building a log cabin. Keep the insides of the wall logs plumb, that is, straight up and down. One way to do this is to spike guide boards upright inside the four corners. Check these with a plumb line to make sure they're perfectly vertical. A string with a stone at its end will serve for this purpose. Or, if such guides are going to be in your way, keep checking the logs with the plumb line as you proceed.

The logs should be kept as level as possible, as each tier rises into place. You'll then have a reasonably level base for your roof, door, and window frames. These levels are very easily regulated by the deepness of the various notches.

The logs can be kept reasonably level, too, by alternating each round of logs so the thin end of one log will always contact the thick end of another. Four kitchen matches will illustrate this point. Lay them with the four heads resting upon one another. You get a fan effect. Then switch every other match so no two tops touch. A reasonably square rectangle is the result.

A flat bottle, filled with contrasting tea with an air bubble in it, will serve as a level. As a matter of fact, you can pretty well improvise throughout. The cover of this book, for example, could be your square. But a good steel tape is one refinement that will save you considerable time.

It's not necessary to become too particular in the matter of getting everything straight and level. When you're working with logs, you can only approximate these ideals at best. However, it's just about as easy to keep everything fairly true and thus allow yourself the widest possible margin for error. You'll end up with a better looking and more substantial cabin. Also, there will be less work when you get around to putting up shelves and cabinets.

CORNERS

Unless you've actually notched in a corner, this is the part of the log cabin building that probably will loom up as the stumbling block. Actually, corner work is simple in the extreme.

The main reason for this is that log walls are not built to fit with any of the tightness of frame buildings. As a matter of fact, you'll end up with a warmer, tighter cabin by making sure that the wall logs remain up to two inches apart. This will make the later chinking considerably easier and more effective.

You can, if you want, avoid notching by spiking the wall logs directly between corner posts. But either of the two corners suggested here will give you a better cabin. If they happen to be new to you, after you've studied them a bit, why not saw a few straight saplings into short lengths? Then experiment with a knife until you have a sound working knowledge of exactly how your corners will fit together.

The general procedure is to get the log into position and move it around until it is resting on its straightest length. Then make sure that the better of the other two sides will be on the inside of the cabin. Now you're ready for your notch.

Saddle Notch

The saddle notch is quickly made. It is good-looking, and it's practical in that no cut is left upturned to gather moisture. The drawing, "Measuring Saddle Notches in a Wall Log," is pretty much self-explanatory. Succeeding notches are made in similar fashion.

As the walls go up, first of all you measure. The notch at its widest spot will, of course, be open only enough to cup the log beneath it. The notch's depth, also governed by the log it is to fit, customarily will be a little less than half the diameter of the log in which it is cut.

Each log should be notched so it will lie fairly level. Suppose the unnotched log lies an inch high on one end? Then either cut the notch on that end an inch deeper or cut the opposite notch an inch shallower.

All this is simplified by the fact that you have a couple of inches to play around with. Wall logs may be laid that far apart at their widest gaps.

Measuring Saddle Notches in a Wall Log

It usually takes a few tries before everything fits to satisfaction. Make your notches, roll the log into place, mark where some more cutting is needed, roll the log off, make the cuts, and try again. When the corners are right, spike them.

Tenon Corner

This type of corner can be cut with a saw. It is fashioned by flattening the top and bottom ends of each log so the resulting tongues will ordinarily be a little more than half as wide as the log ends in which they are made. Leveling and measuring are the same as with all corner construction.

The drawing, "Marking a Tenon Cut," practically explains itself. Each tongue can be made with two vertical and two horizontal cuts. A swiftly working Swede saw or a crosscut saw will take care of all these. Or you can saw down the two vertical marks, then quickly split out each slab with a chisel and mallet.

Leveling Wall Log Held in Saddle Notches

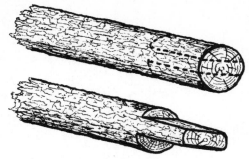

Marking a Tenon Cut

RAISING THE LOGS

The handiest way to lift logs is with a block and tackle, generally available for the borrowing. Leaning pole skids into place will facilitate the raising of the logs even more.

A pole tripod is handy for suspending a block and tackle for lifting cabin logs. Line up three poles on the ground with the bottoms together, and mark where the lashing is to be centered.

Now take two of the poles and lay them with their tops over a log so you can tie them conveniently. Place the third pole between them with its end in the opposite direction. Line up the marks. Separate all three poles with small blocks.

Start the lashing with a clove hitch around one of the outside poles, all the time heeding the marks. Take a half dozen or so loose turns around all three poles. Remove the blocks and take two tight turns around the lashings between an outside pole and the center pole, then between the center pole and the other outside pole. Finish off with a clove hitch around the center pole.

When you set up the tripod, the top of the center pole should be supported by the angle made by the other two.

Tenon Corner

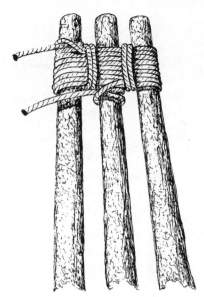

Tripod Lashing

FLOOR

The floor generally goes on after the roof is in place. There's an easy way to provide for it. Spike milled two-by-fours, with their narrow sides up, the length of the two longest bottom logs. Make sure they're level and parallel. Then lay two-by-fours across these from wall to wall, about a foot apart. Spike these joints, which also should have their narrow sides uppermost.

Unless you are able to obtain seasoned flooring, it will be better not to nail it permanently until the second year. Most of the drafts in log cabins swirl in around the feet. You can guard against such cold as much as possible by banking the cabin every fall just before freeze-up. It will also be worthwhile to put in a double floor at the start, laying the second layer at right angles to the first, with heavy, waterproof building paper in between. The covered surfaces can be left rough.

WINDOWS AND DOORS

Where there is no shortage of logs, the quickest procedure is to build solid walls and then saw out the openings.

When you come to the top of the future opening, just frame it inside and outside with perpendicular boards, carefully measured and squared. Then saw out the top log inside these guiding supports. Later on, you can insert a crosscut saw in these openings and complete the work. Milled lumber will simplify the framing.

Quickest Way to Cut Openings

Doors should be built on the spot and should be made solid and massive. A practical door can be constructed of two or more thicknesses of planks, with waterproof building paper between. The exterior layer should be put on vertically so there will be no horizontal cracks exposed to trap moisture.

ROOF

Once the walls are up, the next procedure is generally to put on the roof and make it waterproof. Log construction is rugged, and most cabin roofs are small. Except in very heavy snow country, a steep roof is unnecessary.

A gable roof with a 25 per cent pitch is usually excellent. To determine this pitch, measure between the side walls. Say this distance is ten feet. Then the top of the ridgepole should be roughly five feet higher than the tops of the side walls.

With some five or six short logs, build the two ends of the cabin up to the necessary height. Then center the ridgepole in place.

You'll next need purlins. These are straight, slender logs the same length as the ridgepole. The handiest way to put them up is to cut off the end of each short gable log just enough to allow the purlin to be positioned atop the log below.

Roof Purlins Set in Gables

The purlins should follow the slant of the roof in such a way that they will support boards or poles laid from the ridgepole to the top of the side walls. When all fitting has been done, spike everything down.

Pole Roof

The pole roof is the most beautiful of cabin roofs, something to appreciate when you are dreaming up at it from inside your wilderness retreat. For this type of roof, you'll need a quantity of peeled poles, long enough so they'll butt together atop the ridge and then reach down to the eaves. These poles can be readied all at once on the ground. Butts and tops will be alternated when they are spiked into place.

Cover the top of this pole roof with building paper. Spike on two-by-fours some two feet apart, parallel to the ridge. Fill in between them, if you want, with the dry moss to be found in many woods. Nail on boards and cover with waterproof roll roofing. That will make a warm and picturesque roof.

If, for some reason, you don't want to bother with poles, lumber may be used throughout instead. In really cold weather in the North, it's easy to tell a poor roof from a good roof at a glance. The poorly insulated roof not only becomes bare and icy, but heat waves can be seen shimmering through it. Look around and see who have warm roofs. Then ask how they insulated them.

One fast way to insulate a board roof is to provide a dead-air chamber. Cover the initial layer of boards, nailed to the purlins, with roofing paper. Spike two-by-fours along the edges and parallel to the ridge about three feet apart. Nail on another layer of boards. Cover this with waterproof roofing according to the directions accompanying the product. The result, besides being warm, is trim and clean.

CHINKING

The walls will be completed as soon as they are caulked and chinked. Many wilderness builders take care of the caulking by stringing sphagnum moss, common in numerous localities, liberally between logs and in all joints as the construction proceeds. Oakum, which can be purchased in bulk, is even better.

The chinking usually is an annual matter of mixing up a thick mud, slapping and pressing it into the cracks, and then smoothing it with a flat stick or a small trowel. The numerous ways of chinking also become subjects of considerable local interest, being heatedly discussed and debated through the years. Some earths stay in place better than others, especially if you drive a few nails upright in the cracks for anchors.

Plasters of cheap flour, salt, and water are common in some areas. One of the toughest and most harmonizing of all chinkings is made by mixing sawdust from the job with melted sheet glue.

FURNITURE

"I would rather sit on a pumpkin and have it all to myself," said Thoreau, "than be crowded on a velvet cushion."

Furniture for the wilderness home should be born, not borne, there. Possibilities range from such simplicities as table and stools to individualities like four-poster beds. The particular cabin should be the arbiter.

Rainy afternoons can be enlivened by satisfying your inherent creative urge in the fashioning of seats and other necessities for the forest abode. Furniture is fun.

MATERIALS

Best Woods

Unpeeled birch is a favorite material for indoor furniture. Cedar is a top choice for all kinds of work, the rough sticks being particularly picturesque. Pine certainly is in tradition. The undisputed excellence of such hardwoods as oak and chestnut is tempered only by the increased difficulty in working with them.

Seasoned wood is preferable, not only because it is lighter, but because subsequent shrinkage of undried pieces is apt to cause warping and wobbling. Many find it a profitable practice to store choice sticks to dry for future furniture demands.

Lumber

Planks can be given a hand-made look by having them roughened against a buzz saw at the mill. Or they may be touched up with a hatchet, then rubbed with coarse sandpaper, for a hewn effect. Wood may also be effectively raked with a wire brush, perhaps in conjunction with light charring with a blow torch.

Lumber is not to be passed up too lightly, therefore, for such roles as table tops and chair seats where smooth surfaces are mandatory. Knotty pine is a log cabin favorite. Boxwood is handy for concealed work such as shelves and drawers. It is more desirable if faced with slabs of other rustic materials, however, when used for cupboards and such.

Plywoods are available today in a wide choice of varieties, some of which will enhance both the plainest and the most elaborate wilderness homes. Well-made plywood has the advantage of coming in large, durable, lightweight, easily finished, exceedingly rugged panels which can be quickly and economically cut to any practical shape or size.

Hides, Fillers, and Dyes for Upholstery

Moose and similar hides not only impart a magnificence to log cabin furniture, but their smoky fragrance, if Indian-tanned, will recall many a flickering campfire. They may be used intact, or portions may be tacked to frames for chair seats and backs.

Hides also may be cut round and around with a sharp knife to form a continuous ⅜-inch or so lace for furniture making. An easy way to go about this is to stick the knife into a wide board. Drive a nail beside it the width away desired for the lacing. Then turn a piece of hide around and around this until it is reduced to a single long strip. This babiche or shaganappi, as it is called in the North Woods, should be soaked and then stretched under pressure a number of times.

It then should be resoaked and, while it is wet, tightly laced to a frame to make webbed chair seats or backs. A snowshoe may be used for a pattern. A snowshoe needle, which can be interestingly made of a four-inch bone, sharpened at both ends and with a hole in the middle, will quicken the process. Or the babiche may be simply laced back and forth over a frame or in parallel lines through holes cut in a frame.

The webbing, when dry, should be given several coats of high-grade varnish, a process that may well be repeated yearly.

The making of varicolored cushions will brighten the log cabin and make it more comfortable. Native fillers, such as wild marsh hay, aromatic evergreen needles, and soft sphagnum moss, may be stuffed in to make them invitingly plump.

You may even like to experiment with natural dyes. Cloth immersed in liquid in which swamp maple bark has been boiled will come out a mountain-lake blue. To make it a professional job, you need only add a little iron sulphate to the solution first. If none is lying around the vicinity, a dime's worth may be purchased from a drugstore. Or you may obtain it from a cobbler's shop where it is known as copperas.

Alder bark when boiled gives off a tawny yellow dye that has colored many an Indian's garments. The rich hue of pioneer homespuns was often obtained by boiling the outer nut shells and inner bark of the butternut tree. Sunflower blossoms contain a sunny stain that has the exciting hue of gold.

Glue

Waterproof glue in powder form is available for furniture building. When prepared according to instructions and applied thinly and evenly to tightly fitting, smooth joints, it may be counted upon to make a union stronger than the wood itself. Other satisfactory glues may be purchased at almost any variety or hardware store. Directions accompany them. Glued joints generally should be kept under pressure for some four hours and not subjected to strain for an additional twenty-four hours.

Nails will do for furniture. Screws are better. Countersinking the latter and topping them with glue-immersed pegs is finer still.

STOOLS

A short, upright log is the simplest stool. Place a slab, poles, or a hewn plank over two of these to make a bench. Start with taller blocks, and a table is the result.

Simple Stool, Bench, and Table

Split a short log. Smooth the flat surface, using sandpaper to finish the job. Take a brace and bit, auger, or even a jackknife. Bore four holes in the underside.

Angle in four lengths of saplings or tree limbs, about two inches in diameter. The tops of these should be whittled until they fit snugly. They can be fastened with glue, or small nails may be slanted through them into the slab.

An effective touch is to bore a small hole through the seat and each leg, then to secure the latter by driving in a wooden peg. Softwood dowels adapt themselves easily. Hardwood pegs have to be whittled with more precision. Both will fit more solidly if first dipped in glue.

Stools so made often bring extraordinarily high prices at auctions under the guise of antiques.

BENCHES, CHAIRS, AND TABLES

Handle a longer log similarly for a bench. Bore several holes in the flat surface to support a simple back, and a settee is the next step. Do the same thing with a stool to make a chair. Seat legs can be bored and rungs inserted.

Longer legs will make a table. It may be necessary to brace the legs. A slab shelf can be screwed into position to steady table legs.

Other tops may be substituted for the original split log. Slabs will do. So will planks. Holes will have to be bored all the way through thinner woods, of course. This should be done from the top downward. When the tip of the tool

Stool Made from Split Log

Settee

pricks through, the boring should be completed from the other side so the wood will not be unnecessarily torn and splintered. The legs, after being fitted, can be smoothed until entirely flush.

A spectacular table can be made from the naturally rounded end of a huge log that has been sawed some four inches thick. Effective companion tables may then be topped with similar slices from smaller logs.

Dining Room Set

The simplest eating arrangement for the camp is a table with benches attached. Six poles and several slabs will do the job, as the illustration shows. An additional H-support can be added to the middle, if this seems desirable.

Similar combinations are inviting when put up at outdoor vantage points. Four long posts are first driven solidly into the ground, and the piece is constructed around this nucleus.

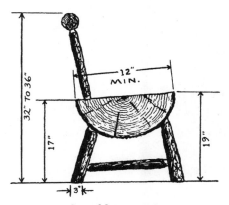

Settee Measurements

Dining Room Set

Drop Leaf Table

Drop leaf tables, both movable and stationary, are space savers in the wilderness home. A frequently valuable provision, too, is a fixed cabinet whose door swings downward for use as a writing desk or typewriter stand.

Proper Proportions

Tables and chairs, when used together, may be respectively thirty and eighteen inches high. If the table is slightly lower, the difference in height between it and the chair should still be one foot. The backs of such chairs should be somewhat more than twice the seat height. They should be practically straight.

If the seat and back are both pitched backward several inches, the seat lowered and widened, and a few rustic cushions added, the result will be a comfortable armchair in which to sprawl and lazily survey blue hills.

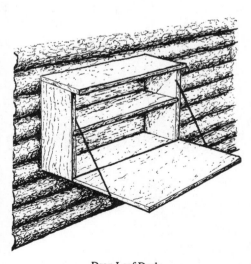

Drop Leaf Desk

USING A MOTIF

Simplicity is the enduring ideal to be stressed above everything else in wilderness furniture building. Actual designs may vary. When one is chosen, it often is pleasing to follow it throughout.

Effective is the use of substantial peeled poles of the same wood as the cabin logs. Post tops need not be flat, but can be slanted at forty-five degree angles and touched up with a sharp hatchet to give a hewn effect.

Well-sandpapered slabs, left round on one side, will often fit in magnificently. Joints held by countersunk screws, boldly pegged, can, many times, add a final fine touch. Interlocking mortise and tenon joints are outstanding.

MORTISE AND TENON JOINT

The mortise and tenon joint is made with surprising ease, as the step by step illustrations show. The entire job can be done with a mallet and chisel. A small saw, such as a keyhole saw, and a brace and bit, will make the work even simpler.

A mortise is a slot, which, in this instance, is cut in a piece of wood so that the tongue of another piece of wood can be inserted through the slot. A hole is

I~ A MORTISE IS A SLOT

A   B   C

MARK   BORE HOLES   CHISEL OUT
TO EASE WORK   SLOT

2~A TENON IS A TONGUE

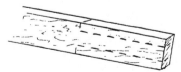   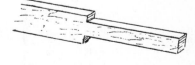

A – MEASURE TO FIT SLOT   B – SAW

Steps in Making a Mortise and Tenon Joint

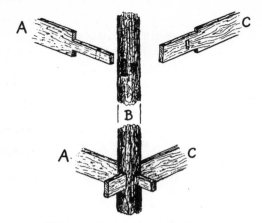

Fitting Mortise and Tenon Joints Together

made in the projecting end of the tongue and a wooden wedge driven in to pin the joint tightly together.

In the use of the interlocking joint suggested later on for a four-poster bed, each tenon may be marked on both sides of the wood with the aid of a try square, then sawed with a fine-tooth tool on the waste side of the guidelines. The wood may then be smoothed with sandpaper.

A slot just big enough to accommodate the tongue is then marked on one side of the piece of wood through which it is to be pushed. An additional location mark may be made on the opposite side, as well, by using the try square to assure accuracy.

The rectangular holes can be cut with a chisel and mallet, trimmed with a knife, and finally smoothed by sandpaper. The wood will knock out more neatly if a number of holes are first bored side by side within the indicated slot. These holes should not extend the full width of the mortise. They should be made by boring through one side until the tool pricks through, then turning the wood and boring from the other side, thus avoiding splintering.

A small narrow slot is similarly marked and cut in the locking tongue. A wooden wedge, whittled to fit tightly, is then driven in to hold the assembled joint together. The distance between the inside of this final slot and the base of the tongue should, of course, equal the width of the main mortise.

BOOKCASE

A bookcase for a log cabin can be built in a very few minutes if lumber is at hand. Decide first on the size. Assemble the four outer pieces. Then, perhaps using the larger of the books that are to be stored as a guide, mark on one of the side boards the location of the shelves. Lay both of these side boards side by side and get the strips on evenly by putting them on in pairs.

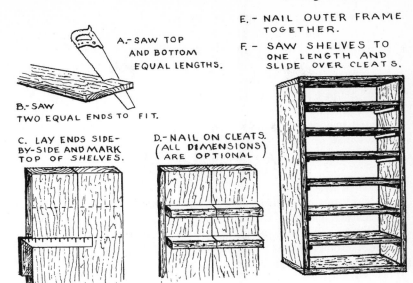

A.- SAW TOP AND BOTTOM EQUAL LENGTHS.

B.- SAW TWO EQUAL ENDS TO FIT.

C. LAY ENDS SIDE-BY-SIDE AND MARK TOP OF SHELVES.

D.- NAIL ON CLEATS. (ALL DIMENSIONS ARE OPTIONAL)

E. - NAIL OUTER FRAME TOGETHER.

F. - SAW SHELVES TO ONE LENGTH AND SLIDE OVER CLEATS.

Steps in Making a Bookcase

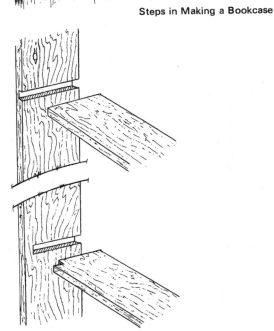

Two Kinds of Slots for Installing Shelves

Now fasten the frame together, nailing the top and bottom boards over the sides for greater strength. Then set this frame in place against the wall, preferably nailing it in position. Saw the shelves to measure and slide them into place.

Blocks of shelves for any purpose can be speedily assembled in this fashion. Add doors, and the result will be a cabinet. A turning piece of wood can be nailed in place so it can be pivoted to hold the door closed.

A more professional way of installing shelves is by sliding them into slots. These slots may be made easily enough by sawing in each instance along two lines drawn the width of the shelf, and carefully knocking out the wood with chisel and mallet.

PICTURE FRAMES

Quartered bits of birch salvaged from the kindling pile will do. Halved cedar saplings and such also are excellent. Neat rustic frames also may be made of boxwood to which thin strips of birch bark have been glued.

Covers of outdoor magazines often are interesting enough to hang. So are some calendar illustrations. Maps of one's locality are invaluable.

BEDS

Bunk

The bunk, as differentiated from the usually movable bed, is attached to the wall. The frame of the ordinary corner bunk requires no more than five poles at most. Since it has but one leg, which supports the only corner not fastened to the cabin logs, it may be put up in several minutes.

If the entire back of a narrow shelter is to be converted into a single large bunk, as is frequently done, the task is not much magnified. The oversize bunk in numerous fishing shacks, for instance, generally has a wooden bottom that is supported between a convenient log in the back wall and a single husky pole stretched across the front. This crosspiece often is spiked between the side walls and is prevented from sagging by one or more pole legs.

Proper Height of Bunk

The need for storage space is what usually governs the height of the bunk or bed constructed in the wilderness home. Such sleeping arrangements often are thirty or more inches high for this practical reason. The area beneath may accommodate drawers or shelves. It is many times found more convenient to store boxes or duffle bags loosely beneath.

The bottom of the frame can be closed in with boards or slabs in which doors or sliding panels are cut. Easiest, though, is curtaining the space.

Two-Story Bunk

The double-deck sleeping accommodation saves space in a way more commendable in cold weather than warm. Any cabin builder who has spent many

Corner Bunk with Pole Spring

Two-Story Bunk

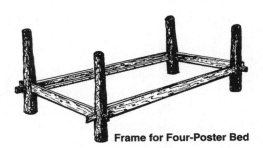

Frame for Four-Poster Bed

nights in the top section of one will not make the mistake of adding frills which, although perhaps picturesque, will interfere with air circulation.

The frame for the upper half of a double bunk may be made similar to that of the lower half, except that posts need not extend between corners and floor, but can be spiked instead between corners and ceiling.

The upper story may be reached by a permanent or portable ladder. The former may be made of cross poles spiked between two vertical poles that are attached either to the bunks or to the cabin wall.

Trundle Bed

The trundle bed conserves space and, at the same time, preserves sleepers from hot upper climes. It may be built atop four posts braced with cross-pieces, except along the inner length, so the stationary bed or bunk, under which the trundle is slid lengthwise, can also furnish a storage area. An end can be left open instead, of course, but then more floor space will have to be left unblocked.

Trundle beds for use in one room may be made to push endwise through wall holes under permanent sleeping accommodations in another room.

Four-Poster Bed

A handsome four-poster bed can be built entirely of seasoned wilderness materials in such a way that it can be taken apart in a few moments, then re-assembled elsewhere in as short a time.

Dimensions will vary to accommodate whatever spring and mattress are used. A comfortable overall height, including these, however, may be set at two feet.

Four matched posts, about five or six inches in diameter, will be needed. These will be worthy of a painstaking search. Four planks about two inches thick will be required, too. These may be roughed against a buzz saw or touched up with a sharp hatchet so as to take on a handmade look. The posts should be carefully worked over with a hatchet or ax for the same reason. The wood then can be smoothed down somewhat with coarse sandpaper.

For the craftsmanlike effect shown in the illustration, this bed should be fitted together with interlocking mortise and tenon joints held by removable hardwood wedges.

The bed springs, which can be improvised with ropes or saplings, may rest on slats supported by strips of wood preferably screwed near the lower interiors of the two longer sides. If the slats are made to fit tightly, their square ends will prevent their turning to slip off the supports and will, therefore, make fastening unnecessary.

RESTRAINT

Some care should be taken not to crowd the cabin too enthusiastically with furniture. Thoreau found three chairs sufficient in his wilderness home: "One for solitude, two for friendship, three for society."

INDEX